AN ENGLISH-KONKANI PRONOUNCING POCKET DICTIONARY

AN ENGLISH-KONKANI PRONOUNCING POCKET DICTIONARY

J. M. PINTO

GYAN

Published by

Gyan Publishing House
5, Ansari Road
Daryaganj, New Delhi-110002
Phone: 011-47034999, 9811692060
E-mail: books@gyanbooks.com

Distribution Network
gyanbooks.com
India, USA, Canada, UK, Australia, France

ISBN : 978-81-212-4329-2(PB)
First Published, New Delhi , 1988

2nd Impression 2020

Printed at: Gyan Press, Delhi.

The book at your disposal is the edition of an old book originally published long back. The Text quality of this book may not be at par as compared to our other books but many readers approached us to reprint this important book so that it could satiate their hunger. We request all the readers of this book to help us to improve its quality by providing the necessary text of those pages which are not properly visible. Your valuable support in this case will be highly appreciated and acknowledged and our future readers will be benefitted immensely.

ENGLISH-CONCANIM
PRONOUNCING
POCKET DICTIONARY.

A, ART. IND. Poilem acxer.

Aback, *e-bác'*. ADV. Patti; thottacon.

Abandon, *a-ban'-ddon*, V. Soddunc; sanddunc; vatter galunc.

Abandoned, *a-ban'-dondd*, P. A. Sanddlolo; niradari.

Abandonment, *a-ban'-ddonment*, N. Ecannem sanddop.

Abase, *a-béz'*, V. Khalto corunc; unnepon diunc.

Abasement, *a-bez-ment'*, N. Unneponn; olkeponn.

Abash, *ie-besh'*, V. Lojeo galunc; lozounc.

Abate, *a-beit'*, V. Unno corunc; VT. unno zaunc.

—*price*, *fever*—deuvunc.

Abatement, *a-bet-ment'*, N. Denvop; moddni; unneponn.

Abbess, *a-bes'*, N. Madrinchi voddiln.

Abbey, *a-bei'*, N. Convent.

Abbot, *ab'-bot*, N. Conventacho voddil.

Abbreviate, *a-bre-vi-eit*, V Unno corunc.

—make short: Mottvo corunc.

Abbreviation, *a-bre-vi-e-xion*, N. Mottveponn; lanponn; attap.

Abdicate, *ab'-di-keitt*, V. Soddunc, soddun diunc; davo soddunc.

Abdication, *ab-di-kei-xion*, N. Soddni.

Abdomen, *ab-do'-men*, N. Pott.

Abduction, *ab-doc'-xion*, N. Chorun vorop eca munxeache duvec vo potinic.

Aberration, *a-ber-rei'-xion*, N. coddsorni; vatt-chuc; vaucddi vatt.

Abet, *a-bett*, V. Vaittac mozot diunc.

Abettor, *a-be-ttor*, N. Vaittac mozot dinar.

Abhor, *ab-hor*, V. Kanttallo dorunc; vitteunc; ubgonc, bejar zaunc.

Abhorrence, *ab-hor'-rens*, N. Vitt; canttallo; vaz, ubgon.

Abide, *a-bai-dd*, V. Ravunc.

—by the law=upordes sambalunc.

—(remain constant) thir zaun ravunc.

Ability, *a-bi'-li-tti*, N. Socot; uxarki; icmot. [olco.

Abject, *ab'-ject*, A. Unno; kircoll;

Abjectness, *ab-ject-nes*, N. Unneponn; olkeponn; kircollai.

Abjuration, *ab-ju-rei'-xion*, N. Pramanar soddnem.

Abjure, *ab-ju-ar*, V. Ann diun soddunc. [aslolo.

Able, *ei-bl*, A. Soctivont; tanc-

Ablution, *ab-lu-xion*, N. duvop.

Abnegation, *ab-ne-gei-xion*, N. Patt cornem; visor.

Aboard (Go), *e-bord.* Tarvar chodd.
Abode, *ei-bôd*, N. Biddar; thicann.
Abolish, *a-bol′-ish*, V. Caddun uddounc; moddunc.
—(school)=dampunc.
Abolition, *a-bo-li-xion*, N. ontraunni; nam cornem; feddnni.
Abominable, *a-bo′-mi-nê-b′l*, A. Canttalleacho.
—(wicked)=khotteponnacho.
Abominate, Polle *Abhor.*
Abomination, *abo-mi-nei′-xion.* N. Canttallo; vitt; khotteponn.
Aborigines, *a-bo-ri-ji′-nez*, N. Mulvasi; thainche munis.
Abortion, *a-bôr-xion*, N. Pottchem; gorb hollnni.
Abound, *ei-baund*, V. Boronc; sompurnai asunc; chodd asunc.
About, *ei-bautt*, AD. PREP. Sumar.
—(almost)=bhon corun,
—(around)=bountonnec,
—(as regards)=thaim.
Above, *ei-bov*, PREP. Voir.
—AD. voir; unch.
Abreast, *ei-brest*, AD. Arin.
—(close)=lagim.
Abridge, *a-brij′*, V. Mottvo cor; lan cor.
Abridgement, *a-brij′-ment*, N. lan corop.
Abroad, *ei-bro′d*, AD. bhair; porganmvant.
Abrogate, *abro-geitt*, Polle *Abolish.*
Abrupt, *ab-rupt*, A. Anchit.
Abscess, *ab-ses*, N. Fodd.
Abscond, *abs-cond*, V. Liponc; pollun vochonc.
Absence, *ab′-sens*, N. Ajirnasnem; goir hazri.
Absent, *ab′-sent*, A. Goir-hazir.
Absent, *ab-sent*, V. Disonam zaunc.
Absinth, *ab-sinth*, N. Manpatri.
Absolute, *ab′-so-liu-tt*, A. Sompurn; paripurn.
—(despotic)=suatamtr ; suadin.
Absolution, *ab-so-liu′-xion*, N. Bogsonnem; suttca.
Absolve, *ab-solv*, V. Absolusaum diunc; bogsunc; map corunc.
Absorb, *ab-sorb*, V. Jironc.
—(in thought)=niallan buddonc.
Abstain, *abs-tein*, V. Chucounc; corinastanam ravunc.
—(from food)=upas dorunc; jinzvar dorunc.
Abstinence, *abs′-ti-nens*, N. Chucounnem; jinzvar; upas dornem.
Abstract, *abs-tract*, V. Caddunc; voddunc.
Abstruse, *abs-truz*, A. Guttacho, gupit; somzonamso; conttin.
Abstruseness, *abs-truz-nés*, N. Cottinai; calloc.
Absurd, *ab-so′rd*, A. Naca zalolo; vareavelo.
Absurdity, *ab-sor-di-tti*, N. Naca zalelem; pisai; golieponn.
Abundance, *a-ban′-dans*, N. Sompurnai; chodd.
Abundant, *a-ban′-dant*, A. Sompurn; dadosi.
Abuse, *a-biuz*, V. Galli sovonc; matiar bosunc.
Abuse, *a-biuz*, N. Gall; visvas gat.
Abusive, *a-biu-ziv*, A. Ocmanacho.
—(words)=galli.
Abyss, *a-bis*, N. Patoll; rahall; emcond.
Academy, *a-ca-de′-mi*, N. Videasall.
Accelerate, *ac-se-le-reit*, V. Vegim vo tactin corunc; dorvoddaunc.
Accent, *ac-sent*, N. Tallear bhar.
Accent, *ae-sent*, V. Tallear bhar galunc.
Accept, *ac-sept*, V. Mandun geunc; raji zaunc.

Acceptable, *ac-sep'-te-bl'*, A. Mogall; apurbaecho; manvoso.
Acceptation, *ac-sep-tei-xion*, N. Gevop; mannop.
Access, *ac-ses*, N. Rig.
Accessible, *ac-se-si-bl'*, A. Rig aslolo; vochoet aslolo.
Accessory, *ac'-se-so-ri*, A. Unnem gorjecho. [chuc.
Accident, *ac-si-dent*, N. Goddop;
Accidental, *ac-si-den-tal*, A. Goddpacho; auchit.
Acclamation, *ac'cla-mei-xion*, N. Navaddni; xebaski.
Accommodate, *ac-com-o'-deitt*, V. Sarco, laic corunc; mandunc; khoxe pormonnem cholonc.
Accommodation, *ac-com'-o-dei'-xion*, N. Mandni; somjaunni; borem gor; iskoll raucho zago; somandan; raji zavop.
Accompaniment, *a-com'-pa-ni-mentt'*, N. Pavni; sangat.
—(of marriage)=hôr.
Accompany, *a-com-pa-ni'*, N. Pavonc; sangata vochunc.
Accomplice, *a-com'plis*, N. Bageli chorien etc., sangati.
Accomplish, *a-com-plish*, V. xarti paunc; cobar corunc.
Accord, *a-cordd'*, V. Coblad diunc; tharau asunc.
Accordance, *a-cor-dans'*, N. Coblad; ecvott.
—(with) pormonnem.
Accordingly, *a-cor-ding-li*, ADV. Tor; decun. [carann.
Account, *é-caunt*, N. Ixeop; FG.
Account, *é-caunt*, V. Caran dacounc; ixeop diunc.
Accumulate, *a-cu'-mu-leit*, V. Punzaunc; ras corunc; choddounc.
Accumulation, *a-kiu-mu-lei'-xion*, N. Ras; zomo; punz (duddjanchi).

Accuracy, *a'-kiu-re'-si*, N. Chuc nasop; zagrutai.
Accurate, *a-kiu-reit'*, A. Chuc cori naslolo; sarco
Accursed, *a-kors'dd'*, PART. A. Xirap poddlolo.
Accusation, *a-kiu-zei'-xion'*, N. Guniauncari corop; feriad.
Accuse, *a-kiuz*, V. Guneauncari corunc; feriad diunc.
Accuser, *a-kiu-zar*, N. Guneauncari cornar; author.
Accustom, *ac cós-tom'*, V. Sovoim corunc; sovoim zaunc.
Acerb, *a-sérb*, A. Orvo; ambott.
Acerbity, *a-ser-bi-tti'*, N. Orvai; amsann; coddsan; FG. connisttai.
Ache, *ék*, N. Duc; foddafodd.
Achieve, *a-chiiv'*, V. Melloun geunc; xarti paunc.
Acid, *a-cid*, A. Ambott. [ambottai.
Acidity, *a-si-di-tti*, N. Amsaun;
Acknowledge, *ac-no-lej*, V. Vollkunc, mannunc, khoro munn somzunc.
—(receipt)=getlo munn sangunc.
Acknowledgement, *ac-no'-lej-ment*, N. Vollkonnem; mannop; decol cornem.
Acquaint, *ak-vaintt*, V. Kollounc; RF. zanno zaunc.
Acquaintance, *ak-veint'-ens*, N. Vollkicho; volloc aslolo.
Acquaintanceship, *ak-vein-ttens-ship*, N. Vollkicho.
Acquire, *a-cua-iar*, V. Zoddunc; jicunc; mellounc.
Acquirement, *a'-cua-iar-ment*, N. Zodd; zanvai.
Acquit, *a'-cuit*, V. Soddunc; niropradi muun suttca diunc.
Acquittal, *a-cui'-ttal*, N. Suttca.
Acrid, *a'-crid*, A. Khor; tic; khoddu; nisttur.
Acrimony, *a-cri-mo-ni'*, N. Coldsann; cottinai.

Across, *e-cros*, P. Polltoddi.
Act, *ect.* N. Corni.
Act, *ect.* V. Corunc.
—(behave)=cholunc.
—(to work in place of another) =bodlí polleunc.
—(fall to effect such as medicine) =guun poddunc.
Acting, *ac'-tting*, N. Bodli; suater choloitolo.
Action, *ec-xion*, N. Corni; cortub.
Active, *ec-ttiv.* A. Suddsuddit; uxear; bolladic.
Activity, *ec-ti-vi-tti*, N. Suddsuddai; uxarcai; boll.
Actor, *ec-ttor*, N. Nattoccar, theatrist, [atancho.
Actual, *ec-chu'-al*, A. Khoroch;
Acute, *a-kiu-tt*, A. Dar aslolo, domsacho; fg. baric.
Acuteness, *a-kiutt-ness*, N. Dar; domos; fg. barcai.
Adage, *a-deij*, N. Munni; proverb.
Adamant, *a-da-mant*, N. Diamanti sarco fator.
Adapt, *a-dapt'*, V. Zoctem zaunc; upcarunc. [di.
Add, *edd*, V. Aninc gal vo aninc
Addict, *a-ddict*, V. Lagonc; bulonc.
Addicted, *a-ddic-tte'd*, P. A. Laglolo munge pieunc etc.
Addition, *e'ddi-xion*, N. Choddau; choddni.
Additional, *e'-ddi-xion-nal*, A. Choddavot; sivai; kerit.
Address, *a'-dres*, N. Naum-gor, naum-gaum; discurs.
Address, *a-dres'*, V. Ulonnc; naum thican borounc; discurs corunc.
Adduce, *a-ddiu'-s*, Dacounc.
Adequate, *a-de-kuëtt*, A. Zocto; camanc poddo sarco.
Adhere, *add-hi'-ier*, Lagunc; cobul zaunc; ecttavonc.
Adherence, *a-ddi-ie-rens'*, N. Lagop; cobul zavop.
Adherent, *a-ddi-ie-rent*, A. Pattlau cornar; istt-montr.
Adjacent, *ad-ja'-sent* A. Lagsilo; mereli.
Adjoin, *ad-jo'-in*, Ecvott corunc, mellounc.
Adjourn, *ad-jörn*, V. Fudde voronc; era disa dovorunc.
Adjudge, *ad-jaj,'* V. Tharau—, nit corunc.
Adjure, *ad-ju-ar* V. Soput diun ulounc; ann,-soput diunc.
Administer, *ad-mi-nis-torr.* V. Cholounc; vosounc.
Administration, *ad-mi-nis-trei'-xion*, N. Cholounni; vosounni.
—(government)=rajcarbar.
—(of justice) nit,-nea cornem.
—(of sacrament)=sacrament dinnem.
Administrator, *ad-mi-nis-treittor*, N. Choloinar; carbari; gorcar.
Admiral, *ad-mi-ral*, N. Zuzacheam tarvancho voddil.
Admiration, *ad-mi-rei'-xion*, N. Ojap zannem; ochoriem; coutuc.
Admire, *ad-ma'iar.* V. Ojap zaun polleunc; thothacun tellunc.
Admission, *ad-mi'-xion*, N. Eunc dinnem; gevop; rig.
Admit, *ad-mitt'*, V. Geunc; eunc diunc; bitor geunc; cobul corunc.
Admonish, *ad-mo'-nish*, V. Bori bud diunc; bobatt corunc; domcaunc.
Admonition, *ad-mo-ni'-xion*, V. Takit; domki; sicoun.
Adopt, *a-dop'-t*, V. Posunc; dorm putr.—Aplo corunc; vinchun caddunc.
Adoption, *a-dop'-xion*, N. Poskeponn: dormputr-ponn.

Adoptive, *a'dop-tiv,* A. Posco; dorm-putr., [caracho.
Adorable, *a-do'-re-bl,* A. Nomos-
Adoration, *ado-rei'-xion,* N. Deupuja; nomoscar; pranipat.
Adore, *a-dor,* V. Nomoscar corunc; bozunc; pranipatunc.
Adorn, *a-dor'-n,* V. Surungarunc; nettounc; sobounc.
Adornment, *a'-dorn-ment',* N. Surungar; sobitai; sobai.
Adroit, *a-droit,* A. Icmoti; mannecar.
Adulation, *a-du-lei'-xion.* N. Lag; khuxamot; fuslaunni.
Adult, *a-dol'-tt,* A. Piraecho; puxtti borlolo; manaim.
Adulterate, *a-dol'-te-reit,* V. Bhelgalunc; bigddunc; fottkiro corunc. [duari.
Adulterer, *a-dol-te-rar,* N. Pro-
Adulteress, *a-dol-te-res,* N. Produvarin. [duavar.
Adultery, *a-dol'-te-ri,* N. Pro-
Advance, *ad'-vans,* V. Mucar galunc; voir caddunc; fudde vochonc; adim faric corunc vo diunc.
Advanced, (*in age*), P. A. Utar piraecho; mataro; malgoddo.
Advancement, *ad-vans'-ment,* N. Don girescaen vaddnem; lab; adau; faida. [jicop.
Advantage, *ad-van'-ttej,* N. faido;
Advantageous, *advan-tte'jias,* A. Adavacho; upcaroso.
Advent, *ad-'vent,* N. Iennem; pavnnem; advent.
Adventure, *ad-ven'-chiar,* N. Oddrust; goddop.
Adversary, *ad-ver'-sa-ri,* N. Inimig, dusman.
Adverse, *ad-vors,* A. Upratto; virodhi; dusmanic.
Adversity, *ad-vor'-si-tti,* N. Avdisa; vign; acant.
Advertise, *ad-vor-ttaiz,* V. Collit, porgott corunc; khobor diunc.
Advertisiment, *ad-vor-taiz-ment,* N. Khobor; collounni; anus.
Advice, *ad'-vais,* N. Bud; somzoni; khobor.
Advisable, *ad-vai'-zé-bl,* A. Kelear boro tosolo.
Advise, *ad'-vaiz,* V. Bud diunc; collounc.
Advocate, *ad'-vo-két,* N. Letrad; vokil.
Adze, *adz,* N. Tasnni.
Aerial, *ë-ri-al,* A. Vareacho.
Aerolite, *é-rô-lait,* N. Cupacho fator.
Aerometer, *e-ro'-me-ttor,* V. Vareachem map.
Afar, *è-far',* AD. pois.
Affability, *a-fa-bi'-li-ti,* N. Mogallponn; boleponn; dulobai; goddai.
Affable, *a-fe-bl,* A. Bolo: mogall; dulob; curpevont.
Affair, *a-fer',* N. Cam: vepar; udiog; dando.
Affect, *a'-fect,* V. Dakounc; bolliam corunc; dong-lng corunc.
Affectation, *a-fec-ttei'-xion,* N. Dakounnem; dong; kopott.
Affected, *af-fec'-tted,* A. Dakoun, laglolo; dongi.
Affection, *a-fec'-xion,* N. Mog; vonddoun; apurbai. [Mogall.
Affectionate, *a-fec'-xio-neitt,* A.
Affiance, *a-fi'-eans,* N. Soiric kelolo. [monn.
Affidavit, *a-fi'-da-vit,* N. por-
Affiliate, *a-fi'-li-eit,* V. Aplo putt corunc; aplem naum diunc.
Affinity, *a-fi'-ni-tti* N. Soiric,
Affirm, *a-for-m,* V. Oi munnonc; khorem—, khonchit—, khondit sangunc.
Affix, *a'-fix,* Lagonnc vo launc.
Afflict, *a'-flict,* V. Ducounc; coistavonc; upodre diunc.

Afflicted, *af-flic'-tted*, A. Dukest; dukaborit.
Afflicting, *af-flic-tting*, A. Ducouncho; lagcho.
Affliction, *a-flic-xion*, N. Khont; duc; coistt.
Affluence, *a'-flu-ens*, A. Loth: londdo; sompurnai.
Afford, *af-ford*, Cobul zaunc; diunc: tanc asunc.
Affront, *af-front*, N. Ocman.
Affront, *af'-front*, V. Ocman corunc.
Afoot, *'e-futt*, AD. Pai-vatton.
Afraid, *a'-freid* A. Bezudd.
Afraid, (I am of) V. Anm bhietam; maca bhirant dista.
Afresh, *e'-fresh*, AD. Portun: aninc ek pautt. [pattlean.
After, *af'-tter*, PR. Uprant: magir;
After all, *af'-tter ol*, AD. Tori; xekim: oxem zalear.
Afterwards, *af-tter-words*, PR. Uprant; magir.
Again, *e-gen*, AD. Aninc ek pautti; portun.
Against, *a-ge'-inst*, PR. AD. Virudh.
Age, *eij*, N. Pirai: vorsam: auc.
Aged, *e'-jed*, A. Mataro; piraecho, vodd.
Agency, *eij-en'-si*, N. Corni: cortob; dolalki; carbar.
Agent, *e-jent*, N. Cornar; Carbari: dolal.
Aggravate, *ag-gra-veitt*, V. Vodic—, ogllo corunc; chodd-dounc: vodic vaitt corunc.
Aggravation, *ag-gra-vei-xion'*, N. Vodic cornem; bhar.
Aggregate, *ag-gre'-geitt*, V. Ecttaim corunc; mellounc.
Aggregation, *ag-gre-gei-xion*, N. Mèll: ecott,
Aggression, *ag-gre-xion*, N. Ocman; zulum; angar poddop.
Aggressive, *a-gre'-siv'*, A. Virodhi: jabardost.
Aggressor, *ag-gre-sor*, N. Angar poddnar; zulumdar.
Agile, *a'-jil*, A. Angsutt; sudd-suddit; utavlo.
Agility, *a-ji-litti* N. Suddsuddai; damdolpon; barcai.
Agitate, *aj-i'-teitt*, V. Alounc; dovlunc; challounc; firounc; gansunc.
Agitation, *aj-i-tei'-xion*, N. Halop; nchambollai; tollmolle.
Agnate, *ag-neitt'*, N. Daiji (bapai eusilo.)
Ago, *ei-go'*, AD. Adim.
Agony, *a-go'-ni*, N. Ghorghor; monnacheo voddi; atte-vitte; toll-molle.
Agree, *ag-ri'*, V. Cobul zaunc; sori corunc.
Agreeable, *ag-ri-e-bl*, A. Godd; roc: sontosi.
Agreement, *ag-ri'-ment*, N. Contrat: somandan.
Agriculture, *ag-ri-col-chiar*, N. Setcam; kurvaddponn.
Ague, *ei'-giu*, N. Tollincho zor.
Ah, *int.* ah! vo aba!
Aid, *eid*, N. Adar; mozot; dir.
Ail, *i'-eil*, V. Duconc: sosunc.
Ailing, *ei-ling*, A. Piddest: vaittacar. [boullic.
Ailment, *eil'-ment*, N. Pidda,
Aim, *eim'*, N. Xevott; carann.
Aim, *ei'm*, V. Tir dorunc; nodor vo dan-mon donrunc.
Air, *er*, N. Varem.
Air, *er*, V. Varem galunc.
Airy, *e-ri*, A. Vareacho; iscoll.
Aisle, *e'-is-li*, N. Bolcanm.
Akin, *a'-kin*, A. Daiji: soiro.
Alacrity, *a-la-cri-tti*, N. Sudd-suddai: uxearcai.
Alarm, *ie'-larm*, N. Bhirant; khont; acantachi campinn.

Alarm, *ie-larm*, v. Beneddaunc.
Alarum, *ie-la'-rum*, N. Zagounnechem goddial.
Alas, *ie-las*, int. ai!
Alcohol, *al-ko-hol'*, N. Soriachi fenni: tic soro.
Ale, *i-el*, N. Bir, cervej.
Alehouse, *i-el-haus'*, N. Soreachem ducan.
Alert, *a'-lert*, A. Zagrut; uxear; toiar.
Algebra, *al-je'-bra*, N. Bijgonnit.
Alienate, *alie-neitt*, v. Mon pois corunc.
Alienation, *a-lie-nei'-xion*, N. Cusin caddop; coddsorop.
Alight, *ie-laith'*, v. Denvunc.
Alike, *ie-laic'*, A. Tosolo; tea jinsacho.
Aliment, *a-li'-ment*, N. Jevon: khan; udarposonn.
Alimentary. *a-li-men-tari*, N. Jevnacho; khannacho; poscho.
Alive, *e-laiv*, A. Jivo: uxear.
All, *ol*, A. Soglo; somest; zonneiclo; sorv.
All, (AT) AD. Bilcul.
Allay, *a'-lei*, v. Somandan corunc; nidounc: duc unni corunc.
Allegation, *a-le-gei-xion*, N. Alegasanm: nimit sangnem; nib.
Allege, *a-lej'*, v. Nimit sangunc; nib sarune: daclo diunc.
Allegory, *a-le'-go-ri*. N. Opar; got.
Alleviate, *a-le'-vi-eit*, v. Hallu corunc: sustaunc: buzounc.
Alleviation, *a-le-vi-ei-xion*, N. Visor: buzvon: luu corop.
Alliance, *a-lai'.ans*, N. Ecott, mêll: isttogot.
Alligator, *a-li-gei-ttor*, N. Americachem mangem.
Allot, *al-lott'*, v. Vanttunc, vantte corun diunc. [tte.
Allotment, *al-lott'-ment*, N. Van-
Allow, *e-lau*, v. Soddunc; rojea diunc; nirmunc. [roja.
Allowance, *elau'-ens*, N. Soddop;
Alloy, *al-loi*, v. Borsunc.
Alloy, *al-loi*, v. Unne kimtichem metal beli corunc.
Allude, *a-liud*, v. Ugddas caddunc; sôr corunc.
Allure, *a-liu'-ar*, v. Fuslaunc; piso corunc.
Allurement, *a-liu-ar-ment*, N, Fuslaunnem; umollai.
Allusion, *a-liu-jion'*, N. Ugddas; suchan.
Ally, *a-li'*, n. Sambandi; istt.
Almanac, *al-ma'-nac*, N. Almanac, panchang.
Almighty, *oll-mai-tti*, A. Sorvpodvedar; sorvocumdar,
Almond, *al'-mond*, N. Amend, bodom.
Almost, *ol'-most*, AD. Sumar; lagim-lagim.
Alms, *a-ms*, N. Izmol, bic; dhorm,
Aloe, *a-loi*, N. Kantte-cuuvor.
Aloft, *a-loft*, AD. Unch.
Alone, *ie'-lon*, A. Eksuro, eclo; ecloch. [lagim; vorvim.
Along, *ei-long*, AD. PR. Codde,
Aloof, *a'-luf*, AD. Pois.
Aloud, *e-laudd*, AD. Voddlean.
Alphabet, *al-fa-bett*, N. Acxermella.
Already, *ol'-re-ddi*, AD. Poiloch; adinch; roeddo; vegim.
Also, *ol-so*, AD. Cunj; tosench; anninc: toi.
Altar, *ol'-ttar*, N. Altar.
Alter, *ol'-ttor*, v. Bodlunc; sori corunc; nittier galunc.
Alteration, *ol-tte'-rei-xion*, N. Bodol: firaunni.
Altercate, *oc-tter'-keit*, v. Zogddung; bandduno; zuzunc.
Altercation, *ol-tter-kei-xion*, N. zogddem; zomba-zombi; basabas.

Alternate, *al-ttor-neitt*, V. Adolbodol corunc; eca meca patti eunc.

Alternately, *al-ttor'-neitt-li*, AD. Sallatpallat.

Alternative, *al-ttor-nei-ttiv*, N. Palli; sodolbodol.

Although, *ol-dou*, C. zori tor.

Altitude, *al-tti-tiud*, N. Unchi; unnatti.

Altogether, *ol-tu-ge-dor*, AD. Soglem mellon; ogdim; bilcul.

Alum, *a-lom'*, N. Fottki.

Always, *ol'-ve-is*, AD. Sodanch; sodanical.

Amalgamate, *a-mal-ga-meitt*, V. Ecttaim corunc; mislluno.

Amalgamation, *a-mal-ga-meixion*, N. Misollni; borsi.

Amanuensis, *ama-nu-en-sis*, N. Borpi; lekhnar.

Amass, *a'-mas*, V. Zomo corunc; punzaunc.

Amaze, *a-meiz'*, V. Ojap zaunc; [thottaconc.

Amazement, *a-meiz-ment*, N Thottacni; auchit dornem.

Ambassador *am-ba-se'-dor*, N. Raibari; munniari.

Ambiguity, *am-bi-gu-itti*, N. Duvarthan; dubav.

Ambiguous, *am-bi-gu-as'*, A. Duvarthi; dubavacho.

Ambition, *am-bi-xion*, N. Suarth; axea; ahancar.

Ambitious, *am-bi-xi-as*, A. Suarthi; axecho; ahancari.

Ambulance, *am-bu-lans*, N. Bountem hospital.

Ambush, *am-bush*, N. Nadd; lipchi suat.

Ameliorate, *a-me-li-eo-reitt*, V. Sudarunc; boro corunc.

Amelioration, *a-me-li-eo-reixion*, N. Sudarop.

Amend, *a'-mend*, V. Sarkem corunc: bodlunc,

Amends, (Make) V. Fariconn diunc.

Amenity, *a-me'-ni-tti*, N. Khoxalai; suc, sontos.

Amiable, *a'-mi-e-bl*, A. Mogall; priticho

Amidst, *ie-midst*, PR. Modem; bitor.

Amiss, (Take), *ie-mis*, V. Vaitt voruuc.

Amnesty, *am'-nes-tti*, N. Bogsonnem; map.

Among, *i-e-mong*, PR. Modem; bitor.

Amount, *i-e-maunt*, N. Rokom; ixeop; cont.

Amount, V. Ixeop zaunc.

Ample, *em'-pl*, A. Zaito; chodd; vistarlolo

Amplify, *em'-pli-fai*, V. Choddounc; vistarunc.

Amputate, *am-piu'-tei-tt*, V. Catrunc; soddounc; capunc.

Amulet, *a-miu'-let*, N. Tottko; utarchit.

Amuse, *a-miuz*, V. Khoxal corunc; Khellounc.

Amusement, *a-miuz-ment*, N. Khoxalai; sontos.

Analogy, *a-na-lo'-ji*, N. Sarkeponn; vopar.

Analysis, *a-na'-li-zis*, N. Vibhag; poricsha.

Ananas, *a-na-nas*, N. Anenes.

Anarchy, *a-nar-ki'*, N. Rai naslelem raj; tirraj; tufan; ghondholl.

Anathema, *a-na-te-ma*, N. Suput, sorgincho xirap.

Anatomy, *a-na'-to-mi*, N. Sorir, sorirac.

Ancestor, *an'-ses-ttor*, N. Mataro; zantto; malgoddo; purvoz.

Anchor, *an'-cor*, N. Nangor,

Anchor, V. Nangor galunc.

Anchorite, *an'-co-rait*, N. Saniasi.

Ancient, *ein'-shent*, A. Porno ; purvilo ; magam.
And, *end*, CONJ. Anim.
Anecdote, *a-nec-dot*, N. Contha; cannim; gosthi.
Anew, *ie-niu'*, AD. Portuo. aninc ek pautt.
Angel, *einj'-el'*, N. Bodvo.
—(Guardian Angel)=bodvo racnno.
Anjelus, (Domini), *an-je-lus*, N. Amori; tinsanam
Anger, *ien-gar'*, N. Rag; kirod.
Angle, *ien-gl'*, N. Gori; sintari; conso.
Angle, V. Masli dorunc; pagunc.
Angry, *ien'-gri*, A. Ragist.
—(to get angry)=ragar zaunc.
Anguish, *ien'-guish*, N. Kollvollo; skant; sontap.
Anil, *a-nil*, N. Niulichem zadd.
Animadversion, *a-ni-mad-ver'-xion*, N. Dusmancai; viclab.
Animal, *a'-ni-mal*, N. Zanvar; monzat. [boll-calliz diunc.
Animate, *a'-ni-meitt*, V. Dhir—,
Animated, *a'-ni-mei-ted*, A. Jivo; bolladic; uxear.
Ankle, *ien-kl'*, N. Khubo
Anna, *a-nna*, N. Anno.
Annals, *an'-nals*, N. Vorsancheo khobro.
Anneal, *a'-nil*, V. Panni diunc.
Annex, *a-nnex*, V. Mellounc; goddsunc.
Annihilate, *a-ni-hi-leitt*, V. Bosmunc; nanch corunc.
Anniversary, *a-ni-ver'sa-ri*, A. Vorsacho; zolmacho dis.
Annolate, *a-nno-leitt*, V. Ticunc; astechi zoddti corunc.
Annotation, *a-no-tei'-xion*, N. Chotrai.
Announce, *a'-nauns*, V. Khobor addunc; porgott corunc; gomounc.
Annoy, *an-noi*, V. Bejar corunc! corcor corunc. [cor.
Annoyance, *an-noi'-ians*, N. Cor-
Annoying, *a-noi'-ing*, A. Corcoracho; bejar corcho.
Annual, *an'-nual*, A. Vorsacho.
Annul, *an-nol*, V. Bomgounc ; moddunc.
Anoint, *a-noint*, V. Cudic tellaunc; makunc; rogddunc.
Anointment, *a-noint-ment*, N. Makhop; rogddop.
Anomalous, *a-nom'-a-las*, N. Caidea pormonnem naslolo.
Anon, *a-non*, AD. Atanch ; thodde pautti.
Anonymous, *a-no-ni-mas'*, N. Naum naslolo.
Another, *ie-no-dor*, A. Aninc eoc; aninc eclo; dusro.
Answer, *an'-sor*, N. Zobab; portipall.
Answer, *an-sor*, V. Zabab diunc.
Ant, *antt*, N. Mui; **black ant**—domllo; **red ant**—umlo; **very small ant**—urna.
Antagonism, *an-ta-go'-ni-zam*, N. Virodh. [mucavelo.
Anterior, *an-te'-ri-ior*, A. Adlo ;
Anthem, *an-tem*, N. Antifon.
Anticipate, *an-tis'-i-peitt*, V. Adim corunc vo polleunc; somzunc. [upai.
Antidote, *an-ti-doutt*, N. Vocot ;
Antipathy, *an-ti-pa'-tti*, N. Napad; dusmancai.
Antiquity, *an-tti'-kui-tti*, N. Adlo call. [fator.
Anvil, *ien-vil*, N. Boddouncho
Anxiety, *anx-sa'-ie-tti*, V. Usco; chintna. [test; uskeache.
Anxious, *anx'-xi-ias*, A. Chin-
Any, *ie-ni*, ART. Cosoloi.
Anywhere, *ie-ni-ver*, AD. Sorvoi suatar. [godd.
Apart, *ie-part*, AD. Kherit ; vin-

Apartment, *ie-part'-ment*, N. cudd.

Apathy, *a-pa'-thi*, N. Mengeponn; zoddai; beporva.

Ape, *eip*, N. Vandor.

Aperture, *ap'-er-chear*, N. Fall; ver; dan.

Apocryphal, *a-poc'-ri-fal*, A Fottkiro.

Apologetic, *a-po-lo-je'-tic*, A. Samballtalo: udaran saugcho.

Apologize, *a-po-lo-jaiz'*, V. Map magunc; farieponn diunc.

Apology, *a-po'-lo-ji*, N. Mapmagnem.

Apoplexy, *a-po-plex-ci*, N. Apaplis; rogtachi pidda.

Apostasy, *a-pos'-ta-zi*, N. Sumurt soddnem.

Apostate, *a-pos'-teitt*, N. Sumurt sandnar: fitur.

Apostatize, *a-pos-ta-taiz*, V. Sumurt soddunc. [xins.

Apostle *a-pos'-sl*, N. Apostl;

Apothecary, *a-po'-te-ca-ri*, N. Voctam victolo; voiz.

Apparatus, *a-pa-ra'-tus*, V. Samonn. [mustaiki.

Apparel, *ap-pa'-rel*, N. Nesounn;

Apparent, *a-pei'-rent*, A. Decol, ugtto, disto ; fottkiro.

Apparently, *a-pei'-rent-li*, AD. Bhailian, bhailia-bhair.

Apparition, *a-pa-ri'-xion*, N. Disttipoddop.

Appeal, *a' pil*, V. Apelasaum coruno, saksi corunc, ; ulo marunc, ilaj magunc. [ilaj.

Appeal, N. Apelasaum, upai,

Appear, *a-pi'-er*, V. Disttipoddonc : ajir asunc.

Appearance, *a-pi'-er-ens*, N. Disop ; rup ; saulli.

Appease, *a-piiz*, V. Sostaunc ; somandau corunc ; movallaunc: faricponn diunc.

Append, *a-pend*, V. Choddounc

Appendix, *a-pen'-dix*, N. Choddop. [zaunc.

Appertain, *a-per-tein'*, V. Favo

Appetite, *a-pi-taitt*, N. Ruch, bhuc : fg. khoxi.

Applaud, *a-plaud*, V. Tallieo pettunc.

Applause, *a-ploz*, N. Tallio pet-nem: xebaski.

Apple, *ie-pl*, N. Apol : bor ; —(apple of the eye), Bauli.

Applicant, *a'-pli-canth*, N. Arjecar.

Application, *a-pli-kei'-xion*, N. Arji, magnem ; lagop.

Apply, *ap-lai'*, V. Magunc, launc ; lagounc.

Appoint, *a-point'*, V. Nomiar corunc ; naum geunc.

Appointment, *a-point-ment*, N. Nomeasaum, nemni.

Appreciate, *a-pre'-xi-eitt*, V. Mandunc ; khoxi zaunc ; mol volkunc.

Apprehend, *a-pre-hend'*, V. Dorunc ; sampddaunc ; somzunc ; volconc ; bhieunc.

Apprehension, *ap-prè-hen'-xion*, N. Bhirant ; chintna.

Apprehensive, *ap-pre-hen'-siv*, A. Bezudd ; chintest.

Apprentice, *ap-pren'-tis*, N. Umedvar, sienar.

Approach, *ap-proch*, V. Lagim soronc vo eunc.

Approbation, *ap-pro-bei'-xion*, N. Manop, approvasaum.

Appropriate, *ap-pro'-pri-eit*, V. Apnnac geunc, aplo corunc.

Appropriate, *ap-pro'-pri-eitt*, A. Borobor, sarco ; zocto.

Approval, *ap-pru'-val*, N. Manop, aprovasaum;

Approve, *ap-pruv'*, V. Mandunc ; puttronc ; posond corunc.

Approximate, *ap-prox'-si-meitt,* A. Lagsarcho, sumaracho.
Approximate, V. Lagim addunc,—vorunc.—pavounc.
Approximation, *ap-prox-si-mei'-xion,* N. Lagim sorop.—pavop.
Apron, *ié'-pron,* N. Mucavelem lugot.
Apt, *i-ept,* A. Soctivont, uxear.
Aquatic, *a-ku-a'-tic,* Udcantlo.
Aqueduct, *a-ku-e'-duct,* N. Noll.
Arbiter, *ar'-bi-ttor,* N. Modest; askari.
Arbitrary, *ar'-bi-tra-ri,* A. Khoxecho, khoxe purto, apnuac zai toso.
Arbitrate, *ar'-bi-treith,* V. Modesthaen nivaddunc; tharaunc; molaunc.
Arbitration, *ar-bi-trei'-xion,* N. Ponchat, carar.
Arbour, *ar'-bor,* N. Mollo; matton.
Arcade, *ar-keid',* N. Vorand.
Arch, *arch,* N. Ark.
Archangel, *arc'-cin-jel,* N. Arcanj.
Archbishop, *arch'-bi-shop,* N. Arcebisp.
Archeology, *ar-cheo'-lo-ji,* N. Adleam callanchi videa.
Archetype, *ark'-taip,* N. Nomuno.
Architect, *ar'-ki-tect,* N. Bandnar, bandpi.
Architecture, *ar'-ki-tec-chear,* N Bandavoll; bandchi videa.
Archive, *ar'-kiir,* N. Dafterkhano.
Ardent, *ar'-dent,* A. Zollto, umalleacho.
Ardour, *ar'-dor,* N. Umallo, khoxi: suddsuddai
Arduous, *ar'-du-as,* A. Conttin.
Area, *a-ria,* N. Suat, zago..
Areca-nut, *a-re-ca-not,* N. Fofoll.
Areca-tree, N. Maddi.
Argil, *ar-gil,* Khedd cumbar-methi.
Argue *ar'-giu,* V. Tocrar corunc; dacounc.
Argument, *ar-gu-ment,* N. Ruzvat; daclo; somzonni.
Arid, *a-rid',* A. Suco.
Aridity, *a-ri'-di-tti,* N Sucop; khorcori; fg. darunnai.
Arise, *ie-raiz',* V. Uttonc, unch vochonc; fg. ubzonc.
Aristocracy, *a-ris-to'-cra-si,* N. Maha-kulli.
Aristocrat, *a'-ris-to-crat,* N. Vodde calliecho munis; poroh.
Arithmetic, *a-rit-me'-tic,* N. Ancanchi videa, gonnit; arithmetica.
Ark, *arc,* N. arc.
Arm, *a'-m,* N. Buz; bhaullo.
Arm, *a'-m,* V. Hatiaram diunc.
Arm-chair, *a-m-cher,* N. Hat asleli bosca.
Arm-pit, *a'-m-pitt,* N. Kac.
Armistice, *ar'-mis-tis,* N. Hatiaram dourop; zuz ravop.
Armour, *ar'-mor,* N. Cuddichi raconn.
Armoury, *ar'-mo-ri,* N. Hatiaranchem gor.
Arms, *a'-ms,* N. Hatiar.
Army, *ar-mi,* N. Lozcor: fouz; soin,
[domdom.
Aroma, *a-ro'-ma,* N. Pormoll; domdom.
Aromatic, *a-ró-ma-tic,* A. Pormolhit; domdomit.
Around, *e-ra'-und,* PR. AD. Bountonim vo bountim.
Arouse, *e-rauz',* V. Uchamboll corunc; uttounc.
Arrak, *a'-rac,* N. Nibor soro.
Arraign, *a-rein,* V. Rombunc; fg. khonchounc; pallam geunc.
Arrange, *ar-réinj',* V. Mandduncl nittier galunc.

Arrangement, *ar-reinj'-mənt,* N. Toiari; manddavoll; bondabost.
Array, *a-rei,* V. Toiari corunc; manddunc.
Array, *a-rei,* N. Manddavoll.
Arrear, *a-ri'-er,* N Baki.
Arrest, *ar-rest',* V. Dorunc; sampddaunc; fg. coidi corunc.
Arrest, *ar-rest',* N. Coidi.
Arrival, *ie-rai-val,* N. Ennem; pavop.
Arrive, *ie-raiv,* V. Eunc; pavunc.
Arrogance, *a'-ro-gans,* N. Gorv; urmottai.
Arrogant, *a'-ro-gant,* A. Gorvi; urmott; aplea vadeacho.
Arrow, *ie-rou,* N. Bhali.
Arrowroot, *ie-rou'-rutt,* N. Cuveachem pitt, ararut. [khar.
Arsenic, *ar'-se-nic,* N. Somal
Art, *artt,* N. Videa; sicop; icmot.
Article, *ar'-ti-cl,* N. Jinos; nog; dagino; vost.
—(of Faith)=Poico.
—(of journal)=Artig.
Articulate, *ar-ti-cu-lleitt',* A. Sostt; sarco.
Articulate, V. Sarkem ucharaunc.
Artifice, *ar'-tti-fis,* N. Cornar, cortobi; fg. goddnar; rochnar.
Artificial, *ar-ti fi'-xial,* A. Kelolo; goddllolo.
Artillery, *ar-tti'-le-ri,* N. Nalli.
Artisan, *ar'-ti-zan,* N. Thovoi.
Artist, *ar'-tist,* N. Casabi, silpi.
As, *ez,* AD. C. Bori.
—zosem; pasun, pasot.
—(far as)=Tethun porian.
—(far as possible)=Tanki pormonnem.
—(much as)=Jitlem.
—(soon as)=Tea uprant.
—(to)=Thaim vo vixeant.
—(follows): oxem.
Asafeatida, *a-sa-fe'-ti-da,* N. Hing.
Ascend, *a'-send,* V. Voir choddonc; unch vochonc.
Ascendency, *a-sen-den-si',* N. Choddni; choddop; fg. podvi; adicar.
Ascension, *a-sen'-xion,* N. Choddop; sorgar choddnem.
Ascent, *a-sentt',* N. Choddto.
Ascertain, *a-ser-tte-in,* V. Khobor geunc; zanno zaunc.
Ascetic, *a-se'-tic,* A. Tapasvantt; devosponnacho.
Ashamed, (Be), *a-xeim'-dd,* V. Lozonc.
Ashes, *ie-xis,* N. Gobor; sinz.
Ash-Wednesday, *iesh-ved-nosddei,* N. Sinzicho budvar.
Ashore, *ei'-shor* AD. Thoddic.
Aside, *ei-said,* AD. Kherit; cusin.
Ask, *asc,* V. Magunc; vincharunc.
Askance, (*Look*) V. Vancddem polleunc.
Asleep, *(Be)* V. Nidonc.
—(Fall) V. Jemenne.
—(Put) V. Nidonnc.
Aspect, *as-'pect,* N. Rup; tondd.
Asphalt, *as-falt',* N. Dambôr.
Aspiration, *as-pi-rei'-xion,* N. Usvas; fg. umed.
Aspire, *as-pa'-iar,* V Laleunc.
Asquint, *as-kuint',* A. Tirso.
—(Look asquint)=tirso polleunc.
Ass, *as,* N. Gaddum.
Assail, *a-seil',* N. Angar poddonc; zulum corunc.
Assassin, *as-sas'-sin,* N. morticar; mort, khun.
Assassinate, *as-sas'-si-neitt',* V. Mort marunc; jivesim marunc;
Assassination, *as-sas-si-nei'-xion,* N. Mort, khun.
Assault, *a-solt',* V. zulum corunc; zomp marunc.
Assault, N. Zulum; zomp.
Assemblage, *a-semb'-lêij,* N. Bous, zomat; ras.

Assemble, *as-sem'-bl*, V. Ecttaim zaunc; zoma zaunc.
Assembly, *as-sem'-bli*, N. Zomat; bous; ecvott.
Assent, *as-sent'*, N. Coblat.
Assent, V. Cobul zaunc.
Assert, *as-sort'*, V. Khondit sangong.
Assertion, *as-sor'-xion*, N. khorem sangnem.
Assessment, *as-ses'-ment*, N. Mol; kimot; andaz.
Assets, *as-sets'*, N. Rinn faric corcheac urlelem samonn.
Asseverate, *as-se'-ve-reith*, V. Sobe mazar decol corunc.
Assiduity, *as-si-du'-iti*, N. Zotnai; chotrai.
Assiduous, *as-sidu'-as*, A. zagrut.
Assiduously, *as-si-du'-as-li*, AD. Tambonastanam.
Assign, *a-sain*, V. Dusreac diunc; nemunc.
Assignation, *as-sig-nei'-xion*, V. Corar bettoncheac; dusreachea naumvar caddunc.
Assignee, *as-sai'-ni*, N. Nemlolo.
Assignment, *as-sain'-ment*, N. Tharaileli vost.
Assimilate, *as-si'-mi-leitt*, V. Tosolo corunc; jironc.
Assist, *as-sist'*, V. Adar vo mozot diunc; pavunc.
Assistance, *as sis-tens'*, N. Mozot; adar.
Assistant, *as-sis'-tant*, N. Ata socol vaur cornar.
Associate, *as-so'-xi-eith*, V. Sangat corunc vo sangati zaunc.
Associate, N. Sangati; istt.
Association, *as-so-xi-ei'-xion*, N. Ecott; mêll.
Assort, *as-sort'*, V. Kherit caddunc; manddunc.
Assortment, *as-sort'-ment*, N. Jinos.
Assume, *as-si'-um*, V. Somzonc; bollan geunc.
Assumption, *as-sam'-xion*, N. Gevop; sorgar vorop.
Assurance, *a-xuar'-ens*, N. Khori bas dinnem; patieop.
Assure, *a-xu'-or*, V. Khorem corunc; thirason diunc; sugur corunc.
Assurer, *a-xu'-o-rar*, N. Sugur cornar.
Asthma, *as'-ma*, N. Lôs.
Astonish, *as-ton'-ish*, V. Ojap corunc; ojap zaunc.
Astonishing, *as-to'-nish-ing*, A Ojapancho.
Astonishment, *as-to'-nish-ment*, N. Ojap.
Astray, (Go) *as-trei'*, V. Vatt chuconc.
Astrict, *as-trict*, V. bandunc vo dambunc.
Astringent, *as-trin'-jent*, N. Bond corchem vocot.
Astrologar, *as-tro'-lo-gar*. N. Gannac, jaisi.
Astronomer, *as-tro'-no-mar*, N. Jiotishi.
Astronomy, *as tro'-no-mi*, N. Jiotis
Asylum, *ie-sai'-lam*, N. Asôr; adar; dhormsal.
Atheist, *a'-te-ist*, N. Nastic; Den asa nunn sotmandinam tosolo munis.
Atlas, *at'-las*, N. Bhuim nocxi.
Atmosphere, *at'-mos-fi'-er*, N. Varem; ontroll.
Atom, *a'-ttom*, N. Cuscutt; tus.
Atone, *a-tton'*, V. Fáric-ponn diunc; pirajit corunc.
Atonment, *a'-tton-ment*, N. Faric-ponn; pirajit.
Atrocious, *a-tro'-xi-as*, A. Darrun; nisttur.
Atrocity, *a-tro'-si-tti*, N. Darrunnai; nisttur ai.

Attach, *a-ttech'*, v. Launc; lagonc.
Attachment, *a-ttech'-ment*, N. Lagop; mog, apurbai.
Attack, *a'-ttec*, v. Angar eunc vo poddonc.
Attack, N. Zulum; boll.
Attain, *a-ttein'*, Jicunc; zod-dunc; paunc.
Attempt, *a-tempt'*, v. Corunc fudde soronc.
Attempt, N. Corunc mucar sorop.
Attend, *a-ttend'*, v. Borobor vochunc vo asunc; hajir asunc; sangat diunc; chacri corunc.
Attendance, *a-ttend'-ans*, N. Chacri corop.
Attendant, *a-ttend'-ant*, N. N. Chacor vo sevoc.
Attention, *a-tten'-xion*, N. Chit divop; chotrai; mon.
Attention (Pay), v. Chit diunc; chotrai dorunc.
Attentive, *a-tten'-tiv*, A. Chit divop.
Attest, *a-ttest'*. v. Atestad—, daclo—, chit diunc; decol corunc.
Attestation, *a-ttes-tei'-xion*, N. Daclo; govai. [rup.
Attitude, *at'-ti-tiud*, N. Acar;
Attorney, *a-ttor'-ni*, N. Vakil; carbari; cam choloinar.
Attract, *a-trect'*, v. Odunc; von-davunc, fuslaunc.
Attraction, *a-ttrec'-xion*, N. Voddni; fuslaunni.
Attribute, *a-ttri-biu'-tt*, v. Aropunc, launc; galunc; thapunc.
Attribute, N. Gunn; vachia.
Attrition, *a-ttri'-xion*, N. Deu-bhirantichi dnc; khont; zall.
Auction, *oc'-xion*, N. Loilanm.
Audacious, *au-dei'-xi-as*, A. Mordivont; dhoiravont; omo-riadi; mosto.
Audacioumess, *au-dei'-xi-as-ness*, AD. Morden; zobordostin.
Audience, *a-di'-ens*, N. Mellagot; dad gennem, aicop.
Audit, *a'-dit*, V. Polleunc; ixeop topasunc.
Auditor, *a-di'-ttor*, N. Ixeop topasnar.
Auger, *a'-gar*, N. Burmo.
Augment, *aug'-ment*, V. Chod-dounc.
Augment, N. Choddop.
Aunt, *antt*, N. Mauxi; acoi; mami.
Aurora, *au-ro'-ra*, N. Arunn; sucr; jenjurthem; fg. udev; oromb.
Auspices, *aus'-pi-sis*, N. Bolmem; boro soheog.
Auspicious, *aus-pi'-xi-as*, A. Nosibacho; folladic.
Austere, *a-us-ti'-er*, A. Cottin; nibor.
Austerity, *aus-te'-ri-tti*, N. Cottinai; nibrai; khont.
Authentic, *au-then'-tic*, A. Khoro, asol.
Author, *o'-ttor*, N. autor; cor-nar. goddnar.
Authoritative, *o-tho-ri-tei'-tiv*, A. Podvedar.
Authority, *au-tho'-ri-tti*, N. Podvi, adicar; sercar; paticnni.
Authorize, *au-tho'-raiz*, V. Pod-vi diunc.
Autocrat, *au-to'-crat*, N. Somraj; patxai.
Auxiliary, *auc-zi'-lia-ri*, A. Ada-racho.
Avail, *a-veil'*, v. Upeog corunc; upearnc poddonc.
Avarice, *a'-va-ris*. N. Sugrat: impttepoun, chatteppoun.
Avaricious, *a-va-ri'-xi-as*, A. Sugrati; impttо.

Avenge, *a-venj'*, V. Faricponn geunc. [odmas ; sora-sori.
Average, *a'-ve-reij*, N. Sumar ;
Averse, *a-vors'*, A. Dusmancaecho ; viclabacho.
Aversion, *a-vor'-xion*, N. Dusmancai ; khantallo ; viclab.
Avert, *a-vart'*, V. Vattaunc ; pois corunc.
Avidity, *a-vi'-di-tti*, N. Hurba ; khuri ; axea.
Avoid, *a-void'*, V. Chucounc ; vattaunc ; pois corunc.
Await, *a-veitt'*, V. Ravunc ; axeunc. [uttounc.
Awake, *ei-veik'*, V. Zagounc,
Aware, *a'-ver*, (I am), V. Maca collta ; aum zaunom.
Away, *ie-ve'*, AD. Pelean.
Awe, *ó*, N. Bhiraut.
Awful, *o'-full*, A. Bhiraucull.
Awkward, *oe-vard*, A. Tarifecho.
Awl, *ol'*, N. Dabon.
Axe, *ex*, N. Curad.
Axiom, *ax'-si-om*, N. Vachan ; orombachem sot,
Axle, *ex'-sl* N. Paroi.
Azure, *a'-ziu-ar*, A. Nillso vo nill rongacho.

B

Babble, *be'-bl*, N. Boddboduem.
Babble, V. Boddboddunc.
Babe, *bei-bi*, N. Burgem ; balloc.
Bachelor, *bech'-e-lor*, N. Ancuar.
Bachelorship, *be-ch'-e-lor-ship*, N. Ancuarponn.
Back, *bec*, N. Patt.
Back, AD. Patti ; pattlean.
Backbite, *bec'-baitt*, V. Chaddieo sangunc.
Backbiting, *bec'-bai-tting*, N. Chaddi.
Backbiter, *bec'-bai-ttor*, N. Chaddieo cornar.
Backbone, *bec'-bon*, N. Pattichi khonno.
Backward, *bec'-vard*, A. Pattlean.
Bacon, *bei'-con*, N. Ducrachem mas.
Bad, *bed*, A. Vaitt ; khotto.
Badge, *bej*. N. Billo.
Bad-hearted, *bed-har-ted*. Khottea monacho.
Bag, *beg*, N. Potem ; theli.
Baggage, *be'-geij*, N. Samonn.
Bail, *beil*, N. Zamin raunar.
Bail, V. Zamin diunc.
Bailiff, *bei'-lif*, N. Naic ; *official das diligencias.*
Bait, *beitt*, N. Ans (maslli dorunc).
Bait, V. Khaunc diunc.
Bake, *beic*, V. Bazunc.
Baker, *bei'-car*, N. Poder.
Bakery, *bei'-ke-ri*, N. Poder-khon.
Balance, *ba'-lans*, N. Tagddi ; baki (ispantli).
Balcony, *bal'-co-ni*, N. Bolcaum.
Bald, *bold*, A. Boddco ; koddo ; kens naslolo.
Bale, *beil*, N. Penddi.
Ball, *boll*, N. Gullo ; europi nach.
Baloon, *balun*, N. Balanm ; sorongo. [tel.
Balm, *bam*, N. Pormollachem
Bamboo, *bam-bu'*, N. Man.
Bamboo-mat, N. Dalli.
Ban, *ben*, N. Cazaracheo chitti.
Band, *bend*, N. Bandop ; birem.
Bandicoot, *ben'-di-cutt*, N. Colliudir.
Banditti, *ban-di'-tti*, N. Pundd ; luttnar.
Banian-tree, *ba-ni'-an-tri*, N. Vodd.
Banish, *be'-nish*, V. Porkea gavant daddunc ; fg. bhair galunc.
Bank, *benc*, N. Noinchi kinari ; vell, thodd ; munnoi ; banc,

Banker, *benk'-ar* N. Saucar; sorap.
Bank-note, *benc'-not*, N. Hundi.
Bankrupt, *benc'-ropt* N. Divallem.
Banner, *be-nnar*, N. Bautto; giaum; bonder.
Banquet, *ban'-kuet*, N. Vodd jevonn; banket.
Banter, *ben-tter*, N. Kesttaeo.
Banter, V. Kesttaeo corunc.
Baptism, *bep-ti'-zam*, N. Bautizm.
Baptize, *bep-taiz'*, V. Bautizm [diunc.
Bar, *bar*, N. Europi soreachem ducan; loconddacho khambo.
Barbarity, *bar-ba'-ri-tti*, N. Nistturai; rannottponn.
Barbarous, *bar-ba-ras*, A. Jongli; rannantlo; nisttur.
Barber, *bar'-ber*, N. Barbeir; navim; malo.
Bare, *ber*, A. Ugtto.
Barefaced, *ber'-fei-sdd*, A. Loznaslolo; mosticho-.
Bargain, *bar'-ge-in*, N. Tharau; corar.
Bargain, *bar'-ge-in*, V. Tharaunc; corar corunc.
Bark, (of trees), *barc*, N. Sal.
-(Boat)=Voddem.
Bark, V. Gonkunc.
Barley, *bar'-li*, N. Barli.
Barn, *barn*, N. Orvacho gudaum.
Barometer, *ba-ro'-me-ttor*, N. Vareachem map.
Barque. *barc*, N. Tarum.
Barrack, *bar'-rac*, N. Soldadanc rauchem gor.
Barrel, *bar-rel*, N. Pip.
Barren, *ber'-ron*, A. Vanz; fg. foll dinaslòlo; nirfoll.
Barrier, *be'-rri-er*, N. Addcoll; oddchon.
Barrister, *ber'-ris-ttor*, N. Voddlo letrad; vokil.
Barter, *bar-tor*, N. Bodol.
Base, *beiz*, A. Unno; fg. holco.
Base, N. Bunhad.
Basement, *bez'-ment*, N. Dorn; dortori.
Bashful, *besh'-ful*, A. Loüist; bezudd.
Bashfulness, *besh'-ful-ness*, N. Loz; bhirant.
Basil *baz'-il*, N. Tullos.
Basilica, *ba-zi'-li-ca*, N. Mukea igroz.
Basin, *bei'-sin*, N. Tost; vattli gulomb.
—(Tank)=tollem,
—(Valley)=vôll.
Basket, *bas'-keitt*, N. Panttli; pettaro.
Bastard, *bas'-tard*, A. Randdecho vo boddkicho; desacho.
Baste. *bêst*, V. Pont marunc.
Bat, *bett*, N. Tonnco; pako.
Bath, *bath*, N. Nan. [ounc.
Bathe, *beidh*, V. Nannounc; biz-
Bathing-room, *bei'-ding-rum*, N. Nauni.
Baton, *bei'-tton*, N. Var; betkatti.
Battalion, *ba-tta'-li-on*, N. Bathalhão; hozar soldadancho zomo.
Batter, *be'-ttor*, V. Nallinim marunc.
Battery, *be'-tte-ri*, N. Nallinchi punz.
Battle, *batt'l*, N. Loddai.
Bay, *bei*, N. Doriachem koll.
Bayonet, *bei-eo'-nett*, N. Armacho balo.
Bazaar, *ba-zar*, N. Pentt.
Be, *bi*, V. Vortounc vo zaunc.
Beach, *biich*, N. Dokho.
Beacon, *be'-kn*, N. Foleir.
Bead, *biid*, N. Moni; sori.
Beadle, *bii'-dl*. N. Pedo.
Beak, *bi-ik*, N. Bonch.
Beam, *bi-im*, N. Patti; danddo; kirn.

Bean, *biin,* N. Ousando; aunro.
Bear, *ber,* N. Asvel; fg. rannot munis.
Bear, *ber,* V. Bar geunc; sosunc; ballont, porsut zaunc; zolmbunc; asonc; fòll diunc.
Beard, *bierd,* N Khard.
Bearer, *be'-rar,* N. Portador; boi.
Beast, *biist,* N. Monzat.
Beat, *biit,* V. Marunc; fofaunc; daddaunc; pettunc.
Beatific, *bi-a-ti'-fic,* A. Bogt, sant.
Beatification, *bi-a-ti-fi-kei'-xion,* N. Bogt cornem.
Beatify, *bi-at'-ti-fai,* N. Bogt, bagevont corunc.
Beatitude, *bi-a'-ti-tiud,* N. Suc; mucti, bagiam.
Beautiful, *biu'-tti-ful,* A. Sobit; sundor; nazuc.
Beautify, *biu'-tti-fai,* V. Sobounc; nettounc.
Beauty, *biu'-tti,* N. Sobai; sundorai.
Becalm, *bi-cam',* V. Fuslaunc; thond corunc.
Because, *bi-coz',* C. kiteac, decun.
Beck, *bec,* V. Tocli-alounc; dolle moddunc.
Become, *bi-com',* V. Zaunc.
Becoming, *bi-com'-ing,* A. Moriadicho; boream gunnancho.
Bed, *bcdd,* N. Antuln; khatt.
Bedstead, *bed-sted,* N. Polong.
Bee, *bii,* N. Movancho mus.
Beef, *biif,* N. Gaichem mas.
Beehive, *bi-haiv',* N. Movancheam musanchem malem.
Beer, *bi'-er,* N. Servej, bir.
Beetle, *bii'-tl,* N. Zorlo; gongurlo; bouvor.
Befall, *bi-fol',* V. Goddonc; zaunc.
Before, *bi-for',* PR. Adim; poilem; magir; mucar; fuddem; poros.
Beforehand, *bi-for'-hend,* AD. Adinch; poilench.
Befoul, *bi-faul',* V. Mellounc; oxigaunc.
Beg, *beg,* V. Poratunc; magunc.
Beget, *bi-get',* V. Zolmonc.
Beggar, *beg'-gar,* N. Bicari.
Begin, *bi-gin',* V. Suru corunc; addaunc.
Beginning, *be-gin'-ning,* Oromb, mull.
Begone, *bi-gon',* V. Chol voch.
Beguile, *bi-gail',* V. Fosounc.
Behalf, *bi-haf',* Partin; pasun, khatir.
Behave, *bi-hev',* V. Cholonc.
Behaviour, *bi-he'-vi-or,* N. Chal; cortub.
Behead, *bi-hed',* V. Xins capunc.
Behind, *bi-haind',* AD. PR. Pattlean; patti.
Behold, *bi-hold',* V. Po'lounc, nodor galunc.
Belching, *belch'-ing,* N. Denc.
Belfrey, *bel-fri',* N. Ganttichi tórr.
Belie, *bi-lai',* V. Lipounc; boglant galunc.
Belief, *bi-liif',* N. Bavarth; sotmandop.
Believe, *bi-liiv',* V. Sotmandunc; patiennc; somzounc.
Believer, *bi-liv'-or,* N. Bavarthi.
Bell, *bell,* N. Ghantt; campinn.
Bellow, *bel'-lou,* V. Ambeunc.
Bellows, *bel'-louz,* N. Bato.
Belly, *bel'-li,* N. Pott.
Belong, *bi-long,* V. Favo zaunc, lagonc.
Beloved, *bi-lov-dd',* A. Mogachoj pritichο, apurbaecho.
Below, *bi-lou,* AD. Socol, khala - unno; ponda.
Belt, *beltt,* N. Potto.
Bemoan, *bi-moun',* V. Roddonc; pirngonc.

Bench, *bench,* N. Banc; bosca.
Bend, *bend,* V. Bagounc: portunc
Bending, *bend'-ing,* N. Bag.
Beneath, *be-nijth'.* AD. Socla. ponda.
Benediction, *be-ne-dic'-xion,* N. Besaum, asirvad.
Benefactor, *be-ne-fec'-ttor,* N. Upcar—, borem cornar.
Benefice, *ben'-e-fis,* N. Upcar, adan.
Benefit, *ben'-e-fit,* N. Upcarouc,
Beneficial, *be-ne-fi'-sial,* A. Upcaracho vo adavacho.
Benevolence, *be nev'-o-lens,* N. Bollepoun; upcarponn; mog.
Benevolent, *be-ne'-vo-lent,* A. Mogal, boro vo bore khoxecho.
Benign, *bi-nain',* A. Upcaracho; mogall.
Bent, *bent,* A. Bagoulolo, vanoddo.
Bequeath, *be-kuiitt',* V. Testamentar dourunc.
Bequest, *bi-kuest,* N. Testamentachem dennem.
Bereave, *bi-riiv',* V. Chucounc; caddung.
Bereavement, *bi-riiv'-ment,* N. Nam zavop.
Berry, *be'-ri,* N. Supurlem foll.
Beseech, *bi-siich',* V. Poratunc.
Beset, *bi-set',* V. Veddo galunc.
Besides, *bi-saidz',* AD. Sivai; kherit. [galunc.
Besiege, *bi-siij',* V. Veddo
Besieging, *bi-sij'-ing,* N. Veddo.
Besmear, *bis-mi-ar,* V. Cosolii vost launc; mellounc.
Besom, *be-zom',* N. Saronn.
Bespeak, *be-spiik',* V. Adim fudde ulounc, dacoun dinnc.
Besprinkle, *be-spring'-kl,* V. Shiuraunc.
Best, *best,* A. Bhou boro; uttom.
Best, AD. Bhou boro.
Bestial, *bes'-ti-al,* A. Monzaticho.
Bestow, *be-stou',* V. Diunc.
Bestride, *bis-traid',* V. Bosunc.
Bet, *bet,* N. Apost, vodda.
Bet, V. Apost vo vodda marunc.
Betake, *bi-teik,* V. Lagunc: adar vo mozot magunc.
Betel, *bi'-tl,* N. Panvel.
Betel-nut, *bi'-tl-nót,* N. Fofoll.
Bethink, *bi-think'.* N. Attou, ugddas corunc, chintunc.
Betimes, *bi-taimz,* AD. Vegim, bhou socallim; fantear.
Betoken, *bi-to'-kn,* V. Daconnc.
Betray, *bi-trei',* V. Gat geunc: fg. Vicunc; ugddapem corunc.
Betrayal, *bi-trei'-al,* N. Gat.
Betroth, *bi-troth',* N. Soirio.
Betrothal, *bi-troth'-al,* N. Mudi galop; ulounem.
Betrothed, *bi troth'-ed,* N. Vocol-vo nouro.
Between, *bit-vuin,* PR. Modem; bhitor.
Bewail, *bi-veil',* V. Roddunc; ducam gollounc.
Beware, *bi-ver',* V. Chotrai geunc.
Biography, *bi-eo-gra'-fi,* N. Jivitachem borop.
Bird, *bord,* N. Sucunnem, sonnnem.
Birdlime, *bord'-laim,* N. Bendor.
Birth, *borth,* N. Zolm; baenteor: zolmacho dis.
Birth-place, *borth-ples,* N. zalolo gaum.
Biscuit, *bis-kit',* N. Biscut, bolaz.
Bishop, *bi'-shop,* N. Bisp.
Bishopric, *bi-sho'-pric,* N. Bispachem raz.
Bit, *bit,* N. Cuddeo; logom.
Bitch, *bich,* N. Colgem
Bite, *baitt,* V. Chabunc, gans marunc; fg. zall eunc; fg, ducounc.
Bite, N. Gans.

Bitter, *bit'-ter,* N. Coddu; fg. coisttancho; nisttur.
Bitterness, *bit'-ter-nes,* N. Coddsann.
Black, *blec,* A. Callo.
Blaken, *ble'-kn,* V. Callo corunc.
Blacksmith, *blec'-smith,* N. Vinnani, lovar.
Blade, *bleid,* N. Canos; dar.
Blame, *bleim,* V. Guniaumcar corunc, nam posond corunc.
Blame, *bleim,* N. Guneaum. oprad.
Blameless, *bleim'-less,* A. Guneaum-naslolo; niropradi.
Blank, *blenc,* N. Khali.
Blank, A. Khali.
Blanket, *blenc'-kett,* N. Bornus; camblem.
Blaspheme, *blas-fiim',* V. Devacher ardd ulounc, deuninda corunc.
Blasphemy, *blas-fe'-mi,* N. Deuninda, blasfem.
Bleed, *bliid,* V. Rogot caddunc, sir marunc.
Bleeding, *bliid'-ing,* N. Sir marop.
Blemish, *ble'-mish,* N. Chuc, aib, khot.
Bless, *bless,* V. Besanm galunc, asirvad diunc; Benzer corunc: argam diunc.
Blessed, *bless'-dd,* A. Besavancho: suki; sant.
Blessing, *bles'-ing,* N. Besaum, asirvazon: borepon; borcot.
Blind, *blaind,* A. Cuddo, anddlo; fg. somzo naslolo vo bud naslolo.
Blindness, *blaind'-ness,* N. Cuddeponn. [ponn.
Bliss, *blis,* N. Suc, sontos, dados-
Blister, *blis'-ttor,* N. Fodd: plastor; lep.
Blood, *blodd,* N. Rogot; fg. cuttom.
Bloodless, *blod'-less,* A. Rogot naslolo; rogtavinn. [varop.
Bloodshed, *blod'-shed,* N. Rogot
Bloody, *blod'-di,* A. Rogtacho.
Bloom, *blum,* N. Ful.
Bloom, V. Fulonc.
Blossom, *blo'-som,* N. Ful.
Blossom, V. Fulonc.
Blot, *blot,* V. Dag galunc, mellonne: pusunc.
Blot, N. Dag: chitti.
Blotting-paper, *blott'-ing-pei-par,* N. Mate-burranm. [noistt.
Blow, *blou,* N. Mar; pétt: fg.
Blow, *blou,* V. Funcunc, eunc; vazonc.
Blow-pipe, *blou-paip,* N. Bato.
Blue, *blu,* A. Nillso rong.
Blunder, *blond'-or,* N. Vodd chuc.
Blunder, V. Chuconc.
Blunt, *blunt,* A. Dar naslolo; fg. somzo naslolo; murc.
Blush, *blosh,* V. Lozonc.
Bluster, *blos'-ttor,* V. Varea baxen gongeunc.
Boar, *bor,* N. Randucor.
Board, *bord,* N. Follem; khan; mell; bann: tarum.
Boarder, *bor'-dar,* N. Jeunnac rautolo.
Boarding-house, N. Puzad, jeunnachem gor.
Boast, *boost,* N. Patrad, boddai.
Boast, V. Boddai dacounc.
Boat, *boot,* N. Voddem. [car.
Boatman, *boot-men,* N. Vodde-
Bodily, *bo'-di-li,* A. Cuddicho.
Body, *bo'-di,* N. Cudd; ang; fg. moll.
Boil, *boil,* V. Sizounc; umallo cadduuc; ucddunc.
Boil, N. fodd.
Boisterous, *bo-is-te'-ras,* A. Uchamboil: tufancar.
Bold, *bold,* A. Nirvonni, callje-vont; gorvi.

Boldly, *bold'-li,* AD. Nirvonnan ; gorvan.
Boldness, *bold'-ness,* N. Nirvonn; gorv.
Bolster, *bols-ttar,* N. Uxem.
Bolt, *bolt,* N. Khili ; bolo.
Bomb, *bomb,* N. Ujeacho gullo.
Bombard, *bom'-bard,* V. Gulleanim marunc.
Bombardment, *bom-bard'-ment,* N. Nalli marop.
Bombastic, *bom-bas'-tic,* A. Tonttonnit, mottiam sobdancho.
Bond, *bond,* N. Khotem, roko ; bondcond.
Bondage, *bon'-dej,* N. Gulamponn.
Bone, *bon,* N. Had.
Bonnet, *bo'-nnet,* N. Topi.
Book, *buk,* N. Livr, pustoc.
Bookbinder, *buk'-bain-dar,* N. Pustocam siunar.
Book-seller, *buk'-sell-er,* N. Pustocam vicnar.
Boon, *buun,* N. Dennem ; curpa ; upcar.
Boor, *buur,* N. Naddcar ; fg. burr.
Boot, *buut,* N. Moche.
Booty, *bu'-ti,* N. Lutt.
Border, *bor'-dor,* N. Deg ; khamb; kinari.
Border, V. Deg bandunc.
Bore, *bor,* V. Topunc, burac corunc ; corcor corunc.
Bore, *bor,* N. Burac ; dompio ; corcori.
Borer, *borar,* N. Girbo.
Born, (*Be*), N. Zolmonc ; ubzonc.
Borough, *bo-ro',* N. Mukom vaddo.
Borrow, *bor'-rou,* V. Usnem geunc ; magun geunc.
Borrowing, *bo'rou-ing,* N. usnem.
Bosom, *bu'-zom,* N. Hordem.
—(Friend)=Callzacho istt.
Botany, *bo'-ta-ni,* N. Udbhidvidea.
Botch, *boch,* N. Suz ; fg. foddposi vaur.
Botch, V. Foddposi corunc.
Both, *both,* PR. Dogni ; dogaim.
Bother, *bo'-dher,* V. Bejar corunc.
Botheration, *bo-do-rei'-xion,* N. Corcor.
Bottle, *bot'-tl,* N. Botl ; sinsli.
Bottom, *bo'-ttom,* N. Pond, thau.
Bound, *baund,* V. Dovorunc ; dampunc.
Bound, N. Aker corunc, mer galunc.
Boundary, *baun-da'-ri,* N. Mer ; aker.
Boundless, *baund'-less,* N. Mernaslolo ; ugonnit.
Bountiful, *baun-ti'-ful,* A. Udar ; moipasi.
Bountifully, *baun-ti'-fulli,* AD. Udarponnan ; moipasan.
Bounty, *baun-tti,* N. Upcar ; inam.
Bouquet, *bo-ke',* N. Fulamcho gons.
Bow, *bau,* V. Bagaunc ; mau [diunc.
Bow, N. Ark.
Bowels, *bauls,* N. Ankiddi.
Bower, *ba'-or,* N. Mollo ; mattou.
Bowl, *bol,* N. Cop ; causo.
Box, *box,* N. Pett ; caix ; tapott.
Box, V. Bizounc ; mutti marunc.
Boy, *boi,* N. Burgo ; cheddo.
Boyhood, *boi'-hud,* N. Burgepon vo burgi pirai.
Bràce, *brês,* N. Bres ; band.
Bracelet, *bres'-lett,* N Cackon ; chuddo. [gigi.
Brackets, *brek'-ets,* N. Dampchi
Brackish, *bre'-kish,* A. Causo.
Brain, *brein,* N. Mendu ; fg. mot.
Bramble, *brem' bl,* N. Kantti ; cantteanchem zadd.
Bran, *bren,* N. Cunddo.
Branch, *brench,* N. Kando ; fantto; talli.

Branch, v. Fantteunc.
Brand, *brend*, N. Colit; dag.
Brand, v. Dag galunc.
Brandish, *bren'-dish*, v. Alounc; dolounc.
Brandy, *bran'-di*, N. Brandi.
Brass, *brass*, N. Pittull.
Brave, *brev*, N. Nirvonni; dhoiravont; uxear. [zaunc.
Brave, v. Mucar soronc; bhienam
Bravely, *brev'-li*, AD. Nirvonnan; bhienastanam.
Bravery, *brev'-e-ri*, N. Nirvonn; calljivont-ponn.
Bravo, *bra'-vo*, INT. Xebas; copaz.
Brazen, *brei'-zan*, A. Pitulcho.
Bray, *brei*, v. Bob marunc.
Breech, *briich*, N. Moddop; dhal; futt; ier.
Bread, *bred*, N. Unddo; bakri.
Breadth, *breth*, N. Rundai.
Break, *breik*, v. Moddunc; foddunc.
—(Get Weak)=Oscot zaunc.
—(Silence)=Gorje sivai ulounc.
—(Rest)=Soncosai pirder corunc.
—(Day)=Uzvaddonc.
—(Asunder)=Cuddkean cuddco corunc.
—(Down)=Moddun galunc.
—(In)=Sado corunc.
—(Into)=Bollan rigunc.
—(In pieces)=Cuddkean cuddco corunc.
—(Loose)=saddo-suddo zaunc.
—(Off)=Moddunc.
—(Open)=Foddunc.
—(Out)=Bhair soronc.
—(Up)=Ustunc.
—(Upon)=Addlonc.
—(With)=Dusmancai ubzaunc.
Break, N. Asôr.
Breakfast, *breik'-fast*, N. Almus; nasto.
Breafast, v. Jinzvar moddunc; almus corunc.
Breaking *breik'-ing*, N. Moddop.
Breast, *breest*, N. Hordem; chiunn.
Breath, *breth*, v. Usvas; dom; fg. jiv.
Breathe, *briid*, v. Usvas soddunc; somonnan zaunc.
—(In)=Usvas geunc.
—(Out)=Usvas soddunc.
—(Upon)=Funcunc.
Breathless, *breth'-less*, A. Usvas naslolo; melolo.
Breeches, *brii'-chis*, N. Calsaum; izar.
Breed, *briid*, v. Zolmonc; posunc.
Breeding, (Good B.)=moriad.
Breeze, *briiz*, N. Varem.
Breviary, *bre-via'-ri*, N. Breviar.
Brevity, *bre-vi'-tti*, N. Thoddeau attapunem.
Bribe, *braib*, N. Lonch.
Bribe, v. Lonch diunc.
Briber, *braib'-ar*, N. Lonch dinar.
Brick, *bric*, N. Itt.
Brick-maker, *bric-mei'-car*, N. Itt-cornar, cumar.
Bridal, *braid'-al*, N. Cazar.
Bridal, A. Cazaracho.
Bridal-dress, *braid'-al-dress*, N. Saddo.
Bride, *braid*, Vocol.
Bride-groom, *braid'-grum*, N. Nouro, horet.
Bridge, *brij*, N. Sancon.
Bridle, *brai'-dl*. N. Logom.
Brief, *briif*, A. Mottvo.
Brief, N. Minut.
Brier, *bri'-ar*, N. Cantti.
Brigade, *bri'-geid*, N. Foujicho Vantto.
Brigadier, *bri-ge-di'-ar*, N. Foujichea vantteacho voddil.
Brigand, *bri'-gand*, N. Pundd; chor.

Bright, *braitt*, A. Porzollit; nitoll; barie.
Brighten, *brait'-ton*, V. Porzollunc; fauconne.
Bright-ness, *braitt'-ness*, N. Uzvadd; porzoll; pracas
Brilliant, *bril-li'-ant*, A. Porzollit; rosrosit.
Brim, *brim*, N. Deg; kantt.
Brine, *brain*, N. Khor udoc.
Bring, *bring*, V. Haddunc; vorunc.
—(Up)=Vaddounc.
—(A man to an opinion)=Somzaunc.
—(Back)=Patti kaddung.
—(Before)=Mucar galunc.
—(Down)=Socol caddunc.
—(Forth)=Porsut zaunc; bhair caddunc.
—(Out)=Bhair vorunc.
Brinjal, *brinj'-ol*, N. Vaingem.
Brink, *brinc*, N. Deg.
Brisk, *brisc*, A. Suddsuddit.
Broad, *brod*, A. Rund.
Broil, *broil*, N. Zogddem.
Broker, *bro'-kar*, N. Dalal.
Bronze, *bronz*, N. Cansem.
Bronze, A. Canseacho.
Brooch, *bruch*, N. Motim; ganj.
Brood, *bruud*, N. Pilancho hind; fg. sonsot vo kuttom.
Brood, V. Rovaunc; fg. niallunc.
Brook, *bruk*, N. Vall.
Broom, *brum*, N. Sarronn.
Broth, *broth*, Cald.
Brothel, *bro'-thel*, N. Cheddianchem gor.
Brother, *bro'-dor*, N. Bhau.
Brother-in-law, *bro'-dor-in-lo*, Mennno; cunhad.
Brotherly (love). Moia-mog.
Brow, *brau*, N. Askitti: copal.
Brown, *braun*, A. Callso.
Browse, *brauz*, V. Khaunc.

Bruise, *bruz*, V. Vattunc; daddaunc.
Bruise, N. Daddaunem.
Brush, *brosh*, N. Brus; iscou.
Brush, V. Dull caddunc; nitoll corunc.
Brutal, *bru'-ttal*, A. Nisttur; monzaticho; ranvott.
Brutality, *brutt-al'-it-ti*, N. Nistturai; monzatpoun.
Brutally, *bru'-tta-lli*, AD. Nistturaen; monzatiporim.
Brute, *brutt*, N. Monzat.
Bubble, *bo'-bl*, N. Bud-buddo: fodd. [baldi.
Bucket, *bo'-ket*, N. Conso; sidi;
Bud, *bod*, N. Collo: bongo; ancri.
Budget, *bo'-jet*, N. Iseop (sercari).
Buffalo, *bo'-ffa-lo*, N. Reddo.
Buffet, *buf'-fet*, N. Mutti marunc.
Buffoon, *bof'-fun*, N. Naddgo.
Bug, *bog*, N. Bikon.
Bugbear, *bog' ber*, N. Bhirantichi vost.
Build, *bild*, V. Bandunc; fg. patieunc.
Building, *bild'-ing*, N. Bandavoll; gor.
Bulk, *bolk*, N. Voddai; map.
Bull, *bull*. (of the Pope) N. Bul.
Bull, N. Paddo.
Bullock, *bul'-loc*, N. Boil: paddo.
Bully, *bul'-li*, A. Zogddemcar; uchamboll.
Bulwark, *bul'-wark*, N. Zoton corchi bandavoll.
Bunch, *banch*, N. Gous: chombo.
Bundle, *ban'-dl*, N. Pottli; boro; borcutti.
Bungle, *ban'-gl*, Mislunc; chuc corunc.
Buoy, *boy*, V. Tharaunc; gottai diunc.
Buoyancy, *bo'-ian-si*, N. Dudospoun; khoxalpoun.

Burden, *bord'n*, N. Vozou ; bar ; zodai ; fg. acant.
Burden, V. Bar galunc ; fg. dog-doganne.
Burdensome, *bord'n-som*, A. Corandaecho ; corcoracho.
Burial, *bu'ri-al*, N. Morn ; interr.
Burlesque, *bur-les-ke'*, A. Facandd : ansounchi khobor.
Burn, *barn*, V. Lasunc ; ujeant galunc ; zollunc ; fg. ragan zollonc.
Burning, *(taste)*, N. Zollti ruch.
Burrow, *bor'-rou*, V. Usnnem duddu geune : rinn caddunc.
Burst, *borst*, V. Foddunc ; moddunc ; futtonc.
Burry, *bo'ri*, V. Matieo launc ; nikipiunc.
Bush, *bush*, N. Jilleutt ; kautti.
Bushel, *bush'-el*, N. Mezpachem map ; xer.
Business, *biz'-ness*, N. Cam ; vaur ; udiog.
Bust, *bost*, N. Voilem lundd buzam pasuu.
Busy, *(is)*, V. Camar assune.
But. *bot*, PREP., C. Sivai ; kherit ; punn ; bogor ; matr.
Butcher, *bu'-cher*, N. Kosai.
Butler, *but'-lor*, N. Mezacho chacor ; butler.
Butter, *bott'-or*, N. Tup ; lounim.
Butterfly, *bo'-tter-flai*, N Pisoem.
Buttermilk, *bo'-ttor-milk*, N. Doim.
Button, *bo'-tton*, V. Butaum galunc.
Button, N. Butanm.
Button-hole. *bo'-tton-hol*, N. Caz.
Buy, *bai*, V. Victo geunc.
Buyer, *ba'-yar*, N. Victo genar.
By, *bai*, PREP. Lagim : pasun.
By the by, AD. Oxem astanam ; uprant. [dem.
By and by, AD. Thoddem-thod-

C

Cabal, *ca-bal'* N. Kutt ; tandd.
Cabbage, *ke'-bej*, N. Côb.
Cabin, *ke'-bin*, N. Tarvachi kotri
Cabinet, *cab'-inet*, N. Camacho ; vachpacho cudd, kherit, khasgi cudd ; mantrisalla.
Cable, *ke'-bl*, N. Dor ; sankoll.
Cacophony, *ca-co'-fo-ni*, N. Fals tallo. [dop.
Cadence, *ca'-dens*, N. Tallo pod-
Cadet, *ca'-det*, N. Dacto put ; Supurlo official.
Cage, *keij*, N. Pandrem.
Cajole, *ca-jol'*, V. Fuslaunc.
Cake, *keic*, N. Keic ; bacri ; polli ; bol.
Calamity, *ca-la'-mi-tti*, N. Coistt ; dogd ; vign ; upodre ; acant.
Calculate, *cal-cu-leit'*, V. Ixeop corunc ; sumar corunc.
Calculation, *cal-cu-lei'-xion*, N. Gonnit.
Caldron, *cal'-dron*, N. Taz ; handdo.
Calendar, *ca'-len-dar*, N. Calendar, panchang.
Calf, *caf*, N. Vasrum.
Calibre, *ca'-li-ber*, N. Rundai ; fg. somjicai.
Caligraphy, *ca'-li-gra-fi*, N. Borem borop.
Call, *col*, V. Apounc, ulo corunc ; munnone
—(Aside)=Kerit dovorunc.
—(Away)=Caddunc.
—(On)=Bettonc.
Calling, *col'-ing*, N. Apounnem, ulo : bhes.
Calm, *cam*, A. Nidan ; thondd ; soucasaecho.
Calm, N. Soncasai ; somandan.
Calm, V. Somandan—, thondd corunc.

Calmly, *cam'-li*, AD. Soucasaen.
Caloric, *ca-lo'-ric*, N. Ushnacho oromb.
Calumniate, *ca-lom'-ni-eitt*, V. Boglautt—, lochand galunc; chaddieo sangunc.
Calumny, *ca'-lom-ni*, N. Chaddi; boglaut, lochand.
Camel, *ke'-mul*, N. Untt.
Camp, *kemp*, N. Moidan; kemp.
Comphor, *cam'-for*, N. Kamfr; kafur.
Can, *ken*, V (maca) Tauctn.
Canal, *ca'-nal*, N. Chor, kholli
Canary-bird, *ca'-na-ri-bord*, N. Kanari-sucnem.
Cancel, *ken'-sl*, V. Nul corunc.
Cancer, *ken'-sor*, N. Cancer; manpulli.
Candid, *ken'-did*, A. Bholo, bholia monacho, sudd; babddo.
Candidate, *can'-di-deitt*, N. Umedvar.
Candlemas-day, *ken'dl-mas-dai*, N. Vati benjar corcho dis.
Candlestick, *ken'-dl-stick*, N. Castisal.
Cane, *kein*, N. Rot; bodd:.
Canister, *ca'-nnis-ttor*, N. Coronddo; panttli.
Cannibal *can'-ni-bal*, A. Munsheachem mas khatolo.
Cannon, *ken'-non*, N. Nall.
Canoe, *ke no'*, N. Pouev, supurlem voddem. [des.
Canon, *ke'-non*, N. Caido; upor-
Canonization, *ka-no-ni-zei'-xion*, N. Bogtanim—leiknem; sant munnchem.
Canonize, *ca-no-naiz'*, V. Bagevont muun pacharunc.
Canopy, *ca'-no-pi*, N. Pal.
Canticle, *can'-ti-cl*, N. Povitr cantig.
Cantonment, *can'-tton-ment*, N. Pollton ranchem thican,
Canvas, *can'-vas*, N. Daddem lugot; sidd.
Cap, *kep*, n. Topi.
Capability, *kei-pa-bi'-li-tti*, N. Socti, cuvet, tanc.
Capable, *kei'-pe-bl*. A. Capaz, soctivont.
Capacity, *ca-pa'-si-tti*, N. Map; socti, cuvet.
Capillary, *ca-pil'-la-ri*, A. Bhou oxir.
Capital, *kep'-it-tal*, A. Mukea; uttim; voddlo.
Capital. N. Mukom xar; gantt.
Capitulate, *ca'-pi-tu-leitt*, V. Cararan sattunc; hatan poddunc.
Caprice, *ca-pris'*, N. Hurluc, khospai.
Capricious, *ca-pri'-xi-as*, A. Fontojcar; zollsar.
Capriciously, *ca-pri'-xi-as-li*, AD. Khospaen.
Captain, *kep'-tein*, N. Copit.
Captivate, *cap'-ti-vaitt*, V. Movallaunc; vondaunc; bulounc.
Captive, *kep'-tiv*, N. Gulam.
Captivity, *kep-ti'-vi-tti*, N. Gulamponn
Capture, *kep'-char*, N. Dornem; pagnem.
Caravan, *ca'-ra-van*, N. Carvan; vattsuraneho zomo.
Carbuncle, *car'-bon-cl*, N. Denttpulli.
Carcass, *car'-cas*, N. Khottaro; panjro.
Card, *card*, N. Datt cagot; chit; kheuchem card.
Cardinal, *car-di'-nal*, A. Mukia.
Cardinal, N. Cardinal.
Care, *ker*, N. Zoton; usco.
Care, V. Zoton corunc; uskeunc.
Career, *ca-ri'-ar*, Bhês; fg. jinn.
Careful, *ker'-ful*, A. Zotnaecho; budivont; uxear.

Careless, *ker'-less,* A. Zoton naslolo; cuidad naslolo.
Caress, *ca-res',* V. Fuslaunc; priti corunc; bulounc.
Caress, N. Fuslaunim; apurbai; bulounim.
Cargo, *car'go,* N. Vojem. [Nokol.
Caricature, *cari-kei'-char,* N.
Carious, *ke'-ri-as,* A. Pokoll.
Carmel, *car'-mel,* N. Carmin.
Carminative, *car'-mi-ne'-tiv,* N. Vattnasac; suzichem vocot.
Carnal, *car'-nal,* A. Cuddicho; masacho; modacho. [khell.
Carnival, *car'-ni-val,* N. Intruz;
Carol, *kei'-rol,* N. Onodachem gaien. [giponn.
Carousal, *ca-rous'-al,* N. Khau-
Carpenter, *car'-pin-ter,* N. Vinnani; suttar, thovoi.
Carpet, *car'-pett,* N. boncal; sumbachi maudri. [mol.
Carriage, *her'-rij,* N. Gaddi; fg.
Carry, *ke'-ri,* V. Vorunc.
—(Away)=Cusin caddunc.
—(Back)=Patti vorunc.
—(Forward)=Mucar cholounc.
Cart, *cart,* N. Gaddo.
Carve, *carv,* V. Cantounc.
Carver, *carv'-ar,* N. Voddli suri.
Carving, *carv'-ing,* N. Cantounchi suri. [dop.
Cascade, *cas'-keid,* N. Udoc-pod-
Case, *kes,* N. Poty; goshtt; doxa; hakicat. [rak.
Casern, *kei'-zorn,* N. Dactem bar-
Cash, *kesh,* N. Nogot duddu.
Cashier, *kesh'-er,* N. Thezoreir, duddu samballnar.
Cashier, V. Chacrevelo caddunc.
Cask, *casc,* N. Pip.
Cassock, *cas'-soc,* N. Lob.
Cast, *cast,* V. Uddounc; soddunc; galunc. [launc.
—(Down the eyes)=Dolle soola
—(Down)=Kontiborit zaunc,

Caste, *kest,* N. Zat.
Castle, *kes'-l,* N. Cott, kilo.
Castor, *cas'-tor,* N. Yendi.
—(Oil)=Yendichem tel.
Casual, *kei'-zu-al,* A. Prasangacho, auchit.
Casually, *kei'-zu-al-li,* AD. Acasmat, auchit.
Cat, *ket,* N. Mazor.
Cataclysm, *ke'-ta-clizm,* N. Poriallo, aunr, budtti.
Catacomb, *ca'-ta-cum,* N. Moddim purchem buiar.
Catafalque, *cat'-a-falk,* N. Es.
Catalogue, *ca'-ta-log,* N. Samnachem list.
Cataract, *cat'-a-ract,* N. Udocpoddop; dolleantlem ful; motim.
Catastrophe, *ca-tas'-trof,* N. Xevott; udrustt.
Catch, *kech,* V. Dorunc; sampddaunc.
—(Cold)=Thondu zaunc.
—(Fire)=Uzo lagonc.
Catching, *kech'-ing,* N. Dórnem; pagnem.
Catechism, *ca'-te-ki-zam,* N. Dotorn, catesizm.
Catechist, *ca'-te-kist,* N. Dotorn sicoitolo.
Catechize, *ca'-te-caiz,* N. Dotorn sicounc.
Catechumen, *ca-te-kiu'-men,* N. Bautizm geunchea adim dotorn sictolo.
Categorical, *ca-te-go'-ri-cal,* N. Khondit, khonchit. [igroz.
Cathedral, *ca-ti'-dral,* N. Voddli
Catholic, *ka'-tho-lik,* N. Catolic, soglean vistarlolo.
Catholicism, *ca-thol'-i-sizm,* N. Christauvanchem xastr.
Cattle, *ket'-tl,* N. Gorvam.
Causality, *kas'-al-i-tti,* N. Khoreponn; nimitponn,

Causative, *kaz'-a-tiv* N. Praiojin.
Cause, *caz*, N. Carann; cam.
Cause, V. nimit diunc.
Caustic, *kos'-tic*, A. Ulpo, gollto, lascho; fg. koddu.
Cauterize, *ko'-ter-aiz*, V. Locond-dan lasunc.
Caution, *co'-xion*, N. Chotrai, bud.
Caution, V. Collounc, bud diunc.
Cautious, *co'-xi-as*, A. Budivont, zagrutt.
Cautiously, *co'-xi-as-li*, AD. Chotraen, cuidadan.
Cavalry, *ca'-val-ri*, N. Goddesuar loscor.
Cave, *kêv*, N. Dol; buiar.
Cavil, *ca'-vil*, V. Uzot corunc; thocounc.
Cavil, N. Uzot.
Caviller, *ca'-vil-or*, N. Uzoti; thôo.
Cease, *siiz*, V. Thambunc; soddunc.
Cedar, *se'-dar*, N. Deudar.
Cede, *siid*, V. Soddun diunc; adin corunc.
Ceiling, *si'-ling*, N. Folleancho forr.
Celebrate, *sel'-e-breitt*, V. Porob corunc; navaddunc, kirtunc.
—(Mass)=Mis sangunc.
Celebrated, *se'-le-breit-ed*, A. Navaddlolo; famad.
Celebration, *se-le-brei'-xion*, N. Navaddni, porgottnem.
Celebrity, *se-leb'-ri-thi*, N. Kirti, navaddni. [jeldi.
Celerity, *se-le'-ri-tti*, N. Jerurai;
Celestial, *se-les'-ti-al*, A. Sorgincho.
Celibacy, *se'-li-ba-si*, N. Anonarponn.
Cell, *sell*, N. Kotri.
Cellar, *sel'-lar*, N. Mallo, jinnoskhanno.
Cement, *se-ment'*, N. Sandnenche collse.
Cement, V. Sandunc; zoddunc; fg. eettaim corunc.
Cemetery, *se'-mi-tte-ri*, N. Simitir.
Cenobite, *se'-no-baitt*, N. Mothvasi; mothvasin.
Cenotaph, *sen'-o-taf*, N. Gori.
Censer, *sens'-ar*, N. turibl; topasnar porgot zaunchea adim.
Censor, *sen'-sor*, N. Borop etc.
Censure, *sen'-char*, V. Guneauncari corunc, nondunc, torzunc.
Censure, N. Semsur, ninda.
Census, *sen'-sus*, N. locachem mezop.
Cents, *sents*, N. Xeoddo.
Centipede, *sen'-ti-pid*, N. Vagonni.
Central, *sen'-tral*, A. Modlo.
Centralise, *sen'-tra-laiz*, V. Modem, mazar vorunc.
Centrally, *sen'-tral-li*, AD. Modem, modecot.
Centre, *sen'-tar*, N. Modian, maz.
Century, *sen'-chu-ri*, N. Xecddo.
Ceremonious, *se-re-mo'-ni-as*, A. Dobajeacho; moriadicho.
Ceremony, *se'-re-mo-ni*, N. Sermon; dobazo.
Certain, *ser'-ttein*, A. Khoro; khondit.
Certainly, *ser'-ttein-li*, AD. Khorench; dubau nastanam.
Certainty, *ser'-ttein-ti*, N. Thirason, katri; sot.
Certificate, *ser-ttif'-i-keitt*, N. Sertificad, daclo, pramonn.
Certify, *sêr'-tti-fai*, V. Khoremruzu, thir corunc.
Certitude, *ser'-tti-tiud*, N. Nirdar, khoreponn, thirason.
Cerumen, *se-ru'-men*, N. Cannlo.
Cessation, *ses-ei'-xion*, N. Ravop; soddni; fg. soncosai.

Cession, *ses'-xion,* N. Soddni; vochop.
Chafe, *chaf,* V. Gansunc; cat caddunc; rag addunc.
Chaff, *chaf,* N. Kunddo; fg. kunddea-pastt.
Chagrin, *sha-grin,* N. Corcor; virasaum.
Chain, *chéin,* N. Sancoll; sankli.
Chair, *cher,* N. Codêl.
Chairman, *cher'-men,* N. Voddil, prezident.
Chalice, *cha'-lis,* N. Cals.
Chalk, *choc,* N. Europi chunno.
Challenge, *chal'-lenj,* V. Zogddonc apounc.
Challenge, N. Zogddonc apounnem.
Chamber, *che-im'-bor,* N. Sal; cudd.
Champion, *cham-pi'-on,* N. Loddaent jicnar; bollist.
Chance, *(By),* Auchit, chinti nastanam.
Chance, *chans,* N. Odrustt; patienem.
Chance, V. Goddonc.
Chancellor, *chan'-sel-lor,* N. Sopo martolo; ministr.
Change, *cheinj,* N. Bodlop.
Change, V. Bodlunc.
Changeable, *che-inj'-ie-bl,* A. Bodolta tosolo.
Channel, *chan'-nel,* N. Valli; khonn.
Chapel, *chep'-el,* N. Irmit, capel.
Chaplain, *chap'-lein,* N. Capelaum.
Chaplet, *chap'-let,* N. Cont; jelo; copel.
Chapter, *chap'-tor,* N. Avesvor; padrinchi vo madrinchi zomat.
Character, *ca'-rac-ter,* N. Letr; gunn; curu; abru-man.
Characteristic, *ca'-rac-te-ris-tic,* A. Lokshannic.
Characterize, *ca'-rac-ter-aiz,* V. Ches, rup diunc.
Charcoal, *char'-col,* N. Collso; inglo.
Charge, *charj,* V. Borunc; angar poddonc; contant galunc; guneauncar corunc; formaunc, hucum diunc; zoton corunc.
Charge, N. Vojem vo vozon; hucum; caido; carann; tiriad; mol; atac.
Chariot, *cha'-ri.ot,* N. Gaddi.
Charitable, *cha'-rit-te-bl,* A. Cacutsar, dhormist; mogall.
Charitably, *cha'-rit-a-bli,* AD. Cacutin; mogan.
Charity, *cha'-ri-tti,* N. Izmol; mog, moiamog.
Charlatan, *char'-la-tan,* N. Borboro, boddboddo.
Charm, *charm,* N. Montr, fg. voddni; suropai,
Charm, V. Khoxal corunc; chodd manounc.
Chase, *cheis,* V. Pattapatt lagonc; cantounc.
Chase, N. Sicar.
Chaste, *cheist,* A. Nitoll, nirmoll.
Chastise, *ches'-taiz,* V. Sicxea diunc; kheastt launc.
Chastity, *chas'-tti-ti,* N. Niclaucponn; nitollponn, nirmollponn.
Chasuble, *shas'-u-bl,* N. Cazul; misachi nesonn.
Chat, *chatt,* V. Gozali marunc. ulounc.
Chat, N. Gozal.
Chattel, *chat'-el,* N. Samon.
Chatter, *chat'-er* V. Naca zalelem ulounc.
Chattering, *cha'-tter-ing,* Boddboddnem, gozali.
Cheap, *chiip,* N. Sovni.
Cheat, *chiit,* N. Thoc, fott.
Cheat, V. Fottounc; donga corunc.

Cheating, *chiit'-ing,* N. Fottoun.
Check, *chek,* V. Addaunc; ixeop sarco asa zalear polleunc.
Check, N. Addcoll.
Cheek, *chiic,* N. Polo.
Cheek-bone, *chiic'-bon,* N. Dadd.
Cheer, *chi'-er,* V. Tallieo pettunc, khoxal corunc.
Cheer, N. Ulas, dadosponn.
Cheerful, *cher'-ful,* A. Khoxal; sontosborit.
Cheerfully, *cher'-ful-li,* AD. Khoxen.
Cheerfulness, *cher'-fulness,* N. Khoxalai; sontos.
Cheese, *chi-iz,* N. Kêz.
Chemist, *kem'-ist,* N. Voctam cornar.
Chemistry, *kem'-ist-ri,* N. Rosa-videa.
Cheque, *chec,* N. Hundi.
Cherish, *che'-rish,* V. mogan chollounc; posunc; buzvondiunc.
Cherub, *che'-rob,* N. Kerobim, dogam zanuancho kel follear zaca asat 64 gonttam.
Chest, *chestt,* N. Pett; horddem.
Chew, *chu,* V. Zabunc; rountunc; golounc.
Chicken, *chik'-en,* N. Pil.
Chicken-pox, *chik'-en-pox,* N. Fugaum.
Chide, *chaid,* V. Insunc.
Chief, *chi-if,* A. Mukeli, voddil.
Chief, N. Mukest vo voddil.
Chiefly, *chiif'-li,* AD. Bhou corun, vodic corun, visês.
Child, *chaild,* N. Burgem, balluc.
Childhood, *chaild'-hud,* N. Burgi pirai; burgeponn.
Childish, *chaild'-ish* A. Burgea baxen.
Childishness, *chaild'-ish-ness,* N. Burgeponn.
Childless, *chaild'-less,* A. Vanz. burgem naslolo.
Chill, *chil,* N. Thonddso.
Chilli, *chil'-li,* N. Mirsang.
Chimera, *ki'-me-ra,* N. Avastu, moia, kholpona.
Chimney, *chim'-nni,* N. Chimnui; dunvrachi vatt.
Chin, *chin,* N. Kaddki; boncho.
Chink, *chink,* N. Futt; verr.
Chisel, *chi'-zel,* N. Irnem. [lat.
Chocolate, *cho'-ko-leit,* N. Chocu-
Choice, *chois,* N. Vinchop.
Choice, A. Uttim; amrut; vinchleli vost.
Choir, *cua'-iar,* N. Igorjechi malloi; cantar cornaracho zommo.
Choke, *chouc,* V. Fugar corunc; gollo dampunc; addcoll gallunc.
Cholera, *co'-le-ra,* N. Sirsiri pidda.
Choose, *chuuz,* N. Vinchun caddunc, soddun caddunc.
Chop, *chop,* V. Cuddkean-kuddke corunc.
Chopper, *cho'-par,* N. Voddli suri.
Chord, *cord,* N. Cordam; sori; dori.
Chorister, *co'-rist-ar,* N. Cantor.
Christian, *kris'-ti-an,* N. Christaum.
Christian, A. Christaunvancho.
Chronic, *cron'-ic,* A. Junnit; sodanchi pidda.
Chronicle, *cron'-i-cl,* N. Contha, vorsancheo khobra.
Chronological, *chron'-o-lo-ji-cal,* AD. Callam pormonnem.
Chronology, *cro-nol'-oji,* N. Callanchi videa.
Chronometer, *cro-nom'-e-tar,* N. Goddial; call man.
Church, *chorch,* N. Igroz; devachem gor.
Church-warden, *chorch-vor'don,* N. Fishali, procurador.

Church-yard, *chorch'-yard*, N. Simiter, matiec launcho zago.
Churl, *chorl*, N. Zongli munis; vauraddi.
Churlish, *chorl'-ish*, A. Bin-moriadicho.
Cicatrize, *si'-ca-traiz*, V. Gai suconc.
Cigar, *sigar*, N. Chirutt.
Cinder, *sind' dor*, N. Inglo, gobor.
Cinnabar, *sin'-na-bar*, Sindur.
Cinnamon, *sin'-na-mon*, N. Tiki, dalchini.
Cipher, *sai'-for*, N. Ziro; anc; guddanchi bhas. [zomo.
Circle, *sor'-cl*, N. Mandal; feri;
Circlet, *sor'clet*, N. Vallo.
Circuit, *sor'-kitt*, N. Bounddi
Circular, *sor'-cu-lar*, A. Chacra-vat, vattcullo, vattangullo.
Circular, *sor-cu-lar*, N. Boundde-car.
Circulation, *sor-cu-lei'-xion*, N. Firnem; bounddi.
Circulate, *sor'-cu-leitt*, V. Boun-tim vochunc; porgot corunc.
Circumlocution, *sor-cum-lo-cu-xion*, N. Girkando.
Circumspection, *sir-cun'-spec-xion*, N. Shannepon, ochircai, tojvit, somjicai.
Circumstance, *sor'-cuns-tans*, N. Doxa, gosht, sangat: bhes; tanc; thar vo jinos.
Cistern, *sis'-tern*, N. Tollem; baim.
Citadel, *si'-ta-del*, N. Cott.
Cite, *saitt*, V. Apounc; ugddas corunc.
Citizen, *si'-tti-zon*- N. Gauncar.
Citron, *sit'-ron*, N. Maulling.
City, *si'-tti*, N. Xar; nogor.
Civil, *si'-vil*, A. Parvasiacho; moriadicho; sadaran.
Civility, *si-vil'-i-tti*, N. Moriad, mausugi, satoria.
Civilize, *si'-vil-aiz*, V. Munshealło corunc, munxean hadduno vo caddunc.
Claim, *kleim*, V. Magunc; por-tun sodunc; direit asa mun sangunc.
Clamour, *clam'-or*, N. Bob, vel.
Clap, *clep*, V. Tallieo pettunc.
Clapper, (of a bell), *clep'-per*, N. Ganttcho lollo.
Clarify, *cla'-ri-fai*, V. Nicklaunc, foddunc; nirmollaunc, nivlunc.
Clash, *clesh*, V. Addlon avaz zaunc; ecachea adavacher ardd eunc.
Clasp, *clasp*, N. Bandunc; veng marunc; zoddunc.
Class, *class*, N. Jat, vorg, jinos; sall, iscol.
Classic, Classical, *clas'-sic*, A. Pathsallicho, iscolacho.
Classify, *clas'-si-fai*, V. Vorg—. zativer corunc.
Clausula, *clau'-zu-la*, N. Pra-karann; vantto.
Claw, *cló*, N. Chopco, dauli.
Clay, *klei*, N. Aveachi mati.
Clean, *cliin*, A. Nitoll; nirmoll.
Clean, *cliin*, V. Nitoll corunc; gansunc.
Cleanliness, *cliin'-li-ness*, N. Nittolai.
Cleanse, *clenz*, V. Nitoll corunc; dunnc.
Clear, *cler*, A. Uzvadic, uzva-dacho; nitoll; kupam naslolo, nivoll; ugddapo, ugtto; sompo.
Clear, *cler*, V. Uzvaddic zaunc etc.
—(Off a debt)=Rinn faric corunc.
—(Away)=Bitor vorunc.
—(Oneself of a charge)=Suttonc.
Clearly, *cler'-li*, AD. Ugddapim, saf, sompepounim.
Clearness, *cler'-ness*, N. Uz-vadd, pracas.

Cleave, *clev*, V. Soddunc; suttounc; futtonc; lagonc.
Cleft, *cleft*, N. Futt; Moddop.
Clemency, *cle'-men-si*, N. Doia; cacut.
Clement, *cle'-ment*, A. Mogall; doiall.
Clepsydra, *clep'-si-dra*, N. Udoachem goddial.
Clergy, *clor'-ji*, N. Padrincho mêll.
Clergyman, *clor'-ji-men*, N. Padri; munniari.
Clerk, *clark*, N. Boroinar; iscrivaum.
Clever, *cle'-ver*, A. Uxear; xanno.
Cleverness, *cle'-ver-ness*, N. Uxearponn; Zantteponn.
Client, *clai'-ent*, N. Giraic; kull.
Climate, *clai'-meitt*, N. Hava; desprakriti.
Climax, *clai'-max*, N. Manddavol; kram.
Climb, *claim*, V. Choddunc.
Cling, *cling*, V. Lagonc.
Clip, *clip*, V. Catrunc; supurlo corunc.
Cloak, *clok*, N. Capot.
Cloak, V. Lipounc.
Clock, *clock*, Goddial, reloz.
Cloister, *clo-is'-ter*, N. convent.
Close, *cloz*, V. Dampunc.
Close, A. Datt; gott; guttacho; mottvo; imtto.
Close, AD. Lagim; sorsim.
Closeness, *cloz'-ness*, AD. Dattai.
Closet, *clo'-zet*, N. Landcudd; cummaum.
Clot, *clot*, N. Meu zomleli mater.
Cloth, *cloth*, N. Lugott; bansirem.
Clothe, *clod*, V. Nesounc.
Clothes, *cloothz*, N. Nesonn, angaulim.
Cloud, *claud*, N. Kup.
Cloudless, *claud'-less*, A. Kup naslolo.
Cloudy, *claud'-i*, A. Callocacho, ouduuco; goir.
Clove, *clov*, N. Lovong.
Clown, *claun*, N. Theatrant ansoncho khell cornar.
Club, *clob*, N. Tounco; ecott.
Clumsily, *clom'-zi-li*, AD. Korkotte ritin.
Clumsy, *clom'-zi*, N. Korkotto.
Cluster, *clos'-ttor*, N. Gons; fenno.
Coach, *koch*, N. Gaddi.
Coachman, *koch'-men*, N. Gaddiecar; bolieiro.
Coadjutor, *co-ad-ju'-tor*, N. Cumoc dinar; asistent.
Coagulate, *co-ag'-u-leith*, V. Zomonc.
Coal, *kol*, N. Inglo; Collso.
Coalesce, *co-al-es'*, V. Mellunc; ecttaim gaunc. [ecott.
Coalition, *co-al-i'-zion*, N. Mêll;
Coarse, *kors*, A. Motto; fg. moriad naslolo.
Coarseness, *kors'-nes*, N. Corddeponn.
Coast, *cost*, N. Vell; kinari; doriachi deg.
Coat, *cot*, N. Judi.
Coax, *kox*, V. Bollaunc.
Cobra, *cob'-ra*, N. Sorop.
—(Capella)=Nag; panro.
Cock, *cock*, N. Combo.
Cock's-comb, *cocks'-comb*, N. Combeachem xencrem.
Cockroach, *cock'-roch*, N. Zorlo.
Cocoanut, *coc'-natt*, Narl.
—(Day)=Narel punoum vo doriachi puja corcho dis.
—(Tree)=Madd.
—(Shell)=Cotti.
—(Juice)=Narlachem udoc.
Cod (*fish*), *codd*, N. Totto.
—(Liver oil)=Totteachem tel.
Code, *cod*, N. Kanujabto.

Codicil, *co'-di-sil*, N. Mrita-patrachi puranni.
Coequal, *co'-i-kual*, A. Borobor-cho (piraen).
Coerce, *ko'ers*, V. Forsan addaunc.
Coffee, *coff'-i*, N. Cafi.
Coffer. *cof'-er*, N. Pett.
Coffin, *cof'-fin*, N. Moddeachi caix; tumb.
Cohabitation, *co-ha-bi-ttei'-xion*, N. Sangata raunem; ecatravas.
Coherence, *co-her'ens*, N. Sangat; ecvott.
Coil, *coil*, N. Covannem.
Coin, *coin*, N. Duddu.
Coin, V. Duddu xapunc; fg. zoddunc.
Coincide, *co-in-said'*, V. Sampatunc; fg. borobor—, eca tempar—, zaunc—, goddunc—, mellunc—, lagunc.
Coincidence, *co-in'-si-dens*, N. Sompat, sompatuni; goddop.
Cold, *cold*, A. Xello; thondd; fg. moipas naslolo.
Coldly, *cold'-li*, AD. fg. Moipasavinn.
Coldness, *cold'ness*, N. Thonddai; fg. beporva.
Colic, *col'-ic*, N. Gullo; pottan chabuem.
Collapse, *col-laps'*, V. Poddonc; moddonc; ibadd zaunc.
Collapse, N. Sirantaram tuttnem.
Collar, *col'-ar*, N. Har; gop; sorpolli; sori.
Colleague, *kol'-lig*, N. Sangati.
Collect, *col'lect*, V. Ecttaim corunc; ras corunc; lunnvonc.
Collected, *col-lekt'-ed*, A. Nirvonnim; gabronaslolo.
Collection, *col-lec'xion*, N. Zomo; punj; vinchni.
Collector, *col-ect'-ar*, N. Ecttaim cornar; administrador,
College, *col'-lej*, N. Colej; videasall.
Collision, *col-li'-zion*, N. addlop; fg. loddai; zogddem.
Colloquial, *col-lo'-kui-al*, N. Chalti bhas.
Colloquy, *col'-lo-kui*, N. Chali; boli; zapsal; uloup.
Collusion, *col lu'-zion*. N. Guddmell; kopattmantr.
Colonel, *colo'-nel*, N. Poltonicho voddlo sardar.
Colosal, *co-lo'-sal*, A. Bhou vodd.
Colosus, *co-los'-us*, N. Mottem bhaulem. [nib.
Colour, *col'-or*, N. Rong; fg.
Colour, V. Rongounc.
Column, *co'-lom*, N. Khambo.
Colt, *colt*, N. Goddeacho pilo.
Comb, *comb*, N. Dantonni.
Combination, *com'-bi-nei'-xion* N. Zoddni; mellouni; ecthavni; carar.
Combustible, *com-bost'-i-bl*, A. Laso sarco.
Come, *com*, V. Euuc; goddonc.
—(Out)=Collit zaunc.
—(To a resolution)=Nicheu corunc.
—(At)=Mellunc.
—(To)=Rocom zaunc.
Come to pieces, Cuddkean cuddco zaunc.
—(Together)=ectaim zaunc.
—(Up)=Zaunc, futtonc.
—(Upon evils)=Poddonc.
—(Away)=Niclonc.
Comedy, *co'-me-di*, U. Comed, zagor.
Comet, *com'-et*, N. Dhumketu.
Comfort, *com'-fort*, V. Buzvon diunc; somandan corunc; dhir diunc.
Comfort, N. Buzvon.
Comfortable, *com'-fort-a-bl*, A Soucasahecho; iscollaecho,

Comic, *com'-ic*, A Anscho.
Coming, *com'-ing*, N. Ennem; paunnem.
Command, *com-mend'*, V. Formaunc; hukum, takit diunc.
Command, *com-mend'*, N. Formonn; upordes.
Commander, *com-mend'-or*, N. Hukumdar; formaitolo munis.
Commemorate, *com-mem'-o reitt* V. Ugddas corunc, attou corunc.
Commemorative, *com-mem-o-rei'-ttiv*, A. Ugddas vo attou corcho.
Commence, *com-mens'*, V. Suru corunc vo zaunc.
Commend *com-mend'*, V. Suadin diunc, adin corunc; bud sangonc; khonchounc.
Commendable, *com-mend'-ie-bl*, A. Abruvont, man favo zalolo
Commensurated, *com-men'-su-'rei-tted*, A. Mezum-ieso; sampariman.
Comment, *com-ment'*, N Orth, vivék.
Commerce, *com'-mers*, N. Vepar.
Commercial, *com-mer'-shal*, A. Veparacho.
Commiserate, *com-miz'-e-reitt*, V. Cacut, disunc; churchureunc.
Commission, *com-mi'-xion*, N. Oppnni, havalo, adicar; dalali, dosturi.
Commissioner, *com-mi'-xion-ar*, N. Dalal; podvi meullolo munis
Commit, *com-mitt'*, V. Corunc. adarunc; adin carunc.
Committee, *com-mit'-ti*, N. Dhazan, commisaum.
Commodious, *com-mo'-di-as*, A. Soucasaccho; iscollaecho.
Common, *com'-mon*,. A. Somestancho, soglleancho; sobarancho, chalto.
Common, N. Sercari zago,
Commonly, *com-mon'li*, AD. Choddavot, bhou corun, sabar pautti; baga, raxic.
Common wealth, *com'-on-welth*, N. Raschem bens, dhazanachem raz vo republic.
Commotion, *com-mo'-xion*, N. Holkandni, uchambollai; goddbodd.
Commune, *com-mun'*, N. prant.
Communicate, *com-miu'-ni-keith*, V. Khollounc, gonounc; eca meca codde ulounc, voivatt asunc; saib geunc.
Communication, *com-miu'-ni-ket'-xion*, N. Khollounni gomounni; chaliboli.
Communion, *com-miu'-ni-on*, N. Sangat, ecvott; saheb, deu.
Community, *com-miu'-nni-tti*, N. Comnidad, ecvott.
Commute, *com-mitt'*, V. Boldunc; baluvadunc.
Compact, *com-pect'*, A. Okhond, ako, gott; gonn, datt.
Compact, N. Carar, contrat.
Compactness, *com-pact'-ness*, N, Khenchounem; dambop.
Companion, *com-pen'-ion* N .Sangati; istt, bagedar.
Company, *com'-pe-ni*, N. Sangat; zomat; mell.
Comparative, *com-pa'-ra-tiv*, A. Soricho, savdhec.
Comparatively, *com-pa-ra'-tiv-li*, AD. Sor corun; dusream mucar.
Compare, *com-per'*, V. Sor corunc.
Comparison, *com-pe'-ri-zon*, N. Sor; vopar.
Compass, *com'-pass*, N. Cumpas, vistar.
Compasses, *com'-pa-sis*, N. Kovar.
Compassion, *com-pe'-xion*, N. Cacut; birmot; churchure,

Compassionate, *com-pe'-shon-eith*, V. Cacut corunc, churchu-ronc.
Compassionate, A. Cacuticho, cacutsar.
Compel, *com-pel'*, V. Boll corunc, forsar corunc.
Compendium, *com-pen'-di-um*, N. Sancshep, attap.
Compensate, *com-pens'-eith*, V. Faric ponn dinnc; inam dinnc; borobor corunc.
Compete. *com-piti'*, V. Ecame-car poddunc; virudunc, dus-sangunc.
Competency, *com'-pe-ten-si*, N. Adicar, hakh; purtepon, kuvet.
Competition, *com-pe-tti'-xion*, N. Eca-mecar poddop, dusamgop.
Compile, *com-pail'*, V. Attapunc, soddunc; baudunc.
Complacency, *com-pla'-sen-si*, N. Khuxamot, bidda; mur-gottni.
Complain, *com-plein'*, V. Xin-nonc; guneaum corunc.
Complainant, *com-plei'-nant*, N. Firiadi; author.
Complaining, *com-plein'-ing*, N. Xinnop. [pidda.
Complaint, *com-pleint'*, N. Xinn;
Complement, *com-ple'-ment*, N. Bhorti. [purto.
Complete, *com-plitt'*, A. Akho;
Complete, V. Bhor corunc; co-bar corunc.
Completely, *com-plit'-li*, AD. Nigut; ogdim; nibel.
Completeness, *com-plitt'-ness*, N. Sompurnai.
Completion, *com-pli'-xion*, N. Xevott, cobar corop.
Complex, *com'-plecks*, A. Gond-dlacho, gondicho; punzo.
Complexion, *com-plek'-xion*, N. Somiog; sarkem.
Complicate, *com'-pli-keit*, V. Augodd corunc; gondaunc; guspaunc.
Complicated, *com'-pli-keit-ed*, A. Oottin; augodd.
Complication, *com-pli-kei'xion*, N. Gottallo; guspaunni; gon-doll.
Complicity, *com-plis'-i-tti*, N. Khottea cortoban sangat.
Compliment, *com'-pli-ment*, N. Cumprument; salam; recad.
Comply, *com-plai'*, V. Khoxe pormonnem cholonc.
Compose, *com-poz'*, V. Mellunc; borounc; fuslaunc.
Composed, *com-pozdd'*, A. Kelolo; fg. nidan.
Composer, *com-poz'-ar*, N. Godd-nar, author.
Composition, *com-po-zi'-xion*, N. Goddni, mandavoll; boroup.
Composure, *com-po'-jear*, N. Sos-nicai; modesti; gottai. [lounc.
Compound, *com-pound'*, V. Mel-
Compound, N. Hort.
Comprehend, *com-pre-hend'*, V. Attapunc; dorunc; chintun sarunc; thau geunc.
Comprehension, *com-pri-hen'-xion*, N. Attapni; somzonni.
Comprehensive, *com-pri-hen'-siv*, A. Somjic; attapacho.
Compress, *com-press'*, V. Dam-bunc; goddi corunc.
Comprise, *com-praiz'*, V. Atta-punc; dorunc.
Compromise, *com'-pro-maiz*, V. Carar—, raji corunc; utor diunc; sampddonc.
Compulsion, *com-pol'-xion*, N. Boll cornem; zobordosti; zulum.
Compulsory, *com-pol'-so-ri*, A. Bollacho; julmacho.
Compunction, *com-pong'-xion*, N. Duc; churchure.

Computation, *com-piu-ttei'-xion,* N. Gannan; lekh.

Compute, *com-piutt',* N. Admasuno; sumarar mezunc.

Concave, *con'-keiv* N. Pokoll.

Concavity, *con-cav'-i-tti.* N. Pokor; poklepoun.

Conceal, *con-siil,* V. Lipounc; guttan dovorunc.

Concealment, *con-siil'-ment,* N. Lipounem; lipohi suat.

Concede, *con-siid',* V. Diunc; soddunc.

Conceit, *con-siit',* N. Pisaechi chintna. [cari.

Conceited, *con-siitt'-ed,* A. Han-

Conceive, *con-siiv',* V. Gorb dorunc; samballunc; chintunc; somzunc.

Concentrate, *con-sen'-treitt,* V. Modem vorunc; eka zagear zomounc; chit diun chintunc.

Conception, *con-sep'-xion,* N. Consesaum. gorb; fg. chintna.

Concern, *con-sorn',* N. Cam: zoton.

Concerned, *con-sorn'-dd,* A. Lagta.

Concerning, *con-sorn'-ing.* PRP. Sovem.

Concert, *con-sort',* V. Ecttaim zaun guddmeu corunc.

Concert, N. Carar; vazop; concerto.

Concession, *con-se'-xion,* N. Dennem; sodduem.

Conch, *congk,* N. Simpo.

Conciliate, *con-si'-li-eitt,* V. Somzaunc, raji corunc; somandan corunc.

Conciliation, *con-si'-li-ei'-xion,* N. Somzaunni; mell; somandan.

Concise, *con-saiz',* A. Thoddeam utrancho; mottvo.

Conclave, *con'-clav,* N. Sabha, parshad, (cardialancho).

Conclude, *con-cliudd',* V. Cobar corunc, attapunc.

Conclusion, *con-cliu'-zion,* N. Aker; xevott.

Concord, *cong'-cord,* N. Ec-chit, ekbhav, mellop.

Concourse, *cong'-cors,* N. Sobar loc vo locacho zommo.

Concubine, *cong'-kiu-bain,* N. Cheddi; dovorleli bail.

Concupiscence, *con-kiu'-pi-sens,* N. Mod; cam; angsuc; cuddichi khoxi; vaitt khoxi.

Concur, *con-cor',* V. Borobor—, ecttaim ravunc, hat-bot galunc, pavunc; mozot diunc.

Concurrence, *con-cor'-rens,* N. Mell: coblot.

Concussion, *con-ku'-xion,* N. Addlop.

Condemn, *con-demn,* V. Sicxechem formon marunc; dondd galunc; guneaumcar corunc.

Condemnation, *con-dem-nei'-xion,* N. Sicxechem formon.

Condensation, *con-den-sei'-xion,* N. Gott cornem, attni, amvlop.

Condense, *con-dens',* V. Gott corunc; attonc, datt corunc; amvlonc.

Condescend, *con-di-send',* V. Khoxe pormounem cholunc; bidda disunc; pottcarunc; puttvonc.

Condescension, *con-di-sen'-xion,* N. Bidda, khuxamot, puttvop.

Condign, *con-dain',* N. Favotea manacho.

Condiment, *con'-di-ment,* N. Sambar, jirem-mirim.

Condition, *con-di'-xion,* N. Got, doxa; prestau; caide; carar.

Conditional, *con-di'-xion'-al,* A. Sertacho.

Conditionally, *con-di'-sio-nal-li,* AD. Prestavan, sertan.

Condole, *con-dol′*, V. Buzvon diunc; cacut corunc.
Condolence, *con-dol′-ens*, N. Pacharop.
Conduce, *con-dius′*, V. Upcarono.
Conduct, *con′-doct*, N. Chal; naddtem.
Conduct, V. Cholounc, vorunc.
Confection, *con-fec′-xion*, N. Mittai.
Confectionery, *con-fec-xio-na′ri*, N. Mittaechem khon.
Confederacy, *con-fe′-de-ra-si*, N. Ecvott; istagott.
Confederate, *con-fe′-de-reitt*, N. Sangati; istt.
Confer, *con-fer′*, V. Diunc; boli-chali corunc.
Conference, *con′-fer-ens*, N. Sori cornem, rujvat, boli.
Confess, *con-fess′*, V. Sangunc, uncharunc, cobul corunc, cum-sar corunc; cumsar zaunc.
Confession, *con-fe′-xion*, N. Cumsar, coblad.
Confessional, *con-fe′-xion-al*, N. Cumsodor.
Confessor, *con-fes′-or*, Confesor.
Confide, *con-faid′*, V. Patiennc, suadin corunc.
Confidence, *con′-fi-dens*, N. Visvas; borvonso; humed.
Confidential, *con-fi-den-xial*, A. Guttacho, gupit.
Configuration, *con-fig′u-rei′xion*, N. Rup, acar.
Confine, *con′fain* N. Mer, sarad.
Confine, V. Dampunc, boncondint galunc; autunnar asunc; porsutt zaunc.
Confined, *con′-faindd*, A. Osir.
Confinement, *con-fain′ment*, N. Bond corop; baintter.
Confirm, *con-form′*, V. Thir corunc; tharavunc; posonc vo cobul corunc; crizm diunc.
Confirmation, *con-fir-mei′-xion*, N. Thirasonn; crizm.
Confiscate, *con′-fis-keitt*, V. Sercaran geunc; jopti corunc.
Confiscation, *con-fis-kei′-xion*, N. Jopti.
Conflagration, *con-fla-grei′-xicn*, N. Vodd uzo; lasop.
Conflict, *con′-flict*, N. Loddai; zuz; fg. zogddem.
Conflict, V. Loddai corunc; zogddunc.
Conflicting, *con-flict′-ing*, A. Virud aslolo.
Confluent, *con′-flu-ent*, N. Noincho fantto,
Conform, *con-form′*, V. Raji asunc, eke budicho zaunc; goddunc, sarco corunc.
Conformation, *con-for-mei′-xion*, N. Rup.
Conformity, *con-for′-mi-tti*, N. Sarkeponn; laikponn, ecvott.
Confound, *con-faund′*, N. Guspaunc; lojec galunc.
Confraternity, *con-fra-ter′-ni-tti*, N. Bhauponn, irmandad.
Confrere, *cong′-frer*, N. Irmaum.
Confront, *con-front′*, V. Mucar raunc.
Confuse, *con-fiuz′*, V. Gusponnc; lojec galunc.
Confusion, *con-fiu′-zion*, N. Gondoll.
Confutation, *con-fiut-ei′-xion*, N. Khamdan, solvop.
Confute, *con-fiutt′*, N. Soluai corunc, Kham-dunc.
Congeal, *con-jiil′*, V. Gar corunc; zomounc.
Congee, *con′-ji*, N. Pez.
Congenital, *con-je′-ni-tal*, A. Soimbacho; zolmacho.
Congestion, *con-jes′-xion*, N. Rogot choddnem-, bornem.
Conglomerate, *con-glom′-er-eith*, V. Zomo vo ras corunc.

Congratulate, *con-grat'-iu-leith,* V. Porbem diunc, dinvasunc.

Congratulation, *con-grat-tu-lei'-xion,* N. Dinvas, porbem magnem.

Congregate, *cong'-gre-geith,* V. Punzaunc, zoma vo ras corunc.

Congregation, *cong-'gre-gei'-xion* N. Zomat, méll, ecvott.

Congress, *cong'-gress,* N. Sabha; mell.

Congruence, *cong'-gru-ens,* N. Laikponn; iuctiponn.

Congruent, *cong'-gru-ent,* A. Mafôc, ecsarco. [biponn.

Congruity, *con-gru'-i-thi,* N. Vaz-

Conjecture, *con-jec'-char,* N. Parconnem; opiniaum; sumar.

Conjecture, V. Parcunc, sumar corunc.

Conjunction, *con-jonk'-xion,* N. Mell; ecvott; zomo.

Conjuncture, *con-jonk'-char,* N. Sangat; soheog.

Conjuration, *con-ju-rei'-xion,* N. Laleunchem magnnem; umalleachem magnnem.

Conjure, *con-ju-ar',* V. Prathun magunc, laleun magunc.

Connect, *con-nect',* V. Bandunc, zoddunc, mellounc.

Connection, *con-nec'-xion,* N. Ekvott; bandop, soiric; fg. isttagot.

Connive, *con-naiv',* V. Bedonc; decon-deco naslelea porim corunc; dolle dampunc.

Connivance, *con-nai'-vens,* N. Dolle dampnnem.

Conquer, *cong'-kor,* V. Jiconc, zoit vorunc; fg. ardd eunc.

Conqueror, *cong'-ker-or,* N. Jicpi, zoit vornar. [zoit.

Conquest, *cong'-ku-est,* N. Jicop,

Consaguinity, *con-sa-guin'-i'-tti,* N. Bapai eusili soiric.

Conscience, *con'-shens,* N. Soiran; somjina; ontoscorn.

—(Remorse of conscience)= ontoscornacho kiddo.

Conscientious, *con-xi-en -xi-as,* A. Borea ontoscornacho; nitivont.

Conscientiousness, *cons-xi-en'-xi-as-ness,* N. Soiran; abru.

Conscious, *cons'-xi-as,* A. Soiranacho, vol!co sarco.

Consciousness, *cons-xi'-as-ness,* N. Soiran, mot.

Consecrate, *con'-se-creit,* V. Povitr corunc; bettounc; somorpiunc; consagrar corunc.

Consecrated, *con-se-krei'-tted,* A. Benjar kelolo; povitr.

Consecration, *con-se-krei'-xion,* N. Bett; somorpinnem, benziment; consegrasaum.

Consecutive, *con-se'-cutiv,* A. Eke ordin; lagim, pattlo.

Consent, *con-sent',* N. Coblad.

Consent, V. Coblad diunc; khoxi voronc.

Consequence, *con'-se-kwens,* N. Fôll; xevott.

—(In consequence of)=pasun; decun.

Consequent, *con'-se-kwent,* A. Sangaticho.

Consequently, *con'-se-kwent-li,* AD. Tor; decun; tea pasun.

Conservation, *con-serv-ei-'xion,* N. Samballop; racnnem.

Conservative, *con-serv'-at-iv,* A. Samballcho; ballguncho.

Conserve, *con-serv',* N. Murumbo; lonchem; samballun dourop.

Conserves, *con-servs',* N. Mittai; alvo.

Consider, *con-si'-dor,* V. Niallunc; monant addunc; chintunc, polleunc; zoton corunc.

Considerable, *con-si'-der-e-bl,* A. Bhon vodd, zaito, sobar.

Considerate, *con-si'-de-reitt,* A. Chotraecho, budvont; zagrut.

Consideration, *con-si-de-rei'-xion,* N. Chintonn, niall, vichar; zoton; chotrai; porva; ochircai; bidda; manbhov; prestau.

Considering, *con-si'-der ing,* PRP. Chintun.

Consign, *con-sain',* V. Vopunc; tabeant diunc; addtiac pattounc.

Consignment, *con-sain'-ment,* N. Havalo; vopni.

Consist, *con-sit',* V. Asunc; goddonc.

Consistence, *con-sis'-tens,* V. Gottai dattai.

Consistent, *con-sis'tent,* A. Thir; ecamecac lagcho.

Consistory, *con-sis'-to-ri,* N. Satsabha.

Consolation, *con-so-lei'-xion,* N. Buzvonn; sontos; ulas.

Console, *con-sol',* V. Buzvonn diunc.

Consolidate, *con-sol'-i-deit,* V. Gottavunc, thiraunc.

Consonance, *con-so'-nans,* N Ectall; suarmal; sompaddop.

Consonant, *con-so'-nant,* N. Sangata ucharchem akxer, venjan.

Consort, *con'-sort,* N. Sangati; poti; potin.

Conspicuous, *con-spic'-u-as,* A. Discho; navaddic vo naum addlolo.

Conspicuously, *con-spik'-u as-li,* AD. Disttic poddo sarko.

Conspiracy, *con-spi'-ra-si,* N. Kutt, guddmell.

Conspirator, *con-spi'-ret-or,* N. Kuttacar, fitturio, kolpololo, koponuo.

Conspire, *con-spa'-iar,* V. Kolpunc; borobori uprasunc.

Constable, *con'-ste-bl,* N. Pulisecho munis, sipaic.

Constancy, *con'-stan-si,* N. Thirasonn; gottai.

Constant, *con'-stant,* A. Thir, gott; sodancho.

Constellation, *con'-stel-lei'-xion.* N. Neketranchi ras.

Consternation, *con-ster-nei'xion,* N. Hairan, sonkirnai, acant.

Constipated (Be), *ulg,* N. Uttcadde bond zaunc.

Constipation, *con'-sti-pei'xion,* N. Barkon; thondd.

Constitute, *con'-sti-tiutt,* V. Goddunc; tharavunc; euzunc; nemunc.

Constitution, *con-sti-tiu'-xion,* N. Goddvonn; tharaoni; kaletri; nem; caido.

Constitutional, *con-sti-tiu'-xional,* A. Caideam pormounem aslolo.

Constrain, *con-strein',* V. Boll corunc; addaunc.

Constraint, *con-streint',* N. Boll cornem; addaunim.

Construct, *con-struct',* V. Bandunc; goddunc.

Construction, *con-stroc'-xion,* N Bandop; akar; mandavol; orth.

Construe, *con'-stru,* V. (Utram) mandunc; somzonni diunc.

Consul, *con'-sul,* N. Consul, sercaracho letrad.

Consult, *con--solt',* V. Bud magunc—, geunc, vicharunc,

Consultation, *con-sol-tei'-xion,* N. Bud, mot magnem, vichar.

Consulter, *con-solt'-or,* N. Budd sangtolo; budd ditolo.

Consume, *con-sium',* V. Khaunc, girasunc; vibadd corunc; lasunc; khorchunc.

Consummate, *con'-sum-meitt,* V. Sompaddunc; sompurn corunc.
Consummation, *con-sum-mei'-xion,* N. Sompaddni; sompurnai; xevott.
Consumption, *con-somp'-xion,* N. Kelladd.
Consumptive, *con-som'-tir,* N. Kelladcar.
Consumptive, A. Kelladicho.
Contact, *con'-tect,* N. Addlop, lagop.
Contagion, *con-tei'-jion,* N. Voso.
Contagious, *con-tei'-ji-as,* N. Voseacho.
Contain, *con-tein',* V. Attaponc; fg. bogounc.
Contaminate, *con-tam'-in-eitt,* V. Khetaunc, bosttaunc, mello corunc; fg. oxig corunc.
Contamination, *con-tam'-in-ei''-xion,* N. Oxigponn; chicol, fg. pozddeponn; burseponn.
Contemplate, *con-tem'-pleitt,* V. Niallunc, dolle laun polleunc, tellunc.
Contemplation, *con-tem-plei'-xion,* N. Niall, tellni; dhian.
Contemplative, *con-tem',plet-iv,* N. Dhianisht; nialli.
Contemporarily, *con-tem'-po-ra-ri-li,* AD. Teach vellar; sovem.
Contemporary, *con-tem-po'-ra-ri,* A. Teach vellacho vo kallacho.
Contempt, *con-temt',* N. Beporvo, desprez.
Contemptible, *con-tem'-ti-bl,* A. Beporvo favo zalolo; holco; unno.
Contend, *con-tend',* V. Zogddonc; loddai coruuc; khondit sangonc.
Content, *con-tent',* N. Dadosponn; sontos; ulas.
Content, A. Sontosacho.
Contention, *con-ten'-xion,* N. Zogddem; loddai; nett.
Contentious, *con-ten'-xi-as,* A. Zogdoncho, niacho
Contest, *con-test',* V. Zogddonc, samballunc. [uzot.
Contest, V. Zogddem, loddai;
Content, *con-tent',* N. Utranchi manddavol; motlob; orth.
Contiguity, *con-ti-gu'-i-tti,* N. Lagop.
Contiguous, *con-tig'-u-as,* A. Lagsilo.
Continence, *con'-ti-nens,* N. Samballop; nidonai; fg. niclancponn.
Continent, *con'-ti-nent,* A. Segunni, nidani, niclancponnacho.
Continent, N. Suki buim vo suco gaum.
Contingency, *con-tin'-gen-si,* N. Goddop.
Contingent, *con-tin'-jent,* A. Acasmatacho; auchit.
Continual, *con-tin'-ual,* A. Sodancho, ravonaslolo.
Continually, *con-tin'-ua-li,* AD. Ravonastanam, sodanch.
Continuation, *con-tin'-u-ei''-xion,* N. Mucar cholop.
Continue, *con-tin'-iu,* V. Mucar cholonc, mucar vochunc; thir ravunc.
Continuous, *con-tin'-u-as,* A. Khali naslolo.
Contortion, *con-tor'-xion,* N. Copel.
Contraband, *con'-tra-band,* N. Chorie-addop; choriecho mal; fg. chorttepoun.
Contraband, A. Choriecho.
Contract, *con-tract',* N. Contrad, karar.
—(Of marriage)=soiric.
Contract, V. Karar corunc; osir corunc.
—(Friendship)=isttogot zodunc.
—(Cloth)=mirio galunc.

Contracted, *con-trect'-ed*, A. Osir, mottvo; dactto; fg somonz naslolo.
Contraction, *con-trec'-xion*, N. Mottveponn.
Contractor, *con-trect'-or*, N. Contradcar.
Contradict, *con tra-dict'*, V. Ardd ulounc.
Contradiction, *con-tra-dic'-xion*, N. Add, virud.
Contradictory, *con-tra-dic'-to-ri*, A. Virud, vivad kelolo.
Contrariety, *con-tra-ra'-e-tti*, N. Virudai.
Contrary, *con'-tra-ri*, A. Porto; virud aslolo; fg. ogunnacho.
Contrast, *con'-trast*, N. Tafavott.
Contrast, *con-trast'*, V. Add asunc.
Contravene, *con-tra-vin'*, V. Moddunc; add vochunc.
Contravention, *con-tra-ven'-xion*, N. Moddop; add ennem.
Contribute, *con-tri'-biutt*, V. Paunc; mozot dinnc; choddounc
Contribution, *con-tri-biu'-xion*, N. Pavop; vantto.
Contrite, *con'-trait*, A. Dukest.
Contrition, *con-tri'-xion*, N. Deu mogachi duc.
Contrivance, *con-trai'-vens*, N. Upai; hicmot; chamatcar; nadd.
Contrive, *con-traiv'*, V. Sodun caddunc; chintunc; naddunc; hicmot corunc.
Control, *con-trol'*, V. Cholounc; samballunc; zoton corunc.
Control, *con-trol'*, N. Kobardari.
Controversy, *con'-tro-vor-si*, N. Tocrar.
Controvert, *con'-tro-vert*, V. vivadunc.
Controvertible, *con-tro-ver'-ti-bl*, A. Tocrari.
Contumacious, *con-tu-mei'-xi-as*, A. Jalgi, salli.
Contumacy, *con'-tu-ma-si*, N. Sall; darunai.
Contumelious, *con-tu-me'lias*, A. Ocmanacho; galli souncho.
Contumely, *con'-tiu-mi'li*, N. Ocman; galli.
Contuse, *con-ttiuz'*, V. Jenzronc; daddounc.
Contusion, *con-ttiu'-zion*, N. Daddounem.
Convalescence, *con-va-les'-sens*, N. Uttarant poddnem; piddechi osoctai.
Convalescent, *con-va-les'-sent*, A. Utarant poddlolo.
Convene, *con-vin'*, V. Apounc; zomatic ecttaim corunc.
Convenience, *con-vi'-ni-ens*, N. Soi; purteponn; laikponn; upeg; soucosai.
Convenient, *con-vi'-ni-ent*, A. Favoto; purto; soicho; soucasaecho.
Convent, *con'-vent*, N. Convent.
Conventicle, *con-ven'-tti-cl*, N. Gudh mell; vivar.
Convention. *con-ven'-xion*, N. Chaliboli; ek zomat; karar; rivaz.
Conventional. *con-ven'-xio-nal*, A. Kararacho.
Converge, *con-vorj'*, V. Bagounc.
Convergency, *con-vorj'en-si*, N. Conso; bag.
Convergent, *con-vorj'-ent*, A. Ekemdrac vallto; eke suatent vecho.
Conversation, *con-ver-sei'-xion*, Gozal, ulonnnem.
Converse, *con-vors'*, V. Eca-meca codde ulounc; gozali marunc.
Conversely, *con'-vors-li*, AD. Portem.
Conversion, *con-vor'-xion*, Portounem; bodlop; novi jinn.
Convert, *con-vort'*, V. Bodlunc; converter zaunc.

Convert, N. Novo christaum; Devac portololo munis.

Convex, *con'-veks*, A. Fugo aslolo, bhailean vattcullo.

Convexity, *con-veks'-i-tti*, N. Ubarai.

Convey, *con-vei'*, V. Vorunc; sundin corunc; orth asunc.

Conveyance, *con-vei'-ans*, N. Gaddi.

Convict, *con-vict'*, V. Guneaumcari corunc.

Conviction, *con-vic'-xion*, N. Guneaumcarponn; khatri.

Convince, *con-vins'*, V. Somzaunc; decol corunc; katri corunc.

Convincing *con-vins'-ing*, A. Katri zai sarco.

Convocation, *con-vo-kei'-xion*, N. Ecttaim zavop; apounnem.

Convoke, *con-voc'*, V. Apounc; zomat borunc.

Convoy, *con-voi'*, N. Vatt-surancho mell.

Convulse, *con-vols'*, V. Voddi [soddunc.

Convulsion, *con-vol'xion*, N. Vodd; camp; morluc.

Cook, *cuc*, V. zizounc; randunc; ucddunc

Cook, N. Randpi; cuzner.

Cookery, *cuk'e-ri* N. Randchi art.

Cool, *cuul*, A. Thondd; fg. xello; fg. nidan; fg. cuidad naslolo.

Cool, N. Thonddai.

Cool, V. Thondd corunc; fg. nivounc; varem gennc; fg. somandan corunc.

Coolie, *cu'-li*, N. Mannai; vauraddi; begari.

Coolness, *cul'-nes*, N. Somandan.

Co-operate, *co-op'-er-eitt*, V. Pavunc; pormonnem cholunc; mozot diunc; sangata vauronc.

Co-operation, *co-op'er-ei-xion*, N. Mozot; pavop.

Cope, *cop'*, N. Cap; padrichi nesonn.

Copious, *co'-pi-as*, A. Chodd; bhou.

Copiousness, *co'pi-as-ness*, N. Sompurnai; dadosponn.

Copper, *cop'-por*, N. Támbem.

Copper, A. Tambeacho.

Copy, *co'-pi*, N. Nocol; nomunno.

Copy, V. Nocol caddunc.

Copyist, *co'pi-ist*, N. Nocol carnar.

Coquette, *co-ket'*, N. Peravecarn, chalac, pattoli.

Coral, *co'ral*, N. Pounlem.

Cord, *cord*, N. Dori; sumb; razu.

Cordial, *cor'di-al*, A. Callzacho; mogacho.

Coriander, *co-ri'-an-dor*, N. confiri

Cork, *cork*, N. Guddi.

Corn, *corn*, N. Danno; khinn.

Corner, *cor'nor*, N. Consc.

Corn-field, *con'-field*, N. Xet.

Corollary, *co'rol-la-ri*, N. Fol; xevott.

Coronation, *co-ro-nei'xion*, N. Gadier bosounném; mocutt galop.

Corporal, *cor'po-ral*, A. Cuddicho; corporal.

Corporation, *cor-po-rei'xion*, N. Zomat; mell.

Corps, *korz*, N. Foujicho vautto.

Corpse, *corps* N. Moddem.

Corpulence, *cor'pu-lens*, N. Mottai; anglott.

Corpulent, *cor'pu-lent*, A. Motto; anglotti.

Corpuscle, *cor'pus-cl* ,N. Cuscut, vost.

Correct, *cor-rect'*, A. Nitt, sarco; boro.

Correct, V. Nittier galunc, bud diunc; boro corunc; sicxea launc.

Correction, *cor-rec'-xion*, N. Sarkem corop, nittier galop.

Corrector, *cor-rec'-tor,* N. Nittier galnar, sarkem cornar ; sicxea lainar.
Correctness, *cor-rect'-ness,* N. Khorepon ; sicxea.
Correlative, *cor-rel'-a-tiv,* A. Lagcho ; somand aslolo.
Correspond, *cor-re-spond',* V. Eca-meca lagim chali boli asuno ; isttogot vo voivatt asuno.
Correspondence, *cor-re-spond'-ens,* N. Chitti borop : chali-boli ; isttogot.
Correspondent, *cor-re-spond'-ent,* N. Potrac kobro boroinar.
Cost, *cost,* N. Mol ; khoroch ; luscon.
Cost, V. (Mol) Poddong vo lagonc.
Costive, *cos'-tiv,* A. Bhair suclolo.
Costiveness, *cos'-tiv-ness,* Bhair bond zavop.
Costly, *cost'-li,* A. Marog ; mola-dic.
Costume, *cos'-ttium,* N. Sovoim, chal ; nesonn.
Cottage, *co'-ttej,* N. Supurlem gor ; comptti.
Cotton, *cot'-tn,* N. Capus.
Cotton-tree, N. Capsin.
Couch, *cauch,* N. Baz, khatlem ; antuln.
Couch, V. Poddonc ; lipon bosonc.
Cough, *cof,* N. Koncli ; usmod.
Cough, V. Konounc.
Council, *caun'-sil,* N. Budvon-tanchi zomat.
Councillor, *caun'-sil-or,* N, Bud-vont ; bud dinar.
Counsel, *caun'sl,* N. Bud ; sang-nem.
Counsel, V. Bud diunc.
Count, *caunt,* V. Mezunc ; ixeop corunc.
Count, N. Porob.
Countenance, *caun'-te-nens,* N. Rupnem ; sarkem ; moriad.
Countenance, V. Vinchun ca-ddunc.
Counteract, *caun-tor-act',* V. Virud vo portem corunc.
Counterbalance, *caun-tor-bal'-ans,* V. Sarkem zoconc ; fg. add-coll galunc.
Counterbalance, N. Sarkem zocop ; fg. addcoll.
Counterfeit, *caun'-ttor-fiit,* V. Eke vosta sarkem corunc.
—(a document)=fottkirem cagot corunc. [punc.
—(money)=fottkire duddu xa-
Counterfeit, A. Fottkiro ; coptti.
Counterfeit, N. Fottounem ; copott.
Countermand, *caun-ttor-mend',* V. Dilolo hocum cadduno.
Countess, *caunt'-es,* Condichi potin.
Countless, *caunt'-less,* A. Cont nam title.
Country, *con'-tri,* N. Ganm ; des.
Countryman, *con'tri-men,* N. Gauncho munis ; vauraddi ; setcamti.
Couple, *co'-pl,* N. Zoddi.
Couple, V. Ecott corunc ; eottaim corunc.
Courage, *ko'-reij,* N. Nirvonn.
Courageous, *co-re-ji'as,* A. Nir-vonni ; zobor.
Courier, *co'-ri er,* N. Pedo.
Course, *cors,* N. Dav ; vatt ; jinos.
Court, *cort,* N. Munsubechem gor.
—(yard)=angonn.
Court; V. Man diunc ; fuslaunc.
Courteous, *cort'-e-as,* A. Moria-dicho ; mogall vo doiall.
Courtesy, *cort'-e-zi,* N. Moriad, mog, doia.
Cousin, *caz'-n,* N. Bapul-bhau ; mauxi-bhau ; bapul-boin etc.

Covenant, *cov'-en-ant*, N. Karar.

Cover, *cov'-er*, V. Dancunc; fg. lipounc.

—(the expeness)=khoroch faric corunc.

Cover, N. Dampnnem.

Coverlet, *cov'-or-let*, N. Pangrop; bornus.

Covet, *cov'.et*, V. Axeunc. khosi voronc; laleunc.

Covetous, *cov'-et-as*, A. Sugrati; axevont; orbosi.

Covetousness, *cov'-et-as-ness*, N. Sugrat vo absuart.

Cow, *cau*, N. gai.

Coward, *cau'-ard*, A. Bezudd.

Cowardice, *cau'-ard-is*, N. Bezuddai; olkem mon.

Cowdung, *cau'-dong*, N. Xenn.

Coxcomb, *coks'-com*, N. Xencrem; fg. danddi.

Crab, *creb*, N. Curli.

Crack, *crec*, V. Futtonc, dau vochonc.

Crack-brained, A. Piso.

Craft, *craft*, N. Hicmot; chamatcar; naddgeponn.

Cram, *crem*, V. Borunc; fg. decor corunc.

Cramp, *cremp*, N. Xir gusponnem.

Crater, *crai'-ttor*; N. Tondd.

Cravat, *cra-vat'*, N. Gorvat.

Crave, *crev*, N. Laleun magunc.

Crazy, *creiz'i*, A. Piso; vid laglolo; oscot.

Cream, *criim*, N. Sai: fg. uttim

Create, *cri-eitt'*, V. rochunc; goddunc.

Creation, *cri-ei'-sion*, N. Rochna; sounsar.

Creator, *cri-ei-ttor*, N. Rochnar.

Creature, *cri'-char*, N. Rochna.

Credentials, *cre-den'-si-al*, N. Xifarazichem potr.

Credibility, *cre-di-bil-i'-tti*, N. Patienni; sotmandop.

Credible, *cred'i-bl*, A. Patiencho; sotmandcho.

Credit, *cred'-it*, N. Borem naum; abru; man.

Creditable, *cred'-it-ei-bl*, A. Abrucho; moriadicho.

Creditor, *cre'-di-ttor*, N. Rinn ditolo munis.

Credulous, *cre'-du-las*, A. Sompeponnim sotmandi sarco.

Creed, *criid*, N. Sotmandtam.

Creep, *creep'*. V. Choronc.

Creeper, *crip'-ar*, N. Val; bêl.

Crescent, *cres'-sent*, A. Vaddto.

Crest, *crest'*, N. Xencrem; xenddi.

Crest-fallen, *crest'-fol-lon*, A. Khalto.

Crevice, *cre'-vis*, N. Futt; ver.

Crew, *cru*, N. Tarvachem loscor vo kalasi.

Crib, *crib*, N. Dhavem, khavonn; gotto.

Crick, *cric*, N. Voddi; gott gollo.

Cricket, *crik'et*, N. Birmotti; bettancho kell.

Crime, *craime*, N. Crime; vodd guneaum, oprad, patoc.

Criminal, *crim'in-al*, A. Khotto; patki.

Criminate, *crim'in-eitt*, V. Firiad diunc; guneaumcari corunc.

Cripple *cri'pl*, N. Thontto.

Crises, *crai'zes*, N. Rogh-bavantar; xevott; risk. [shan.

Criterion, *cri-te-ri'on*, N. Lakh-

Critic, *cri'tic*, A. Khoddi caddtolo·

Critical, *cri'ti-cal*, A. Zocmecho; khoddi caddcho.

Criticize, *cri'ti-saiz*, V. Varia diunc; khoddi caddunc, torea doruuc.

Critique, *cri'tic*, N. Crit, khoddi caddnem.

Croak, *croc*, N. mankeanchi bob; sinn.

Croak, *croc*, V. Bob marunc; sinn ulonnc.
Crocodile, *cro'co-dail*, N. Mangem.
Crook, *cruc*, V. Bagoùnc.
Crook, N. Ganch. [donkn.
Crooked, *cruk'ed*, A. Vanoddo;
Crookedness, *cru'ked-ness*, N. Vanoddeponn.
Crop, *crop*, N. Pic.
Crop, V. Chabunc; catrunc, mottvo corunc.
Cross, *cros*, N. Khuris; fg. coistt.
Cross, A. Add aslolo; cor-corancho.
Cross, V. Zoddunc.
—(A river)=Polltoddi vochunc.
Cross-examination, *cros-ex-za-mi-nei'xion*, N. Adda-sovall.
Crossing, *cros'sing*, N. Vattancho mell.
Crouch, *crauch*, V. Bagounc.
Croup, *crup*, N. Guntton.
Crow *crou*, N. Cau-llo.
Crowd, *craud*, N Urponz; zomo.
Crowd, V. Urponz ecttaim zaunc.
Crowded, *craud'ed*, N. Zomlolo.
Crown, *craun*, N. Mucutt, curou; fg. razvottki.
Crown-prince, *craun-prins*, N. Malgoddo cuuvor.
Crucible, *cru'si-bl*, N. Kovo.
Crucifix, *cru'si-fiks*, N. Suam Jesu Christachi imaz; khuris.
Crucifixion, *cru-si-fik'xion*, N. Khursar marnem.
Crucify, *cru'si-fai*, V. Khursar marunc vo zoddunc.
Crude, *crud*, A. Jivo; horvo; peconaslolo.
Cruel, *cru'el*, A. Nisttur.
Cruelty, *cru'el-thi*, N. Nistturai.
Cruet, *cru'et*, N. Misacho soro galcheo sinsleo.
Cruise, *cruz*, V. dorian bonvunc.
Cruising, *cruz'ing*, N. Doriant boundi.
Crumb, *cromb*, N. Lan cuddeo.
Crumble, *crom'bl*, V. Cuddkean cuddke corunc.
Crush, *crosh*, V. Chenchunc; daddaunc; pitto corunc; jiconc; fg. nanch corunc.
Crust, *crost*, N. Uuddeachem oottem; mand.
Cry, *crai*, N. Roddnem; bob.
Crystal, *cris'tal* N. Arso; rup aslolo fator.
Crystalline, *cris'tal-in*, A. Arseacho; porzollit.
Crystallization, *cris'tal-liz-ei'-xion*, N. Fatranchem rup.
Crystallize, *cris'tal-laiz*, V. Rup metlonc.
Cube, *cob*, N. Pilo.
Cube, *kiub*, N. Satchoucancho cuddeo.
Cuckoo, *co-cu'*, N. Cogul.
Cucumber *cu'cum-bor*, N. Touxem.
Cudgel, *cad'jel*, N. Boddi; tonco sotto.
Culpability, *colp-a-bil'i-tti*, N. Guneauncarponn.
Culprit, *cal'pritt*, N. Guneauncar.
Cultivate, *cal'ti-reitt*, V. Vosounc, camais corunc; zoton corunc.
Cultivated, *cal-ti-vei'tted*, A. Vosoilolo zago; siclolo.
Cultivator, *cal-ti-vei'ttor*, N. Setcamti.
Culture, *cal'char*, N. Sicop; zanvai.
Cumbersome, *com'bor-som*, A. Bhou zodd; toudreacho.
Cumin-seed, *com'in-siid*, N. Jirem.
Cumulative, *co'mu-lat-tiv*, A. Borobor. [nadd.
Cunning, *can'ing*, N. Naddgo,
Cup *cop* N. Cop; chier.
Cupboard, *cop'bord*, N. Almar.
Curate, *kiu'reitt* N. Cur.
Curb, *corb*, N. Supurli vollout, doro.

Curdle, *cor'dl*, V. Doim corunc.
Cure, *kiu'ar*, N. Vocot; bolaiki.
Cure, V. Vocot diunc; boro corunc; mittac galunc.
Curiosity, *kiu-ri-o'-zi-tti*, N. Nazucai; otreg; kuriozidad.
Curious, *kiu'-ri-as*, A. Nazuc; chamatcarancho; khobranche axecho.
Curl, *carl*, V. Kensanchi panti galunc.
Curl, N. Panti.
Currency, *car'-ren-si*, N. Sovoim; cholop; cholte duddu vo nannem.
Current (*is*), V. Cholonc.
Current, *car-'rent*, N Udcacho neott; vall.
Curry, *co'-ri*, V. Goddeac malis corunc.
Curry, N. Coddi; amb; umon.
Curse, *cors*, V. Xirap galunc; galli sonvon; bodlam galunc.
Curse, N. Xirap; gall.
Cursed, *cors'-dd* A. Xirap poddlolo.
Curtail, *cor-teil'*, V. Unno corunc; mottvo corunc.
Curtain, *cor'tein*, N. Porddo.
Curved, *corv'-dd*, A. Vancddo; bagaulolo.
Cushion, *cush'-on*, N. Uxem.
Custard-apple, *cos'tard-ep-pl*, N. Ant.
Custody, *cos'-tho-ddi*, N. Raconn; para; boncondd.
—(Put in custody)=Bouconddint galunc.
—(Custody)=Coïdi corunc.
Custom, *cos'-tom*, N. Sovoim; rit; alfand.
Custom-house, N. Alfandachem gor.
Customary, *cas'-to-ma-ri*, A. Sovoincho; sodancho.
Cut, *cat*, V. Catrunc.
—(In two)=Don cuddke corunc.
—(Off)=Nas corunc.
—(Short)=Mottvo corunc.
Cut, N. Catrop; gao; mar.
Cutler, *cat'lor*, N. Surio cornar vo vicnar.
Cutlet, *cat'-let*, N. Cutles.
Cut-throat, *cat'throot*, N. Morticar.
Cylinder, *si'-lin-dar*, N. Addcullem.
Cypress, *sai'-press*, N. Chabcacho ruc.

D

Dab, *deb*, V. Addlonc; bosonc.
Dabble, *deb'-bl*, V. Udcant khellonc.
Dabbler, *deb'-blor*, V. Voilea-voir cornar.
Dagger, *deg'-gar*, N. Balo.
Daily, *dei'-li*, A. Dispotto.
Daily, AD. Disandis.
Daintiness, *dein'ti-ness*, N. Nazucai.
Dainty, *dein'-ti*, A. Nazuc; suadic.
Damage, *dem'-eij*, V. Luksan corunc; vaitt corunc.
Damage, N. Luksan; noistt.
Damask, *dam'-ask*, N. Damasc.
Damn, *dem*, V. Condenar corunc; formonn marunc.
Damnation, *dem-nei'-xion*, N. Condenasaum.
Damp, *demp*, V. Xello, volo corunc.
Damp, A. Xellicho.
Dampness, *demp'-ness*, Xell; bato.
Dance, *dens*, V. Nachonc.
Dance, N. Nach.
Dancing-girl, N. Colvont.
Danger, *dein'-jar*, N. Perig; asant.
Dangerous, *dein'-je--ras*, A. Perigoz, lusconacho.

Dangerously, *denn'-je-rus li,* AD. Bhou perig.
—(Sick)=mornant asa.
Dare, *der,* V. Nirvonn asunc.
Dark, *dark,* A. Callocacho, callso; somzo naslolo.
Darken, *dark'n,* V. Calloc corunc; uzvad pois caddunc.
Darkish, *dark'ish,* A. Callso.
Darkness, *dark'ness,* N. Calloc; gutt. [mogall.
Darling, *dar'ling,* A. Apurbaecho;
Darling, N. Burgem.
Dart, *dart,* N. Bhali.
Dash, *desh,* V. Addlonc.
Date, *deit,* N. Toroc; kazur.
Date, V. Toroc borounc.
Daughter, *do'ttor,* N. Dhuu.
Daughter-in-law, *do'ttor-in-lo',* N. Sun.
Daunt, *dont,* V. Bhem galunc; benoddanne.
Dauntless, *dont'less,* A. Bhirant naslolo; nirvonnim.
Dawn, *don,* N. Fantem; uzvadd.
Dawn, V. Uzvaddonc.
Day, *dei,* N. Dis.
Daybreak, *dei'brek,* N. Fantem; dis udeunc.
Day-light, *dei'-laith,* N. Disacho uzvadd.
Dazzle, *dez'-zl,* V Dolleam mucar zogzogunc vo zoglaunc.
Deacon, *di'-con,* N. Diacn.
Dead, *dedd.* A. Mel-lo.
Dead, N. Melole.
Deadly, *dedd'-li,* A. Chodd vaitt; jiu caddcho; coddu.
Deaf, *def,* A. Bhero.
Deafen, *def'-n,* V Canfuttonc.
Deafness, *def'-ness,* N. Bhereponn.
Deal, *di-il,* N. Chodd; sobar.
Deal, V. Vepar, corunc; cholonc; gollounc.
Dealer, *dil'-or,* N. Vepari.
Dealing, *dil'-ing,* N. Vepar; isttogot.
Dear, *di'-er,* A. Mogall; marog.
Dearness, *di'-er-ness,* N. Margai.
Dearth, *darth,* N. Ducoll, margai.
Death, *deth,* N. Morn.
Debar, *de-bar',* V. Cusin cădduno.
Debase, *di-bez',* V. Beli corunc; lojec galunc; unneponn, diunc.
Debate, *di-beit',* V. Discusaum corunc; uzot corunc.
Debauch, *di-bauch',* V. Pirder corunc; ibaddunc.
Debauchery, *de-bauoh'-e-ri,* N. Potatt; bebdicai.
Debilitate, *de-bil'-i-teith,* V. Osoct corunc.
Debility, *de-bi'-li-tti,* N. Osoctai.
Debt, *dét,* N. Riun; caido.
Debtor, *de'-tor,* N. Riuncari; chuclolo.
Debut, *du-bu',* N. Oromb.
Decade, *de'-keid,* N. Khon.
Decadence, *de-ka'-dens,* N. Nas, utrop.
Decamp, *di'-kemp,* V. Liponc; pollonc.
Decant, *di-kent',* V. Votunc, dusrea aidonant galunc.
Decapitate, *de-ca-pi'-teitt,* V. Tochi catrunc, xins capunc.
Decapitation *de-ca-pi-ttei'-xion,* N. Xins capnem.
Decay, *di-kei'.* V. Bavonc; suconc; pirdder zaunc.
Decease, *di siiz',* V. somponc.
Deceased, *di-siiz'-d,* A. Somplolo.
Deceit, *di-siit',* N. Fott; nadd.
Deceitful, *di-siit'-ful,* A. Fottkiro; naddgo,
Deceive, *di-siiv',* V. Fottounc; chucounc.
Decency, *di'sen-si,* N. Moriad; mausugi.

Decent, *di'-sent,* A. Mansugecho.
Decently, *di'-sent-li,* AD. Mansugen. [kirponn.
Deception, *di-sep'-xion,* N. Fott-
Decide, *di-said',* V. Nicheu corunc, chintunc; tharavunc; todduuc, nical corunc.
Decided, *di-said'-ed,* A. Bhem naslolo; thir.
Decidedly, *di-said'-ed-li,* AD. Dubavavinn, khorench.
Decipher, *de-sif'-for,* V. Somzonni diunc, orth sangunc.
Decision, *di-si'-zhon,* N. Nicheu; tharav.
Decisive, *di-sai'-ziv,* A. Khondit; nirvadi. [nettounc.
Deck, *dec,* V. Surungarunc:
Declaim, *di-cle-im',* V. Dobajean ulounc; hindsunc; bobmarunc; galli sonvonc.
Declamation, *de-cla-mei'-xion,* N. Ulounem. sub-bashan.
Declaration, *de-cla-rei'-xion,* N. Decoll, collit cornem, sangni; daclo.
Declare, *di-cler',* V. Saph-sangunc, collit corunc; nemunc.
Decline, *di-clain',* V. Bagaunc; denvunc; naca munnonc.
Decline, N. Paddpoddop.
Declivity, *de-cli'-vi-tti,* N. Deunti.
Decoction, *di-coc'-xion,* N. Ucoddni, sijounni; koddo.
Decompose, *di-com-poz',* V. Vingattunc, viscattunc; cusunc.
Decomposition, *de-com'-po-zi-xion,* N. Vingattni, viscattni; cus, cusop.
Decorate, *dec'-co-reitt,* V. Surungarunc, nettounc.
Decoration, *dek-co-rei'-xion,* N. Surungar, nettouni.
Decorum, *de-co'-rum,* N. Mansugi; moriad.
Decoy, *di-coi',* V, Fottounc; fuslaunc.
Decrease, *di-criiz',* V. Unno corunc vo zaunc, denvounc.
Decree, *di-crii',* N. Hucum, formonn; raj-potr; jabto.
Decree, V. Hucum diunc; formaunc, nemunc.
Decrepit, *de-crep'-it,* A. Matarddo, donkro, jorantt.
Decrepitude, *de-crep'-it-iud,* N. Matarponn, jorddeponn, donkreponn. [potr.
Decretal, *de-cret'-al,* N Srisason-
Dedicate, *ded'-i-keith,* V. Bettounc; somorpiunc.
Dedication, *de-di-kei'-xion,* N. Bett; somorponn.
Deduce, *de-dius',* V, Denvunc; concluzaum caddunc.
Deduct, *di-doct',* V. Bad galunc
Deduction, *di-doc'-xion,* N. Bad galnem.
Deed, *diid,* N. Corni, daclo.
Deem, *diim,* V. Chintunc.
Deep, *diip,* A. Khol; nibor, guttacho; gott.
—(Silence)=gopchip.
Deepen, *dip'-n,* V. Kholaunc; fg. choddounc. [fg. purtem.
Deeply, *di-ip'-li,* AD. Bhou chodd;
Deer, *di'-er,* N. Chitoll.
Deface, *di'-fes,* V. Vidrup corunc.
Defamation, *de-fa-mei'-xion,* N. Man ubounem—, ogddaunem, chaddi.
Defame, *di-feim',* V. Man ubounc—, ogddaunc; bodlam galunc
Default, *di-folt',* N. Goirhazri; nasop.
Defeat, *de-fiit',* V. Zoit vorunc, jiconc, pirdder corunc.
Defect, *di-fect',* N. Aib, khodd.
Defection, *di-fec'-xion,* N. Fituri; pollni. [unno.
Defective, *di-fec'-tiv,* A. Aibacho;

Defence, *di-fens'*, N. Samball; asro; adar.

Defenceless, *di-fens'-less*, A. asro naslolo; niradhari.

Defend, *di-fend'*, V. Samballunc, racunc, chuconnc.

Defendant, *di-fend'-ant*, N. Pra- [tivadi.

Defensive, *di-fen'-siv*, A. Racnne-cho, samballacho; nivarac.

Defer, *di-for'*, V. Patti galunc; magir corunc; abru diunc.

Deference, *de'-fe-rens*, N. Man, abru.

Deficiency, *de-fi'-shen-si*, N. Unnau, totto, lutt, comti, cosor.

Deficient, *de-fi'-shent*, A. Unno, comti, vicoll.

Defile, *di-fail'*, V. Khotaunc, mello corunc, bosttaunc.

Defilement, *di-fail'-ment*, N. Khot; bosttonnem.

Define, *di-fain'*, V. Iscottun sangunc; orth sangunc; nemunc.

Definite, *de'fin-it*, A. Khondit, khonchit.

Definition, *de-fi-ni'xion*, N. Nirvachan, lokshen.

Definitive, *de-fin'-it-iv*, A. Khondit; nirvadi.

Deform, *di-form'*, V. Rup—, acar caddunc—, padd corunc.

Deformity, *di-form'-i-tti*, N. Nirup vidrupai; vicollai.

Defraud, *di-frod'*, N. Fosonnc.

Defray, *di-frei,'* V. Khoroch faric corunc.

Defy, *di-fai'*, V. Vodda marun, beporva corunc.

Degeneracy, *de-jen'e-ra-si*, N. Khottepon; cusop.

Degenerate, *de-jen'-e-reitt*, V. Bigddunc, utronc, bosttavunc; padd zaunc.

Degradation, *de-gradei'-xion*, N. Podvi caddnem; kircollai; kircollponn,

Degrade, *di-greid'*, V. Podvi caddunc, man caddunc; bhairo corunc; holco corunc.

Degree, *di-gri'*, N. Potto vo diplom; zutti.

Deification, *de-if'i-kei'-xion*, N. Deva-sarco-cornem.

Deign, *dein*, V. puttvonc.

Deism, *de'-izm*, N. Kevalesvaramat.

Deity, *de'i-ti*, N. Deuponn; deu.

Deject, *di-ject'*, V. Sonkirn corunc; ducounc.

Dejected, *di-ject'-ed*, A. Ducoilolo.

Dejection, *di-jec'-xion*, N. Duc; upodre

Delay, *di-lei'*, V. Patti dourop; usir launc, soucas corunc.

Delay, N. Usir, kalau.

Delegate, *de'-le-geitt*, V. Aple bodlec daddunc; apli podvi diunc.

Delegate, *de'le-geitt*, N. Vakil, muctiar.

Delegation, *de-le-gei'-xion*, N. Opnni; niyog; dileli podvi

Deliberate, *de-lib'e-reitt*, V. Vichar-math corunc.

Deliberate, A. Budvont, xanno; khoxecho.

Deliberately, *de-lib'e-reitt-li*, AD. Khoxen, zotnaen.

Deliberation, *de-li-be-rei'xion*, N. Vichar, chali-boli; munsubi.

Delicacy, *de'li-ca-si*, N. Nazucai; ruch.

Delicate, *de'li-keith*, A. Nazuc, ruchicho; riskecho; osoct.

Delicious, *de-li'xi-as*, A. Suadic; khuxalaecho; ruchicho.

Delight, *de-laith'*, N. Sontos; khuxalai; suc.

Delight, V. Sontos bogunc; manuonc.

Delightful, *di-laith'ful*, A. Suadic; ruchicho,

Delineate, *de-lin'i-eitt,* V. Acarunc; chitrunc; manddavoll corunc.
Delineation, *de-lin'i-ei'xion,* N. Acar; chitr; nirupoun.
Delinquent, *de-lin'ku-ent,* N. Guneaumcari; opradi.
Delirious, *de-li'ri-as,* A. Zancnecho; uchamboll.
Delirium, *de-li'ri-am,* N. Zanc; khubdollni.
Deliver, *de'-li-vor,* V. Soddunc; samballunc; adin corunc; mozot diunc, nivarunc.
Deliverance, *de-liv'er-ens,* N. Soddvonn.
Deliverer, *de-liv'er-er,* N. Soddvonddar.
Delivery, *de-liv'e-ri,* N. Pursuttponn; baunteor; ulouncho jinos
Deluge, *del'iuj,* N. Poriallo; budti.
Deluge, V. Aunr eunc; fg. boronc.
Demagogue, *dem'a-gog,* N. Locacho vostad. [magonc.
Demand, *dim-end',* V. Soten
Demand, N. Soten magnnem.
Demean, *dem'in,* V. Cholunc; acharunc; vortunc; puttvonc.
Demeanour, *de-min'nor,* N. Chal.
Democracy, *de-mo'cra-si,* N. Locachem raj.
Demolish, *de-mol'ish,* V. Vibaddunc; nas-corunc; moddunc; conslaunc.
Demolition, *de-mo-li'xion,* N. Moddni, conslaunni.
Demon, *de'mon,* N. Devchar, bhut, soitan.
Demoniac, *de-mo'niac,* A. Devcharacho, soitanacho; devchar laglolo vo boslolo.
Demonstrate, *de-mon'streitt,* V. Ruzu corunc; dacounc.
Demonstration, *de-mon-strei'xion,* N. Dacoun; ruzvat,
Demonstrative, *de-mon-stre'tiv,* A. Ruzvaticho, thir.
Demoralization, *de-mo'ra-li-zeixion,* N. Cusop; holkeponn.
Demoralize, *de-mo'ra-laiz,* V. Cusounc.
Demure, *de-mi'ur,* A. Moriadi.
Den, *den,* N. Doll; buiar.
Denial *de-na'ial,* N. Negar zavop.
Denominate, *de-nom'in-eitt,* V. Naum diunc; pacharunc; ulo corunc.
Denomination, *de-nom'in-ei'xion,* N. Naum; ulo.
Denote, *di'not,* V. Dacounc.
Denounce, *di-nauns',* V. Collit corunc; porgottunc; firiad corunc. [gonn.
Dense, *dens,* A Khench; datt;
Density, *dens'i-tti,* N. Dattai, gonnai.
Dentist, *den'tist* N. Dantancho voiz
Denunciation, *de-nun'si-ei'xion,* N. Gomouni; collounni; porgottni.
Deny, *di-nai',* V. Negar zaunc; naca munnonc; apler zoit voronc.
Depart, *di-part',* V. Bhair soron vochonc.
—(This life)=Moronc; soronc.
Departed, *di-part'ed,* A. Sorlolo, somplolo.
Department, *di-part'ment,* N. Khotem.
Departure, *di-part'char,* N. Bhair soron vochnem; morn.
Depend, *di-pend',* V. Umcallonc; khalto asunc; favo asunc; patieunc; hatant asunc.
Dependence, *di-pend'ens,* N. Khalteponn.
Dependency, *di-pend'en-si,* N. Adin aslolo gaum.
Dependent, *di-pend'ent,* A. Khalto.

Depict, *de-pict'*, v. Pintarunc.
Depletion, *di-ple'xion*, n. Rito cornem ; sir-marnem.
Deplorable, *di-plor'ei-bl*, a. Du-councho ; roddcho.
Deplore, *di-plor'*, v. Roddunc, rudon corunc ; churchurone ; ducam gollounc.
Depopulate, *de-po'piu-leitt*, v. Nisonton corunc.
Deport, *di-port'*, v. Gaunva bhairo corunc ; nirvasunc.
Depose, *di-poz'*, v. Zuttievello caddunc ; soddunc; govai diunc.
Deposit, *de-poz'it*, v. Amanat dovorunc, thevunc.
Deposit, n. Dovorni, thevni.
Depository, *de-poz'it-o-ri*, n. Thevnar, amanat dovortolo.
Deposition, *de-po-zi'xion*, n. Caddni ; govai.
Depravation, *de-pra-vei'xion*, n. Vaittponn, khotteponn, nostte-ponn ; holkeponn.
Deprave, *de-preiv'*, v. Vaitt—, khotto corunc.
Deprecate, *de'pre-keitt*, v. Bogso-nnem magunc ; vinoti corunc.
Depreciate, *de-pre'xi-eitt*, v. Mol—, dor denvounc ; kircoll corunc ; man caddunc.
Depress, *di-pres'*, v. Khalto corunc ; urba denvonc ; fg. ducounc.
Depression, *di-pres'xion*, n. Khal-teponn ; upodre.
Deprive, *di-praiv'*, v. Chucounc ; caddunc.
Depth, *dept*, n. Kholai.
Deputation, *de-pu-tei'xion*, n. Podvi—, adicar dennem ; vakil-ponn ; nemun daddlele munis.
Depute, *de-piutt'*, v. Sotea diun daddunc.
Deputy, *de'-pu-tti*, n. Nemun daddlolo ; dalal.
Derange, *di-reinj'*, v. Guspaunc, gondlaunc, foskottaunc.
Deranged, *di-reinj'-dd*, a. Piso, vid lagïolo.
Dereliction, *de-re-lic'-xion*, n. Soddni ; niradhar.
Deride, *di-raid'*, v. Kendunc ; kesttaeo corunc.
Derivation. *de-ri-rei'-xion*, n. Oromb.
Derive, *di-raiv'*, v. Caddunc, haddunc.
Derogate, *de'-ro-geitt*, v. (Cai-deacho bag) caddunc, nisraunc.
Descend, *dis-send'*, v. Denvunc ; utronc ; fg. ubzonc ; eunc.
Descendant, *dis-send'-ant*, n. Sonsticho pinddeo.
Descent, *dis-sent'*, n. Devnem ; oromb, kuttom.
Describe, *dis-craib'*, v. Vornunc, nirupunc, varnan corunc.
Description, *dis-crip'-xion*, n. Varnan, nirupan ; akar.
Desert, *de'-zert*, a. Ecsuro.
Desert, n. Oronnem ; chacri.
— n. soddop ; niradhar.
Desert, v. Soddunc.
Deserve, *di-zorv'*, v. Favo zaunc.
Design, *di-zain'*, v. Nocxi caddunc, chintun borounc.
Design, n. Tensaum ; kolpon ; :ojvit.
Designate, *de'-zig-neith*, v. Da-counc, collit corunc, nemunc.
Designation, *de-zig-nei'-xion*, n. Dakounim, nemni.
Desire, *di'-za-iar*, n. Khoxi, ruch ; urba.
Desire, v. Khoxi vorunc ; la-leunc ; magonc.
Desirous, *de-za'-ea-ras*, a. Kho-xecho ; urbest.
Desist, *de-zist'*, v. Thambunc ; monna corunc.
Desk, *desc*, n. Dacttem mez.

Desolate, *de'-zo-leitt*, A. Ecsuro; nas kelolo; dukest; oronnem.
Desolation, *de-zo-lei'-xion*, N. Due; khont.
Despair, *di-sper'*, V. Axea soddunc.
Despair, N. Beborvanso, nirasa.
Despatch, *dis-pech'*, V. Daddunc; cobar corunc; fg. jivesim marunc.
Despatch, N. Daddop; cagot; hucum.
Despicable, *des-pik'-ic-bl*, A. Unnac, olco
Despise, *dis'-paiz*, V. Beporva corunc
Despond, *di-spond'*, V. Axea soddunc.
Despot, *dis'-pott*, N. Nisttur patxai; aple sotecho rai.
Despotism, *dis'-pott-i-zam*, N. Nisttnrai; aploch adicar.
Dessert, *de'-zert*, N. Follar.
Destination, *des-ti nei'-xion*, N. Xevott; nirmon.
Destine, *des'-tin*, V. Nirmunc, nemunc.
Destiny, *des'-ti-ni*, N. Odrustt, nosib.
Destitute, *des'-ti-ttiut*, A. Dublo; Sanddlolo; nirbagui.
Destitution, *des-ti-tiu'-xion*, N. Nasnem, dublocai; acant; coistt.
Destroy, *dis-troi'*, V. Vibaddunc, moddunc; conslaunc.
Destructible, *dis-truct'-i-bl*, A. Moddum-eso. moddcar.
Destruction, *di-struc'-xion*, N. Ibadd, nas.
Desultory, *de-zul-tto'-ri*, A. Uddto.
Detach, *di-tech'*, V. Niclaunc; pois corunc; vegledar corunc.
Detachment, *di-tech'-ment*, N. Niclavop, cusin caddop.
Detail, *di-teil'*, N. Vistar, topsil.
Detain, *di-ttein'*, V. Patti dourunc; ravounc.
Detect, *di-tect'*, V. Sodun caddunc; tolas corunc.
Deter, *di-tor'*, V. Addaunc; pois dourunc.
Deteriorate, *de-te'rio-reitt*, V. Padd corunc, bigddaunc, utrunc.
Determination, *de-tter-min-ei'-xion*, N. Nicheu; nirmon; formon.
Determine, *di-ttor'min*, V. Nitt—, borobor dacounc; tharaunc; chintunc; cobar corunc,
Determined, *di-ttor'mind*, A Tharailolo; khondit.
Detest, *di-test'*, V. Canttallo dorunc; vitt disunc.
Detestable *di-ttest'ei-bl*, A. Canttalleacho.
Detestation, *de-ttest-ei'xion*, N. Canttallo, omcaro.
Dethrone, *di-ttron'*, V. Patxeac caddunc.
Detract, *di-trect'*, V. Man caddunc; chaddio sangunc.
Detraction, *di-ttrec'xion*, N. Chaddi.
Devastate, *de'-vas-tteit*, V. Gorthoun— , dull doxea corunc.
Devastation, *de'-vas-ttei'xion*, N. Dulldoxa cornem; gorthonn.
Develope, *de-vel'op*, V. Vistarunc; somzouni diunc; vaddunc.
Development, *de-vel'op-ment*, N. Vaddau; xevott.
Deviate, *de'vi-eitt*, V. Vatt soddunc; vatt chuconc; fg. vaitt zaunc.
Deviation, *de-vi-ei'xion*, N. Chuc; guneaum.
Device, *di-vais'*, N. Hicmot; upai.
Devil *de'vil*, N. Devchar, soitan, bhut. [khotto.
Devilish, *de'vi-lish*, A. Soitanacho.

Devise, *de-vaiz'*, V. Sodun caddunc, chintunc.

Devolve, *di-volv'*, N. Dusreac diunc; portun eunc; mellonc.

Devote, *di-vot'*, V. Bulonc; bettounc; khorchunc; lagunc.

Devote, *de-vot'ed*, A. Laglolo.

Devotion, *de-vo'xion*, N. Devosponn; bogtiponn; santiponn; fg. bulop; apurbai.

Devour, *di-va'or*, V. Gillonc; bocrunc.

Devout, *di-vautt'*, A. Bagevont; devosponnacho.

Dew, *diu'*, N. Dou.

Dewy, *diu'i*, A. Dovacho, dovanborlolo.

Diadem, *da-ia'dem*, N. Mocutt; curou.

Diabolic, *di-a-bol'ik*, A. Nistiur, deucharacho.

Diagnosis, *da-iag-no'zis*, N. Piddechi poricsha.

Dial, *dai'al*, N. Suriachem goddial.

Dialect, *dai'a-lect*, N. Chalti bhas; holki bas.

Dialogue, *dai'a-log*, N. Ulounem; gozal.

Diameter, *dai-am'e-tor*, N. Addmezop; dattai.

Diametrically, *da-ia-met-ri-ca'-lli*, AD. Purtem; Ligut.

Diamond, *dai'a-mond*, N. Diamant, vajir.

Diaphoretic, *dai'a-fo-re-tic*, A. Gam caddcho.

Diarrhœa, *da-ia're'-iu*, N. Agoun, utcadde, bhair.

Diary, *dai'a-ri*, N. Disachem pustoc.

Dictate, *dic-tteit'*, V. Formaunc; vachun sangunc.

Diction, *dic'xion*, N. Ulouneachi rit.

Dictionary, *dic'sio-na-ri*, N. Sobdakos, disionar.

Die, *dai*, N. Chonc.

Die, V Morunc, sorunc.

Diet, *da'iet*, N. Poth.

Differ, *dif'for*, V. Ecott nasunc; voglodar asunc.

Difference, *dif'fer-ens*, N. Fêr, bhed, veglachar, veglepoun.

Different, *dif'fer-ent*, A. Veglo, dusro, nirallo.

Differently, *dif'fer-ent-li*, AD. Dusre jinsim, nam zalear.

Difficult, *dif'fi-colt*, A. Cottin; sonkest, angodd.

Difficulty, *dif'fi col-ti*, N. Coistt; angoddai; sonkesttai; acant.

Diffidence, *dif'-fi-dens*, N. Bezuddai, bhem; beborvanso.

Diffident, *dif'-fi-dent*, A. Bezudd, patienaslolo.

Diffuse, *di-fiuz'*, V. Vanvounc vistarunc; eunc.

Diffuse, A. Vistarlolo; choda.

Dig, *dig*, V. Konddonc; ustunc.

Digest, *dai-jest'*, V. Jironc, pochunc.

Digestible, *dai-jest'-i-bl*, A. Jirvonnec; bolaikecho.

Digestion, *dai-jest'-xion*, N. Jirvonn, pochop.

Digestive, *dai'jcst-iv*, A. Jirvonnecho.

Digger, *dig'-gar* N. Kondtolo.

Digit, *di'-jit*, N. Bott, angull,

Dignitary, *dig'-ni-ta-ri*, N. Motte podvecho munis.

Dignity, *dig-ni'-tti*, N. Voddvi, man, thorponn; moriad.

Digress, *di-gress'*, V. Soddunc; bhair soronc.

Digression, *di-gre'-xion*, N. Soddnem; poi top.

Dilapidate, *di-la'-pi-deitt*, V. Modduuc, conslaunc, vatt launc.

Dilapidated, *di-la'-pi-dei-ted*, A. Moddlolo, consoullolo.

Dilate, *di-laitt',* v. Posrunc, vistarunc; vaddounc; choddounc.
Dilemma, *di-lem'-ma,* N. Ubhaisambhav; lochand
Diligence, *di-li'-jens,* N. Zagrutai, uxarki, fikir, suddsuddai.
Diligent, *di-li'-jent,* A. Zagrut, uxear; suddsuddit.
Dilute, *di-liutt',* V. Mellounc.
Dim, *dim,* A. Callso, onduukuro.
Dim, v. Callso corunc.
Dimension, *dai-men'-xion,* N. Voddai; mezop.
Diminish, *di-min'-ish,* V. Unno corunc; denvounc.
Diminution, *di-mi-niu'-xion,* N. Unav, utar, tutt.
Dimness, *dim'-ness,* N. Calloc.
Din, *din,* N. Hac-bob.
Dine, *dain,* V. Jeunc; jevounc.
Dining-room, *dai'-ning-rum,* N. Jeunachi cudd.
Dinner, *di'-nnor,* N. Jevonn.
Diocese, *da'-io-siz,* N. Bispachem raj.
Dip, *dip,* V. Buddounc.
Dip, N. Buddop.
Diploma, *di-plo'-ma,* N. Sanad, potr, diplom.
Diplomacy, *di-plo'-ma-si,* N. Chodounchi videa.
Diplomatic *di-plo-mat'-ic.* N. Raiacho vokil, mantri.
Direct, *dai-rect',* V. Cholounc; vosounc, kamavunc,
Direction *dai-rec'-xion,* N. Chalaunni; carbar; caido; sicoun.
Directly, *dai-rect'-li,* AD. Nitt; sida; tambonastanam; atanch.
Director, *dai-rect'-tor,* N. Choloinar, vosoinar, voddil, adikari.
Directress, *dai-rect'-ress,* N. Vodiln.
Dirt, *dort,* N Coir; chicol; bursepou.
Dirty, *dort'-i,* A. Mello; ollsic
Dirty, V. Mellounc; mello corunc.
Disability, *dis-a-bil'i-tti,* N. Icmot nasop; osoctai.
Disable, *dis-ei'ble,* V. Osoct corunc.
Disaccustom, *dis-a-cos'ttom,* V. Sovoim moddunc.
Disadvantage, *dis ad-van-tej,* N. Luscan.
Disadvantageous, *dis-ad-van'-tei-ji-as,* A. Lusconacho.
Disaffect, *dis-affect',* V. Mon pois corunc.
Disaffection, *dis-affec'xion,* A. Noi moipasi, noi mogacho.
Disagree, *dis-a-gri',* V. Cobul zainam zaunc.
Disagreeable, *dis-a-gri'ei-bl,* A. Laic naslolo; corcorancho; bejar corpacho; cottin.
Disagreeableness, *dis-a-gri-'ei-bl-ness,* N. Korcor, bejar corop.
Disagreement, *dis-a'-gri-ment,* N. Ecott nasnem; vetias.
Disappear, *diz-a'-pi-ear,* V. Disttipoddonam zaunc.
Disappoint, *diz-a-point',* V. Gondoll, gorencar corunc.
Disapprove, *dis-ap-pruv',* V. Porsond corinam zaunc; guneauncar corunc.
Disarm, *diz-arm',* V. Hatiaram cann geunc.
Disarrangement, *diz-a-reinj'-ment,* N. Manddavoll, bondabost nasop; gusop.
Disaster, *diz-as'-ttor,* N. Maro, ghat, vigu, noistt.
Disavow, *dis-a-vau',* V. Cobul zaina zaunc.
Disbelief, *dis-bi-liif',* N. Onbavarth, dubau.
Disburse, *diz-bors',* V. Faric corunc, khorchunc.
Disc, *disc,* N. Mandd.

Discard, *dis-card'*, V. Bhair vuddounc.
Discern, *di-sorn'*, V. Bhed caddunc ; sarkem disonc.
Discernment, *dis-sorn'-ment*, N. Bud ; budi-pracas.
Discharge, *dis-charj'*, V. Vojem caddunc, voucone ; soddunc ; cholounc ; corunc.
Discharge, N. Far ; pallo.
Disciple, *dis-sai'-pl*, N. Xins ; iscolacho burgo.
Discipline, *dis'-si-plin*, N. Sisop; torbet ; moriad ; chal.
Disclose, *dis-cloz'*, V. Dancnnem caddunc ; uctto corunc ; fg. porgottunc ; dacounc.
Discolour, *dis-col'-or*, V. Rong vochonc.
Discoloured, *dis-co-lor'-dd*, A. Rong gelolo.
Discomfit, *dis-com'-fit*, V. Daunddaunc.
Discomfort, *dis-com'-fort*, N. Bejearponn ; husco ; corcor ; duc ; khont.
Discomposure, *dis-com-po'-jar*, N. Gusop, gondoll.
Disconcert, *dis-con-sort'*, N. Mod-dunc, guspaune ; nirfoll corunc.
Discontent, *dis-con-tent'*, N. Dadosponn—, somandan nasop.
Discontinue, *dis-con-tin'-iu*. V. Bond corunc, choloinam zaunc.
Discord, *dis'-cord*, N. Veglachar; dusmancai ; zogddem.
Discount, *dis'-caunt*, N. Vattau ; unnau. [corunc.
Discount, V. Vattau diunc ; unno
Discountenance, *dis-caun'-tin-ens*, V. Lozounc, posond corunc ; canttallonc.
Discourage, *dis-co'-rej*, V. Benod-daunc ; axea caddunc.
Discouragement, *dis-co'-rej-ment*. N Nirvonn nasop.
Discouraging, *dis-co'-re-jing*, A. Nirvonn nam corcho.
Discourse, *dis-cors'*, V. Gozal marc corunc ; sermaum sangunc.
Discourse, N. Ulop ; sermaum.
Discourtesy, *dis-cor-te'-zi*, N. Bemoriad.
Discover, *dis-co'-vor*, V. Uctto corunc ; sodun caddunc ; da-counc. [caddop.
Discovery, *dis-co'-ve-ri*, N. Sodun
Discredit, *dis-cre'-dit*, V. Mah caddunc.
Discredit, N. Ocman.
Discreet, *dis-criit'*, A. Budivont ; mogall.
Discretion, *dis-cre'-xion*, N. Bud ; khoxi.
Discuss, *dis-coss'*, V Gansunc, torcunc, vivadunc.
Discussion, *dis-co'-xion*, N. Gans-ni ; mathni, vivec.
Disdain, *dis-dein'*, V. Beporva corunc ; canttalonc.
Disdain, N. Beporva, canttallo.
Disease, *di-siiz*, N. Pidda.
Diseased, *di-siiz-d'*, A. Piddest, piddevont.
Disembarrass, *diz-em-ba'-rass*, V. Suttonc ; meclo zaunc.
Disembark, *diz-em-bark'*, N. Tar-va velo denvonc.
Disengage, *dis-en-geij'*, V. Bestto zaunc, meclo zaunc.
Disengaged, *diz-en-gejdd'*, A. Cam naslolo, bestto.
Disentangle, *diz-en-teng'gl*, V. Suttonc.
Disesteem, *diz-es-tiim'*, V. Apur-bai corinn zaunc.
Disesteem, N. Beporvo.
Disfavour, *dis-fei'-vor*, N. Ocman.
Disfigure, *dis-fi'-gar*, V. Rup pirder corunc.
Disgrace, *diz-greis'*, N. Ocman ; khoxe zocto nasunc; nirbagponn.

Disgrace, *diz-greis'*, V. Man cad-dunc.; ocman corunc.

Disgraced, *diz-greis-dd'*, A Khoxe zocto naslolo; moriad naslolo.

Disgraceful, *diz-greis-ful*, A. Ocmanacho, ollxic; lojist.

Disguise, *diz-gaiz'*, N. Sarkem bodlop, moiem; atvi nesonn.

Disguise, V. Moiem galunc; veglo bhes geunc.

Disgust, *diz-gost'*, V. Vaz eunc, bejar zaunc; canttallo disonc.

Disgusting, *diz-gost'-ing*, A. Ruchnaslolo: ollxic.

Dish, *dish*, N. Pollgon.

Dish-cover, *dis-co-var*, Pollgo-nauchem dancnem.

Dishonest, *diz-ho'-nest*, A. Man naslolo; khotto, visvasi noi, chor.

Dishonesty, *diz-ho'-nes-tti*, N. Khotteponn; chorponn.

Dishonour, *diz-ho'-nor*, N. Be-abru; ocman.

Dishonour, V. Man caddunc; [kotaunc.

Dishonourable, *diz-hon'-o-rei-bl*, A. Abru naslolo.

Disinclination, *diz-in'-cli-nei-xion*, N. Canttallo, vielab, dus-mancai.

Disinfect, *diz-in-fect'*, V. Vas—, gann caddunc. nitoll corunc.

Disinherit, *diz-in-he'-rit*, V. Daiz caddunc; daiza bhair galunc.

Disinter, *diz-in-tor'*, V. Matientlo caddunc.

Disinterested, *diz-in'-te-res-ted*, A. Adau—, asil naslolo.

Disjoin, *dis-join'*, V. Veglo corunc; soddunc.

Disjunction, *dis-jonc'-xion*, N. Veglachar; sutt.

Disjunctive, *dis-jonc'-tiv*, Veg-lachar corcho.

Dislike, *diz-laic'*, V. Canttallonc, vaitt lagonc, mandonam zaunc.

Dislike, N. Ruch nasop; can-ttallo.

Dislocate, *diz'-lo-keitt*, V. Codd saravunc, sorcavunc, konslaunc.

Dislocation, *diz'-lo-kei-xion*, N. Coddsorni, sorcavni.

Dislodge, *dis-loj'*, V. Bhair galunc.

Dismal, *diz'-mal*, A, Callso; biraneull.

Dismember, *dis-mem'-bor*, V. Cuddke corunc, sande catrunc; cusin corunc.

Dismiss, *dis-miss'*, V. Bhair ga-lunc; soddunc; roja diunc.

Dismissal, *dis-mis'-sal*, N. Bhair galop; soddop.

Dismount, *diz-maunt'*, V. Den-vunc.

Disobedience, *diz-o-bi'-diens*, N. Nam man-nnem, nam aiconnem.

Disobedient, *diz-o-bi'-di-ent*. A. Beporvi, fotting, sanglelem aiconaslolo.

Disobey, *diz-o-bei'*, V. Nam pall-unc, nam manunc, nam aicunc.

Disoblige, *diz-ob-laij'*, V. Ocman corunc, ducounc.

Disobliging, *diz-ob-lai'-jing*, A. Onupcari: imtto.

Disorder, *diz-or'-dor*, N. Gondoll; charkond; chuc; pidda.

Disorder, V. Gondoll—, chavon, goddbodd corunc

Disorderly, *diz-or'-dor-li*, A, Gonddlacho, akar naslolo.

Disorganisation, *diz-or'-ga-ni-zei'-xion*, N. Mandavoll—, goddvonn moddnem.

Disorganise, *diz-or'-ga-naiz*, V. Goddvonn—, mandavoll mo-ddunc.

Disown, *diz-oun'*, V. Aplo noi munnonc.

Disparage, *dis-pa'-rçij*, V. Man caddunc, be abru corunc.

Disparagement, *dis-pa'-reij-ment* N. Ocman; be abru. [unav.
Disparity, *dis-pa'-ri-tti,* N. Tutt,
Dispassionate, *dis-pes'-xio-neith* A. Nidhan; thondd; fg. somandonacho.
Dispel, *dis-pel'* V. Caddunc; bhair galunc.
Dispensary, *dis-pens'-a-ri,* N. Butic,
Dispensation, *dis-pen-sei'-xion,* N. Mapi, sodd.
Dispense, *dis-pens',* V. Dispens dinnc, map corunc, soddunc.
Disperse, *dis-pors',* V. Simpddaunc, ud Jounc, tin tera corunc.
Dispersion, *dis-por'-xion,* N. Simpoddni, uddouni.
Display, *dis-pley',* V. Dacounc; uctto corunc.
Display, N. Dakoun.
Displease, *dis-pliiz',* V. Ruch—, khoxi caddunc; nam manonc; ubgonc, vajounc
Displeasure, *dis-ple'-jar,* N. Disgost, dukh, vielab.
Disposal, *dis-po'-zal,* N. Manddavoll; ruzu—, ajir asunem.
Dispose, *dis-poz',* V. Mandduno, dallunc, tharaunc; toiar corunc; vondavunc; formaunc; vosounc.
Disposition, *dis-po-zi'-xion,* N. Aitomon; vondavon; gunn.
Dispossess, *dis-poz-zes',* V. Suadin aslelem voronc; caddunc.
Disproportion, *dis-pro-por'-xion,* N Ontor, nam laiekpoun; namecott.
Disproportionate, *dis-pro-por'-xio-neitt,* A. Ontor aslolo,
Disputable, *dis-piu'-tte-bl,* A. Tocrari.
Disputant, *dis-piu'ttant,* N. Vadi, parvadi; tocrar cornar.
Disputation, *dis-piu-ttei'xion,* N. Tocrar,
Dispute, *dis-piutt',* N. Tocrar: zogddem; tontto.
Disqualification, *dis-kua-li-fi-kei'xion,* N. Goroz ti menni nasop, osoctai,
Disregard, *dis-ri'-gard,* V. Beporva corunc.
Disregard, N. Beporvo.
Disregardful, *dis-ri-gard'-ful,* A. Beporvo corcho.
Disrespect, *dis-re-spect',* N. nam man vo abru.
Disrespect, V. Man dinam zaunc.
Disrespectful, *dis-ri-spect'-ful,* A. Ocmanacho; man dinaslolo.
Disruption, *dis.rop'-xion,* N. Moddop.
Dissatisfaction, *dis-sa-tis-fec'-xion,* N. Nam mannuop, dadoxi nasop.
Dissect, *dis-sect',* V. Catrunc; cuddkéan-cuddco corunc
Dissection, *dis-sec'-xion,* N. Chirop; catrop.
Dissemble, *dis sem'-bl,* V. Lipounc; lipoun dourunc.
Disseminate, *dis-se'-mi-neitt',* Vompunc, simpddaunc; porgottunc.
Dissension, *dis-sen'-xion,* N. Veglachar, vaittachar.
Dissent, *dis-sent',* V. Nam mannunc, portem dorunc.
Dissertation, *dis-ser-tei'-xion,* N. Patt; lamb ulounem.
Dissimilar, *dis-si'-mi-lar,* A. Dusre jaticho.
Dissimilarity, *dis-si'-mi-la-ri-tii,* N. Ontor.
Dissimulation, *dis-si-mu-lei'-xion,* N. Lipoun dovornem, can matrem
Dissipate, *dis'-si-peitt,* V. Uddounc, nam corunc; sorounc, ogddaunc,

Dissipated, *dis-si-peit'-ed*, A. Chintinam tosolo ; vaittam khoxeanc lobdollo.

Dissipation, *dis-si-pei'-xion*, N. Nam cornem, ubouni, ogddanni; bongostoll.

Dissolute, *dis'-so-liutt*, A. Vaittam khoxeauc lobdollo, chonchol, simdal.

Dissolution, *dis-so-liu'-xion*, N. Khirop, virop ; moddop.

Dissolve, *dis-solv'*, V. Khirounc. gollounc ; virgaunc ; mellounc,

Dissonance, *dis'-so-nans*, N. Absoar, suar-bhed.

Dissuade, *dis-su-eidd'*, V. Moddavunc, mon-chit firounc.

Dissuasion, *dis-su-ei'-xion*, N. Moddavni, mon firaunem.

Distaff, *dis-taff'*, N. Kirki.

Distance, *dis'-tans*, N. Pal-lo, lambai.

Distant, *dis'-tant*, A. Pois, dur, lamb.

Distaste, *dis-teist'*, N. Nam ruch; canttallo.

Distasteful, *dis-teistt'-ful*, A. Ruch naslolo ; canttalleacho.

Distemper, *dis-tem'-por*, N. Pidda.

Distend, *dis-tend'* V. Vistarunc, rundaunc ; suzonc.

Distention, *dis-ten'-xion*, N. Vistarop ; zuz.

Distil, *dis-til'*, V. (Soro arak) Caddunc, battiec launc; gallunc, pogllunc.

Distillation, *dis-til-ei'-xion*, N. Caddnem, battiec lavnem ; lavni.

Distillery, *dis-ttil'-e-ri*, N. Bhatti.

Distinct, *dis'-tingct*, A. Vises ; veglo ; kherit.

Distinction, *dis-tingkt'-xion*, N. Veglauni ; veglicai ; man, abru.

Distinctive, *dis-tingkt'-iv*. A. Veglaitalo ; manadic, abruvont ; sost.

Distinctly, *dis-tingct'-li*, AD. Ecamec ve-veglim, saf, barcaen.

Distinguish, *dis-ting'-guish*, V. Veglo—, nirallo corunc ; man diunc, navaddunc; man addunc; aicunc.

Distinguished, *dis-ting'-gu-ishd*, A. Uttom ; navaddlolo, famad.

Distort, *dis-tort'*, V. Vollonc.

Distortion, *dis-tor'-xion*, N. Vollop.

Distract, *dis-trect'*, V. Nam chit diunc ; addaunc ; moddunc.

Distracted, *dis-trect'-ed*, A. Chit dinaslolo.

Distraction, *dis-trec'-xion*, N. Visor ; add chintna, baili chintna.

Distress, *dis-tress'*, N. Acant ; coistt ; oprad.

Distress, V. Corcor corunc ; coistt diunc ; bejar corunc.

Distribute, *dis-tri'-biutt*, V. Vanttunc, vanttun diunc.

Distribution, *dis-tri-biu'-xion*, N. Vanttni, vanttop.

Distributive, *dis-tri'-but-iv*, A. Vantteacho.

District, *dis'-trict*, N. Jillo, [mahal.

Distrust, *dis-trast'*, V. Patienam zaunc, dubavonc.

Distrust, N. Nam patienem ; oborvanso.

Distrustful, *dis-trast'-ful*, A. Patiennslolo, dubavi.

Disturb, *dis-torb'*, V. Dosunc ; uchamboll corunc ; bejar corunc.

Disturbance, *dis torb'-ans*, N. Corandai ; uchambollai ; revolusaum.

Disunion, *diz-iu'-ni-on*, N. Veglochar, ecott nasop.

Disunite *diz-iu-naitt'*, v. Veglo corunc.
Disuse, *diz-iuz'*, v. Sovoim moddunc, siclelem visronc.
Ditch, *dich*, N. gottor ; kholli ; khon.
Ditty, *dit'tti*, N. Pod.
Dive, *daiv*, v. Buddonc, udcant rigonc ; niallunc.
Diverge, *dai-vorj'*, v. Vatt soddunc ; dusre eusilean cholonc ; fanttunc.
Divergence, *dai-vorj'-ens*, N. Vetias ; vingoddai,
Divers, *dai'-varz*, A. Veglo.
Diverse, *dai-vors'*, A. Veglo, bodol.
Diversion, *dai-vor'-xion*, N. Khell, gomot ; veglachar.
Divert, *dai-vort'*, v. Khuxal corunc, visraunc. khellunc ; sorcavunc, pelean caddunc.
Divest, *dai-vest'* v. Nagddo corunc ; bhair galunc, soddunc.
Divide, *di-vaid'*, v. Doxim corunc ; vantte corunc, catrunc ; cusin caddunc.
Dividend, *di'-vi-dend*, N. Vantto.
Divination, *di-vi-nei'-xion*, N. Parkhonuem.
Divine, *di-vain'*, A. Devacho, Devagelo ; deuponni ; fg. ojapancho.
Divine, v. Parkunc, nimit sangunc.
Diviner, *di-vain'-ar*, N. Nimit sagnar.
Divinity, *di-vi'-ni-ti*, N. Deuponn ; Deu.
Divisibility, *di-viz-i-bil'-i-tti*, N. Vantti sarkem.
Division, *di-vi'-jion*, N. Vanttop, vantto ; veglachar, doxim cornem ; khon.
Divorce, *dai-vors'*, N. Cazar moddnem.
Divorce, v. Cazar moddune cusin soronc.
Divulge, *di-volj'*, v. Porgottunc ; sobemazar collounc, fancounc.
Dizziness, *di'-zi-ness*, N. Gunvoll.
Do, *du*, v. Corunc ; zaunc.
—(Away with)=Bhair caddun vuddounc.
—(Without)=Goroz nasunc.
Docile, *do'-sail*, A. Sico-sarco ; sado ; khalto.
Docility, *do'-si-li-tti*, N. Siccho gun, somjicai ; dulobai ; khalteponn.
Dock, *doc*, N. Godd.
Doctor, *doc'-tor*, N. Voiz.
Doctrine, *doc'-trin*, Sicop, sicoun; dotorn.
Document, *do'-ku-ment*, N. Daklo, lekpotr.
Doe, *do*, N. Bail merum, bail sonso,
Doer *do'-ar*, N. Cornar.
Dog, *dog*, N. Sunnem ; petto.
Dogma, *dog'-ma*, N. Snmurt ; bavartachi sicoun ; bavarth.
Dogmatic, *dog-ma'-tic*, N. Bavartachi videa.
Dolorous, *do'-lor-as*, A. Dukest, khontiborit.
Dolour, *do'-lor*, N. Duk.
Dolphin, *dol'-fin*, N. Doriantlo ducor.
Domain, *do-mein'*, N. Raj ; bhuim.
Dome, *dom*, N. Kolos, ghumott.
Domestic *do-mes'-tic* N. Garantlo chacor ; ravoilolc
Domestic, A. Garacho, gorcho ; ravoilolo ; sado.
Domesticate, *do-mes-ti-keitt'*, v. Goravo—, munxallo corunc, gorachi sovoim corunc.
Dominate, *dom'-i-neitt*, v. Sotia—, podvi cholounc, adicar asunc ; matear chodduuc, razvott corunc.

Dominion, *do-min'-i-on*, N. Dhonipoun; jamindhari, jaghir, razvottki.
Donation, *do-nei'-xion*, N. Dernem; izmol, bio.
Donkey, *don'-ki*, N. Gaddum.
Door, *dor*, N. Dar; darvontto.
Door-keeper, *dor-kip'-ar*, N. Porteir; dar racnar.
Dormitory, *dor'mi-tho-ri*, N. Nidcho cudd.
Dose, *doz*, N. Mezop, map.
Dot, *dott*, N. Tibo; khot.
Dote, *dôt*, V. Mogan morunc; laleunc.
Double, *do'bl*, A. Doddo; don pautti chodd.
Double, V. Doddunc; doddo corunc; don pautti chodd corunc; bounttonim vochunc.
Doubleness, *do'bl-ness*, N. Dupott.
Doubt, *dautt*, V. Dubavonc.
Doubt, N. Duban.
Doubtful, *dautt'ful*, A. Dubavacho.
Doubtless, *dautt'less*, AD. Dubava-vin, vo duban-nastanam; olbot.
Dough, *dof*, N. Moullelem pitt.
Dove, *dov*, N. Conddo.
Dovecot, *dov'cott*, N. Covddeancho gudd.
Dowager, *da'ra-gar*, N. Gou meleli hostori jicho putr cazar zala.
Down, *daun*, N. Pac.
Down, AD. Socol; dornir, khala.
Down, A. Socoilo, khailo.
Down-cast, *daun'-cast*, A. Socol galolo; pondcho.
Down-fall, *daun'-fol*, N. Socol poddop.
Down-right, *daun'-rait*, A. Khoroch, khoro; ecanı ɔm.
Dowry, *dau'ri*, N. Dôt.
Doze *doz*, V. Jemeunc.
Dozen *do'zon*, N. Bara.
Doziness *do'zi-ness*, N. Jem; alsai.
Draft, *draft*, N. Noksha.
Drag, *dreg*, V. Voddunc.
Drain, *drein*, N. Udoc paglounchi zalli.
Drain, *drèin*, V. Udoc caddunc; paglounc; rito corunc.
Drake, *dreik*, N. Dadlem ans.
Drama, *dra'ma*, N. Nattoc.
Dramatic, *dra'mat-ic*, A. Nattcacho, nattki.
Dramatist, *dra'ma-tist*, N. Nattcant kell-cornar.
Drape, *dreip*, V. Nesounc; pangrounc.
Draught, *drott*, N. Voddop; pieunchem vo pieonn; varem; nocol;- chek.
Draw, *dro*, V. Voddunc; caddunc
—(Tears)=Ducam gollounc.
—(Near)=Lagim pavunc.
—(Up)=Borounc.
Drawer, *dro'-ar*, N. Govet.
Drawers, *dro'ars*, N. Izar, serul.
Drawing, *dro'ing*, N. Pintur; nacsha.
Dread, *dred*, N. Bhem, bhirant, camp.
Dreadful, *dred'-ful*, A. Bhirancull tortoreancho.
Dream, *dri'im*, N. Soponn.
Dream, V. Soponn poddonc; sopnenne.
Dreamer, *driim-'ar*, N. Sopnnacar.
Dreary *dre'ri*, A. Bhirancull.
Dregs, *dregs*, N. Soreachi mur.
Drench, *drench*, V. Bizonc; fugonc.
Dress, *dress*, N. Nesonn.
Dress, V. Nesonc; gai borc corunc; jevon toiar corunc.
Dresser, *dress'ar*, N. Voiz.
Dressing, *dres'sing*, N. Toiari.
Dried, *draid*, A. Suco.

Drift, *drift*, N. Xevott; ras.
Drill, *drill*, V. Topunc; pokoll corunc; Soldadponn sicounc.
Drink, *drink*, V. Pieunc; cop marunc.
Drinkeable, *dringk'-e-bl*, A. Pieuncho; pie-sarco.
Drinker, *dringk'-ar* N. Pienar vo pinar.
Drinking, *drink'-ing*, N. Pieonn.
Drip, *drip*, N. Vau.
Drip, V. Thembeunc.
Drive, *draiv*, N. Lottunc; boll corunc; bhollan cholo..c; mucar cholounc; daunddaunc; goddear boson vochunc.
—(About)=Ennem-tennem alounc.
—(Out, forth)=Bhair galunc.
—(Together)=Mellounc, ecttaim corunc.
Drive, N. Gaddiechi suari.
Driveller, *dri'-vi-llar*, N. Piso munis; sopnnacar; soirboir.
Driver, *drai-'car*, V. Gaddi choloinar.
Droll, *droll*, N. Anso.
Drone, *dron*, N. Dadlo mounvancho mus; fg. auxi.
Droop, *druup*, V. Umcollounc; bavonc; denvunc.
Drop, *drop*, N. Thembo.
Drop, V. Thembeunc, ponvonc; fg. soddunc.
Drop-in, *drop-in*, V. Bettonc.
Dropsy, *drop-'si*, N. Naicut.
Dross, *dross*, N. Coir.
Drossiness, *dros-si'-ness*, N. Burseponn.
Drossy *dros'-si*, A. Burso.
Drought, *drott*, N. Suki dadd.
Drown, *dra-un*, V. Buddonc; buddounc.
Drowsiness, *drau-zi'-ness*, N. Jem, nid; ausai.
Drowsy, *drau'-zi*, A. Nidest; ausi.
Drudge, *droj*, V. Coisttavonc.
Drudge, N. Gulam.
Drug, *drog*, N. Vocot.
Druggist, *drog'-ist*, N. Butiqueir; voctam vicnar.
Drum, *drom*, N. Dol.
Drunk, *dronk*, A. Bebdo.
Drunkenness, *drongk'-en-ness*, N. Bebdeponn, bebdicai.
Dry, *drai*, A. Suco.
Dry, V. Sucounc.
—(tears)=dukam pusunc.
Dryness, *drai'-ness*, N. Suki-dadd.
Dubious, *du'-bi-as*, A. Dubavacho, dubavi.
Duck, *dock*, N. Ans.
Due, *diu*, A. Devo; favo.
Due, N. Rinn.
Duel, *du'-el*, N. Doganchem zogddem.
Duke, *diuk*, N. Duque.
Dull, *doll*, A. Callso; dar naslolo; somzo-naslolo; chintest.
Dull, V Callso corunc, dar pirder corunc.
Dullness, *doll'-ness*, N. Auseponn; murcponn.
Duly, *diu'-li*, AD. Sarkem, favo te jinsim; caidean.
Dumb, *domb*, N. mono; munco.
Dumbness, *domb'-ness*, N. Moneponn.
Dun, *don*, A. Callso.
Dunce, *dons*, A. Brut; piso.
Dung, *dong*, N. Xenn.
Dung, V. Sarem galunc.
Dungeon, *dan'-jon*, N. Dornipondchi bonkondd.
Dunghill, *dong'-hill*, N. Sareachi ras; thapo.
Dupe, *diup*, V. Fottounc, thocunc
Dupe, N. Vegim fottousarco.
Duplicate, *du'-pli-keitt*, N. Nocol.
Duplicity, *du-pli'-si-tti*, N. Falsponn; copott. [Togop.
Durability, *diu-ra-bil'-i-tti*, N.

Durable, *diu'-ie-bl*, A. Tognar.
Duration, *diu-rei'-zion*, N. Call; togop.
During, *diu'-ring*, Prep, vellar; modem. [vell.
Dusk, *dosk*, N. Dis dare Vecho
Dusky, *dosk'-i*, A. Callso.
Dust, *dost*, N. Dull; pudd; coir.
Dust, V. Dull pusunc; coir caddunc.
Dusty, *dostt'-i*, A. Dullicho; mello.
Dutiful, *diu'-ti-ful*, A. Khalto; mogall.
Dutifulness, *diu-ti-ful'-ness*, N. Khalteponn.
Duty, *diu'-tti*, N. Caido; cam.
Dwarf, *du-orf'*, N. Mottvo munis.
Dwell, *du-ell'*, V. Ravonc; fg. niallunc, soncas chintunc.
Dwelling, *dwel'-ing*, N. Biddar, gor.
Dwindle, *du-in'-dl* V. Bavunc; denvunc; nam zaunc.
Dye, *dai*, V. Rong launc.
Dynasty, *dai'-nas-ti*, N. Patxae-anchem garannem.
Dysentry, *dis'-en-tri*, N. Zorom bhair; hagonn.
Dyspepsia, *dis'-pep-sia*, N. Ajirn.

E

Each, *iich*, PRO. Dogui.
—(a)=zonn eiclo.
Eager, *ii'-gar*, A. Bhou axecho; urbevont; umalleacho.
Eagerness, *ii'-gar-ness*, N. Vodd axea; urba; umallo.
Eagle, *i'-gl* N Gonn.
Ear, *er*, N. Can.
Ear-ache, *er'-eik*, N. Canachi duc vo can-foddnem.
Earl, *arl*, N. Vodde culliecho munis.
Early, *er'-lli*, A. Socallincho; porno; suru zauncho.
Early, AD. Socallim; vegim.
Earn, *arn*, V. Mellounc; zoddunc.
Earnest, *arn'est*, A. Khoroch; suddsuddaecho,
Earnest, N. Sinalache duddu.
Earnestly, *arn'-est-li*, AD. Thambonastanam; moriadiu.
Earnestness, *arn'-est-nes*, N. Suddsuddai; zagrutai.
Ear-ring, *er'-ring*, Mudi, argolinho.
Earth, *arth*, N. Sounsar; mati; bhuim.
Earthly, *arth'-li*, A. Sounsaracho; matiecho.
Earth-quake, *arth'-hu-eic*, N. Dorn-camp.
Ear-wax, *er'-vex*, N. Canulo.
Ease, *iiz*, N. Soucasai; sompeponn; moriad,
Easily, *iiz'-i-li*, AD. Soucasaen, sompeponnim.
East, *iist*, N. Udenti.
Easter, *iis'-tar*, N. Pascanchi porob.
Eastern, *iis'-tarn*, A. Udenticho.
Eastern, N. Udenti.
Eastward, *iist'-vard*, AD. Udente eusilean.
Easy, *iz'i*, A. Sompo; coistt naslo lo; soucasaecho; soimbacho.
Eat, *iitt*, V. Khaunc; jeunc.
Eatable, *it'-ie-bl*, N. Khauncheo vostu.
Eating, *ii'-tting*, N. Khan.
Eaves, *iivs*, N. Paunlleo; nolli.
Ebb, *eb*, N. Sucti.
Ebb, V. Sucti eunc.
Ebony, *eb'-on-i*, N. Abnus, temttu
Ebriety, *e-brai'-e-tti*, N. Bebdi-cai.
Ebullition, *e-bul-li'-zion*, N. Khotcoto; umallo; uchambollai
Eccentric, *ec-sen'-tric*, A. Mazabhailo; tarifecho.
Ecclesiastic, *ec-cle'-zi-as-tic*, N. Igorjecho munniari.

Ecclesiastic, A. Igorjecho.
Echo, *i'-ko,* N. Porto tallo, porto avaz, gaz, nad.
Echo, V. Gazunc, nadunc; gazounc nadounc.
Eclat, *e-cla',* N. Pracas, porzoll; onod, man.
Eclectic, *ec-lec'-tic,* A Vinchun caddcho.
Eclipse, *ec-clips',* N. Giran; suria-grahan.
Ecliptic, *ec-clip'-tic,* A Girauacho.
Economic, *e-con-om'-ik,* A. Ispan khorchitolo, gorvosthi.
Economize, *e-kon-'om-aiz,* V. Zogounc, thevunc.
Economy, *i-kono'mi,* N. Khoroch, thau, veiavoste, zogounni, sugrat, thevni.
Ecstasy, *ec-'sta-zi,* N. Distti poddop; sontos.
Ecstatic, *ec-stat'-ik,* A. Distti-poddpacho, sontosacho.
Ecumenical, *e-cu-men'-i-cal,* A. Sogle igorjecho.
Eddy, *ed'di,* N. Bovor
Edge, *ej,* N. Deg, dhar.
Edict, *e-dict.* N. Hocum; vartaman, formonn, dangro.
Edification, *e-di-fi-kei'-xion* N. Bori dek.
Edifice, *ed'-i-fis,* N. Bandop.
Edify, *e'difai,* V. Bori dek diunc.
Edit, *ed'-itt,* V. Porgottunc. xapunc.
Edition, *e-di'-xion,* N. Xapnni, porgottponn.
Educate, *e-du-keitt,* V. Sicounc; vaddounc. lan vodd corunc.
Educated, *e-du-kei'tled,* A. Moriadicho, sicpi, manacho.
Education, *e-du-kei'-xion,* N. Sicounni, rovis, mansugi, moriad.
Educe, *e'-dius,* V. Bhair caddunc.
Eel, *il,* N. Marimugud.
Efface, *if-fes'* V. Pusunc.
Effect, *if-fect',* N. Foll, gunn; samonn.
—(In effect)=Khorench.
Effective, *i-fect'-tiv,* A. Boll aslolo; khoroch, gunnacho.
Effectual, *i-fec'-chu-al,* A. Gunn aslolo; khoroch.
Effectuate, *if-fec'-chu-eitt,* V. Gunn poddonc.
Effeminacy, *ef-fem'-in-a-si,* N. Baileponn: baibolponn.
Effeminate, *ef-fem'-in-eitt,* A. Baibolo, bailanddo.
Effervescense, *ef-fer-ves'-sens* N. Umallo; uchambollai.
Efficacious, *ef-fi-kei'-xi-as,* A. Gunnacho. gunvont, follachi, sufoll, gott, bolladic.
Efficacy, *ef'-fi'-ca-si,* N. Boll, gunn, tej. [nest; laik.
Efficient, *ef-fi'-si-ent,* A. Gun-
Efflorescence, *ef-flo-res'-sens,* N. N. Fullni; tonvri, tonvor; gamollem.
Effort, *ef'-fort,* N. Minot; pechoddop.
Effrontery, *ef-fron'-te-ri,* N. Loz-nasnem; möst.
Effusion, *ef-fiu'-jion,* N. Otni, varonni; fg. umallo.
Eft, *eft,* N. Pal.
Egg, *egg,* N. Tantim.
Egotism, *e'-got-izm,* N. Aumponn, apleponn, absuart, aplo mog.
Egotist, *eg'ot-ist,* N. Absuarti, motlobi, apnnacho mog cornar.
Egregious, *e-gre'-jias* A. Uttim bhou uxar; voddlo, aprup.
Egress, *i'-gress* N. Bhair sorop,
Egyptian luffa, N. Gonsallem.
Either, *ai'-dor,* A. Dontlem-ec.
Ejaculation, *e-jac'-u-lei'-xion,* N. Uscar; ontoscarnachem magnem.
Eject, *i-ject',* V. Bhair galunc, doiacho varjunc.

Eke out, *eik-aut*, V. Urounc.
Elaborate, *e-lab'-o-reitt*, V. Cobar corunc, chotraen corunc.
Elaborate, A. Sarco vo chotraen kelolo.
Elapse, *i-leps'*, V. Pasar zaunc.
Elastic, *e-las'-tic*, A Vistaro-sarco ; votti ; lavchic.
Elasticity, *e-las-tis'-i-tti*, N. Lavchicponn.
Elate, *e-leitt'*, V. Fugounc.
Elated, *e-leitt'-ed*, A. Hancaracho ; gorvi.
Elation, *e-lei'-xion*, N. Choddop ; gorv ; fugop.
Elbow, *el'-bo*, N. Kompor.
Elder, *eld'-er*, N. Malgoddo ; voddlo.
Elect, *i-lect'*, V. Vinchun caddunc; nomiarunc.
Elect, A. Vinchun caddlolo.
Election, *i-lec'-xion*, N. Vinchnem.
Elector, *i-lec'-tor*, N. Vinchun caddtolo.
Electricity, *e-lec-tri'-si-tti*, N. Viz vo vizachi videa.
Elegance, *el'-e-gans*, N. Rup ; unch bhas ; sobitai.
Elegant, *el'-e-gant*, A. Rupest ; sobit ; suudor ; nitoll.
Element, *el-e'-ment*, N. Mullacho vautto ; poili sicoun.
Elementary *el-e-ment'-a-ri*, A. Mullacho ; fg. sado ; sompo ; coistt naslolo.
Elephant, *el'-e-fant*, N. Hoti.
Elevate, *el-e-veitt'*, V. Uclunc vo ubarunc ; fg. man diunc.
Elevated, *e-le-vei'-tted*, A. Ubar ; fg. gorvist ; voddnacho ; vorto.
Elevation, *e-le-vei'-xion*, N. Uclop ; ubar zago ; matiechi ras ; gorv ; man, voddponn.
Elicit, *e-lis'-itt*, V. Caddunc.
Eligibility, *e-li-ji-bi'-li-tti*, N. Vinchi sarkem.
Eligible, *el'-i-ji-bl*, A. Vinchi sarco.
Eliminate, *e-lim'-in-eitt* V. Bhair galunc.
Elexir, *e-lik'-sir*, N. Rosaian.
Ellipse, *ell-ips'*, N. Pandalop : anddakar.
Ellipsis, *el-lip'-sisi*, N. Pandalop ; utram soddnem.
Elocution, *e-lo-cu'-xion*, N. Ucharan ; vachea.
Elope, *e-lop'*, V. Pollonc.
Eloquence, *el'-o-kv-ens*. N. Unch bhas, vachea-eukti ; supralap.
Else, *el-s*, A. Ad. nam zalear; anim. [suater.
Elsewhere, *els'-rer*, Ad. Dusre
Elucidate, *e-lu'si-deitt*, W. Ugddapem corunc, somzaunc.
Elucidation, *el-u-si-dei'xion*, N. Somzaunni : pracas, vivaran.
Elude, *e-liud'*, V. Chuconnc ; fottonnc.
Emaciate, *e-ma'-xi-eitt*, V. Baric corunc ; bagonc.
Emaciated, *e-ma-xi-ei'tted*, A. Baric, bagottio, haddieo.
Emanate, *em'-a-neitt*, V. Utpon zaunc, nipjunc, bhair soronc.
Emanation, *e-ma-nei'xion*, N. Bhair sorop ; kirlop ; ub ; vaitt varem.
Emancipate, *e-man'-si-paitt*, V. soddonnc, suttea diunc.
Emancipation, *e-man'si-pei-xion*, N. Suttea.
Embalm, *em-bam,'* V. Pormollaunc ; moddeac pormollachem tel launc.
Embank, *em-benc'*, N. V. baud galunc.
Embankment, *embangk-'ment*, N. Band.
Embargo, *em-bar-'go*, N. Addcoll, addauni.
Embark, *em-barc,'* V. Tarvar choddonc ; fg. launc.

Embarrass, *em-bar'-ras*, V. Oddchunc, gondaunc, guspaunc, addcoll galunc.

Embarrassed, *em-bar'-rasd*, A. Gondlolo ; addcollicho.

Embarrassment, *em-bar'-ras-ment*, N. Addcoll, oddchon, gondoll.

Embassy, *em'-bas-si*, N. Raibari.

Embellish, *em-bel'-lish*. V. Sobounc, surungarunc.

Embers, *em-'bers*, N. Gobor, murmuro ; ujeacho inglo.

Embezzle, *em-bez'-zl*. V. Nagounc.

Embitter, *em-bit'ar*. V. Ducounc ; rag addunc.

Emblem, *em'-blem*, N. Kuru. khuna : sarkem.

Embody, *em-bo'-ddi*, V. Fg. rupdiunc.

Embolden, *em-bold''-en*, V. Dhir diunc.

Embowel, *em-bou'-l*, V. Ankiddi caddunc.

Embrace, *em-bres'*, V. Pottlun dorunc : veng marunc, fg. vinchun caddunc.

Embrace, *em-bres'*, N. Veng.

Embrocation, *em-bro-kei'-xion*, N. Bizop.

Embroider, *em-broi'-dar* V. Lugttai fulam caddunc,

Embryo, *em'-bri-o*, N. Gorb, gabh : fg. mull, oromb.

Emend, *e-mend'*, V. Chuki sarkeo corunc.

Emerald, *e'-me-rald*, N. Maninc.

Emerge, *e-merj,'* V, Udcautlo voir eunc.

Emergency, *e-merj'-en-si*, N. Bhair sorop, udcantlo voir sornem : goroz.

Emetic, *e-met'-ic*, N. Onkchem

Emigrant *em'-i-grant*, N. Porkea gaum ant vochnar.

Emigrate, *em'-i-greit*, V. Aplo gaum soddun vochunc, porgaunvant vochunc.

Eminence. *em'-in-ens*, N. Thorponn, unchponn, vorteponn.

Eminent, *em'-in-ent*, A. | Vodd, thor, vorto.

Emissary, *em'-i-sa-ri*, N. Daddlolo, pattoilolo.

Emission, *e-mis'-xion*, N. Bhair daddop.

Emit, *e-mit,'* V. Bhair uddounc, soddunc, fekunc.

Emmet, *em'-met*, N. Mui.

Emollient, *e-mol'-li-ent*, A. Mou corchem, samak.

Emolument, *em-ol'lu-ment*, N. Labh, adav ; upcar, faida, prapti.

Emotion, *e-mo'-xion*. N. Movallai; voddni, uchambollai ; gusop.

Emperor, *em'-pe ror,* N. Maharaj. imperador.

Emphasis, *em'-fa-zis*, N. Boll, ucharneacho nett.

Empire, *em'-pa-iar*, N. Razvott.

Empiric, *em-pi'-ric*, A. Ambavacho. sidh ; okhti.

Employ, *em.ploi,'* V. Khorchunc ; vaurac lagunc ; camar asonc.

Employment, *em-ploi'-ment*. N. Prayog, cam, udiog, dando.

Emporium, *em-po'-ri-um* N. Veparacho zago.

Empower, *em-pau'-or*, V. Podvi vo adicar diunc.

Empowered, *em-pau'-ord*, A. Podvi aslolo.

Empress *em'-press*, N. Maharanni.

Emptiness, *emp'-tti-ness* N. Rite ponn, Khaliponn.

Empty, *emp'-tti*. A. Khali ; rito.

Empty, V. Khali corunc, votunc.

Emulate, *em'-u-leitt*, V. Udandim corunc, eca mecachi dok geun cholunc,

Emulation, *em-u-lei'-xion*, N. Uddop.
Enable, *en-ei'-bl* V. Boll diunc.
Enact, *en-ect'*, caido goddunc; posond corunc.
Encamp. *en-kemp'*. V. Thombu marunc.
Enceinte, *ang-seingt'*, N. Gorbest, gurvar.
Enchain, *en-chein'*, V. Bandunc, sanclleo galunc.
Enchant, *en-chant'*, V. Montrunc; fg. pisaunc; bhou Khuxal corunc [tri.
Enchanter, *en-chant'-ar* N. Mon-
Enchantment, *en-chant'-ment*, N. Montri; fg. pisainnem.
Enchanting, *en-chant'-ing*, A. Fg. Ojapancho; bhou sobit; pisounchoo.
Enchantress, *en-chant'-ress*, N. Montrin.
Encircle, *en-sor'-cl*, V. Veddo galunc; guttlaunc.
Enclosure, *en-clo'-jar*, N. Addo, voddop.
Encomium, *en-co mi'-um*, N. Varnan, tarif, vakanni.
Encompass, *en-com'-pass*, V. Veddo galunc, guttlaunc.
Encounter, *en-caun'-ttar*, V. Mellonc; fudde ravonc.
Encourage, *en-co'-rej*, V. Dhir—, Boll diunc.
Encouragement, *en-co'-rej-ment*, N. Urba, dhir, adar.
Encumber, *en-cum'-bor*- V. Addcoll galnnc, addaunc'
Encyclical, *en-si'-cli-cal*, N. Somestanc boroileli chitt.
Encyclopedia, *en-sic-lo-pe'-dia*, N. Sorv-videia.
End, *endd*, N. Xevott, fim.
End, V' Cobar corunc; thambounc; xevott asunc.
Endanger, *en-dein'-jar*, V. Riscar galunc.
Endear, *en-di-ar*,' V. Mogall corunc.
Endearment, *en-diar'-ment*, N. Fuslaunni, bulounni.
Endeavour, *en-dev'-or*, V. Upai geunc, goddta tem corunc.
Endeavour, N. Praiattan.
Endorse, *en-dors*,' V. Pattier naum borounc.
Endow, *en-ddau*,' V. Diunc, dot diunc.
Endowed, *en-daudd'*, A. Aslolo, borlolo.
Endurance, *en-duar'-ens*, N. Sosnicai.
Endure, *en-ddiu-ar'* V. Sosunc, bogunc, thir zaun ravunc, togonc.
Enduring, *en-ddu-ar'-ing*, A. Sosnik, togtolo.
Enema, *en-i'-ma*, N. Ajut galcho poscotto.
Enemy, *e-ne'-mi*, N. Dusman.
Energetic, *en-er-jet'-tic*, tejvont, gott, suddsuddit.
Energy, *en'-er-ji*, N. Boll, tej, jiv. nett.
Enervate, *en'-er-veitt*, N. Osoct corunc.
Enervation, *en-er vei'-xion*, N. Osoctai.
Enfeeble, *en-fi'-bl*, V. Osoct corunc.
Enforce, *en-fors'*, V. Pallo diunc launc.
Engage, *en-geij'*, V. Bhas—utor diunc; cazar corunc; zuz manddunc.
Engagement, *en-geij'ment*, N. Dileli bhas, soiric, zuz; cazar. cam.
Engaging, *en-geij'-ing*, A. Mogall, manancho; khuxalaecho; sobit. [unc.
Engender, *en-jen'-dar*, V. Zolmo-
Engine, *en'-jin*, N. Injin, ujeachem macn.

Engineer, *en-ji-ni'-ar*, N. Yantracar, injiner.
Engrave, *en-grev*,' V. Cantounc.
Engraver, *en-grev'-ar*, N. Cantoinar. [tounchi videa.
Engraving, *en-grev'-ing* N. Can-
Engross, *en-gross'*, V. Occupad asonc; buddonc.
Enhance, *en-hens*,' V. Choddounc; vaddounc; sobit corunc; marog corunc.
Enhancement, *en-hens'-ment*, N. Vistarop, choddop.
Enigma, *e-nig'-ma*, N. Gudd, umaonem. [Guddacho.
Enigmatical, *e-nig-mat'-ical*, A.
Enjoin, *en-join*,' V. Formaunc.
Enjoy, *en-joi'*, V. Bogunc; upeog corunc; upcarac poddonc.
Enjoyment, *en-joi'-ment*, N. Khuxalcai; dadosponn.
Enlarge, *en-larj*,' V. Choddounc, vistarunc, rundaunc.
Enlargement, *en-larj'-ment*, N. Vistar.
Enlighten, *en-laitt'-on*, V. Uzvaddaunc, ginean diunc.
Enlist, *en-list*,' V. Poltonint zoma zauncheao naum diunc.
Enliven, *en-liv'-on*, V. Uxar corunc (gozalint).
Enmity, *en'-mi-tti*, N. Dusmancai; virudai.
Ennoble, *en-no'-bl*, V. Man mellounc; vorto corunc.
Enormity, *e-nor'-mi-tti* N. Khotteponn.
Enormous, *e-nor'-mas*, A. Bhou vodd; khotto; nisttur.
Enough, *i-naf*,' A. Puro.
Enquire *in-kua'-iar*, V. Vincharunc, khobor caddunc.
Enrage, *en-reij*,' V. Rag addunc; uchamboll corunc.
Enraged, *en-reijd*,' A. Ragist.
Enrich, *en-rich*,' V. Girest corunc.
Enrol, *en-rol'*. V. Listar naum borounc; entrad corunc. [runc.
Enslave, *en-sleiv'*, V. Gulam co-
Ensnare, *en-sner'*, V. Gondlant—addcolint galunc.
Entail, *en-teil'* V. Eo batt kherit, caddunc jeral daijeantlem.
Entangle, *en-ten'-gl*, V. Guspaunc, dorunc, gondounc; revdunc.
Enter, *en'ter* V. bitor vochunc.
Enterprise, *en'ter-praiz*, N. cosoleim cam corunc hatant getlelem.
Enterprising, *en'-ter-prai-sing*, A. nirvonni; cosoleim cam corunc toiar aslolo.
Entertain, *en'-ter-tein* N. biddar diunc; chacreo dourunc: khoxal corunc.
Entertainment, *en'-ter-tein-ment*, N. Biddar; khuxalcai, upcar.
Enthrone, *en-thron*,' N. Gaddier bosounc; voir dourunc.
Enthusiasm, *en-thu'-zi-azm*. N. Urba, chodd axea; uchambollai, umallo.
Enthusiastic, *en-thu'-zi-as-tic*, A. Urbevont; uchamboll.
Entice, *en-ttais'*, V. Fottounc; fuslaunc; piso corunc.
Enticement *en-ttais'-ment*, N. Voddni; fuslaunni.
Enticing, *en-ttai'-sing*, A. Bullounno; fottkiro; voddnecho.
Entire, *en-tta-iar'*, A. Soglo.
Entirely, *en-tta-iar'-li*, AD. Purtem: sompurnaen.
Entitle, *en-ttai'tl*, V. Hak asunc, pustocac naum dourunc.
Entity, *en-ti'-ti*, N. Asop; vostu.
Entrails, *en'-treils*, N. Ankiddi.
Entrance, *en-trens*,' N. Rig, robjes, dar.
Entrap, *en-trep*,' V. Rateor manddunc, rateran dorunc; addcoll galunc.

Entreat, *en-trit,'* V. Laleun' magunc.
Entrust, *en-trost'*, V. patiennc; adin corunc, tabeant diunc.
Entry, *en'-tri*; N. Rig; pustocar borounc.
Entwine, *en-twin'*, V. Revoddunc; vollunc.
Enumerate, *en-iu'-me-reitt*, V. Mezunc; munnonc.
Enumeration, *e-nu-me-rei'-tion*, N. Mezop, ixeop.
Enunciate, *e-nun'-si-eitt*, V. sangunc; ucharunc.
Envelope, *en-ve'lop*, N. Cap (chittichem).
Envelope, V. Guttlaunc.
Envenomed, *en-ven'-onde*, A. Bhou khotto: chodd nostto
Enviable, *en'-vi-e-bl*, A. Axeuncho; apurbaecho.
Envious, *en'-vi-as*, A. Mosri; cusddo.
Environs, *en'vi-rons*, N. Bounton.
Envoy, *en'-voi*, N. Munniari.
Envy, *en'-vi*. N. Imvej, adavot, niscuchar.
Envy, V. Adavot–, mosor disunc, bogunc.
Epidemic, *e'-pi-de'-mic*, N. Vosenchi pidda; chorchorit mari.
Epigram, *ep'-i-gram*, N. Borop.
Epilepsy, *e'pi-lep-si*. N. Morluc.
Episcopal, *e-pis'-co-pal*, A. Bispacho.
Episcopate, *e-pis'-co-peitt*, N. Bispachi podvi, bispachem raj.
Episode, *e'-pi-zod* N. Addcontta; addgoshtt.
Epitaph, *ep'i-taf*, V. Fondavelem borop.
Epitome, *e-pit'-om*. V. samkshep; attop.
Epitomize, *e-pit'-om-aiz*, V. Samkshep corunc.
Epoch, *i-'poc*, V. Call, somoi.
Equability, *e-kua-bil'-i-tti*, N. Nidanai.
Equable, *e'-kue-bl*, A. Nidan.
Equal, *e'-kual*, A. Sarco; samco.
Equal, V. Sarco corunc. [cavnni.
Equality, *e-kual'-i-tti*, N. Sar-
Equally, *e'-kua-li*, Ad. Teach jinsim.
Equator, *e-kue'-ttor*, Samabhagagit.
Equilibrium, *e-kui-li'-bri-um*, N. Somtoll.
Equinox, *e'-kui'-noks*, N. Raticdisac sor.
Equip, *e-kuip,'* V. Toiar corunc.
Equipage, *ek'-ri-pej*, N. Foujichem samonn; savari, arabo.
Equity, *ek'-vi-tti*, N. Nit.
Equivalent, *e-kuiv'-a-lent*, A. Sarco; eke torecho.
Equivocal, *e-kuiv'-o-cal*, A. Dubavi; don orthanche.
Equivocation, *e-kuiv'-vo-kei-xion*, N. Dubau; dubavachim utram.; dusrem dornem; chuc.
Era, *e'-ra*, N. Call, somoi.
Eradicate, *e-rad'-i-keitt*, V. Humblunc: rukachim pallam caddunc; mullan than caddunc.
Erase, *i-reiz,'* V. Pusunc; dag caddunc.
Erasure, *i-reiz'-ar*, N. Pusun caddop, nam corop.
Erect, *i-rect,'* A. Nitt; ubo.
Erect, V. Uclunc; bandunc.
Erection, *i-rec'-xion*, N. bandop.
Err. *e'-rr*, V. Chuconc; fottvonc; parpoll zaun bonvonc.
Erratic, *er-rat'-ic*, A. Parpoll; acram.
Erroneous, *er-ro'-ni-as*, N. Fottkiro; sotavinn.
Error, *e'-ror*, N. Chuc; patoc.
Eructation, *e-ruc-tei'-xion* N. Denk.
Erudition, *e'-ru-di-xion*, N. Sicop.

Eruption, *i-rop'-xion,* N. Ujeachi vouk; fodd, gamollem.
Erysipelas, *e-ri-si'-pe-las,* N. Dhamvrem.
Escape, *is-keip',* V. Vattounc; chucone; pollonc; liponc.
Escape, N. Pollop.
Escort, *es'-cort,* V. Racon vorunc: saugat corunc; bollandunc.
Escort, N. Paro, scolt.
Esoteric, *e-so-te'-ric,* A. Guttacho.
Especial, *s-pe'-shal,* A. Visesh, omcoch.
Especially, *is-pe'-shal-li,* AD. Bhou—, chodd—, vodic corun.
Espionage, *es'-pi-o-neij,* N. Bediponn.
Esplanade, *s-ple-neid',* N. Moidan.
Espousal, *es-pouz'al,* N. Cazar.
Esquire, *s-qua'-iar,* N. Saib.
Espy, *es-pai',* V. Poisthan pollounc; sodun caddunc.
Essay, *es-se',* N. Poricsha; dactem borop.
Essence, *es'-sens,* N. Tattv. soimb.
Essential, *es-sen'-shal* A. Tattvacho, soimbacho, choddegorjecho.
Establish, *es-tab'-lish,* V. Thiravunc, tharaunc; goddunc, rochunc, ubarunc, mauddunc'
Establishment, *es-tab'-lish-ment* N. Karkhanno; bandop.
Estate, *s-tteit',* N. Bhuim; bhens.
Esteem, *s-tiim',* N. Man: borem naum.
Esteem, V. Man dacounc, apurbai corunc.
Estimate, *es-tim'-eitt,* V. Andaz corunc.
Estimate, N. Andaz.
Estrange, *is-treinj',* V. Aivo—, veglo disunc, lagunc, nam borem lagunc; mon pois corunc.
Eternal, *i-ttorn'-al,* A. Sasuancho, ogonnit; mornavinn.
Eternally, *-i-ttorn'-a-li,* Ad. Sasnanchea sasnanc, sodancal.
Eternity, *e-ttorn'-it-ti,* N. Sasonn.
Ethic, *e'-thic,* A. Chalicho.
Ethics, *eth -ics* N. Chalixastr.
Etiquette, *et'-i-kett,* N. Rajrit, dostur.
Etymology, *e-ti-mol'-o-ji,* N. Sobdanchi videa.
Eucharist, *eu'-ca-rist,* N. Santism sacrament.
Euphonic, *iu'-fon-ic,* A. Boro vaztolo.
Euphony, *eu'-fo-ni,* N. Borem vazop.
Evacuate, *e vac'-u-eitt,* V. Khali corunc; soddunc.
Evacuation, *e-vak'-u-ci-xion,* N. Khali corop, soddni.
Evade, *i-veid',* V. Chucounc, pollounc-
Evanescent, *e-van-es'-ent,* A. Nopoinch zauncho; fg. Khali, fottkiro.
Evangelical, *e-van-jel'-i-cal,* A. Evanjelan sicoil-lo.
Evangelist, *e-van-jel'-ist,* A. Evanjelist.
Evangelize, *e-van-jel'-aiz,* V. Evanjel porgot corunc.
Evaporate, *e-va'-po-reitt,* V. Baficaddunc ubounc. [nib.
Evasion, *e-vei'-jion,* N. Chucop;
Evasive, *i-ve'-ziv,* A. Chucouncho
Eve, *iv,* N. Adlo dis.
Even, *i'-oon,* A. Telto; sarco; fg. nidan.
Even, Ad, legun, soit poriaut.
Evening, *e-vn'-ing,* N. Sanz.
Evenness, *i-vn'ness,* N. Telteponn; nidanai.
Event, *i-vent',* N. Goddop; xevott.
Eventual, *e-vent'-u-al,* A. Xekim.
Ever, *ev'-ar,* Ad. Sodanch.
Everlasting, *ev-er-last'-ing,* A. Sasuancho.

Evermore, (for). Ad. Sodanch.
Every, *ev-ri′*, A. Zonn-eiclo; eoc-eoc; cosoloi.
Everybody, *ev′-ri-bo-di*, N. Conn-uim munis; eo-ieclo.
Everyday, *ev′-ri-dei*, Ad. Disandis.
Every-day, A. Dispoddto.
Every-thing, N. Sokott.
Every-way, N. Soglleam vatt-anim.
Everywhere, A. Sorvoi suatar.
Evidence, *ev-i-dens′*, N. Gõvai; ruzvat.
Evident, *ev′-i-dent*, A. Ugtto, ugddapo, thavo, safh
Evidently, *e-vi′-dent-li*; Ad. Ugddapim, deool, zaun; safh.
Evil, *i′-vil*, N. Vaitt, vign; khotto.
Evil-doer, *i′-vil-do-ar*, N. Vaitt cornar.
Evil-minded, *i′-vil-main-ded*, A. Mosor cornar.
Evil-speaking, *evil-spiik′-ing*, N. Chaddieo sangnnem; galli.
Evince, *e-vins′*, V. Sostt corunc; dacounc. [vorunc.
Evoke, *i-vok′*, V. Apounc; apoun
Evolve, *i-volv′*, V. Soddounc.
Ewe, *iu′*, N. Bokri.
Exact, *egz-akt′*, V. Soten magunc; formaunc.
Exact, A. Sarco, borobor.
Exaction, *egz-ac′-xion*, N. Khoch-khochit ukallo; nigutai, hiemot.
Exactly, *egz-akt-li,′* Ad. Borobor, sarkem.
Exactness, *egz-akt-ness*, N. Zagrutai.
Exaggerate, *egz-aj′-e-reitt*, V. Choddounc, vodio corunc; fg. Gopam sangunc.
Exaggeration, *egz′-aj-e-rei-xion*, N. Choddoun; fg. gop.
Exalt, *egz′-olt*, V. Vorto corunc, ubarunc, man diunc, taril corunc.

Exaltation, *egz′-olt-ei′-xion*, N. Vortepon; man, ucol, ucollni.
Examination, *egz-am-in-ei′-xion*, N. Poricxa; doriaf; ugddas.
Examine, *egz-am′in*, V. Poricxa—vichar—, corunc; doriaf corunc; polleunc.
Examiner, *egz-am′-in-ar*, N. Polletolo, poricxa getolo.
Exceedingly, *ek-sid′-ing-li*, Ad. Bhou vo bhou chodd.
Excel, *ek-sel′*, V. Ogllo—, vodio—, vorto zaunc.
Excellence, *ek′sel-lens*, N. Vorte-ponn; apurbhai, gunpragarsh.
thorai.
Excellent, *ek′sel-lent*, A. Uttim, zobor boro, nazuc, chokott.
Excellently, *eks′-el-lent-li*, Ad. Bhore bhaxen.
Except, *ek-sept′*, Prep. Sivai.
Exception, *ek-sep′xion*, N. Var-jannem; apavad.
Exceptional, *ek-sep′xion-al*, N. Aprup.
Excess, *ek-sess′*, N. Ogllepon, nosteponn, visesh; chuc.
Excessive, *ek-ces′-siv*, A. Chodd, vodio, ogllo.
Exchange, *eks-cheinj′*, V. Bod-lunc; vattaunc.
Exchange, N. Bodlop; vattau.
Exchequer, *eks-chek′er*, N. Kha-jinno.
Excise, *ek-saiz′*, N. Sunc.
Excitability, *ek-sai-ta-bi-li′tti*, N. Uchambollai, chalvuncho gun.
Excitable, *ek-sait′e-bl*, A. Zolsar; Tikott.
Excite, *ek-saitt′*, V. Uthaunc; tiddaunc; boll diunc.
Excitement, *ek-saitt′ment*, N. Uthauni, huskauni; chalvani, tiddoo.
Exclaim, *esk-claim′*, V. Ardduno, arattunc, arddun sangunc.

Exclamation, *eks-clam'ei-xion.* N. Arodd; aratt; bob.

Exclude, *eks-cliud',* V. Kherit caddunc; bhair galunc.

Exclusion, *eks-cliu'jion,* N. Bhair galop.

Exclusive, *ex-cliu'ziv,* A. Kherit; khaxa; mukhdi; eicsuro.

Exclusively, *eks-clu'ziv-li,* AD. Bhair dourun; kherit; bhair.

Excommunicate, *eks-com-miu'-ni'keitt,* V. Igorjentlo bhair galunc, excommungar corunc; zati bhair galunc.

Excommunication, *eks-com-miu'ni-kei''xion,* N. Excommunhaum.

Excrement, *eks'cre-ment,* N. Pozodd; gu.

Excrescence, *eks-cres'sens,* N. Dhung, khoddum, bukodd.

Excruciating, *eks-cru-shi-ei'-ting* A. Conttin; coisttancho; dogdauncho.

Exculpate, *eks-cul'peitt,* V. Bogsunc; niropradi corunc.

Exculpation, *eks-cul-pei'xion,* N. Bogsonnem.

Excursion, *eks-cur'xion* N. Pasoi, bounddi; sovari.

Excusable, *eks-kiuz'e-bl,* A. Bogsonnem favo to, maf corunc-eiso

Excuse, *eks-kiuz',* V. Maf corunc, bogsunc.

Excuse, N. Maf, bogsonnem; nib.

Execrable, *ek'se-cre-bl,* A. Sirapacho; khotteponhacho; khanttalleacho.

Execrate *ek-se'creitt,* V. Sirap galunc; bosttaunc. [Sirap.

Execration, *ek'se-crei'xion,* N.

Execute, *ek'se-kiutt,* V. Corunc, sompadunc.

Execution, *ek'se-kiu'xion,* N. Corni, sompaddni, mornachi sicxa.

Executioner, *ek-se-kiu'xion-ar,* N. Fasi galtolo.

Executive, *ez-ek'iut-iv,* A. Cortolo; nibor, khor, gunvontt.

Executor (of a will,) *egs-ek'iutt or,* N. Testamentac pallo ditolo,

Exemplar, *egz-em'lar,* N. Nomuno; dek.

Exemplary, *egz'em-pla-ri,* A. Dekivont.

Exemplify, *egz-em'pli-fai,* V. Daclo diunc.

Exempt, *egz-empt',* A. Viret.

Exempt, V. Rojea diunc; maf corunc; soddunc.

Exemption, *egz-em'xion,* N. Maf, suttca.

Exercise, *ekz'er-saiz,* N. Chalauni, cam, bounddi; caido; sonvoim.

Exercise, V. Cholounc; sonvoim corunc; poricxa coruno; kovat sicounc.

Exercised, *ekz'er-saizd,* A. Sonvoim aslolo.

Exercises, *ekz'er-sai-zis,* N. Vorsacho caido; niall.

Exert, *ekz'-art,* V. Govllavunc, rattunc; dacounc.

Exertion, *egz-ar'-zion,* N. Galavnni, rahatt.

Exhalation, *eks-hal-ei'xion,* N. Bafh; pormoll; ub; ghan.

Exhale, *egz-heil',* V. Bhair galunc; bhair sorunc.

Exhaust, *egz'ost,* V. Boll moddonc, puro zaunc; oscot corunc.

Exhausted, *egz-host'ed,* A. Puro zalolo, osoct.

Exhaustion, *egz-os'xion,* N Voddosoctai.

Exhibit, *egx-ib'-it,* V. Dacounc. dolleam mucar galunc.

Exhibition, *eks-i-bi'-xion,* N. Dakonn.

Exhilarate, *egz-hil'e-reitt,* V. Khoxal corunc.

Exhilaration, *egz-il-e-rei'xion*, N. Khoxalponn.

Exhort, *egz-hort'*, V. Bori bud diunc ; uttounc.

Exhortation, *eks-hor-tei'xion*, N. Bud ; sermaum.

Exigency, *eks-i'jen-si*, N. Goroz.

Exile, *egz-ail'*, N. Pordes.

Exile, V. Pordesac daddunc, goddpar coruno.

Exist, *egz-ist'*, V. Asonc.

Existence, *egz-ist'ens*, N. Asop ; jinn.

Existent, *egz-ist'-ent*, A. Jiouncho; atancho.

Exit, *eks'-it*, N. Bhair sorop ; osir pau-vatt.

Exonerate, *egz-on'-e-reitt*, V. Bogsunc ; caideantlo soddunc ; meclo-—, sutt zaunc.

Exorbitant, *egz-or'bi-tant*, A. Bhou chodd.

Exorcise, *eks'or-saiz*, V. Deuchar-—, pixem cadduuc.

Exordium, *egz-or'di-um*, N. Upaneas ; addavni, suru.

Exorteric, *eks-or-te',ric*. A. Porgott ; ugtto.

Exotic, *egz-ot'tic*, A. Bhailo.

Expand, *eks-pend'*, V. Vistarunc ; soddounc, fulounc.

Expansion, *eks-pen'xion*, N. Vistarop, fulni, ugollni.

Expatiate, *ex-pash-eitt'*, V. Lamb ulounc ; vistarun ulounc.

Expatriate, *eks-pa'tri-eitt*, V. Gavam-bhairo corunc; pordesani daddunc.

Expectation, *ek-spect'ei-xion*, N. Borvonso.

Expectorate, *eks-pec'to-reitt*, V. Oncunc, kancarun uddounc.

Expediency, *eks-pi'-di-en-si*. N. Kirop, huxarki : upai.

Expedient, *eks-pi-di-ent*, N Favo ; upcaracho.

Expedition, *eks-pe-di'-xion*, N. Daddni, pattounni (fouzichi).

Expel, *ex-pel'*, V. Bhair daddunc, nivraunc.

Expend, *ek-spend'*, V. Korchunc.

Expenditure, *eks-pend'ichar*, N. Khoroch, [Cust.

Expense, *ek-spens'*, N. Khoroch,

Expensive, *ek-spens'iv*, A. Marog, Khorchacho.

Experience, *eks-pi'-ri-ens*, N. Anbhog ; poricsha.

Experience, V. Sosunc, bhogunc ; poricsha corunc, siconc.

Experienced, *ex-pi-ri-ensd'*, A. Anbogi.

Experiment, *eks-pe'-ri-ment*, N. Poricsha, ajmas.

Expert, *eks-pert'*, A. Uxar : zantto.

Expiate, *eks-pi'-eilt*, V. Pirajit corunc, faricpon diunc.

Expiation, *eks-pi-ei'-xion*, N. Pirajit, faricponn.

Expiatory, *eks'-pi-a-to-ri*, A. Pirajitacho ; faricponnacho.

Expiration, *eks.pi-rei'-xion*, N. Usvas, fg. vaideacho xevott.

Expire, *eks-pai-ar'*, V. Morunc, pran soddunc.

Explain, *eks-plain'*, V. Orth sangunc, somzaunc.

Explanation, *eks-pla-nei'-xion*, N. Orth somjaoni.

Explicit, *eks-pli-sit'*, N. Ugddapo, decoll. safh,

Explicity, *ex-plis-it'-ti*, Ad. Ugddapem-—, decoll corun, safh.

Explode, *eks-plod'*, V. Far zaunc ; fg. sonsonunc.

Exploit, *eks-ploit'*, N. Vorti corni ; dhoiravont cortob.

Explore, *eks-plor'*, V. Sodunc, sodun cadduuc. sud genuc.

Explosion, *eks-plo'-jion*, N. Far.

Explosive, *eks-ploz'-iv*, A. Far zai sarco.

Export, *eks-port'*, V. Porganvac—, bailea ganvao (mal) daddunc.

Exportation, *eks-port-ei'-xion*, N. Porganvanc mal daddnem.

Expose, *ex-poz'*, V. Bhair dovorunc; ugtto galunc, dacounc; risker galunc,

Exposed, *eks-pozd'*, A. Dacoilolo; soddlelem burgem.

Exposition, *eks-po-zi'-xion*, N. Dacoun; sacramentachem besaum.

Expostulate, *eks-pos'-tu-leit*, V. xinnonc; guneauncar corunc.

Exposure, *eks-po'-jar*, N. Bhair dourop, ugttem dourop.

Expound, *eks-paund'*. N. somzaunc, orth sangunc.

Express, *eks-press'*, V. Pillunc; ucharunc; dacounc; ulounc.

Express, *eks-press,'* A. Safh. mudom pattoilolo.

Expression, *ek-pres'-xion*, N. Uchar; utor.

Expressive, *eks-pres-'iv*, A. Somzo sarco.

Expressly, *eks-pres'-li*, Ad. Mudom corun, khondit.

Expulsion, *eks-pol'-xion*, N. Bhair galop.

Expunge, *ek-sponj'*, V. Pusunc.

Expurgate, *eks-pur'-geit*, V. Nitoll—, nirmoll corunc.

Exquisite, *eks'kuvi-zit*, A. Uttim, najuc, ruchicho, suadic.

Exquisteness, *eks'-kuvi-zit-ness*, N. Najucai; vorteponn.

Extant, *eks'tant*, A. Urta to.

Extempore, *eks-tem'-po-re*, AD. Ecach fara; auchit.

Extend, *eks-tend'*, V. Vistarunc. lamb corunc; rundaunc.

Extension, *eks-ten'-sion*, N. Vistarop.

Extensive, *eks-ten'-siv*, A. Vistarlolo; chodd.

Extent, *eks-tent'*, N. Vistarop.

Extenuate, *eks-ten'-u-eitt*, V. Mafcorunc, lau corunc; boll moddunc.

Exterior, *eks-ti'-ri-or*, A. Bhailo.

Exterminate, *eks-ter'-min-eitt*, Ganva bhair galunc; fg. vibadd corunc.

Extermination, *eks-ter-min-eixion*, N. Nas; vibadd.

External, *eks-ter'-nal*, A. Bhailo;

Extinct, *ek-stingt'*, A. Palovlolo. moddlolo; caddlolo; nam zalolo; melolo.

Extinction, *ek-stingt'-xion*, N. Nas, bosm.

Extinguish, *ek-sting'-gwish*, V. Palounc.

Extinguisher, *ek-sting'-guish-er*, N. Palounchem aidon.

Extirpate, *eks-tirp'-eitt*, V. Mullan caddunc, umttunc; umblunc.

Extort, *eks-tort'*, V. Beneddaunbollan geunc.

Extortion, *eks-tor'-xion*, N. Zulum.

Extra, *eks'-tra*, N. Khusur; visesh.

Extract, *eks-tract'*, N. Kashai, kadho, nis.

Extraction, *eks-trac'-xion*, N. Kuttom; rogot.

Extraneous, *eks-tra'-ni-as*, A. Porgauncho.

Extraordinarily, *eks-tra-or'-dina'-ri-li*, AD. Chali bhair, bharim, zobor.

Extraordinary, *eks-tra-or'-di-na'-ri*, A. Chali bhailo, aprup.

Extravagance, *eks-trav'-a-gans*, N. Akram, kospai; pixeponn.

Extravagant, *eks-trav'-a-gant*, A. Chali bhailo, piso, vid laglolo.

Extreme, *eks--triim'*, A. Akercho. nimanno.

Extremity, *eks-trim'-i-ti*, N. Tonk, pont; xevott.

Extricate, *eks'-tri-keitt*, V. Soddounc; sarkem corunc.
Exuberance, *eks-u'-be-rans*, N. Sompurnai.
Exuberant, *eks-u'-be-rant*, A. Matlolo, fg. fuscoll.
Exult, *egz-olt'*, V. Sontos bognnc,
Exultation, *egz.al-tei'-xion*, N. N. Onond, suc.
Eye, *ai*, N. Dollo.
—(Brow), N. Askiddi.
—(Glass), N. Vocl.
—(Lid), N. Dolleachem dampnem.
—(Witness), N. Deololo govai.

F

Fable, *fe'bl*, N. Canni; vopar.
Fabric, *fa'bric*, N. Bandop; lugot, vostur.
Fabrication, *fa-bri-kei'xion*, N Fott; collpon.
Fabulous, *fa'bu-las*, A. Khoro noi; fottkiro; canniem sarco.
Face, *fe's*, N. Mucamboll; rup; tondd.
Face, V. Mucar ravunc, fudde vochunc.
Facetious, *fe-se'xias*, A. Chesttaecho, fakandi, gomti; lofango.
Facetiousness, *fa-se'xias-ness*, N. Gomot, fakand.
Facilitate, *fa-si-li-teitt'*, V. sompo corunc; hallu corunc; adin corunc.
Facility, *fa-si'li-tti*, N. Sompeponn; sovalponn; tank, cuvet.
Fac-simile, *fac-si'mi-le*, N. Sarki, borobor nocol.
Fact. *fect*, N. Zalelem cam vo goddleli vost.
—(Infact). khorench vo albot.
Faction, *fec'xion*, N. Mat, kutt, partid.
Factious, *fec'-xi-as*, A. Partidacho; uchamboll,
Factious, *fec-'xi'-as*, A. Chamatcaracho; icmoti.
Factor, *fec'ttor*, N. Dolal; bodli; carbari.
Factory, *fec'to-ri*, N. Kharcanno.
Faculty, *fac'ul-tti*, N. Podvi. socot.
Fade, *fei'd*, V, Suconc; bavonc;
Fag, *feg*. V. coisttaunc, minotin vauronc.
Fagot, *fe'got*, N. Moulli; bhoro.
Fail, *feil*, V. Chuconc; beporva corunc; fottounc; divallem caddunc; pirder zaunc.
--(Without), N. Chuconastanam.
Failure, *fei'li-ar*, N. Chuc; guneaum.
Fain, *fein*, adv. Zalear borem.
Faint, *fe'int*, A. Sonkirn; osoct.
—(Rmembrance), Matso ugddas.
Faint *fe'int*. V. Jintt marunc; gunvoll eunc; puro zaunc.
Faintness, *fe'int-nes*, N. Gunvoll, jintt; osoctai.
Fair, *fer*, A. Sobit, sundor; goro; gunnacho; nitivont; sumarso boro.
Fair, N. Shant; jatra.
Fairness, *fer'ness*, N. Sobitai; sobai, sundorai, nit.
Faith, *feith*, N. Bavarth; patien ni; xastr.
Faithful, *feith'ful*, A. Bavarthi; patienuicho.
Faithfulness, *feith'fuln-ess*, N. Visvasponn, patienni.
Fakeer, *fakir'*, N. Fokir.
Falcon, *fal-cou'*, N. Giddgo.
Fall, *fo'l*, V. Poddonc; denvunc; vibadd zaunc; moddonc.
—(Away), kusin soronc; baric zaunc. bhagonc.
—(Back), patti eunc.
—(Foul of), addlonc; galli sangonc.
—(Headlong), vompto poddonc

—(Into), vaunc.
—(In with) melluuc; mandunc.
—(Off), nisronc; padd zaunc; poddonc.
—(On), angar poddonc.
—(Out), zaunc, vo goddonc; zogddonc.
—(Short), chuconc; unno zaunc.
—(Sick), vaittant poddonc.
Fall-under, V. Khala poddonc
—(Among robbers), choram modem poddonc.
Fall, N. Poddop; dennni; vibadd.
Fallacious, *fal-lei'shas*, A. Fottkiro.
Fallacy, *fal-la'si*, N. Chuc; bigoddni.
Fallibility, *fal-li-bi'-li-tti*, N. Chucho gunn.
Fallible, *fal-li'bl*, A. Chuco sarco; zait nam zait tosolo.
Falling, *foll'ing*, A. Poddta tosolo.
Falling off, N. Lodolni; revolusaum.
Fallow, *fall'ow*, A Camais keleli zomin.
False, *fols*, A. Fottkiro; khoro noi; lottic.
Falsehood, *fols'-hud*, A. Fott.
Falsify, *foll si'-fai*, V. Bodol corunc: fottkiro corunc.
—(Money), fottkire duddu corunc.
Falter, *fol'ttor*, V. Gageunc; ravun-ravunc ulounc.
Fame, *fem*, N. Kirti, fam; khobor.
Familiar, *fa-mi'liar*, A. Gorcho; goravo; chodd volloc aslolo.
Familiarity, *fa-mi-li-a'ri-ti*, N. ennem-vochnem; voivatt; salzi.
Family, *fe'mi-li*, N. Famil, gorchim munxeam; bail-burgim.
Family-name=Alcunh.
Famine, *fe'min*, N. Ducoll; margai,
Famous, *fei'mas*, A. Navaddiç: kirtivont.
Fan, *fen*, N. Aino.
Fanatic, *fa'na-tic*, A. Dhorm piso; devpiso.
Fanaticism, *fana-ti'si-zam*, N. Devpisai; dhorm pixem.
Fanciful, *fen'si-ful*, A. Fontazicho; sopneta tosolo.
Fancy, *fen'si*, N. Chintna; kolponn; pixeponn.
Fancy, V. Chintunc; somzunc.
Fantastic, *fan-tas'tic*, N. Fontojicar. [kiro.
Fantastic, A. kolponnecho: fottkiro.
Far, *far*, AD. Pois.
—(As far as), Poriant.
—(So far), Titlem.
—(How far). Kitlem.
Fare, *fer*, N. Khun; mol.
Farewell, *fer'vel*, N. Deu borem corum.
Farm, *far'm*, N. Zomin; asti; set.
Farm, V. Set vosounc; gorvam posunc anim setcamot corunc.
Farmer, *far'mor*, N. Setcamti. buincar.
Farther, *far'-dor*, AD. Mucar; fudde.
Farthing, *far'ding*, N. Inglez mor aunnar poiseache kimtichi.
Fascinate, *fa'ci-neitt*, V. Bul galunc; montrunc; pisaunc.
Fascination, *fas-ci-nei'shon*, N. Bul; bulvonn: montr; voddni.
Fascine, *fas-sin'*, N. Moulli: bhoro.
Fashion, *fesh'ion*, N. Mod: sovoim.
Fashion, V. Rup diunc.
Fast, *fast*, A. Gott; thir.
—AD. Gott zaun.
—V. Jinzvar dorunc.
Fasten, *fas'sen*, V. Gott corunc; bandunc.
Fastening, *fas'sen-ing*, N. Bandop; bandpas.

Fastidious, *fas-ti'di-as*, A. Bejar zai sarco; korcori; nazuc.
Fastidiousness, *fas-ti'di-as-ness*, N. Bejar zavop; korcor; nazneai.
Fasting, *fas'ting*, N. Upas; jinzvar.
Fasting, A. Upasi; jeunc khaunc naslolo.
Fat, *fett*, N. Vos; chorob.
Fat, A. Motto; pustti.
Fatal, *fei'ttal*, N. Daivacho; jivcaddcho; bhou lusconacho.
Fatalism, *fei'tta-lizm*, N. Daivvad; acant.
Fate, *fei'th*, N. Odrustt.
Father, *fa'dor*, N. Bapui; pai; bap.
Father-in-law, N. Maum.
Fathom, *fe'dom*, V. Kholai mezunc.
Fathom. *fe'dom*, N. Kholai; kôr.
Fathomless, *fe'dom-less*, A. Kor naslolo
Fatigue, *fa-tig'*, V. Puro corunc vo zaunc.
Fatigued, *fa tig'dd*, A. Puro zalole; cansad.
Fatness, *fet-ness'*, N. Mottai.
Fatten, *fe tton'*: V. Motto corunc.
Fatuity, *fa-tu'i tti*. N. Pixeponn.
Fault, *fol'tt*, N Chuc; guneaum.
Faultless, *foll'tt-less*, N. Guneaunva vinn; vo guneaum naslolo.
Faulty, *foll'tti*, N. guneuncar.
Favour, *fei'vor*, N. Upcar; mog; doia, adar.
—(In favour of), Khatir vo vinot
Favour, V. Upcar corunc; doia corunc.
Favourable, *fei-vo-rei'bl*, A. Adavacho; gunnacho; doiall.
Favourite, *fei'vo-rit*, A. Mogall.
Fawn, *fo'n*, V. Fusllaunc; pattlean vochonc.
Fear, *fi'er*, N. Bhem; bhirant.
Fear, V. Bhieunc; camponc.
Fearful, *fi'er-ful*, A. Bhiraneul; bhiranticho; bezudd.
Fearfulness, *fi'er-ful-ness*, N. Bhirant; camp.
Fearless, *fi'er-less*, A. Bhirant naslolo.
Fearlessness, *fi'-er-less-ness*, N. Bhirant nasnem; nirvonn.
Feast, *fii'st*, N. Fest; porob.
Feather, *fe'dor*, N. Pac.
Feathered, *fe-dor'dd*, A. Pacam aslolo vo pacam futtlolo.
Feature, *fi'char*, N. Rup; tondd; sarkem; gunn.
Feculence, *fe'cu-lens*, N. Chicol; bursepon.
Feculent, *fe'cu-lent*, A. Chiclacho; burso.
Federal, *fe'de-ral*, A. Caracho; Katteacho.
Fee, *fii'*, N. Fi; pag; dondd.
Feeble, *fii'bl*, A. Osoct, frac; sonkirn.
Feebleness, *fii'bl-ness*, N. Osoctai; bolaiki nasnem.
Feed, *fii'd*, V. Posnuc; khavounc; jeunc; fg. udoc dinnc.
Feel, *fii'l*, V. Bogunc; apoddonc; hat launc; sosunc.
—(Glad), sontcs bogunc.
Feeler, (of an insect) *fii'lar*, N. Misio.
Feeling, *fii'ling*, N. Bogop; voddni; munxeponn; somzoni.
Feign, *fe'in*, V. Bolliam oorunc; fottounc.
—(Tears), fottkirim ducam gollounc.
Feigning, *fei'ning*, N. Bolliam corop; fotvon.
Feint. *fe'int*, N. Copott.
Felicitation, *fe'li-ci-tei-shon*, N. Dhinvas; parbem.
Fell, *fell'*, V. Catrun galnnc.
Fell, N. Pervot; cat.

Fellow, *fell'o*, N. Sangati; sando vo membr; munis; lucho.
Fellowship, *fell'ou-ship*, N. Sangat; isttogot.
Female, *fi'meil*, N. Bai! munis.
Feminine (gender), A. Bailancho.
Fence, *fens*, N. Addo; voddop.
Fence, V. Voddop bandunc; addo galunc.
Fennel, *fen'nel*, N. Boddishep.
Ferment, *for'ment*, N. Fug; fg. umallo; uchambollai.
Ferment, V. fg. sizounc.
Fermentation, *for-men-tei'-shon*, N. Fug.
Ferocious, *fe-rou'xi-as*, A. Nistur; cacut naslolo; khotteponnacho.
Ferocity, *fe-ro'si-tti*, N. Nisttnrai; khotteponn.
Ferret, *fer'ret*, V. Bhair caddunc.
Ferruginous, *fer-ru'ji-nas*, a loconddi, locondd aslolo.
Ferrule, *fer'rul*, N. Anos.
Ferry, *fer'ri*, N. Tar.
Ferry-boat, *fe'ri-bott*, N. Tarichem voddem.
Ferry-man, N. Tarcar.
Fertile, *for'ttai-l*, A. Picacho; folladic.
Fertility, *for'tti-li-tti*, N. Suffollai; picaveponn.
Fervent, *fer'vent*, A Suddsuddaecho; urbevont.
Fervently, *fer'vant-li*, Ad. Suddsuddaen; axen; umallean.
Fervour, *fer'vor*, N. Khottkoto; umallo; axea.
Festival, *fes'ti-val*, N. Festacho; Porbecho dis.
Festive, *fes'tiv*, A Festacho; onodacho. [porob.
Festivity, *fes'ti-vi-tti*, N. Fest;
Festoon, *fes'tun*, N. Fulam.
Fetch, *fech*, V. Apoun addunc: vochon geun eunc.
—(A sigh), V. suscar soddunc.
Fetid, *fetid*, A. Gannero; voncareacho.
Fetter, *fe'ttor*, N. Sancli; Khoddo.
Fetter, V. Khoddo galunc; addaunc.
Fetus, *fe'tus*, N. Gorb.
Fever, *fi'var*, N. Zor, tap.
Feverish, *fi-ve'rish*, A. Zoracho; u.etso zor aslolo.
Few, *fiu*, A. Thodde.
Fibre, *fai'br*, N. Kato.
Fickle, *fic'l*, A. Thir naslolo; bodolcho.
Fickleness, *fic'cl-ness*, N. Doundollitponn; thir nasop.
Fiction, *fic'shon*, N. Kopott; canni; dhong.
Fictitious, *fic-ti-xi'as*, A. Kolponnacho; dhongi.
Fiddle, *fi'dl*, N. Rebec.
Fiddlestring, N. Cordam.
Fidelity, *fai-de'li-tti*, N. Patienni. visvas; khoreponn. [liacho;
Fiduciary, *fi-du'sia ri*, N. Hava-
Fie, *fai'*, INT. Ohi.
Field, *fiild*, N. Set; moidan.
Field-marshal, N. Mukia adepoti.
Fiend, *fi'end*, N. Bhut, denchar.
Fierce, *fi'ers*, A. Bhou ragist; nisttur, ranvott.
Fierceness, *fi'ers-ness*, N. Nisttnrai; mharuponn; ranvotponn.
Fiery, *fa'-ia-ri*, A. Ujeacho; uchamboll.
Fife, *faif*, N. Pirluc.
Fig, *fig*, N. Anjir; runbod.
Fight, *faith*, V. Zogd'd nc; zuzonc.
Fighting, *fai'thing*, N. Zuz, loddai; zogddem.
Figure, *fi'gor*, N. Akar; rup; pintur; rupnem.
Figure, V. Chintunc.
Figurative, *fi-gr-ra'tic*, A. Khunacho; upam.

Filch, *filch',* v. Gupteam chorune.
File, *fail',* N. Soldadanchi ar; potti; çanos.
File, V. Arin gal: cansin gansune; fg. nitoll corune.
Filial, *fi'li-al,* A. Burgeacho; putracho.
Filings, *fai'lings,* N. Charo; pudd.
Fill, *fill,* V. Borune.
Filled, *fill'd,* A. Borlolo; dadosi.
Filter, *fill'ttor,* V. Gallune.
Filter, N. Gauchem aidon.
Filth, *filth',* N. Coir: mhell; bursepoun.
Filthy, *fil'di,* A. Mhello; olisic; burso.
Fin, *fin',* N. Shempatto.
Final, *fai'nal,* A. Akercho; nimanno.
Finally, *fai'na-lli,* AD. Xekim; sevtim.
Finance, *fai'nans,* N. Rajvosul; jamavosul.
Find, *faind,* N. Mellune: sicone; bogune; disone.
(Fault), Guneauñcari corune.
—(By experience), Onbogune.
—(Out), Sodun caddune.
Fine, *fain',* A. Baric; nazuc: sobit; boro; moladic.
Fine, N. Siesha; dondd.
Fineness, *fai'n-ness,* N. Barcai: nazucai.
Finger, *fing'or,* N. Bott.
Finish, *fi'nish,* V. Cobar corune: thambune: sompadune; ontrone.
Finite, *fai'nailt,* A. Xevott aslolo: khondit.
Fire, *fa'iar,* N. Uzo; far; FG. boll; suddsnddai.
Fire-box, N. njeachi pett.
(Brand), N. Colit.
—(Fly), Cazulo.
—(Lock), Bonduc.
—(Pan), Cail.
Firewood, *fa'iar-vud,* V. Lancudd; khanttiam.
Fire-work, N. Fog.
Firm, *for'm,* A. Gott; alonaslolo; thir.
Firmament, *for'ma-ment,* N. mollob.
Firmly, *for'm-li,* AD. Gott zaun; thir zaun.
Firmness, *for'm-ness,* N. Boll; gottai; thirasonn.
First, *for'st,* A. Poilo; mukeli.
First-born, A. Malgoddo; poilo zolmotolo.
Fiscal, *fis'cal,* N. Vosuldarpoun, sercari khajino.
Fish, *fish,* N. Maslli; nistem.
Fish, V. Maslli dorune vo pagune, gorounc fg. sarkem corun sodune.
Fisherman, *fish'er-men,* N. Kharvi.
Fish-hook, N. Gori. [gop.
Fishing, *fish'ing,* N. Maslli pa-
Fist, *fist,* N. Mutt.
Fit, *fit,* N. Boll; fors.
Fit, A. Mona zocto; zantto.
Fit, V. Mandone; galune; laik corune; toiar corune.
Fitness, *fit'ness,* N. Laikponn.
Five, *fai'r,* A. Panch.
Fix, *fix',* V. Lagoune: gott corune; corar corune; khonchoune.
Fixed, *fix'd,* A. Nomiarlolo: khondit.
Flabby, *fleb'bi,* A. Soddill.
Flag, *fleg,* N. Bonder; gieaum; bautto.
Flag, V. Baune; unno zaune.
Flagellate, *fla'je-lleitt,* V. Jerbondanim marune.
Flagellation, *fla-je-llei'shon,* N. Jerbondache mar.
Flaggy, *fleg'gi,* A. Bagouncho; osoet.

Flagrant, *fla'grant,* A. Khotto.
Flag-staff, N. Bantuo katti.
Flambeau, *flam-bo',* N. Diutti; uzvaddi.
Flame, *flei'm,* N. Ujeachem kendd; agttom.
Flannel, *fla'nel,* N. Flanel.
Flap, *flep,* V. Fapuddunc.
Flash, *flesh,* N. Porzoll.
Flash, V. Porzollunc.
Flask, *flask,* N. Kodrad botl vo siso.
Flat, *flett,* A. Sountoll; fg. ruch naslolo
Flat, N. Sountoll suvat; malloi.
Flatter, *fle'ttor,* V. Fuslaunc; bulounc.
(Oneself), Axea dorunc.
Flatterer, *fle'tte-rar,* N. Fuslaitolo: fottkiro.
Flattery, *fle'tto-ri,* N. Fuslaunnem.
Flatulence, *fla'tu-lens,* N. Vai.
Flaunt, *flau'nt,* V. Bounc; ubonc.
Flavour, *flei'vor,* N. Suad; ruch.
Flaw, *flo,* N. Aib: chuc.
Flawless, *flo'less,* A. Aib-naslolo.
Flax, *flex,* N. Sonn.
Flay, *flei,* V. Cat vo chambddem voddunc.
Flea, *fli,* N. Chiru; uloc.
Fledged, *flejd',* A. Pakam futtlolo.
Flee, *fli',* V. Pollonc; danvunc; chucounc.
Fleer, *fli'er,* N. Chesttai: beneddannem.
Fleet, *fliit,* N Tarvam.
Flesh, *flesh,* N. Mas; fg. Cudd.
Fleshy, *flesh'i,* A. Masall.
Flexibility, *flex-i-bi'li-tti,* N. Bagou sarkem; soddilai.
Flexible, *flex'i-bl,* A. Bagonta tosolo; soddil.
Flicker, *flick'ar,* V. Pacam alounc: ubonc
Flight, *flaight,* N. Pollop; danvop.
Flimsiness, *flim-si'ness,* N. Barcai; pattolai.
Flimsy, *flim'si,* A. Baric; pattol; osoct.
Flinch, *flinch,* V. Patti soronc.
Fling, *fling,* V. Uddounc.
Flint, *flint,* V. Pakonni, fator.
Flirt, *fl'ort,* V. Alounc; Uddounc.
Flit, *flit,* V Bounc; ubonc.
Float, *flo'tt* V ufeunc; ubonc; umcollonc.
Flock, *floc,* N. Hind; kensachi jil.
Flog *flog,* V. Marunc; boddounc.
Flogging, *flog'ing,* N. Mar.
Flood, *flod,* N. Aunr; buddti.
Floor, *flor,* N. Dorn; malloi.
Flora, *flo'ra,* N. Fulam.
Florid, *flo'rid,* A. Tamso. tambdoch.
Flour, *fla'or,* N. Pitt.
Flourish, *flo'rish,* V. Fulanim borunc; fulonc, fg. nondoncvosonc.
Flow, *flo',* V. Vaunc; soddil zaun umcollonc.
Flower, *flau'or,* N. Ful, fg. surungar.
Fluctuate, *floc'chu-eitt,* V. Ennem-tennem alonc, dubau voronc ;ufeunc.
Fluency, *flu'en-si,* N. Vavponn; fg jibechi haluvai
Fluent, *flu'ent,* A. Vaito; fg. zapsali; laiar.
Fluently, *flu'ent-li,* Ad. soddsod, dil, chorchorit.
Fluid, *flu'id,* A. Vaunto.
Fluid, N. Vavti vost.
Flute, *fliut',* N. Flaut; pirluc.
Flutter, *flott'or,* V. Ennem-tennem ubonc; fg. simpddaunc
Flux *flocks',* N. Varop, vavonn.
Fly, *flai,* N. Mus.
Fly, V. Ubonc.

Foal, *fol*, N. Goddeachem pil.
Foam, *fom*, V. Fenno.
Foam, F. Fenno eunc.
Fob, *fob*, V. Dacttem bols.
Fodder, *fodd'or*, N. Gorvanchem khan ; chorou.
Fodder, V. Chorounc ; posnnc.
Foe, *fo*, N. Dusman.
Fog, *fog*, N. Duunri ; calloc.
Foggy, *fo'gi*, A. Duunrecho.
Foh, *foh*, INT. Shi.
Foible, *foi'bl*, N. Aib.
Foil, *foil*, N. Domos-nasleli torvar.
Foist, *foist*, V. Choriam vo adicar nastanam kiteim vodic borounc.
Fold, *foldd*, N. Gotto.
— (Of a garment) miri; goddi.
Fold, V. Goddi corunc ; doddunc.
Foliage, *fo'li.ej*, N. Palo ; kholieo.
Follow, *fol'o*, V. Pattlean vochunc ; patlau corunc ; dek geunc.
—(advice), aicunc.
—(an opinion), raji zaun
—(on), thir ravonc.
Follower, *foll'o-ar*, N. Xins ; mandtolo ; pattlan cornar.
Following *foll' o-ing*, N. Pattlan.
Following, A. Dusro ; euncho.
Folly, *foll'i*, N. Pixeponn.
Foment, *fo-ment'*, V. Xekunc ; fg. uchamboll corunc ; uscaunc.
Fomentation, *fo ment-ei'shon*, N. Xecnni, xec.
Fond, *fond*, A. Piso ; mogall ; modur.
Fondle, *fon'dl*, V. Apurbai, priti corunc ; laleunc.
Fondness. *fond'nes*, N. Apurbai.
Font. *font'*, N. Jar ; font.
Food, *fu'dd*, N. Khan ; jevonn ; gras.
Fool, *fu'l*, A. Piso : bud-naslolo.
Foolish, *ful'ish*, A. Pixea sarco.
Foolishness, *ful'ish-ness*, N. Pixeponn.
Foot, *futt'*, N. Paim ; zoc 12 inch.
—(on foot), pai vatten.
Foot-bath, N. Paim xekop.
Footing, *futt'ing*, N. Gott tharo ; fg. acar.
Foot-man, *futt'men*, N. Gorcho chacor vo sipai-
Footpath N. Osir vatt ; pai-vatt.
Footstep, *futt'step*, N. Panvol ; paianchi khuna.
Footstool, *futt'stul*, N. Monnoi ; bankin.
Fop, *fop*, N. Danddi; polkist.
For, *for'*, PREP. Pasun vo pasot ; khatir; vorvim; pormonnem.
For, CONJ. Kiteac ; decun.
Forage, *fo'reij*, V. Goddeanc khan diunc.
Forage, N. Khan.
Forbear, *for'ber*, V. Xinnonam zaunc ; soddunc.
Forbearance, *for-ber'ens*, N, Sosnicai.
Forbid, *for-bid'*, V. Addvarunc; formaunc.
Forbidden, *for-bidd'n*, A. Addvarlolo.
Force, *fors'*, N. Boll; socot ; zulum: fouz.
Force, V. Boll corunc; corunc launc; zulmen rigonc.
Forcible, *fors'i-bl*, A. Bollan kelolo.
Forcibly, *fors'i-bli*, AD. Bollan.
Ford, *ford*, V. Utva udcantlean cholon vochunc.
Ford, N. Uttou udoc nodint vo era zagear zantlean cholun vochuet.
Fore, *for'*, AD. Mucavelo; adlo.
Fore-arm, *for-arm'*, V. Adim. toiar corunc.
Forebode, *for-bodd'*, V. Adinch sangonc; dacounc; collounc.

Forefather, *for-fa'dor*, N. Purvoz; voddil.
Forefend, *for-fend'*, V. Mona corunc; addvarunc.
Forego, *for-go'*, V. Soddunc.
Forehead, *for'hed*, N. Copal.
Foreign, *fo'rin*, A. Porco; bhailo; atvea gauncho.
Foreigner, *fo'rin-ar*, N. Pordesi; bhailea gauncho; porco
Foreknow, *for-now'*, V. Adinch zanno zaunc.
Foremost, *for'most*, A. Poilo; mucavelo.
Forenoon, *for'nun*, N. Donparam adim; socallim.
Foreordain, *for-or-dain'*, V. Adinch vinchun caddunc.
Fore-runner, *far'ran-ar*, N. mucar vecho munis.
Forsee, *for-si'*, V. Adim vollconc vo polleunc.
Foresight, *for'sait*, N. Barcai; mucaveli volloc.
Forest, *fo'rest*, Dronnem; ran.
Forestall, *for-stoll'*, V. Adim victem geunc.
Forester, *fo'res ttor*, N. Ran racnar.
Foretaste, *for'teist*, N. Ruch.
Foretell, *for-tell'*, V. Adim sangonc.
Forfeit, *for'fitt*, N. Guneannva udexim pirder zavop; dondd; hogddaunnem.
Forfeit, V. Dondd faric corunc; chuconnc; hogddaunc.
Forefeiture, *for'fi-char*, N. Hogddaunnem.
Forge, *forj*, N. Vinnaneachi sall.
Forge, V. Corunc vo goddunc; fottkiri asinad corunc.
Forger, *forj'or*, N. Fottkiri asinad cornar.
Forgery, *forj'e-ri*, N. Fottkiri asinad; fottkiro document.
Forget, *for-get'*, V. Visronc; ugddas nasonc.
Forgetful, *for-get'ful*, A. Ugddas naslolo.
Forgetfulness, *for-get'ful-ness*, N. Visor.
Forgive, *for-giv'*, V. Bogsunc; maf corunc.
Forgiveness, *for-giv'ness*, N. Bogsonnem.
Fork, *forc*, N. Garf.
Forlorn, *for-lorn'*, A. Vatter poddlolo; sanddlolo; upai naslolo; kircoll.
Form, *form*, N. Rup; rit; jinos.
Form, V. Corunc; manddunc; chintunc.
Formal, *form'al*, A. Riti pormonnem; bhailea bhair.
Formally, *form'al-li*, AD. Sarkench.
Formation, *form-ei'shon*, N. Corop; goddop.
Former, *form'or*, A. Poilo; adim aslolo.
Formerly, *form'or-li*, AD. Adim; purvim.
Formidable, *for'mi-de-bl*, A. Bhiyaneul; thortoreancho.
Formless, *form'less*, A. Rup vo soia naslolo.
Formula, *for'mu-la*, N. Rit; dostur; nomunno.
Formulary, *form'u-la-ri*, N. Riticho mêll; vidhan mala.
Fornicate, *for'ni-keitt*, V. Vebichar corunc.
Fornication, *for-ni-kei'shon*, N. Vebichar.
Fornicator, *for'ni-kei-ttor*, N. Vebichari.
Forsake, *for-seik'*, V. Soddunc; sanddunc; ubot galunc.
Forsooth, *for-suth'*, AD. Khorench; albot.
Forswear, *for-suer'*, V. Juramenta khal soddunc; fals jurar zaunc.

Fort, *fort*, N. Cott.
Forth, *forth*, AD. Bhair; than.
Forthcoming, *forth-com'ing*, A. Euncho; discho.
Forthwith, *forth-with'*, AD. Atanch; callau corinastanam.
Fortification. *for-ti-fi-kei'shon*, N. Cott: vonott; gottai.
Fortify, *for'ti-fai*, V. gott corunc: boll diunc.
Fortitude, *for'ti-ttiud*, N. Gottai; boll; dhir.
Fortnight. *fort'naitt*, N. Don sumanam.
Fortress, *fort'res*, N. Cott; dusmanauc addaunchem ghor.
Fortuitous, *for'tu'i-tas*, A. Anchit; sabsubo.
Fortunate, *for'chu-neitt*, A Feliz; sukhi; bhagi.
Fortunately, *for'chu-neitt-li*, AD. Borea noxiban.
Fortune, *for'chun*, N. Furtun: nosib; odrustt; bhag.
Fortune-teller, *for'chun-tell-ar*, N. gaddi; fudde zauncheo asleleo vostu sangnar.
Forum, *fo'rum*, N. Cacheri: tribunal.
Forward, *for'vard*, AD Mucar.
Eorward, A. Adim euncho: calljevont.
Forward, V. Daddunc; mozot corunc; voir caddunc.
Forwardness, *far'vard-ness*, AD. Rocddeponn; suddsuddai; uxari'
Fossil, *fos'sil*, N. Konddleli vost.
Foster, *fos'-thor*, V. Samball corunc; voir caddunc; posunc.
Foster-father, *fos'-ttor-fa'dor*, N. Posco-pai.
Foster-mother. *fos'-ttor-mo-dor'*, N. Poski-avoi.
Foul, *faul*, V. Mello corunc; mellounc; khotaunc.
Foul, A. Mello: khot aslolo; vittecho.
Foulness, *faul'-ness*, N. Mêll. mellepona.
Found. *faund*, V. Giddunc, baudunc.
Foundation, *faund-ei'shon*, N. Bunbad; mull
Founder, *faund'or*, N. Goddnar.
Fountain, *faunt'ein*, N. Zhor; fg. mull; oromb.
Four, *for*,' A. Char.
Fourfold, *for'fold*, A. Char pautti chodd.
Fowl, *faul'*, N. Suknnem; combi, vo pil.
Fowler, *faul'ar*, N. Sicari, Casador.
Fox, *fox*, N Colo.
Fraction. *frak'shen*, N. Cuddeo; bag, vantto
Fracture. *frek'char*, N. Moddop.
Fragile, *fra'jail*, A. Moddsar; Oseet.
Fragility, *fra-gil-i'tti*, N. Moddo sarkem.
Fragmet. *freg'men't*, N. Cuddeo.
Fragrance, *fra'grans*, N. Pormoll; suad.
Fragrant. *fra'grant*, A, Suadic; pormollacho.
Frail, *freil'*, A. Moddo-sarco; oscet.
Frailty, *frail'-tti*, N, Osoetai.
Frame, *frem*, N. Choue, rup: sobai.
Frame, V. Manddune; poson corunc; goddunc: choue corunc.
Frame-work, *frem'vork*, N. Choue.
Franchise, *fran'chaiz*, N. Vot; sotea votar corcheac:
Frank, *frenk'*, N. Addcoll naslolo; ugtto; nirmoll, nivoll; sado.
Frankincense *frenk'in-sens*, N. Pormollacho dhump.
Frankness, *frenk'ness*, N. Nirvonn; nenttuvi; sadem mon.

Frantic, *fren'tic*, A. Vid laglolo; piso; uchamboll.
Fraternal, *fra-ter'nal*, A. Bavancho, bauponnacho.
Fraternity, *fra-ter'ni-tti*, N. Bauponn; baubondki.
Fratricide, *fra'tri-said*, N. Bavac marnem, bratrigat.
Fraud, *frodd*, N. Lobaddi, nadd, thokbaji.
Fraudulent, *frod'u-lent*, A. Lobaddicho, naddicho, lobadd.
Fray, *frei*, N. Zogddem.
Freak, *frik*, N. Morji.
Freckle, *frek'l*, N. Ouduvi cat.
Free, *fri*, A. Sotecho; bandinaslolo; fmcott; ngtto.
Free, V. Soddunc; suttea diunc.
Free-booter, *fri bu'ttor*, N. Chor.
Free-booting, *fri-but'ing*, N. Chori.
Freedman. *frid'men*, N. Suttea meullolo munis.
Freedom, *fri'dom*, N. Suttea; sotea.
Freehold, *fri'hold*, N. Vorg; svantacho zago.
Freeholder, *fri'hold-ar*, N. Vorgadar.
Freely, *fri'li*, AD. addcoll nastanam; khoxen; borea monan.
Freeman, *fri'men*, N. Aplo sotecho munis.
Freewill, *fri'will*, N. Sotea; khaxa khoxi.
Freeze, *friiz'*, V. Core zomonc; thonddan gott zaunc.
Freight, *freit,h* N. nor; gaddiechem vo vaporachem baddem.
French. *french* N. A. Francez.
Frenzy, *fren'zi*, N. Pixeponn; ragachem pixeponn.
Frequency, *fri'kuen-si*, N. Ennem vochnem; chaliboli.
Frequent, *fri'kuent*, A. Goddie—goddiecho; bhou pautti zatalo.
Frequent, V. Sobar pautti vochonc.
Frequented, *fri-kuent'ed*, A. Euncho-vecho.
Frequently, *fri-kuent'li*, AD. Sobar pautti; goddie-goddie.
Fresh, *fresh*, A. Novo; baulolo noi; bolaikecho.
Freshen, *fresh'n*, V. Thond corunc; nivounc.
Fresh-man, *fresh'men*, N. Umedvar.
Freshness, *fresh'ness*, N. Jivall tazo-asnem.
Fret, *fret*, V. Chabun caddunc; fg. desunc; corcor corunc.
Fret, N. Corcor.
Fretful, *fret'ful*, A. Chavoulolo; ragist.
Friable, *fri'ie-bel*, A. Sompeponnim chenchi sarco.
Friar, *fri-ar'*, N. Frad.
Friction, *fric'shon*, N. Gansnem; gansop.
Friend, *frend'*, N. Istt; isttin; dost.
Friendless, *frend'less*, A. Istt naslolo; babddo.
Friendliness, *frend'li-ness*, N. Mogallponn; doia.
Friendly, *frend'li*, A. Mogall; doiall; gunnacho.
Friendship, *frend'ship*, N. Isttogot; dosti.
Fright, *fraitt*, N. Bhem; bhirant.
Frighten, *fraitt'un*, V. Beneddaunc; bhirant launc.
Frightful, *fraitt'ful*, A. Bhirancull.
Frigid, *fri'jid*, A. Thondd; fg. urba naslolo.
Frill, *frill*, N. Miric.
Fringe, *frinj*, N. Rend.
Frippery, *frip'e-ri*, N. Fallieo; chindieo.
Frisk, *frisk*, V. Nachonc; uddonc.

Frith, *frith*, N. Doriachi osirai.
Fritter, *fritt'ar*, N. Supurlo bazlolo cuddco kekacho vo masacho.
Fritter, V. Supurle cuddke catrune; khorchune.
Frivolity, *fri-vol'i-tti*, N. Pokllai; kircollai; cuscuti.
Frivolous, *fri'vol-as*, A. Bestto; poclo; olko; kircoll.
Frizzle, *friz'l*, V. Inni galunc.
Fro, (To And) Ennem-tennem.
Frock, *froc*, N. Kutaum; voilem angostr.
Frog, *frog*, N. Manko; manki.
Frolic, *fro'lic*, A. Khoxal; uddcho.
Frolic, N. Morji khell.
Frolic, V. Uddonc.
From, PREP. Than; poriant.
Front, *front*, N. Muc; poilo; fuddo; muro.
Front, V. Fuddo vo muro corunc.
Fronting, *front'ing*, N. Mucar.
Frontispiece, *fron'tis-pis*, N. Mucpotr; fuddo; muro.
Frost, *frost*, N. Core; gar.
Frosty, *frost'i*, N. Garacho vo thonddaecho.
Froth, *froth*, N. Fennom.
Froward, *fro'vard*, A. Aplea vadeacho; dharun; khalto noi.
Frown, *fraun*, V. Toudd vancddem corunc; copalac mirieo galunc. [zalolo.
Frozen, *froz'n*, P. A. Invan-datt
Frutification, *fruc'ti-fi-kei'xion*, N. Foll diunchem; foll.
Fructify, *fruc'ti-fai*, V. Folladic corunc.
Frugal, *fru'gal*, A. T h o d d e a khannacho; alpaboji.
Frugality, *fru-gal'i-tti*, N. Thoddem khan,—jevonn.
Fruit. *frutt*, N. Foll; frut.
Fruitful, *frutt'ful*, A. Folladic; sufoll.
Fruitfulness, *frutt'ful-ness*, N. Follaboritponn; togni; sufollai.
Fruitless, *frutt'less*, A. Foll dinaslolo; nirfoll.
Fruit-tree, N. Follanchem zadd.
Frustrate, *frus'treitt*, V. Fosounc; bigdhavunc; FG. nirfoll corunc.
Frustration, *frus-trai'xion*, N. Fosounni; bighdaunni; bhong.
Fry, *frai*, N. Zomo.
Fry, V. Bazunc.
Fry, N. Bazlelem khan.
Frying-pan, *frai'ing-pen*, N. Cail.
Fudge, *fuj*, INT. Chi.
Fuel, *fu'el*, N. Canttiam; zollo.
Fugitive, *fu'jit-iv*, A. Pollpotto; danvro.
Fulfil, *ful-fil'*, V. Pallunc; samballunc; sompounc.
Fulfilment, *ful-fil'ment*, N. Pallop; pallni.
Full, *full*, V. Lovenchem lugot daddaunc.
Full, A. Borlolo; puro; sompurn; dados.
Full-moon, *ful'mun*, N. Punov
Fully, *ful'li*, AD. Ecannem; sogloch; purto.
Fulminate, *ful'min-eitt*, V. zoglaunc.
Fulness, *ful'ness*, N. Bortiponn; sompurnai.
Fulsome, *ful'som*, A. Canttaleacho; kircoll.
Fumble, *fum'bl*, V. Sanspunc.
Fume, *fium*, N. Dunvor; ub; fg gormi.
Fume, V. Dunxor bhair sodounc; FG. ragar zaunc.
Fumigate, *fum'i-geitt*, V. Dunvor diunc; dumvraunc.
Fun, *fan*, V. Chesttai; facandd.
Function, *funk'xion*, N. Dando; caido; kam; socott; gunn.

Functionary, *funk'shon-a..i*, N. Kamdar; adicari.
Fund, *fund*, N. Bandvoll; banddar.
Fundamental, *fun-da-ment al*, A. Bunhadicho; mullacho.
Funeral, *fiu'ne-ral*, N Morn; purop; inter.
Funeral, A. Mornacho vo interracho.
Fungus, *fung'gus*, N. Aimbero.
Funnel, *fun'el*, N. Funel.
Funny, *fun'i*, A. Chesttaecho; anscho.
Fur, *fôr*, N. Loum; lonvenchem chambddem.
Furbish, *fur'bish*, V. Sullsullit corunc; gansunc.
Furious, *fiu'ri-as*, A. Ragist; piso; fg. rannot.
Furl, *forl*, Revoddunc; covllunc.
Furlong, *for'long*, Mailacho attvo vantto. [cens.
Furlough, *for'lo*, N. Rojea; li-
Furnace, *for'nes*, N, Khorn; agttem.
Furnish, *for'nish*, V. Diunc; toiar corunc; addun dinnc.
Furred, *farr'd*, PT. A. Lovenche vo loum aslolo.
Furniture, *for'ni-cher*, N. Samonn; gorvota.
Furrow, *fu'ro*, N. Vóro: chori.
Furrow, V. Cosunc; naugrunc.
Furrowed, *for'roud*, A. Mirieo poddlolo.
Further, *for'dor*, AD. Hea sivai; anim; mucar.
Further, V. Vaddounc.
Furtherance, *for'dor-ens*, N. Mozot; adar.
Fury, *fiu'ri*, N. Khuri; doddpadd; rag; tufan.
Fuss, *fass*, N. Bestto boball.
Future, *fiu'chur*, A. Euncho; fuddlo.
Future, N. Fuddar; fuddlo temp. —(In future), Fuddem.

G

Gabardine, *gab'ar-din*, N. Lambam hatanchem bandian.
Gabble, *gab'l*, V. Boddbodduuc; gozali marunc.
Gabbler, *gab'lar*, N. Boddboddo vo borboro.
Gabbling, *gab'ling*, N. Gozali.
Gad, *gad*, V. Parpoll bonvonc.
Gadder, *gadd'or*, N. Parpoll.
Gadfly, *gad'flai*, zollar.
Gag, *geg*, V. Thounddac chomddo marunc.
Gage, *geij*, V. Utor diunc; basannc; zamin dinnc.
Gaiety, *gei'e-ti*, N. Ulas, khoxalai; sontos.
Gaily, *gei'li*, Ad. Dadosponnan.
Gain, *gein*, N. Jicop; zodd; adau; lab; faido; nofa.
Gain, V. Jiconc, zoddunc.
Gainful, *gein'ful*, A. Adavacho; faideacho.
Gait, *geit*, N. Chal.
Gala, *gal'a* N. Peravo, nett, sungar; dobajo.
Galaxy, *ga'lak-si*, N. Dudavatt; to lamb fancarlolo marog mol-bar, gonttinim nekettranim kelolo.
Gale, *geil*, N. Nibor varem, vareachi daun.
Gall, *gol*, N. Pint; fg. coddsan.
Gall, V. Zenzraunc; gausunc.
Gallant, *gal'ant*, A. Danddi; sobit nirvonni munis, vo bahadur.
Gallantry, *gal'ant-ri*, N. Bulounni; mirdvni.
Galleon, *gal'e-on*, N. Vodd-tarum,
Gallery, *gal'e-ri*, N. Galeri; vorand, osro.

Gallnut, *gol'nott*, N. Oddo.
Gallop, *gel'op*, N. Fer, ferroi ; dan-vodd.
Gallop, V. Feroi maruuc ; danud-davim vochunc.
Gallows, *gal'oz*, N. Gollar marcho khambo.
Gamble, *gem'bl*, V. Jugar khel-lonc.
Gambler, *gem'blar*, N. Jugari ; duddvanim keunar.
Gambling, *gem'bling*, N. Jugar.
Game, *geim*, N. khell ; khuxalai.
Game, V. Khellonc.
Gamut, *gam'ot*, N. Solfancheo risco.
Gander, *gen'dor*, N. Dadlem ans.
Gang, *geng*, N. Zomo, urponz.
Gaol, *gaul*, N. Boncondd.
Gangrene, *gang'rin*, N. Gangren; sadeponn.
Gaoler, *gau'lor*, N. Carserer.
Gap, *gep*, N. Futt, dau ; ugddop.
Gape, *geip*, V. Thond ugttem corunc.
Garb, *garb*, N. Nesonn, auglem.
Garble, *gar'bl*, V. Bodluuc, fott-kiro corunc.
Garden, *gar'dn*, N. Hort ; bag.
Gardener, *gar'den-ar*, N. Mali.
Garland, *gar'land*, N. Jelo; kopel.
Garlic, *gar'lic*, N. Losun.
Garment, *gar'ment*, N. Nesoun, angostr.
Garnet, *gar'net*, N. Moladic fa-tor, bhou corun thambddo.
Garret, *gar'ret*, N. Mallo.
Garrison, *ge'ri-zon*, N. Soldadan-cho zomo, dovorlolo cottant, vo xarant.
Garrulous, *ge'ru-las*, A. Bodd-boddo ; lamb jibecho.
Garter, *gar'ttor*, N. Meia voir dor-cho band ; eoc vodd titl zo ditat Englaterrac.
Gas, *gas*, N. Vai ; ub.
Gash, *gesh*, N. Vodd gai.
Gash, V. Vodd gai galunc.
Gasp, *gasp*, V. Khorseuuc.
Gasp, N. Khoros.
Gate, *geit*, N. Darvontto.
Gate-keeper, *geitt-keep'ar*, N. porteir.
Gather, *ged'ar*, V. Ecttaim co-runc ; lunvonc.
—(In), zoddunc.
Gathering, *ged'er-ing*, N. Zomat, mell.
Gauge, (goj), V. Mezunc.
Gauntlet, *gont'let*, N. Lumv.
Gay, *gei*, A. Khoxal ; sontosborit ; porzollit.
Gaze, *geiz*, V. Dolle laun tellune
Gaze, N. Distt ; nodor
Gazette, *ga-zet'*, N. Gazet, potr.
Gazetteer, *ga-zet-ter'*, N. Potra-car.
Gear, *giar*, N. Mustaiki ; samonn.
Gelatine, *jel'a-ttain*, N. Gelatin ; gum.
Gem, *jem*, N. Moladic fator.
Genealogy, *gen'i-al-o-ji*, N. Fami-lichi, khobor ; kulli
General, *jen'e-ral*, A. Sadaran ; somestaucho, sogtancho ; por-gott.
—(Become general), porgott [zaunc.
General, N. Foujicho voddil ; general.
Generalize, *jen'é-ra-laiz*, V. So-mestanc labounc ; sogleanc vistarunc.
Generalissimo, *jen-e-ral'is-si-mu*, N. Mukia-senapati vo voddlo general.
Generality, *jen-e-ral'i-tti*, N. Sa-daranponn ; sara sori.
Generally, *jen'é-ral-li*, AD. Sada-ranponnim ; vodic corun.
Generate, *jen'e-reitt*, V. Utpon corunc ; zolm diunc ; rochunc ; goddunc.

Generation, *jen-e-rei'xion*, N. Utpoun cornem; sonsot, soin; piuddca; gotr; eca somoiacho loc.

Generosity, *jen-e-roz'-i-tti*, N. Udarpoun; vodd mon.

Generous, *jen'e-ras*, A. Udar; vodd monacho.

Genesis, *jen'e-zis*, N. Oromb.

Genial, *ji'ni-al*, A. Khoxalaecho; mogall; bore morjecho.

Genius, *ji'ni-as*, N. Sobau; mahatuiya; sudhi; gunn.

Genteel, *jen'til*, A. Cullivont; sobit; manculo; dulob; bolo; modur.

Gentile, *jen-ttail*, N. Onbavarthi; concuno.

Gentle, *jen'tl*, A. Moriadicho; lin; soucasaecho.

Gentleman, *jen-tl'men*, N. Sardar; saib.

Gentleness, *jen-tl'ness*, N. Moriad; chal chomcon.

Gently, *jent'li*, AD. Moriadin; soucasaen.

Genuine, *jen'u-in*, A. Niz; khoroch, borsinaslolo, nigoll.

Geographer, *je-og'ra-far*. N. Buim-sastri.

Geography, *je-og'ra-fi*, N. Bugoll-videa.

Geographical, *je-o-graf-i'cal*, A. Bhuim vivoracho vo buincho.

Geological, *je-o-lo'ji-kal*, A. Buimorombacho.

Geologist, *je-ol'o-jist*, N. Buimorombacho mister.

Geometer, *je-om'et-ar*. N. Buim-mapnar.

Geometry, *je-om'et-ri*, N. Buinchem map.

German, *jer'man*, N. Soiro; bhau vo bhoin; dhaiji.

Germinate, *jerm'i-neill*, V. Ubzonc; kirlonc.

Germination, *jer-min-ei'xion*, N. kirlop, comb futtnem.

Gesticulate, *jes-tik'ul-eit*, V. Hat portunc; ang vollunc.

Gesticulation, *jes-tik-u-lei'xion*, ang moddnem, moddamodd; ang bhong.

Gesture, *jes'char*, N. modd, isarat, halauni.

Get, *get*, V. mellunc; poddonc.

—(Abroad), collit zaunc.

—(Across), ūtronc.

—(Along), mucar vochunc.

—(Among), poddonc.

—(At), paunc.

—(Away), pollonc.

—(Back), portun geunc vo patti soronc.

—(Clear of), chuconnc.

—(Down) Denvounc.

—(Hold), dorunc.

—(Rid of), chuconnc.

—(Through), paunc; cobar corunc.

—(Upon,) choddonc.

Ghastliness, *gast'li-ness*, N. mornachi vo moddeachi soia.

Ghastly, *gast'li*, A. Campereacho, biranculI.

Ghost, *gost*, N. Munxeacho otmo; pran; distti poddop; saulli.

Giant, *jai'ant*, N. Orisht, khoddegant.

Gibbet, *jib'bet*, N. Goll; fasi.

Gibbosity, *jib-os'it-ti*, N. Pong.

Giddiness, *gid'di-ness*, N. Gunvol.

Giddy, *gid'i*, A. Gunvolicho; fg. bud naslolo.

Gift, *gift*, N. Dennem; chit.

Gifted, *gif'ted*, A. Mot aslolo.

Gigantic, *ji-gan'tic*, A. Bhou vodd; orisht.

Giggle, *gig'l*, V. Amburco ansonc.

Gild, *gild*, V. Bangar caddunc.

Gilded, *gild'ed*, A. Bangar caddlolo.

Gilder, *gild'ar,* N. Bangar caddpi.
Gilding, *gild'ing,* N. Bangar caddop.
Gill, *gill,* N. Paintacho chouto vantto; xenkrem.
Gimlet, *gim'let,* N. Supurlo girbo asun baric pont mucac.
Gin, *jin,* N. Genebra; capus nitou corchem macn.
Gin, V. Capus nittol corunc.
Ginger, *jin'jer,* N. Alem; suntt.
Gipsy, *jip'si,* N. Parpoll.
Gird, *gard,* V. Revoddunc; lagunc.
Girl, *gorl,* N. Cheddum; duv; choli
Girth, *gorth,* N. Band.
Gist, *jist,* N. Mukea vost; mull.
Give, *giv,* V. Diunc.
--(A blow), Marunc.
—(To understand), Somzaunc.
—(Back), Portun diunc.
—(Chase), Daunddaunc.
—(In one's name), Aplem naum borounc.
—(Over), Adin corunc.
—(Up), Soddunc; ghat corunc.
—(Way), Pirder zaunc; khoxe pormonnem corunc.
—(A dinner), Vaddunc.
Glacial, *gla'shi-al,* A. Borpacho; chodd thondd; fg. urba naslolo.
Glacis, *gla'sis,* N. Borpacho zago; deunti.
Glad, *gled,* A. Dadosi; sontosborit; onod aslolo.
Gladden, *gled'n,* V. Dadosi vo khoxal corunc.
Glade, *gleid,* N. Chorvacho zago eca ranant.
Gladiator, *glad'ie-tor,* N. Torsadinim kusti khellnar.
Gladly, *gled'li,* AD. Sontosan; dadosi zaun.
Gladness, *gled'ness,* N. Sontos.
Glance. *glans,* V. Polleunc; nodor galunc.
Glance, N. Distt; nodor.
Glare, *gler,* N. Porzoll; baric bhi rancnll nodor; kirn; ulop.
Glare, V. Porzollunc.
Glass, *glas,* N. Arso; vidr.
Glassy, *glas'i,* A. Arseacho.
Glaze, *gleiz,* V. Arso galunc vo launc; zogzokit corunc.
Gleam, *glim,* N. Porzoll; kirn
Gleam, V. Porzollunc; zogzogunc.
Glen, *glen,* V. Batacheo conxeo vinchunc, lunvon velea uprant.
Glide, *glaid,* V. Nisronc.
Glimmer, *glim'ar,* V. Porzollunc.
Glimpse, *glimps,* N. Matso uzvadd.
Glitter, *glit'ar,* V. Porzollunc; zogzogunc.
Glitter, N. Porzoll.
Gloat, *glot,* V. Jiv soddun polleunc; khottea dadosponnan niallunc.
Globe, *glob,* N. Gullo; sounsar.
Globular, *glob'u-lar,* A. Vaddkulo.
Gloom, *glum,* N. Ondoc; calloc; fg. khont.
Gloomy, *glum'i,* A. Calso; ondunko; chintest; dukest.
Glorification, *glo'ri-fi-kei'xion,* N. Onodponn; muctipad dennem.
Glorify, *glo'ri-fai,* V. Onod vo man diunc; man vaddounc.
Glorious, *glo'ri-as,* A. Zoitvont, manadic; onodborit.
Glory, *glo'ri,* N. Onod; man; voddvi.
Glory, V. Manounc; yes addunc.
Gloss, *glos,* V. Porzollunc.
Glossary, *glos'a-ri,* N. Utrancho vivor; sobda-kos.
Glossy, *glos'i,* A. Porzollit.
Glove, *glov,* N. Lumv; hatachem nesonn.
Glow, *glo,* N. Gormi; umallo; porzoll.
Glow, V. Taponc; tapounc; un zaunc; fg. zollonc.

Glowing-terms, N. Umalleachim utram.
Glow-worm, *glo'vorm,* N. Cazulo.
Gloze, *gloz,* V. Fuslaunc.
Glue, *glu,* N. Gom ; pank.
Glut, *glot,* V. Upott pott borunc.
Glut, N. Pottachem borop ; khaugeponn.
Glutinous, *glo'tin-as,* A. Chicott ; pancacho.
Glutton, *glutt'n,* N. Pottieo munis.
Gluttonous, *glott'n-as,* A. Pottieo; khangi.
Gluttony, *glott'n-i,* N. Pottard ; pottarponn.
Gnash, *nesh,* N. Dant chabonc vo kirkiraunc.
Gnashing, *nesh'ing,* N. Dant chabnem.
Gnat, *nett,* N. zollar ; mus.
Go, *go,* V. Vochunc; bhair soronc.
—(About), Bonvunc.
—(Astray). Chuconc.
—(By), Lagim vochonc ; pattlau corunc.
—(Down), Denvunc.
—(For), Apoun addunc.
—(In), Rigonc,
—(Off), Zaunc.
—(On), Mucar vochonc; goddonc; jiconc.
Go (over), Utron vochonc ; soddunc ; cobul zaunc ; voilea voir vachunc.
—(Up) choddonc.
Goad, *god,* N. Domsachem atiar zanvaranc daunddaunc.
Goad, V. Domsachem atiar topun daunddaunc ; challounc.
Goal, *gol,* N. Xevott.
Goat, *gott,* N. Gauncho boeddo vo boeddi.
Go-between, *go-bit'vin,* N. Malo; dalal,
Gobble, *gob'l,* V. Doddvoddean khaunc.
Goblet, *gob'let,* N. Cop ; pucr.
Goblin, *gob'lin.* N. Drusttacai.
God, *godd,* N. Deu.
God-child, N. Filiad.
Goddess, *godd'es,* N. Devi.
God-father, N. Podorn.
Godhead, *godd'hed,* N. Deuponn.
Godless, *godd'less,* A. Deu naslolo.
Godliness, *godd'li-nes,* N. Santiponn, bogtiponn.
Godly, *godd'li,* A. Devagelo, sant.
God-mother, N. Modorn.
Godsend, *godd'send,* N. Chintinaslolem mellop vo borem noxib.
Goggle, *gog'l,* A. Gugicho ; ambaddeam dolleancho.
Goitre, *goi'tor,* N. Gordon ; foll.
Gold, *gold.* N. Bangar.
Golden, *gold'n,* A. Bangarachem
Gold-leaf, *gold'lif,* N. Bangarachi fol'
Goldsmith, *gold'smith,* N. Sonar.
Gong, *gong,* N. Ghantt ; thali.
Good, *gudd,* A. Boro.
—A good deal), bhou chodd.
Good, N. Borem ; ast ; dan-vostu.
Good-breeding, *gudd-brid'ing,* N. Bori chal-chomcon; moriad.
Good-bye, *gudd'-bai,* N. Adeus.
Good-Friday, *gudd'frai-dei,* N. Nimanno suncrar.
Good-humour, *gudd-hiu'mor,* N. Austem mon.
Good-looking, *gudd'-luk-ing,* A. rupest, bolaikent aslolo.
Good-nature, *gudd-nei'char,* N. Mogallponn.
Goodness, *gudd'ness,* N. Borem mon, mogallponn.
Goods, *gudds,* N. Mhal, asti ; samon, [Borem mon.
Good-temper, *gudd-tem'par,* N.

Good-tempered, *gudd-tem'pard*, A. Mogall ; lin.
Good-will, *gudd-wil'*, N. Bori khoxi ; mog ; dosti.
Goose, *gus*, N. Bail-ans.
Gordian, *gor'di-an*, A. Coisttancho ; conttin.
Gore, *gor*, N. Xinkelelem rogot.
Gore, V. Xing topunc.
Gorge, *gorj*. N. Gomtto, gollo ; fg. osrai.
Gorgeous, *gor'jas*, A. Sobit ; dobajeacho.
Gormandize, *gor'mand-aiz*, jivsoddun khaunc.
Gormandizer, *gor'mand-aiz-ar*, N. Pottieo ; khaugi.
Gory, *go'ri*, A. Rogtacho vo rogtan borlolo.
Gospel, *gos'pul*, N. vanjel, Jesu Christachi sumurt, Devachem utor.
Gossip, *gos'-ip*, V. Gozal ; fotasi marnar.
Gourd, *gord*, N. Dudin.
Gout, *goutt*, N. Vat.
Govern, *go'-vern*, V. Cholounc ; razvottki corunc.
Governess, *go'vern-es*, N. mistin ; aya.
Government, *go'vern-ment*, N. sercar ; adhicar.
Governor, *go'ver-nor*, N. Raza ; adhicari.
Gown, *gaun*, N. Vistid ; gagro.
Grace, *gres*, N. Curpa ; dosti ; nettouni ; argam.
Grace, V. Nettouc ; sobounc.
Graceful, *gres'ful*, A. Moriadicho ; sundor
Gracefulness, *gres'ful-nes*, N. moriad ; sobitai.
Gracious, *grei'xas*, A. Gunacho ; bolo ; mogall.
Graciousness, *grei'xas-nes*, N. Mogallponn.
Gradation, *gra-dei'xion*, N. Grau.
Graft, V. Garf corunc.
Grain, *grein*, N. dhanno.
Gram, *grem*, N. Chonnem ; kullit.
Grammar, *gram'ar*, N. Viakaran.
Grammarian, *gram-mei'ri-an*, N. Viakaranist.
Grammatical, *gram mat'ic-al*, A. Viakaranacho.
Grammatically, *gram mat'ic-al-li*, AD. Viakarana pormonnem.
Granary, *gra-na'ri*, N. Tupem ; orvacho gudaum.
Grand, *grend*, A. Dobajeacho.
Grand-child, *grend'-chaild*, N. Natnum.
Grand-daughter, *grend'do-tor*, N. Nat.
Grand-father, N. Azo.
Grand-mother, N. Aji.
Grand-son, N. Natu.
Grandee, *gren-di'*, N. Vhdd munis ; sardar ; rao.
Grandeur, *grend'yuar*, N. Dobazo ; voddponn.
Grange, *greinj*, N. Vosounni ; camgot.
Granite, *gran'ait*, N. Pakonn.
Grant, *grent*, V. Dinnc ; soddunc ; cobul zaunc.
Granulous, *gren'ul-as*, Revencho.
Grape, *grep*, N. Dak.
Graphic, *gra'fic*, N. Akarlolo ; chitarlolo.
Grapnel, *grep'nel*, N. Lan nangor.
Grapple, *grep'l*, V. Dorunc ; zogddonc.
Grasp, *grasp*, V. Dorunc ; fg. Somzonc.
Grass, *gras*, N. Tonn.
Grassy, *gras'i*, A. Tonnacho.
Grate, *greit*, N. Gorgoro.
Grate, V. Vattunc ; gansunc ; zollounc.
Grateful, *greit'ful*, A. Upcari ; manuyoncho.

Gratefulness, *greit'ful-ness*, N. Upcarponn.
Gratification, *grat'i-fi-kei'shon*, N. Khoxalai ; dadoskai.
Gratify, *grat'i-fai*, V. Upcar corunc ; dados corunc.
Grating, *greit'ing*, N. Gorgoro ; dori.
Gratis, *gra'tis*, AD. Funkea.
Gratitude, *gret'i-tiud*, N. Upcarponn vo upcar.
Gratuitous, *gra-tu'it-as*, A. Funkeacho.
Gratuity, *gra-tu'i-tti*, N. Dennem ; inam.
Grave, *grev*, N. Fondd.
Grave, A. Zodd ; bhari.
Grave-digger, *greiv'dig-or*, N. Fondd-caddtolo.
Grave-stone, N. Fonddacho fator.
Grave-yard, N. Simiter.
Gravitate, *grav'i-teit*, V. Zoddai corunc ; gurutvacarshanna pavunc— ; vochunc.
Gravity, *grav'i-tti*, N. Bhar ; zoddai.
Gravy, *gre'vi*, N. Po-ou; cald; ros
Gray, *grei*, A. Gobro ; dovso.
Gray-hairs, *grei'hers*, N. Pike kens.
Graze, *greiz*, V. Choronnc.
Grazing, *greiz'ing*, N. Chorou.
Grease, *griiz*, N. Chorob
Grease, V. Chorob launc.
Great, *greit*, A. Vodd ; vorto ; bhari.
Greatly, *greitt'li*, AD. Chodd ; bhou.
Greatness, *greitt'ness*, N. Voddponn ; vorteponn ; rundai.
Greedy, *grid'i*, A. Axecho ; khaugi.
Green, *grin*, N. Torno ; pachvo.
Green, N. Torneponn ; pachvo reng.
Greenhorn, *grin'horn*, N. Bollo munis ; spiriens naslolo.
Greenish, *grin'ish*, A. Tornoso ; pachnoso.
Greet, *grit*, V. Salam corunc vo sangunc ; besaum magunc.
Greeting, *grit'ing*, N. Salam ; recad.
Grenade, *gre-neid'*, N. Khon-no.
Greyhound, *grei'haund*, N. Sikarechem sunnem.
Grid-iron, *grid'ai-ern*, N. Bazcheo sorieo.
Grief, *grif*, N. Khont, duc.
Grievance, *griv'ans*, N. Sinn; coistt ; coddsan.
Grieve, *griv*, V. Ducounc ; coisttaunc.
Grievous, *griv'as*, A. Coisttaucho. ducouncho ; coddu.
Grievousness, *griv'as-ness*, N. Coddsan.
Grill, *gril*, V. Bazunc.
Grim, *grim*, A. Vaneddes tonddacho vo vaneddo ; rannot.
Grimace, *gri-meis'*, N. Vaneddem tondd.
Grim, *grim*, V. Dant kirkiraunc ; dant dacounc ; ansear galunc.
Grind, *graind*, V. Dollunc, fg. dogdogaunc.
Grinder, (**Tooth**). *graind'or*, V. daddi.
Grind-stone, N. Dantem ; van.
Gripe, *graip*, V Dorunc ; mudddonc.
Gripes, *graips*, N. Muddonnem vo muddonni.
Griping, *graip'ing*, part. A. Muddouneacho ; fg. conttin.
Grist, *grist*, N. Pitt ; dhanni.
Groan, *gron*, V. pirngonc ; roddonc.
Groaning, *gron'nig*, N. Pirngoni ; rodduem.
Grocer, *gro'sar*, N Posorcar.

Groom, *grum*, N. Goddevalo.
Groove, *gruv*, N. Gero.
Groove, V. Gero corunc.
Grope, *grop*, V. Sansponc.
Gross, *gros*, A. Datt ; Omoridadicho ; lanno.
Grossness, *gros'nes*, N. Datt ui ; omoriad.
Grot, *grot*, N. Dol.
Grotesque, *gro-tesk'*, A. Vegloso, addgot, Vilakshan.
Ground, *graund*, N. Dorn ; zago ; carann.
—Gain Ground,= V. Jiconc, vistaronc.
—Lose Ground,= V. Pirder zaunc.
Ground-floor, *graund-flor*, N. Dorn.
Groundless, *graund'less*, AD. Carannavin.
Ground-work, *graund'work*, N. bunbad.
Group, *grup*, N. Zomo, mell.
Grove, *grov*, N. Zilleuttachem savott.
Grovel. *gro'vel*, V. Choronc (dornir).
Grow, *gro*, V. Futtonc ; vaddonc ; zaunc.
Grown-up, *gron-op*, A. vadutolo ; manai.
Growl. *graul*, V. Gonkunc, bobatt marunc.
Growth, *groth*. N. Vaddavol.
Grudge, *groj*, V. Mosor corunc
Grudge, N. Mosor ; dusmancai.
Gruel, *gru'el*, N. Ambil.
Gruff, *groff*, A. Omoriadicho ; darrun ; coddu.
Gruffness, *groff'nes*, N. Omoriadd ; cottinai.
Grumble, *grom'bl*, V. Sinnonc ; pattlean ulounc.
Grunt, *gront*, V. Gorgoronc.
Guarantee, *ga-ran-tli'*, N. Zamin.
Guard, *gard*, V. Samballunc, raconc ; paro corunc.
Guard, N. Asro ; racuno ; paro ; torsadichi mutt.
Guardian, *gard'i-an*, N. Racnno ; tutor.
Guardianship, *gard'i-an-ship*, N. asro ; paro.
Guava, *gua'va*, N. Per.
Guess, *ges*, V. Parkunc, sumaran sangunc.
Guess, N. Parkiunem.
Guest, *gest*, N. Soiro ; voullo.
Guide, *gaid*, N. Vatt dacoinar ; choloinar ; sicoinar.
Guide, V. Vatt dacounc ; cholounc ; sicounc, pavounc.
Guide-post, *gaid-post*, N. Vatt dacouncho fator vo khambo.
Guild, *gild*, N. Bageleancho zomo.
Guileless, *gil'i les*, A. Sado ; innosent.
Guillotine, *gil'o-ten*, N. Kuddar xins capunc.
Guilt, *gilt*, N. Guneanm ; oprad.
Guilty, *gilt'i*, A. Guneauncar.
—Become Guilty=guneauncari zaunc.
Guinea, *gin'i*, N. Inglezachi porni mor vo 21 shillingam.
Guise *gaiz*, N. Bhailean disrem ; rup.
Gulf, *golf*, N. Somdirachi vanc.
Gulp, *golp*, N. Goutt ; gans.
Gulp, V. Ecach gottan gillonc
Gum, *gom*, N. Molla ; Gondd ; dic.
Gummy, *gum'i*, A. Pancacho, gondacho.
Gun, *gon*, N. Nall ; arm.
Gunpowder, *gon'pau dor*, V. Daru.
Gurgle, *gor'gl*, V. Gorgol corunc.
Gurgling, *gorg'ling*, N. Gorgol.
Gush, *gosh*, V. Vauvunc ; bhair votonc.
Gut, *got*, N. Ankiddeo.
Gutter, *got'or*, N. Gottor ; mellem udoc vechi kholi.

Guttural, *gut'tor-al*, A. Gongteantlo.
Guzzle *gaz'l*, V. Dorvoddiam piennc; cop marunc.
Gymnasium, *jim-na'zi-um*, N. Cosrat corchem gor; voddlea sicpachem iscol.
Gymnast, *jim'nast*, N. Cosrat cornar vo sicoinar. [ticho.
Gymnastic, *jim-nast'ic*, A. Cosra-

H

Haberdasher, *ha'ber'dash-er*, N. flanel, sed, ribbon etc. vicnar.
Habit, *he'bit*, N. Nesonn; soviom; caletri.
Habitable, *ha'bit-ê-bl*, A. Ravosarco.
Habitation, *ha-bit-ei'zion*, N. Gor; biddar; thicannem.
Habitual, *ha-bit'u-al*, A. Sovoincho; porno.
Habitually, *ha-bit'u-al-li*, AD. Sovoim-ie pornonnem.
Habituate, *ha-bit'u-eitt*, V. Sovoim corunc; gorvasi corunc.
Hack, *heck*, V. Catrunc; cuddke corunc.
Hack, N. Baddeacho goddo.
Hackney, *hec'ni*, N. Baddeac dovorlolo goddo.
Haggard, *hag'ard*, A. Zongli; besurvanno.
Haggle, *heg'gl*, V. Chodd vanponn corunc.
Hail, *heil*, N. Core; coreancho paus.
Hail, V. Gar poddonc; salam diunc vo corunc.
Hail-stone, *heil'ston*, Coro.
Hair, *her*, N. Kens.
Hair-cloth, *her'cloth*, N. Kensanchem lugot; pirajitachem lugot.
Hairy, *her'i*, A. Lovencho; sobar kens aslolo.
Half, *haf*, A. Ordo.
Half-brother, *haf'bro-dor*, N. Mau sibau; bapulbau.
Half-dead, *haf'ded*, A. Ordo melo
Hall, *hol*, N. Sal.
Hallo, *hal'lo*, IN. Are.
Hallucination, *hal'lu-si-nei-shon*, N. Bhorm; soponn; fg. chuc.
Halo, *ha'lo*, N. Suriacho vo chondrimacho mandd.
Halt, *holt*, V. Raunc; mukom corunc; kunttonc.
Halt, N. Ravop.
Halter, *hol'tor*, N Goll; dori.
Halve, *haf*, V. Donn vantte corunc.
Ham, *hem*, N. Ducrachem kharem kelelem pern; hem.
Hamlet, *hem'lett*, N. Vaddo.
Hammer, *hem'or*, N. Tutio.
Hammock, *hem'oc*, Hindlo; painem.
Hamper, *hem'pör*, V. Addaunc; addcollint galunc.
Hand, *hend*, N. Hat; tallat; goddielacho cantto.
Hand, V. Dinnc; adin corunc.
Hand-bell, *hend'bel*, N. Campin.
Hand-bill, *hend'bil*, N. Ecoddem xaplelem cagot vanttcheac.
Hand-book, *hend'buc*, N. Manual; at pustoc.
Handbreadth, *hend'bredth*, N. Eca hatacho rundaecho zago.
Hand-coff, *hend'cof*, N. Khoddo.
Handful, *hend'ful*, Muttbor.
Handicraft, *hend'i-craft*, N. Hatan kelelem cam.
Handkerchief, *hend'kor-chif*, N. Lens.
Handle, *hen'dl*, N. Thorum; mutt;
Handsome, *hend'som*, A. Sobit sundor; dobajeacho; vodd.
Handwriting, *hend'rait-ing*, N. Hatborop; borop
Hang, *heng*, V. Umcallaunc; lambounc; fasi marunc.

Hanging, *heng'ing*, N. Umcallaunem ; fasi.
Hangman, *heng'men*, N. Gollar marnar.
Hanker, *heng'kor*, V. Laleunc.
Hankering, *heng'ker-ing*, N. Laleunem.
Haply, *hep'li*, AD. Ecadevella.
Happily, *hep'i-li*, AD. Noxiban ; felizment.
Happiness, *hep'i-nes*, N. Suc ; bhag; dadospoun.
Happy, *hep'i*, A. Dadoxi ; bhagi ; bagevont ; sufol.
Harangue, *ha'reng*, V. Dobajean discurs corunc ; sobe mazar ulounc.
Harangue, N. Discurs ; sobe mazar ulounnem.
Harass, *ha'ras*, V. Zollounc ; corcor corunc.
Harbinger, *har'bin-jer*, N. Fuddem eun saugnar ; khunna.
Harbour, *har'bor*, N. Bondir ; khadd ; fg. asro.
Harbour, V. Arso diunc ; arso mellonc.
Hard, *hard*, a nibor, gott ; cottin.
Harden, *hard'n*, V. Gott corunc.
Hard-hearted, *hard'hart-ed*, A. churchure naslolo, darun callzacho.
Hardness, *hard'nes*, N. Nirvonn ; gottai ; darunai.
Hardly, *hard'li*, Ad. Conisttaen.
Hardship, *hard'ship*, N. Upodre ; coistt ; minot.
Hardy, *hard'i*, A. Gott ; darun ; lozbanddo.
Hare, *her*, N. Sonso.
Hark, *hark*, V. Int, aic-re.
Harm, *harm*, N. Lucsan ; noistt ; vaitt.
Harm, V. Ducounc ; vait corunc.
Harmful, *harm'ful*, A. Lusconacho ; vaitt.
Harmless, *harm'less*, A. Guneaum naslolo ; nentto.
Harmonious, *har-mo'ni-as*, A. ecach talleacho ; isttogoticho.
Harmoniously, *har-mo'ni-as-li*, AD. Eke-motin ; isttogotin ; somandonan
Harmony, *har-mo'ni*, N. Borem cantar ; soucasai ; ec chit ; mell.
Harness, *har'ness*, N. Goddesuarachem nesson ; goddeachem samonn,
Harp, *harp*, N. Arp, kinnari.
Harpy, *har'-pi*, N. Dolleant rag naslolo munis.
Harrow, *ha'ro*, N. Danto.
Harrow, V. Danto marunc.
Harsh, *harsh*, A. Ambott ; gorgori ; cottin.
Harshness, *harsh'ness*, N. Nibrasann ; cottinai.
Hart, *hart*, N. Rangoddo.
Harvest, *har'vest*, N. Set luuncho call.
Hash, *hesh*, V. Cuddkean cuddco corunc
Hasp, *hasp*, N. anceddo ; kill.
Hassock, *has'hoc*, N. Dimbi galchem vo bosonchem uxam.
Haste, *hest*, N. Dorvodd, ausar.
Haste, V. Ausar corunc, vegim corunc.
Hastily, *hest'i-li*, AD. Vegimvegim ; dorvoddean.
Hasty, *hest'i*, A. Dorvoddeachochintinaslolo.
Hat, *het*, N. Chepem ; topi.
Hatch, *hech*, V. Rovaunc, rovannec bosonc.
Hatchet, *he'-chet*, N. Supurli curadd.
Hate, *heit*, V. Cosonc ; cantallonc.
Hateful, *heit'ful*, A. Canttaleacho ; Khotto.
Hatred, *het'red*, N. Canttalo, mosor ; dusmancai.

Haughtiness, *hot'i-nes* N. Gorv.
Haughty, *hot'i*, A. Gorvi.
Haul, *hol*, V. Voddunc.
Haunt, *hont*, V. Goddie-goddie enn bejar corunc eca melelea munxea porim; coisttaunc.
Have, *hev*, V. asonc; dovorunc.
Haven, *hevn*, N. bondir, khadd; arso.
Havock, *hev'ec*, N. Ibadd, bosm; nas.
Hawk, *hok*, N. Gidd.
Hawk, V. Khancaronc.
Hawker, *hok'ar*, N. Bouvon pornem samon gennar anim vicnar.
Hay, *hey*, N. Sucoilelem tonn.
Hay-cock, *hei'cock*, N. tonnachem, cuddem.
Hazard, *ha'zard*, N. Eoc khell daimancho; risk, zokum.
Hazard, V. Riscar galunc.
Hazardous, *ha'zar-dus*, A. Perigoz; odrusttacho.
He, *hi*, V Pron, to.
Head *hed*, N. Tocli; matem; boddic.
Headache, *hed'eik*, N. Toclechem foddop, vo copolachi duc.
Headlong, *hed'long*, AD. Tocli fudde galun, dorvoddean.
Heading, *hed'ing*, N. Matea velem borop; titl.
Headless, *hed'less*, A. Toclinaslolo, murc.
Headman, *hed'men*, N. Mukeli; voddil.
Headmost, *hed'most*, A. Mucavelo; poilo.
Head-quarters, *hed,kuar-ters*, N. Mukom.
Headsman, *heds'men*, N. Gollar marnar.
Headstrong, *hed'strong*, A. Aplea vadeacho.
Heal *hil*, V. Boro corunc; pecounc.
Health, *helth*, bolaiki, saud.
Healthy, *helth'i*, A. Bolaikecho, bolaikent aslolo.
Heap, *hip*, N. Ras; zomo; punj.
Heap, V. Ras corunc; punji corunc; zomounc.
Hear, *hier*, V. Aiconc; canant poddonc; chit diunc.
Hearer, *hier'er*, N. Aiconar; chit dinar.
Hearing, *hie'ring*, N. Aicop; bhet; ulo.
Hearken, *hark'n*, V. Can diunc; chit diunc.
Hearsay, *hier'sei*, N. Funca; pucaro.
Heart, *hart* N. Calliz; ontoscorn; nirvonn; modem.
—(Learn by heart), Decor corunc.
Hearth, *harth*, N. Randon.
Heartily, *hart'i-li*, AD. Callzan than; ontoscornan than.
Heartless, *hart'less*, A. Bezudd; darrun.
Hearty, *hart'i*, A. Callzacho vo ontoscornacho; mogall.
Heat, *hit*, N Ulop; unau; gormi; fg. uchambolai.
Heat, V. Tapounc; un corunc; coddounc.
Heathen, *hi'don*, N. Onbavarti; concne.
Heathenism, *hi'don-izm* N. Onbavartpoun; conconpunn.
Heating, *hit'ing*, N. Taponnem; ulop.
Heave, *hiiv*, V. Uclunc; suzounc; fg. uchamboll zaunc.
—(A sigh), suscar soddunc.
Heaven, *hev'n*, N. Sorg, voincutt; mollob.
Heavenly, *hev'en-li*, A. Sorgincho.
Heavenwards, *hev'en-vads*, AD. Sorga eusilean.
Heaviness, *he'vi-nes*, N. Bhar; zoddai; khont; duc.

Heavy, *he'vi*, A. Zodd ; baradic ; fg. auxi ; fg. dukest ; sonkest.
Hebrew, *hi'bru*, N. Izrael Judeu.
Hedge, *hej*, N. Voddop.
Heed, *hiid*, N. Chotrai ; zagrutai.
Heedless, *hiid'les*, A. Chotrainaslolo.
Heel, *hiil*, N. Khott.
Heifer, *hef'ar*, N. Paddi ; supurli gai.
Heigho, *hi'ho*, IN. Xebas.
Height, *haith*, N. Unch suat ; unchai ; fg. voddponn.
Heighten, *haith'en*, V. Choddounc ; ubarunc.
Heinous, *hein'as*, A. Canttaleacho ; bhou khotto.
Heir, *er*, N. Herdeir ; daiji.
Heiress, *er'es*, N. Bail herdeir ; daijin.
Heirloom, *er'lum*, N. Cosoleim gharachem samonn jem caidean herderac meutta.
Hell, *hel*, N. Infern ; emcondd.
Hellish, *hel'ish*, A. Infernacho ; soitanacho.
Helm, *helm*, N. Sukannem.
Help, *help*, N. dhir ; adar ; mozot.
Help, V. adar, dhir diunc.
Helpless, *help'les*, A. Upainaslolo ; adarnaslolo ; dublo.
Helplessness, *help'less-nes*, N. Lacharponn vo lachari.
Hem, *hem*, N. Deg.
Hem, V. Deg launc.
Hemisphere, *he'mi-sfiar*, N. Gulleachem ord ; ordo sounsar.
Hemorrhage, *he'mor-eij*, N. Rogot vanvnem ; amolpint.
Hemp, *hemp*, N. Sonn.
Hen, *hen*, N. Combi ; cuncodd.
Hence, *hens*, AD. Anga than ; aizlegun ; hea mucar ; tor vo decun.
Henceforth, *hens'forth*, AD. hea mucar vo hea uprant.
Hennery, *hen'er-i*, N. 'Cuncddancho gudd.

Henpecked, (husband), *hen'-pekt*, A. Baillonddo dadlo ; bailec bhieta tosolo.
Hepatic, *he'pat'ic*, A. Callzacho.
Heptagon, *hep'ta-gon*, N. Saptacoun ; satconxeanchem rup.
Heptarchy, *hep'tar-ki*, N. Sat zannanchem raj ; vo sat rajeancho ecott.
Her, *har*, PRON. Ticho.
Herald, *he'rald*, N. Rajdut ; ravani.
Herb, *herb*, Tonn ; supurlem zadd.
Herd, *hard*, N. Hind.
Herdsman, *hardz'men*, N. Goulli.
Here, *hier*, AD. Anga.
—(And there). Eusin-teusin.
—(About), Sumar anga.
—(After), Ache uprant ; melea uprant ; dusre jinnint.
Hereby, *hier'bai*, AD. Vorvim.
Hereditary, *he-red'i-ta-ri*, A. Daizantlo.
Herein, *hier'in*, AD. Antum.
Heresy, *he're-zi*, N. Herezi, bavarthar virudai.
Heretic, *he're-tic*, N. Yerej ; bavarthac virudi.
Heretical, *he-re'ik-al*, A. Bavarthac add aslolo.
Here-upon, *hier-ap-on*, AD. Tache uprant ; ternam.
Herewith, *hier'with*, AD. Ache vorvim.
Heritage, *he'rit-eij*, Daiz; herans.
Hermeneutic, *her-me-nu'tic*, A. Orthacho ; somzonnecho.
Hermeneutics, N. Orth ; somzonni.
Hermit, *her'mit*, N. Ecsuro raunar ; saniasi.
Hermitage, *her'mit-eij*, A. Ecsuro raunarachem ghor ; convent.
Hero, *hi'ro*, N. Nirvonni munis ; pilvonn.
Heroic, *he-ro'ik*, A. Bhou vorto munis.

Heroine, *hi'ro-in*, N. Virinn ; doiravont hostori
Heroism, *he'ro-izm*, V. Bhou vortem nirvonn.
Hers, *hers*, PRON. Ticho.
Hesitate, *he'zi-teitt*, V. Dubavone ; guspone, patti-fudde sorone.
Hesitation, *he'zi-ttei-shon*, N. Dubau ; luddbeoni ; gagevni.
Hesperian, *hes-pe'ri-an*, A. Ostomticho.
Heterodox, *he'te-ro-dox*, N. Yerej.
Heterogeneous, *he'te-ro-ji'ni-as*, A. Dusre torecho vo jaticho.
Hew, *hiu*, V. Tasunc ; catrunc.
Hey, *hei*, Int. xebas.
Hiatus, N. Uktepoun ; khautem.
Hibernate, *hi-ber'neitt*, V. Pausacho vo invancho temp caddunc.
Hiccup, *hik'op*, N. Bakio.
Hiccup, V. Balkio eunc
Hidden, *hid'n*, A. Guttacho.
Hide, *haidd*, V. Lipounc; dancunc; guttan dovorunc
Hide, N. Cat ; chambddem.
Hideous, *hid'i-as*, A. Ollsic ; bhirancull ; canttaleacho.
Hideousness, *hid'i-as-nes*, N. Ollsikponn ; bhirancullai,
Hiding, *haidd'ing*, N. Lipounem ; dancun galnem.
Hiding-place, N. Lipun raunchi suat.
Hie, *hai*, V. Vegim cholonc.
Hierarch, *hi'er-ark*, Mukia dormadeakshachi podvi.
Hierarchy, *hi'er-ar-ki*, N. Povitr adhicar.
Hieroglyphic, *hi'er-o-glif'ik*, N. Guttachem borop.
Higgle, *hig'l*, V. Vann-ponn corunc.
High, *hai*, A. Unch ; voir.
Highland, *hai'lend*, N. Dograncho gaum,
High-mass, *hai'mas*, N. Cantar mis ; voddlem mis.
High-priest, *hai'prist*, N. Voddlo padri.
High-treason, *hai'trez-on*, N. Voddlo abgat raiacher vo gaun cher.
High-water, *hai'ro-ttor*, N. Borti.
Hilarity, *hi-la'ri-tti*, N. Khoxalponn, sontos.
Hill, *hil*, N. Supurlo dongor.
Hillock, *hil'oc*, N. Ghatti.
Hilly, *hil'i*, A. Xencareancho vo gunddeancho.
Hilt, *hilt*, N. Mutt torsadichi.
Himself, *him'self*, PRON. Toch.
Hind, *haindd*, N. Bail merum.
Hinder, *hain'dor*, A. Pattlo.
Hindmost, *haind'most*, Nimanno; akericho.
Hindrance, *hin'drans*, N. Addcoll ; horcot.
Hinge, *hinj*, N. Vato.
Hinge, V. Vateur portonc.
Hint, *hint*, N. Ugddas.
Hint, V. Montint addunc ; sor corunc.
Hippopotamus, *hip-o-pot'a-mus* N. Noincho goddo.
Hire, *ha'iar*, N. Baddem.
Hire. V. Baddeac corunc vo dinnc.
Hireling, *hair'ling*, N. Baddeac getlolo ; kulcar.
Hirer, *haiar'er*, N. Baddeac genar.
Hiring, *haiar'ing*, N. Baddem.
Hirsute, *her'sut*, A. Lovencho.
His, PRON. Tacho.
Hiss, *hiss*, V. Fusfusonc.
Historian, *his'to-ri-an*, N. Histor boroinar.
History, *his'to-ri*, N. Contha ; khobor ; cannim.
Hit, *hit*, V. Marunc ; pettunc.
Hit off-Sarki somzonni diunc
—(Upon)-mellonc.
—(The mark)-sarcoch lagonc.
—(Together), addlonc.

Hit, N. Mar; pett.
Hitch, *hich*, N. Addcol.
Hitherto, *hith'er-tu*, AD. Yedoll; atam poriant.
Hive, *haiv*, N. Movanchem malem.
Ho, *ho*, INT. Ye; cotta-cotta.
Hoar, *hor*, A. Douso.
Hoar-frost, *frost*, N. Dou.
Hoarse, *hors*. A. Sorantla; tallo poddla.
Hoarseness, *hors'ness*, N. Sorantto; motto tallo, poddop.
Hoary, *hor'i*, A. Dovo; douso fg. piko.
Hoax, *hoks*, V. Fottounc; chesttaeo corunc.
Hoax, N. Cosoleim facann vo chesttaeo.
Hobble, *hob'l*, V. Cunttonc; thontten baxen cholonc.
Hobby, *hob'i*, N. Axa.
Hobby-horse, *hob'i-hors*, N. Lanceddacho goddo burgueanc khellonc; cosolii apurbaechi vost.
Hobgoblin, *kob-gob'lin*, N. besurvanno deunchar; drusttakoi.
Hobnob, *nob'nob*, V. Isttogotin piennc.
Hock, *hoc*, N. Vinho.
Hoe. *ho*, N. Panaddoi; khorantti.
Hog, *hog*, N. Ducor.
Hogshead, *hogz'hed*, N. Pip; borl.
Hold, *hold*, V. Dorunc; veng marunc; cholounc.
—(back), patti caddunc; addaunc.
—(cheap), beporva corunc.
—(fast), gott dorunc.
—(peace), vogo ravonc.
—(out), sosnicaen ravonc.
—(in), patti dovorunc.
—(up), ukolunc vo uclun dorunc.
Hold (your tongue), uloinaca, gop rau.
Holding, *hold'ing*, N. Baddeac keleli suat vo zomin.
Hole, *hol*, N. Burac; domplo.
Holiday, *ho'li-dei*, N. Rojea, feriad.
Holiness, *ho'li-nes*. N. Santiponn, bagevontpoun.
Hollow, *hol'o*, A. Pokoll; khali.
Hollow, N Dhol.
Hollow, V. Pocrunc
Holy, *ho'li*, A. Bagevont; povitr; sant, sagrad.
Holy-water, N. Agment vo alment.
Homage, *hom'eij*, N. Man, respeit.
Home, *hom*, N. Ghor; biddar; tharo.
Homeless, *hom'les*, A. Ghor nasslolo.
Homely, *hom'li*, A. Chalto; sado.
Home-sickness, *hom'sick nes*. N. Ghorchi chintna.
Homicide, *ho'mi-said*, N. Morticar.
Homily, *ho'mi-li*, N. Bud-ball; sermaum.
Homogeneous, *homo-ji'nias*, A. Ekech torecho.
Honest, *hon'est* A. Moriadicho; manadic; boro.
Honesty, *on'est-i*, N. Moriad; bari jinn; abru.
Honey, *hon'i*, N. Moum, mel.
Honey-bee, N. Movancho mus.
Honey-comb, *hon'i-kom*, N. Movanchi polli.
Honorary, *on'or-a.ri*, A. Manadic.
Honorary, N. Inam.
Honour, *on'or*, N. Man; borem naum, onod; moriad; caido.
Honour, V. Man diunc.
Honorable *on'or-a-bl*, A. Manadic, abruvont.
Honorably, *on'or-a-bli*, AD. Manau; abrun.

Hood *hud*, topi; kholl.
Hood-wink, *hud'wink*, v. Fottoune.
Hoof, *huf*, N. Gell paddeachem.
Hook, *huk*, N. Ancddo, gori.
Hooked, *hukt*, A. Ancddo galolo vo aslolo.
Hooping-cough, *hup'ing-kof*, N. Sunni koncli.
Hoot, *hut*, V. Bob marunc.
Hop, *hop*, V. Eca donkeau uddonc.
Hope, *hop*, N. borvonso; patieuni.
Hope, v. Borvonso dovorunc; patieunc.
Hopeful, *hop'ful*, A. Patieuncho; borvonso aslolo.
Hopeless, *hop-less*, A. Nir axecho; borvonso naslolo.
Hopelessness, *hop'les-nes*, N. Niraxa; vomtea colxear udoc.
Horde, *hord*, N. Penddareanchi urponz.
Horizon, *ho-rai'zon*, N. Molbachi deg, dhar; akas, mollob.
Horizontal, *ho-ri-zon'tal*, A. Add, addvo.
Horn, *horn*, N. Xing.
Horned *hornd*, A. Xingam aslolo vo xingallo.
Hornet, *horn'et*, N. Kirant.
Horny, *horn'i*, A. Xinganclio.
Horologe, *ho'ro-loj*, N. Goddial, reloj
Horrible, *hor'ri-bl*, A. Bhirancul; tortorauncho; fg. bhou ollxic.
Horror, *hor'ror*, N. canttallo, ollxic, vitt; corcoddo, sirsiro.
Horse, *hors*, N. goddo.
Horse-keeper, *hors-kip'ar*, N. goddevalo.
Horsemen, *hors'men*, N. Goddear Bosnar.
Horse-shoe, *hors'sho*, N. Nal.
Hose, *hoz*, N. Mei, izar.
Hospice, *hos'pis*, N. Dhorm-sal, devpuri.
Hospital, *hos'pit-al*, N. Vaittacaranchem ghor, hospital.
Hospitality, *hos-pit-al'i-tti*, N. paramas, udarponn.
Host, *host*, N. Biradd ditolo, yezmani, ghorcar; fouz, zomo.
Hostage, *host'eij*, N. Zamin.
Hostess, *host'es*, N. Yezman, gorcan.
Hostile, *hos'tail*, A. Vairi, dusmanic; fg. coria cornar.
Hostility *hos-til'i-ti*, N. dusmancai; Loddai, coria.
Hot, *hot*, A. Un, khor; votacho; uball fg. umalleacho; uchamboll.
Hotel, *ho'tel*, N. Jeunachem ghor, hotel; puzat.
Hotch-potch, *poch'poch*, N. Khichddi.
Hound, *haund*, N. Sicarechem sunnem.
Hour, *aor*, N. Or, gantto.
Hour-glass, *aor'glas*, N. Ampnlheit, revenchem goddial.
Hour-hand, *aor'hend*, N. Orancho cantto.
House, *haus*, N. Ghor, biddar; gharannem.
House, v. Biddar vo arso diunc.
Household, *haus'hold*, N. Kuttom; ghor.
Householder, *haus'hold-ar*, N. Gorcar.
Houseless, *haus'les*, N. Gornaslolo.
House-maid, *haus'meid*; N. Chacorn.
House-wife, *haus'waif*, N. Gorcan.
Howel, *ho'wel*, V. Umcollonc; ubonc.
How, *hau*, AD. Coso, kedo.
—Many—Kitle.
—Much—Kitlo vo kedo.
However, *hau-ev'er*, AD. Tor, zalear, cosolei jinsim.

Howl, *haul*, V. Bob marunc; goroz galunc.
Howl, N. Bob, goroz.
Hubbub, *hob'bob*, N. Boball.
Huckster, *hock'ster*, N. Jeripuranavala; dacto posorcar.
Huddle, *hod'l* V. Dorvoddiam ecttaim corunc. [bob.
Hue, *hiu*, N. Rong; chorac dorchi
Hug, *hog*, V. Veng marunc; axe. unc.
Huge, *hiuj*, A. Bhou vodd; oristt
Hulk, *holk*, N. Pirder zalelem porneni tarum.
Human, *hui'man*, A. Munxeacho vo munxeaponacho, vo munxeaponni; sounsaracho.
Humane, *hiu'mein*, A. Munxeaponnacho, mogall, doiall.
Humanity, *hiu'man-i-ti*, N. munxeponn; śoimb; boleponn; doia
Humanize, *hiu'man-aiz*, V. Mansugi sicounc.
Humble, *hom'bl*, A. Khalto; lin; moriadicho.
Humble, V. Khalto corunc; unneponn diunc.
Humbug, *ham'bog*, N. Naca zaleli vost; zanc; fottvon.
Humidity, *hiu-mid'i-tti*, N. Xell; olsann; bato.
Humility, *hiu-mil'i-tti*, N. Khalteponn; linttuvai.
Humorous, *hiu'mor-as*, A. Facanddi; chesttaecho.
Humour, *hiu'mor*, N. Morji; voddni; sobau.
Humour, V. Fuslaunc.
Hump, *hamp*, N. Pong.
Humped, *hamp'd*, A. Pongo.
Hundred, *hon'dred*, A. Xembor.
Hundred-fold, *hon'dred-fold*, N. Xembor pautti.
Hunger, *hong'er*, N. Bhuk.
Hunger, V. Bhukeunc; bhuc lagonc.
Hungry, *hang'ri*, A. Bhukelolo; bhuk-laglolo.
Hunt, *hant*, V. Sicari corunc; cas marunc.
Hunt, N. Sicari; cas.
Hunter, *hant'or*, N. Sicari; casador.
Hurdle, *hor'dl*, N. Totti; voddop.
Hurl, *horl*, V. Soddunc; uddounc.
Hurrah, *hu-re*, INT. Xebas.
Hurricane, *hor'ri-kein*, N. Tufan; vaddol.
Hurried, *har'rid*, A. Dorvoddeacho.
Hurry, *ha'ri*, N. Ausar; dorvodd.
Hurry, V. Ausar vo vegim corunc launc; dorvoddaunc.
Hurt, *hart*, N. Luksan; ghai.
Hurt, V. Luksan corunc; ducounc.
Hurtful, *hart'ful*, A. Lusconacho; noisttacho.
Husband, *haz'band*, N. Poti; gou; gorcar.
Husbandman, *haz'band-men*, N. Setcamti; buincar.
Husbandry, *haz'band-ri*, N. Setcamot; gorchea camachi zoton.
Hush, *hash*, INT. Chip.
Hush, V. Vego ravounc; fuslaunc.
Husk, *hask*, N. Sal; motto cunddo.
Hustle, *has'sl*, V. Compor marunc.
Hut, *hot*, N. Khomp.
Huzza, *huz-za'*, INT. Xebas.
Hydraulic, *hai-dral'ic*, N. Chala-java-vidia.
Hydrophobia, *hai-dro-fo'bi-a*, N. Pisaulelea sunneacho vikar.
Hydropic, *hai-drop'ic*, A. Naicutcar.
Hydrostatics, *hai-dro-stat'iks*, N. Udcasamandan videa.
Hyena, *hai-e'na*, N. Sunnem-vagott.
Hygrometer, *hai-grom'et-ar*, N. Olsann mezchem map.

Hymn, *himn*, N. Cantig ; onodachem gaian.
Hyperbole, *hai-per'bol*, N. Vodic saugnem.
Hypercritic, *hai-per-krit'ik*, A. Bhou khoddi caddcho.
Hyphen, *hai'fun*, N. Ecttaim corchi khunna.
Hypochondria, *hai-po-kon'dri-a*, N. Khont ; usco.
Hypocrisy, *hi-pok'ri-zi*, Copott ; fottkirem devosaum.
Hypocrite, *hi'po-krit*, A. Coptti ; fottkiro munis.
Hypostasis, *hai-pos'ta-zis*, N. Sotantirachem soimb.
Hypostatic, *hai-pos'ta-tic*, A. Aplea sotantrar aslolo.
Hypothesis, *hai-poth'e-zis*, N. Sert ; colponna.

I

I, PRON. Aum.
Ice, *ais*, N. Gar ; borof.
Ice-cold, *ais-cold'*, A. Thondd-gar.
Icicle, *ais'i-kl*, N. Borfacho fator.
Idea, *ai-di'a*, N. Chintna ; volloc ; kolponna.
Ideal, *ai-di'al*, A. Nomunneacho ; chintlolo.
Idealism, *ai-di'al-izm*, N. Moya ; yoga moya.
Identical, *ai-den'tik-al*, A. Toch ; ecach ; sarco ; ecsarco.
Identify, *ai-den'ti-fai*, V. Ecsarco, ecuch corunc; ec corun dacounc.
Identity, *ai-den'ti-tti*, N. Sarkeponn ; ecsarkeponn ; sambhav.
Idiom, *id'i-om*, N. Bhas ; lokbhas; bhasechi rit ; chal.
Idiomatic, *id'i-om-at-ik*, A. Bhasecho ; vises.
Idiot, *i'di-ot*, N. Nennar ; gollio ; khullo.
Idiotic, *id-i-ot'ik*, A. Golliacho ; piseacho.
Idle, *ai'dl*, A. Ricambi ; cam naslolo ; allsi.
Idle, V. Allsai corunc ; vell faraunc.
Idleness, *ai'dl-nes*, N. Allsai; jem.
Idler, *ai'dler*, N. Becar, allsi munis.
Idol, *ai'dol*, N. Cuddo deu ; murti; fg. bhou mogall vost.
Idolater, *ai-dol'at-er*, N. Concno ; onbavarthi.
Idolatry, *ai-dol'al-ri*, N. Murtipuja ; conconponn.
Idolize, *ai-dol'aiz*, V. Mogan morunc ; laleunc ; apurbai asunc.
If, *if*, CONJ. Zor tor.
If not, Sivai.
Ignoble, *ig-no'bl*, A. Unno ; kircoll ; olko.
Ignominious, *ig-no-mi'ni-as*, A. Ollxic ; fg. lozist ; ocmanacho.
Ignominy, *ig'no-mi-ni*, N. Loz ; ocman.
Ignoramus, *ig-no-ra'mus*, N. Daddo munis ; vlg. reddo ; boil.
Ignorance, *ig'no-rans*, N, Nennarponn ; nenttuvai.
Ignorant, *ig'no-rant*, A, Nennar ; vo siconaslolo ; nentto.
Ignorantly, *ig'no-rant-li*, AD. Nennarponnan.
Ignore, *ig-nor'*, V. Nenno zaunc ; soddunc.
Ill, *ill*, N. Vaitt.
—(Fall ill), Vaittant poddunc.
—(Speak ill), Vaitt ulounc.
Ill-affected, *ill-a'fec-ted*, A. Khoxi naslolo.
Ill-bred, *ill-bred'*, A. Noi moriadi ; corddo.
Ill-breeding, *ill-brid'ing*, N. Aumoriad.
Ill-health, *ill-helth*, N. Nam bolaiki.

Illegal, *il-le'gal*, A. Caidea pormonnem naslolo.
Illegible, *il-le'ji-bl*, A. Vachunc nozo aslolo vo vachinanso.
Illegitimate, *il-le-gil'i-meith*, A. Pottacho; khoro bapui naslolo; caidea virodi.
Illiberal, *il-lib'e-ral*, A. Sugrati; imtto.
Illicit, *il-lis'it*, A. Caidea pormonnem noi.
Illiterate, *il-lit'er-eitt*, A, Siconaslolo.
Ill-natured, *il'nei-chard*, A. Vaitt sobavacho etc.
Illness, *il'ness*, N. Pidda; rog.
Illogical, *il-lo'jik-al*, A. Iuktivirudh; aiukt.
Ill-tempered, *ill'tem-perd*, A. Vaitta monacho; coddsanicho.
Illuminate, *il-lum'in-eitt*, V. Pracasunc; uzvadd corunc; dive launc.
Illumination, *il-lum'in-ei-shon*, N. Pracas; uzvadd; fg. budipracas.
Illusion, *il-liu'zhon*, N. Fottvonn; chuc; soponn; bhul.
Illustrate, *il-lus'treit*, V. Navaddunc; pracasunc; vivarunc.
Illustration, *il-lus-trei'shon*, N. Navadhni; vorto cornem, vivor.
Illustrious, *il-lus-tri'as*, A. Uttom; navadhgo; tejvont; sriman; vodd.
Ill-will, *il'will*, N. Mosor; niscuchar.
Image, *im'ej*, N. Imaz; rupcar; rupnem; sarkem: rejist.
Imaginable. *im-aj'in-e-bl*, A. Colpum-yeso; chintuet tosolo.
Imaginary, *im-aj'i-na-ri*, A. Colponnacho; chintnecho.
Imagination. *im-aj'in-ei-shon*, N. Colponn, chintna.
Imagine, *im-aj'in*, V. Colponna corunc, chintunc; sodun caddunc.
Imbecile, *im'be-sil*, A. Osoct, mengo, durboll; khullo.
Imbibe, *im'baib*, V. Attonc. jironc, monaut geunc.
Imbrue, *im-bro'*, V. Bizounc, khonchounc, rigounc.
Imitable, *im'i-te-bl*, V. Dek geum sarco, anucaria.
Imitate, *im'i teit*, V. Dek geunc, pattlau corunc.
Imitation, *im'i-tei-shon*, N. Dek gennem, pattlau; nokol.
Immaculate, *im-ma'ku-leit*, A. Nirmoll, nittoll, povitr; papkhot naslolo.
Immaterial, *im-ma-ti'ri-al*, A. cuddnaslolo; anang, amurt, nirakar.
Immature, *im-ma'chuar*, A. Pico naslolo. torno, horvo.
Immediate, *im-mi'di-eitt*, A. Tenclolo, lagsilo. sorsilo, teach vellacho.
Immediately, *im-me'di-eitt-li*, AD. lagun, tencun; rocdoch uprant, tea fara.
Immemorial. *im-me-mo'rial*, A. Ugddas-khobor naslolo.
Immense, *im-mens'*, A. Mitmer nasloio, okondit, ogónnit: bhou vodd, bhou chodd.
Immensity, *im-mens'i-tti*, N. Aparimitai, okhonditai; chodd. voddai.
Immerge, *im-merj'*, V. Buddounc.
Immersion, *im-mer'shon*, N. bud. dop, buddui, buchkoll.
Immigrate *im'mi-greit*. V. Porganvant vochunc,--ravunc.
Imminent, *im'mi-nent*, A. Lagim,—lagsarac aslolo, godduncaslolo,—paulolo.

Immoderate, *im-mo'der-eit*, A. Choddit, mitmer naslolo; utavlo, urmot, akar naslolo.
Immoderately *im-mo'der-eit-li*, AD. Mitmer uastanam.
Immoderation, *im-mo'de-rei-shon*, N. Nir moriad, adikai, utavlai, urmottai, danddgepònn.
Immodest, *im-mo'dest*, A. Loj,—bidda, akar naslolo; omoriadi.
Immodesty, *im-mo'desti*, N. omoriad, bemoriad, nilajreponn.
Immolate, *im'mo-leit*, V. Marun bettounc; somorpunc.
Immolation, *im-mo-lei'shon*, N. Bettounni, sacrifis.
Immoral, *im-mo'ral*, A. Onitivont, anayi, khotto, pojddo, choncholl.
Immorality, *im-mo'ra-li-tti*, N. Onit, anai; pojdeponn, sodeponn, choncholai.
Immortal, *im-mor'tal*, A. Mornavinn, morn naslolo; xevott naslolo.
Immortalize, *im-mor'-ta-laiz*, V. mornavinn corunc; aplem naum,—sasvat corunc, ajaravor zaunc.
Immortality, *im-mor-tal'i-tti* N. amoran, amrut, nirjarai, ajaravorponn.
Immovable, *im-mov-ie'bl*, A. Halo nozo aslolo, halo naslolo.
Immunity, *im-miu'ni-ti*, N. Sodd, sutt, mapi, modleponn.
Immutability, *im-mu-ta-bi'li-ti*. N. Thirason, nam-bodlop.
Immutable *im-miu-te'bl*, A. Bodolnaslolo; thir.
Imp, *imp*, N. Supurlo deuchar, buth; thidd hurgo.
Impair, *im-per'*, V. Pirder corunc; unno corunc, osoct corunc; man caddunc.
Impale *im-peil'*, V. Topunc; jiu caddunc.
Impalpable, *im-pal'pe-bl*, A. Hat lavum, hafdum nozo aslolo,
Impanel, *im-pan'el*. V. Kacherechea listar borounc.
Impart, *im-part*, V. Vantto diunc; ugddapem corunc.
Impartial, *im-par'shal*, A. Nitivont; tondd polle naslolo.
Impartiality, *im-par'shi-a-li-ti*, N. Modestai; nit.
Impassable, *im-pas'ie-bl*, A. Duka meclo; utronam-so.
Impassibility, *im-pas'i-bil-i-ti*, N. Nirdukh; sosinam-sarkem.
Impassible, *im-pas'i-bl*, A. Sosinam-sarco.
Impassioned, *im-pe'shond*, A. Uchambol; ragan pettlolo; Umalleacho.
Impatience, *im-pei'shens*, N. Sosnicai; tokos nasnem; dorvodd; chollboll; uchambollai.
Impatient, *im-pei'shent*, A. Sosnicai; usorpct naslolo; chollbollo vo uchamboll.
Impeach, *im-pich'*, V. Firiad diunc; guneauncari corunc.
Impeccability, *im-pec'a-bil-i-tl*, N. Patcantli suttca; papa-sambhav.
Impeccable, *im-pek'ie-bl*, A. Papcorum nozo aslolo; papa-sambhavi.
Impede, *im-pid'*, V. Addaunc; monam corunc; addvarunc.
Impediment, *im-ped'i-ment*, N. Addcoll; nadd; modd; vign.
Impel, *im-pel'*, V. Doclunc; lottunc.
Impend, *im-pend'*, V. Umcollunc; poddcho asunc.
Impending, *im-pend'ing*, A. Poddcho; bhou lagim aslolo.
Impenetrability, *im-pe'ne-tra-bil'i-ti*, N. Rigonam sarkem.
Impenetrable, *im-pe'ne-tre-bl*, A. Rigunc nozo aslolo.

Impenitence, *im-pe'ni-tens*, N. Dharunnai ; nam prajit.

Impenitent, *im-pe'ni-tent*, A. Dharun, prajit cori naslolo.

Imperative, *im-pe'rat-iv*, A. Podvecho ; sotecho ; gorjecho.

Imperceptible, *im-per-sept'i-bl*, A. Distti poddo naslolo ; callogomo-naslolo.

Imperfect, *im-per'fect*, A. Ordokhuro ; apurto ; vikhon ; aibi ; khorab.

Imperfection, *im-per-fec'shon*, N. Apurtai ; napurvonn ; aprapti, kosor.

Imperial, *im-pi'ri-al*, A. Maharajeacho.

Imperious, *im-pi'ri-as*, A. Sotecho ; podvecho ; nettacho ; jerudicho.

Imperishable, *im-pe'rish-ie-bl*. A. Mornavinn ; pirder zai naslolo.

Impermeable, *im-per'mi-a-bl*, A. Udcac rig naslolo.

Impersonal, *im-per'son-al*, A. Zonn dacoi naslolo.

Impertinence, *im-per'ti-nens*, N. Nacazalelem ; camac enaslelem ; corandai.

Impertinent, *im-per'ti-nent*, A. Naca zalolo ; bhailo ; bejar.

Imperturbable, *im-per-turb'a-bl*, A. Thondd ; shant ; thir.

Impervious, *im-per'vi-as*, A. Rig naslolo.

Impetuosity, *im-pe'tu-as'i-tti*, N. Japatto ; thoddaco ; veg ; urmottai.

Impetuous, *im-pe'tu-as*, A. Bollist ; urmott ; nettacho.

Impetus, *im'pe-tus*, N. Nett ; kinv ; fg. uchambollai.

Impiety, *im-pai'e-tti*, N. Devninda ; khotteponn.

Impious, *im'pi-as*, A. Dev-dhorm naslolo ; nisttur ; khotto.

Implacable, *im-pla'ke-bl*, A. Thambo nasloló ; darrun ; bogsi naslolo.

Implant, *im-plent'* V Launc ; rovunc ; khonchounc.

Implement, *im'ple-ment*, N. Aidon ; upai.

Implicate, *im'pli-keitt*, V. Guttlaunc ; guspaunc ; addcolin galunc ; dacoun diunc.

Implication, *im-pli-kei'shon*, N. Gonttalo ; revodd-conkem ; fg. addcoll.

Implicit, *im-pli'sit*, A. Nam uchcharlolo ; gupit.

Implore, *im-plor'*, V. Prathun hatpaim dorun, paiarh poddun magunc. attapunc.

Imply, *im-plai'*, V. Somzunc eunc;

Impolite, *im-po-laitt'*, A. Chalchomcon naslolo, Khorddo, rannot, jongli.

Impoliteness, *im-po-laitt'nes*, N. Mansugi nasnem.

Impolitic, *im-po'lit-ik*, A. Bud nasnaslolo ; rajnitic porto.

Imponderable, *im-pon'der-ie-bl*, A. Bhar naslolo,

Import, *im-port'*, N. Bhailem addnem ; orth,

Import, *im-port'*, V. Bhailo,—porgauncho addunc ; orth asunc ; somzon eunc.

Importance, *im-por-tans'*, N. Mol, kimot ; bhar ; porva, bixat.

Important, *im-port'ant*, A. Molacho, moladic ; bhari, vozondar, orthacho.

Importune, *im-pon-tun'*, V. Vaz addunc, ubgaunc, patt geunc.

Importunity, *im-por-tun'i-tti*, N. Corcor ; tondre.

Impose, *im-poz'*, V. Formannc ; fottounc.

Impossibility, *im-poss'i-bil-i-tti*, N. Nam tanc, osoctai. nam socti.

Impossible, *im-poss'i-bl*, A. Zai,—goddo naslolo, asambhavi.

Impostor, *im-pos'tor*, N. Dhongi, fotting, thoc.

Imposture, *im-pos'char*, N. Dong, kopott, nadd.

Impotence, *im'po-tens*, V. Osoctai, nirball. mengeponn.

Impotent, *im-po,tent*, A. Socot naslolo; osoct.

Imprecate, *im'pre-keitt*, V. Sirapunc, sirap galunc, sovunc.

Imprecation, *im-pre-kei'shon*. N. Sirap, soput; gall, maldisaum.

Impress, *im-press'* V. Mhor marunc; moVallunc; boro lagonc.

Impression, *im-pre'shon*. N. Khonchonnem; mhor; pagop, uchambollai.

Impressive, *im-press'iv*, A. Lagcho; monant,—callzant rigcho.

Imprint, *im-print'*, V. Sico,—xap marunc, xapunc.

Imprison, *impri'zn*, V. Prez galunc, bonconddint galunc.

Improbable, *im-pro'be-bl*, A. Sotmandunc nozo tosolo,

Improper, *im-pro'por*, A. Aiukt, borobor naslolo; nam-laik.

Improperly, *im-pro'por-li*, AD. Nittaevinn, apurtayen, aumoriadin.

Impropriety, *im-pro-prai'e-tti*, N. Ayukti, namlaiki.

Improve, *im-pruv'*. V. Sudarunc, boro corunc.

Improvement, *im-pruv'ment* N. Gunn vaddonnem, boro cornem, sudaron.

Imprudence, *im-pru'dens*, N. Bechotrai, urmottai; pixeponn.

Imprudent, *im'pru.dent*, A. Xanneponn. chotrai naslolo; urmott; hullhullo.

Impudent, *im'pu-dent*, A. Loz,—moriad naslolo, lapitt; tovnas, divallkor, bansiro.

Impugn, *im-pun'*, V. Virod ulonuc, addvarunc.

Impulse, *im'pols*, N. Lott, tol, nett, dhoko.

Impulsive, *impul'siv*, A. Nettacho, vegacho; huskauncho.

Impunity, *im-pu'ni-tti*, N. Khastintli suttca.

Impure, *im-piu'or*, A. Ollxig, mhello; burso.

Impurity, *im-piu'ri-tti* N. Mhelleponn; pozdeponn; cuddicheo khoxeo.

Imputation, *im-pu-ttei'shon*, N. Galni, thapni; lochand.

Impute, *im-piutt'*, V. Galunc, thapunc, Vahunc; opradi corunc.

In, *in*, V. Prep. bhitor, thaim.

Inability, *in-a-bil'i-ti*, N. Osoctponn, osoctai.

Inaccessible, *in-ac-ses'i-bl*, A. Pavum,—tenkum nozo aslolo; succduc naslolo.

Inaccuracy, *in-ak'kiu-ra-si*, N. Nam chotrai.

Inaccurate, *in-ak'kiu-reitt*, A. Zagrut noi aslolo; chotrai naslolo.

Inactive, *in-ak'tiv*, A. Betho; bestto; ricami.

Inactivity, *in-ak-tiv'i-tti*, N. Becarponn; ricamponn; nirudioz.

Inadequate, *in-ad'e-kuet*. A. Apurto; ayukt; camano poddo naslolo.

Inadvertence, *in-ad'vert-ens*, N. Avichar; bechotrai, chuc.

Inalienable, *in-al' yen-ie-bl* A. Dusreac diunc soddum nozo aslolo.

Inanimate, *in-an'i-meitt*, A. Jiu naslolo.

Inapplicable, *in-ap'pli-ke-bl*, A. Lozo naslolo ; onupeogi.
Inappreciable, *in-ap-pre'shi-ie-bl*, A. Mol corum nozo aslolo; faricponn naslolo; uncha molacho.
Inapproachable, *in-ap-proch'ie-bl*, A. Pavom-tenkum nozo aslolo.
Inaptitude, *in-apt'ti-tiud*, N. Nam laiki ; nirupiog.
Inarticulate, *in-ar-tik'u-leitt*, A. Gungunnit ; sande naslolo.
Inasmuch, *in-ez'mach*, AD. Decunn ; tea pasun.
Inattention, *in-at-ten'xion*, N. Nam chit ; nam chotrai.
Inattentive, *in-at-tent'iv*, A Chit di naslolo.
Inaugurate, *in-a'gu-reitt*, V. Suru curunc ; benjar corunc ; dobajean gennc.
Incalculable, *in-cal'ku-le-bl*, A. Gonnit, lek naslolo ; fg. chodd; zaito ; sobar.
Incandescence, *in-can-des'ens*, N. Ag cosi zannem.
Incandescent, *in-can-des'ent*, A. Uzo coso ; inglo coso.
Incantation, *in-can-tei'shon*, N. Bolinem ; bhul; ghaddi.
Incapability, *in-ke-pa-bil'i-tti*, N. Osoctponn ; osoctai ; nam laiki.
Incapable, *in-kei'pe-bl*, A. Tanc ; cuvet naslolo ; osoct ; apurto ; nam-laik.
Incarnate, *in-car'neitt*, V. Munxeachem soimb gennc ; munis zaunc.
Incarnation, *in-car-nei'shon*, N. Munxeavatar ; incarnasaum.
Incautious, *in-ko'shas*, A. Chotrai—, sidducai naslolo ; bechotur.
Incense, *in'sens*, N. Dump.
Incense, V. Dumpaunc.
Incentive, *in-sen'tiv*, N. Urba ; hurluc ; umallo.
Incertitude, *in-ser'ti-tiud*, N. Dubau ; athirponn ; samdhev.
Incessant, *in-ses'ant*, A. Thambo— ; kollo naslolo.
Incessantly, *in ses'ant-li*, AD. Nirontarim ; thambonastanam.
Incest, *in'sest*, N. Soiriam bhitor producvar.
Inch, *inch*, N. Angull.
Incidence, *in'si-dens*, N. Poddni ; ecmecac tenknem.
Incident, *in'si-dent*, N. Add cam ; goddni.
Incison, *in-si'zon*, N. Katrop ; katro.
Incisor, *in-siz'er*, N. Mucavelo dant.
Incite, *in-sait'*, V. Uchamtoll corunc ; huskaunc ; uttounc.
Incitement, *in sait'ment*, N. Urba ; umallo.
Incivility, *in-si-vil'i-tti*, N. Mansugi nasnem ; onitivontponn.
Inclemency, *in-cle'men-si*, N. Durunnai ; nistturponn ; kottinai.
Inclination, *in-cli-nei'shon*, N. Bagavni ; vankouni ; voddni ; apurbai.
Incline, *in-clain'*, V. Bagaunc ; vondounc ; borem disonc.
Inclined, *in-claind'*, (*park*) A. Toiar.
Include, *in-cliud'*, V. Bhitor galunc ; dorunc ; attapunc.
Inclusive, *in-cliu'ziv*, A. Soit.
Incognito, *in-cog'ni-tu*, A. Olloc ; khobor naslolo ; gupit.
Incoherence, *in-co-her'ens*, N. Ontor ; tafarat ; fer.
Incoherent, *in-co-he'rent*, A. Lago naslolo ; tuttco.
Income, *in'com*, N. Adau ; zodd.

Incommensurable, *in-com-men'-su-re-bl,* A. Mezum nozo aslolo; ogonnit.

Incommodious, *in-com-mo'di-as,* A. Soucosai naslolo.

Incommunicable, *in-com-miu'-ni-ke-bl,* A. Sangum nozo aslolo; ulouncho bond kela aslolo.

Incomparable, *in-com'pe-re-bl,* A. Sor corum,—sor dium nozo aslolo; aprub.

Incompatible, *in-com-pat'i-bl,* A. Mello,—lago naslolo, virudh, add.

Incompetence, *in-com'pe-tens,* N. Adicar nasnem; ayukti.

Incompetent, *in com'pe-tent,* A. Podvi naslolo, khaxa noi aslolo, ayukt.

Incomplete, *in-com-plit',* A. Ordho kuro, apurto, vicoll.

Imcompleteness, *in-com-plit'-ness,* N. Asampurnai.

Incomprehensible, *in-com'pre-hen-si-bl,* A. Somzunc nozo aslolo, attapum nozo aslolo.

Inconceivable, *in-con-siv'e-bl,* A. Chinti sarco naslolo, chintunc nozo aslolo.

Inconclusive, *in-con-klus'iv,* A. Aker naslolo, tall-mull naslolo.

Incongruity, *in-cong-gru'i-tti,* N. Virod, bascollponn.

Inconsiderable, *incon-sid'er-ic-bl,* A. chodd noi; olco; unnac.

Inconsiderate, *in-con-sid'e-reitt,* A. Chotrai naslolo, utavli.

Inconsiderateness, *in-con-sid'e-reitt-nes,* N. Uttavolponn.

Inconsistency, *in-con-sist'en-si,* N. Gottai nasnem; dounddo-litai; chomchollai.

Inconsistent, *in-con-sist'ent,* A. Gottai naslolo, halaito; fusfu-sit, dounddollit.

Inconsolable, *in-con-sol'ie-bl,* A. Bhuzoi sarco naslolo, asama-dhami,

Inconstansy, *in-con'stan-si,* N. Chonchollai; firteponn.

Inconstant, *in-con'stant,* A. Choncholl, uddto, variavelo; tir-tiro.

Incontinence, *in-con'ti-nens,* N. Amoriad; simdalponn.

Incontrovertible, *in-con'tro-vert-i-bl,* A. Tocrar—,vivad naslolo; dubava-vinno.

Inconvenience, *in-con-vi'ni-ens,* N. Favo-purai nasleli; bash-colponn.

Incorporate, *in-cor'po-reitt,* V. Mellounc.

Incorrectness, *in-co-rect'ness,* N. Assuddponn; fottkirponn.

Incorrigible, *in-co'ri-ji-bl,* A. Boro zai naslolo, belebann.

Increase, *in-criz',* V. Choddounc; vaddounc.

Increase, N. Choddop vo chod-dan.

Incredible, *in-cred'i-bl,* A. Sot-mandinanso.

Incredulity, *in-cre-du'li-tti,* N. Ovisvas, onbavarth.

Incredulous, *in-cre-du'las,* A. On-bavarthi, sotmandinam tosolo.

Incriminate, *in-crimin eith,* V Gunneuncari.—opradi corunc, guneaum galunc.

Incrust, *in-frost',* V.Cat enne: mau zaunc.

Incubate, *in'ku-beitt,* V. Rovan-nenc bosunc, rovaunc.

Inculcate, *in-cul'keitt,* V. Khon-chounc, motint galunc; portun portnn sangunc.

Inculcation, *in-culkei'shon,* N. Tarif sangnem, bori khobor dinnem.

Inculpable, *in-cul'pe-bl* A. Nent-to, guneaum naslolo.

Inculpate, *in-cul'peitt*, V. Guneauncari,—opradi corunc, dossunc.
Incur, *in-kor'*, V. Mellunc; khoroch corunc, guneaunvac sampddonc.
Incurability, *in-cur'a-bi-li-tti*, N. Boro zai naslolo, nirupai.
Incurable. *in-cur'e-bl*, A. Boro zai,—okot naslolo.
Incursion, *in-kor'shon*, N. Suari, punddai.
Indebted, *in-debt'ed*, A. Rin aslolo.
Indebted (Be), V. Devo asunc.
Indecency, *in-di'sen-si*, N. Niraj, omoriad, pozddeponn; ollxic.
Indecision, *in-di-si'jion*, N. Nivadd nasnem, dubau, Vicolp.
Indecisive, *in-di-si-zi'v*, A. Dubavi, dubavacho; tharan—nivadd cori naslolo.
Indecisive, *in-di-saiz'iv*, N. Duban, tharan cori naslolo.
Indeclinable, *in-de-klin'ie-bl*, A Chucoum; vattaum nozo aslolo.
Indecorous, *in-de-ko'ras*, A. Man mansugi—, akar naslolo; sobha naslolo.
Indecorum, *in-de-ko'rum*, N. Aumoriad. [albot.
Indeed, *in-did'*, AD. Khorench;
Indefatigable, *in-de-fat'ig-ie-bl*, A. Puro zainam tosalo; bejar zainam tosolo.
Indefinable, *in-de-fin'ic-bl*, A. Orthum nozo aslolo.
Indefinite, *in-def'i-nit*, A. Nitmer naslolo; ogonnit; aparampor.
Indelicate. *in-de'li-keitt*, A. Arbott; nazuc noi aslolo.
Indelicacy, *in-de'li-ca-si*, N. Arbottponn; omoriad.
Indemnification, *in dem'ni-fi-kei'shon*, N. Faricponn; borun dennem; luscan bornem.
Indemnify, *in-dem'ni-fai*, V. Borun diunc; luscan borunc.
Indent, *in-dent'*, V. Catre galunc.
Independence, *in-de-pend'ens*, N. Apli sotea; svatamtr.
Independent, *in-de-pend'ent*, A. Suadin naslolo; aple sotecho.
Independently, *in-de-pend'ent-li*, AD. Aple soten; aple khoxen.
Indestructible, *in-de-strukt'i bl*, A. Moddum nozo aslolo.
Indeterminable, *in-de-ter'min-ie-bl*, A. Anischei; annirnei.
Indeterminate, *in-de-ter'mi-neitt* A. Anischit; pullpullit; allmallit.
Indetermination, *in-de-ter'mi-nei'shon*, N. Anischai; anirdhar.
Index, *in'deks*, N. Paznanchi potti; dacounchem bott.
Indian, *in'di-an*, A. Indiecho vo Hindustancho.
Indicate, *in'di-keitt*, V. Bott; hat dacounc; polleunc diunc.
Indication, *in-di-kei'shon*, N. Dacoun.
Indicative, *in-dik'ie-tiv*, A. Dacouncho.
Indict, *in-dit*, V. Guneaum corunc caidea pormonnem.
Indifference, *in-dif'er-ens*, N. Beporva; befikir; thondmon; sambav.
Indifferent, *in-dif'er-ent*, A. Udasin; udas; beporvi; thondd.
Indifferently, *in-dif'er-ent-li*, AD. Udaspannim; ontor corinastanam; adavavinnem.
Indigence, *in'di-jens*, N. Durbolcai; dolldir; goribponn.
Indigenous, *in'di-jen-as*, A. Gauncho.
Indigent, *in'di-jent*, A. Dublo; gorib; gorjevont.
Indigestible, *in-di-jest'i-bl*, A, Jiro naslolo.

Indigestion, *in-di-jest'shon*, N. Ajirn; moddsi.
Indignant, *in-dig'nant*, A. Ragist; kirodacho.
Indignation, *in-dig-nei'shon*, N. Vaitt disnem; rag.
Indignity, *in-dig'ni-tti*, N. Ayukti; namlaiki; favo naslelem; naca zalelem, ocman.
Indigo, *in'di-go*, N. Nil.
Indirect, *in-di-rect'*, A. Addvo; vancddo.
Indirectly, *in-dai-rect'li*, AD. Addvem; vancddem.
Indiscreet, *in-dis-krit*, A. Uttavli; bechotur; jibec add naslolo.
Indiscretion, *in-dis-kre'shon*, N. Uttavlai; bechoturai; pixepon.
Indiscriminate, *in-dis-crim'in-eitt*, A. Kusin; veglo naslolo.
Indiscriminately, *in-dis-crim'in-eitt-li*, AD. Ontorevinnem.
Indispensable, *in-dis-pens'ie-bl*, A. Bhou gorjecho; chuco naslolo; jeruricho.
Indispose, *in-dis-poz'*, V. Vondounam zaunc; bongounc; bore bolaiken nasunc.
Indisposed, *in-dis-pozd*, A. Bolaiki naslolo.
Indisposition, *in-dis-po-zi'shon*, N. Jivac borem nasnem; soucasai nasnem.
Indisputable, *in-dis'piut-ie-bl*, A. Vivadum nozo aslolo; betocrar.
Indissoluble. *in-dis'so-liu-bl*, A. Soddum-, moddum nozo aslolo.
Indistinct, *in-di-stingkt'*, A. Veglo—,kherit noi aslolo.
Indistinctly, *in-dis-tingkt'li*, AD. Ontor—, veglicai nastanam; goir.
Indistinguishable, *in-dis-ting' gwish-ie-bl*, A. Boro aicum,—polleum uozo aslolo. [munc.
Indite, *indait* V. Borounc; nemunc.

Individual, *in-di-vid'u-al*, A. Aplo, viacticho, visesh; ecacho.
Individual, N. Jan, ekjan, asami, kull.
Individuality, *in-di-vid-u-al'i-tti*, N. Svabav, visesh; ecleacho gunn.
Indivisibility, *in-di-viz'i-bil-itti*, N. Abhediata.
Indivisible, *in'di-viz'i-bl*, A. Dosim corum nozo aslolo.
Indocile, *in-do'sail*, A. Sicounc nozo aslolo, sicunc upcaro naslolo.
Indocility, *in-dos'si-lit-ti*, N. Ashisheponn, siconam saskem.
Indolence, *in'do-lens*, N. Allsai; mengeponn; mosagot.
Indolent, *in'do-lent*, A. Auxi; jemetolo.
Indomitable, *in-dom'it-ie-bl*, A, Domaum nozo aslolo; attpo naslolo.
Indoor, *in'dor*, A. Gara bhitorlo.
Indubitable, *in-du'bit-ie-bl*, A. Dubavavinn konchit, khoro.
Induce, *in'dius'*, V. Fuslaunc, somzaunc combo caddunc.
Inducement, *in-dius'ment*, N. Fuslaunni, somzaunni, bulounni.
Induct, *indukt'* V. suru corunc.
Indulge, *in-dolj'*, V. Soucasaen cholonnc; soucas cholonc, soddunc; khoxe pormounem cholonc.
Indulgence, *in-dolj'ens*, N. Induljens, convollai, movollai; patcanchem bogsonnem.
Indulgent *in-dolj'ent*, A. Dulob movall, convallo, mogall.
Indurate, *in-diu-reitt*, V. Nibor corunc, gott corunc.
Industrious, *in-dus'trias*, A. Kami, coistti, udiogi; hicmoticho.
Industry, *in-dus'tri*. N. Hicmot, minot; hatcam.

Inebriate, *in-e'-bri-eit*, V. Bebdo corunc.

Ineffable, *in-ef'fe-bl*, A. Sangum--, ucharun nozo aslolo ; fg. coutic nazuc.

Ineffective, *n-ef-fek'tiv*, A. Gunn —boll naslolo, nirfoll.

Inefficacy, *in-ef'fi-ka-si*, N. Gunn nasnem ; osoctai.

Inelegant, *in-el'e-gant*, A. Sob,—akar nasiolo.

Inelegance, *in-el'e-gans*, N. Sob, nasnem, nir-acar.

Ineligibility, *in-el'i-ji-b-li-tti* ; N. Vinchun caddinam sarkem.

Ineligible, *in-el'i-ji-bl*, A. Vinchun caddum nozo aslolo.

Inequality, *in-i-kwal'i-tti*, N. Soi nasnem ; ontor.

Inert, *in-ort'*, A. Halunc nozo aslolo.

Inestimable, *in-es'tim-ie-bl*, A. Amolic, bhou moladic.

Inevitable, *in-ev'it-ie-bl*, A. Chucounc nozo aslolo.

Inexcusable, *in-eks'kiuz-ie-bl*, A. Mof favo naslolo ; vodde gorjecho.

Inexhaustible, *in-egz-ost'i-bl*, A. Uspum nozo aslolo.

Inexorable, *in-eks'or-ie-bl*, A. Canar ge naslolo ; cottin, khorkos.

Inexpediency, *in-eks-pi'di-en-si*, N. Nam vazbiponn.

Inexpedient, *in-eks-pi'di-ent*, A. Camanc poddo naslolo.

Inexperience, *in-eks-pi'r-iens*, N. Kocheponn, nenarpponn ; nam anbogh, nam sovoim.

Inexplicable, *in-eks'pli-ke-bl*, A. Orth—, somzoni dium nozo aslolo.

Inextinguishable, *in-eks-ting'-gwish-ie-bl*, A. Palov naslolo ; fg. soro naslolo ; tambo naslolo.

Inextricable, *in-eks'tri-ke-bl*, A. Sutto nasloio, gonddlacho.

Infallibility, *in-fal'i-bil-i-tti*, N. Achucponn, chuc nasnem.

Infallible, *in-fal'i-bl*, A. Chuco naslolo ; dubau naslolo.

Infamous, *in'fe-mus*, A. Beabrucho ; mancaddcho ; bodlami.

Infamy, *in'fa-mi*, N. Naum ubounnem ; man caddnem ; chaddi.

Infancy, *in'fan-si*, N. Burgeponn; ballponn.

Infant, *in'fant*, N. Ball ; balloc.

Infanticide, *in-fant'i-said*, N. Burgeacho morticar ; ball-gatki vo gatkin.

Infantry, *in-fant'ri*, N. Paim loscor.

Infatuate, *in-fa'tu-eitt*, V. piso corunc.

Infatuation, *in-fa'tu-a-shon*, N. Pixeponn.

Infect, *in-fect'*, V. Voso launc ; fg. cusounc.

Infection, *in-fec'shon*, N. Voso.

Infer, *in-for'*, V. Anumanunc : torcunc.

Inference, *in'fer-ens*, N. Anumantorc.

Inferior, *in-fi'ri-or*, A. Socoilo ; khailo ; khala aslolo.

Inferiority, *in-fe'r-io-ri'-tti*, N. Khalteponn ; unneponn ; camiponn.

Infernal, *in-fer'nal*, A. Emconddacho ; norokacho.

Infertility, *in-for-ti-li'tti*, N. Nam pikponn ; vanjponn ; dukoll.

Infidel, *in'fi-del*, A. Onbavarthi.

Infidelity, *in-fi-del'i-tti*, N. Onbavarthiponn ; abghat ; fottkirponn.

Infinite, *in'fi-nit*, A. Ogounit ; opormit ; okhondit.

Infinitely, *in'fi-nit-li*, AD. Sorivinn ; okhondit.

Infinitive, *in'fi-n-itiv*, A. Khondit naslolo.

Infirmary, *in-fer'ma-ri*, N. Piddechem gor vo hospital.
Inflame, *in-fleim'*, V. Pettounc; zollounc; ulpaunc.
Inflamed, *in-fleimd'*, A. Ragan borlolo; ragan khotkotlolo
Inflammation, *in-flam-ie'xhon*, N. Pettni; zolni; lasnni; vaidomon; agrum.
Inflate, *in-fiet'*, V. Suzounc; fulonc; fugounc.
Inflect, *in-flekt'*, V. Bagounc.
Inflexibility, *in-fleks'i-bil'i-tti*, N. Nittai; thatto; fg. kottinai; chicottai.
Inflexible, *in-fleks'i-bl*, A. Bagavo naslolo; nitt. [nem.
Inflexion, *in-fleks'xhon*, N. Bagou-
Inflict, *in-flikt*, V. (Khastt; dondd) launc; diunc; galunc.
Influence, *in'flu-ens*, N. Sokti; upai; pang.
Influence, V. Vollunc; boll corunc; voso lagonc.
Influential, *in-flu-en'shal*, A. Soctivont; biddecho; vozoudar.
Influx, *in-floks'*, N. Voton; bhorti.
Inform, *in-form'*, V. Collit corunc; khobor diunc; gomounc.
Informal, *in-form'al*, A. Caidea pormonnem naslolo; rit naslolo.
Information, *in-form-ie'xhon*, N. Khobor; volloc.
Infraction, *in-frek'xhon*, N. Moddop; guneaum.
Infrequency, *in-fri'kwen-si*, N. Kernaim goddnem.
Infrequent, *in-fri'kwent*, A. Kernaim goddtalo; patoll.
Infuriate, *in-fiu'ri-eitt*, V. Ragan zollounc.
Infuse, *in-fiuz'*, V. Bhitor galunc; votunc; labounc.
Infusion, *in-fiu'jion*, N. Otnni; galni; kosoi: fg. borounni; rigounni.

Ingenerate, *in-jen'er-eitt*, V. Zolmounc.
Ingenious, *in-je'ni-as*, A. Coistti; baric.
Ingenuity, *in-jen-u'i-tti*, N. Barkai; chamatcar.
Ingenuous, *in-jen-u'as*, A. Bolia monacho; sado; bollo.
Ingenuousness, *in-jen-u'as-ness*, N. Boleponn; sadeponn.
Inglorious, *in-glo'ri-as*, A. Yes—, kirti naslolo; ocmanancho; lojistt.
Ingrate, *in'greitt*, A. Onupcari.
Ingratiate, *in-gra'shi-eitt*, V. Movallaunc; mog launc.
Ingratitude, *in-grat'i-tiud*, N. Onupcarponn.
Ingredient, *in-gre'di-ent*, N. Sambar; aien.
Ingress, *-n'gres*, N. Rig.
Ingulf, *in-golf'*, V. Gillong.
Inhabit, *in-he'bit*, V. Asunc; raunc; jieunc.
Inhabitable *in-ha'bit-ie-bl*, A. Ravo sarco; biddar diuncho.
Inhabitant, *in-he'bit-ant*, N. Loc; eca thicannar sodaucal rautolo.
Inhale, *in-heil'*, V. Usvas geunc.
Inharmonius, *in-har-mo'ni-as*, A. Tallea mel naslolo; sampoddnaslolo.
Inherent, *in-her'ent*, A. Laglolo; thaincho.
Inherit, *in-he'rit*, V. Daiz poddonc, bens poddonc.
Inheritable, *in-he'rit-ie-bl*, A. Bens poddo sarco.
Inheritance, *in-he'rit-ens*, N. Daiz, bens.
Inheritor, *in-he'rit-or*, N. Daiji.
Inhebit, *in-heb'it*, V. Addvarunc, monam corunc.
Inhospitable, *in-hos'pit-ie-bl*, A. Biddar dinam tosolo, porkeanc ravonc dinam tosolo.

Inhuman, *in-hiu'man*, A. Munxeponn naslolo; nisttur.
Inhumanity, *in-hiu-man'i-tti*, N. munxeponn nam.
Inimitable, *in-im'it-ie-bl*, A. Dek geunc nozo aslolo, sangat corunc nozo aslolo.
Iniquitous, *in-ik'wit-as*, A Khotto, onkhotto, adhormacho.
Iniquity, *in-ik-wi-ti*, N. Onit, anai, onkottem, cusddeponn.
Initial, *in-i'shal*, A. Poilo, orombacho, mudolcho.
Initiate, *in-i'shi-eitt*, V. Suru corunc, oromb diunc.
Inject, *in-ject'*, V. Bhitor galunc vo borunc.
Injection, *in-jek-shon*, N. Bitor galnem, vo bornem.
Injunction, *in-jangk-shon*, N. Hucum, takid, caido.
Injure, *in'jer*, V. Luscan corunc, ducounc, noistt corunc.
Injurious, *in-ju'ri-as*, A. Ocmanacho, ducouncho, nimdecho.
Injury, *in'ju-ry*, N. Ocman; noistt; luscon; vaitt, duc.
Injustice, *in-just'is*, N. Onit, oprad, julum.
Ink, *ink*, N. Tint, xai.
Inkstand, *ihgk'stend*, N. Tinteor·
Inlay, *in-lei'*, V. Katre galunc.
Inlet, *in'let*, N. Rig, bhitor sorcho vall.
Inmate, *in'meitt*, N. Raunnar, loc.
Inmost, *in'most*, A. Bhou bhitorlo.
Inn, *in*, N. Hotel, puzad.
Innate, *in-neitt'*, A. Thaincho, soimbacho.
Innavigable, *in-na'vig-ie-bl*, A. Tharum choloum nozo aslolo doria.
Inner, *in'er*, A. Bhitorlo.
Inkeeper, *in'kep-er*, N. Puzadcar vo puzadcan.
Innocence, *in'no-sens*, N. Nentteponn, niroprad; lanponn, goribponn; babddeponn.
Innocent, *in'no-sent*, A. Nentto; patoc naslolo, guneauncar noi, bagevont. [kari, savo.
Innocuous, *in-nok'u-as*, A. Avi-
Innovate, *in'no-veitt*, V. Novo corunc, bodlunc.
Innovation, *in-no-vei'shon*, N. Bodlop; novi rit; novi moriad; novem cornem.
Innovator, *in-no-vei'tor*, N. Novem cortolo.
Innumerable, *in-nu'mer-ie-bl*, A. Gonnit-lek naslolo; ogonnit.
Inobservant, *in-ob-ser'vant*, A. Samballi naslolo, beporvi.
Innoculate, *in-ok'iu-leitt*, V. Tottko corunc; sikho,—dag diunc.
Inoffensive, *in-of-fens'iv*, A. Ocman corinaslolo, nir—opradi; bagevont.
Inopportune, *in-op'por-tun*, A. Favonaslelea vellar, avellacho.
Inordinate, *in-or'di-neitt*, A. Krama vinn; mirouncho.
Inorganic, *in-ar-gan'ik*, A. Sandhe,—jiv naslolo.
Inquest, *in'kwest*, N. Vicharop.
Inquire, *in-kwa-iar'*, V. Vicharunc; somzun geunc; khobor geunc.
Inquisition, *in-kwi-zi'shon*, N. Choucosi; vajpusi; dormasamik—shannasabha.
Inquisitive, *in-kwiz'i-tiv*, A. Choucosi corcho; vichari,
Inroad, *in'rod*, N. Angar poddop; lutt.
Insalubrious, *in-sa-lu'bri-as*, A. Bolaikec—, jivac vaitt; rogi.
Insane, *in-sein'*, A. Piso; vid lagul—lo.
Insanity, *in-san'i-ti*, N. Pixeponn; vid.

Insatiable, *in-sa'shi-ie-bl*, A. Osvosi; dadosi zai naslolo.
Insatiability, *in-sa'shi-a-bil'i-tti*, N. Osvosponn; havreponn.
Inscribe, *in-scraib'*, V. Borounc; khodunc; sivdder—, pottier galunc.
Inscription, *in-scrip'xhon*, N. Borop; lekhni; sercari roco.
Inscrutable, *in-scru'te-bl*, A. Vicharunc nozo aslolo; guttacho.
Insect, *in-sekt'*, N. Kiddo; kidd.
Insensibility, *in-sens'i-bil'i-tti*, N. Bohireponn; nirdukh.
Insensible, *in-sens'i-bl*, A. Visoe naslolo; bohiro; nirdukhi; sucdukh naslolo.
Inseparable, *in-sep'a-rei-bl*, A. Cusin—vingodd corunc nozo aslolo.
Inseparability, *in-sep'a-ra-bil'i-tti*, N. Vingodd—cusin zainam sarkem.
Insert, *in-sart'*, V. Bhitor galunc; khonchounc; kovunc.
Insertion, *in-sor'shon*, N. Sircavni, khovni.
Inside, *in'said*, PREP. Bitor.
—A. Bitorlo. [cuddo; gatki.
Insidious, *in-sid'i-as*, A. Kopti;
Insight, *in'sait*, N. Purti volloc.
Insignia, *in-sig'ni-a*, N. Nixan; doja.
Insignificant, *in-sig-ni'fi-cant*, A. Orth naslolo; kircoll; kuscutacho.
Insincere, *in-sin-si-ar'* A. Fottkiro; khotto; tondda purto.
Insincerity, *in-sin-ser'i-ti*, N. Fottkirponn; lobaddponn; kopott.
Insinuate, *in-sin'u-eit*, V. Monant galunc; callzant khonchounc; fuslaunc.
Insinuation, *in-sin'u-ei'xhon*, N. Vanoddim utram; fuslaunnim.
Insipid, *in-sip'id*, A. Ruch—suad naslolo.
Insipidity, *in-si-pid'i-ti*, N. Chachurai; capeponn; naca zalolo.
Insist, *in-sist'*, V. Gansunc; bhasunc; portun portun magunc.
Insolence, *in'so-lens*, N. Danddgai; urmottai; most.
Insolent, *in'so-lent*, A. Chalibhailo; urmott.
Insoluble, *in-sol'u-bl*, A. Soddum nozo aslolo; suttonaslolo; fg. viro—, khiro naslolo.
Insolvent, *in-sol'vent*, A. Bancrutti; thoclolo.
Insomuch, *in-so'mach*, AD. Tittlo ki; he jiusim.
Inspect, *in-spekt'*, V. Torjun polleunc; racunc.
Inspection, *in-spec'xhon*, N. Torjun pollop; choucosi corop.
Inspector, *in-spect'or*, N. Tellnar adikari; karbari.
Inspiration, *in-spi-rei'xhon*, N. Usvas; fuslaunni; devaprakas.
Inspire, *in-spa-iar'*, V. Usvasaborobor geunc; motint galunc; dhir diunc.
Instability, *in-sta-bil'i-ti*, N. Athirponn; thir naslelem mon; choncholai.
Install, *in-stal'*, V. Sodrer bosounc; pos diunc; ritin zagiar tharavunc; mudol gulunc.
Instalment, *in-stol'ment*, N. Pos dennem; mocruri; vaido.
Instance, *in'stans*, N. Zorurai; magnnem; daclo.
Instance, V. Motint haddunc; ugddas corunc.
Instant, *in'stant*, A. Gorjecho; joruri.
Instant, N. Khinn; vell.
Instantaneous, *in-stant-e'ni-as*, A. Ecach faracho, eke goddiecho, eca khinna bhitorlo.

Instantaneously, *in-stant-e'ni-as-li*, AD. Khinnam bhitor, eke goddien.

Instantly, *in'stant-li*, AD. Pallanc lagun; ecach fara.

Instead of, *in-sted'*, V. Prep. bodlec; suater.

Instep, *in'step*, N. Panvol.

Instigate, *in'sti-geit*, V. Sicounc, fulounc, uchamboll corunc.

Instil, *in-stil'*, V. Thoddem thoddem bhitor galunc.

Instinct, *in'stingkt*, N. Soimbacho—, jolmacho gunn; soimbachi zanvai.

Instinctive, *in-stingkl'iv*, A. Amgche budicho, soimbacho.

Institute, *in'sti-tiut*, V. Goddunc, rochunc; tharavunc.

Institute, N. Karcano, sall; videa math; goddop, bandop.

Instruct, *in-strukt'*, V. Sicounc; hukum diunc.

Instruction, *in-struc'shon*, N. Sicop vc sicon; hukum.

Instructive, *in-struct-iv*, A. Siconncho, upcarac poddcho; bud diuncho.

Insructor, *in-struct'er*, N. Sicoitolo mistir.

Instrument, *in'stru-ment*, N. Aidon, atiar; upai; daklo.

Instrumental, *in-stru-ment'al*, A. Upcari, cumki.

Insubordinate, *in-sub-or'din-eitt*, A. Khalto naslolo, kholpololo.

Insubordination, *in-sub-or'din-ei-shon*, N. Kholponnem, fituri.

Insufficiency, *in-suf-fi'shen-si*, N. Napurvon, comti, apurtai.

Insufficient, *in-suffi'shent*, A. Pavonaslolo, apurto, unno.

Insular, *in'su-lar*, A. Ecoddo, sutto.

Insult, *in'sclt*, N. Ocman, gall, beman.

Insult, V. Ocman coruno, insul tar corunc, man caddunc.

Insulting, *in'solt-ing*, A. Ocmanacho, bemanacho.

Insuperable, *in-su'per-ie-bl*, A. Jicunc nozo aslolo; zoit voronc nozo aslolo.

Insupportable, *in-sup-port'ie-bl*, A. Sosum, tallum nozo aslolo, bhou khor.

Insurance, *in-shor'ans*, N. Zamimicho mell, bima.

Insure, *in-shor'*, V. Risk naslolo corunc; zamindar zaunc.

Insurgent, *in-sor'jent*, A. Bonddi, fiturio.

Insurgent. N. Sercaracher kolpololo, bodol-lolo mnnis.

Intact, *in-tekt'*, A. Hat lagunc naslolo, amanat, aputt.

Integer, *in'ti-jer*, N. Purto anc.

Integral, *in'te-gral*, A. Soglo, sompurn.

Integrity, *in-teg'ri-ti*, N. Soglepoun; moriad; ancuarponn.

Intellect, *in'tel-lekt*, N. Ginean, mot.

Intellectual, *in'tel-lec-chu-al*, A. Budicho, moticho, gineanacho.

Intelligence, *intel'i-jens*, N. Somjicai; ginean.

Intelligent, *in-tel'li-jent* A. Somjic; uxar.

Intelligible, *in-tel'i-ji-bl*, A. Somzum-eso, somzo sarco.

Intemperance, *in-tem'per-ans*, N. pottartti; attibhojan.

Intemperate, *in-tem'per-eitt*, A. Khanna-pinneank pettlolo, pottarthi.

Intend, *in-tend'*, V. monant asunc, monant dorunc; chiutnne.

Intense, *in-tens'*, A. Koddoc, bhari, umalleacho.

Intensity, *in-ten'si-ti*, N. Umallo; cottinai.

Intent, *in-tent'*, A. Laglolc ; chit diuncho.
Intent, N. Xevott ; mon.
Intention, *in-ten'shon*, N. Tensaum, mon, euzonn.
Intentional, *in-ten'shon-al*, A. Khoxen kelolo.
Intentionally, *in-ten'shon-al-li*, AD. Khoxen, chintun.
Intently. *in-tent'li*, AD. Chit diun.
Inter, *in-tor'*, V. Puruno. matiec launc.
Intercede, *in-ter-sid'*, V. Dusrea katir magunc ; vinoti corunc.
Interceder, *in-ter-sid'er*, N. Dusrea khatir magnar ; vinoti cornar.
Intercept, *in-ter-sept'*, V. Vatter dorunc ; ravounc ; bond corunc.
Intercession, *in-ter-se'shon*, A. Magnem ; vinot ; mozot.
Intercessor, *in'ter-ses-or*, N. Mozotdar ; xarati ; modest.
Interchange, *in-ter-cheinj'*, V. Bodlunc.
Intercourse, *in'ter-kors*, N. Ennem vochnem; chali—boli; voivatt.
Interdict, *in-ter-dikt'*, V. Addvarunc ; monam corunc. [corop.
Interdict, N. Addvarop ; mona—
Interest, *in'ter-est*, V. Addav—, phol diunc; zoddunc, mellounc; boro—, ruchic lagunc.
Interest, N. Adan ; labh ; nofa ; asil , porva ; fikir ; bhar ; jur.
Interested, *in'ter-est-ed*, A. Adau—, nofa aslolo ; bhar getolo ; bageli ; vanttecar.
Interesting, *in'ter-est-ing*, A. Boro lagcho; ruchic, suadic; coutic; najuc ; chit mon voddun vorcho.
Interfere, *ih-ter-fiar'*, V. Modembhitor eunc ; hat-thondd galunc ; gusunc.
Interference, *in-ter-fer'ens*, N. Modem ennem ; modestai ; gusnni. [alaiti chacri vo cam.
Interim, *in'ter-im*, N. Modlo call ;
Interim, AD. Itlea—bhitor.
Interior, *in-te'ri-or*, A. Bhitorlo.
Interjacent, *ig-ter-ja'sent*, A. Bhiter—, modem aslolo.
Interlace, *in-ter-leis'*, V. Ecttaim vinounc.
Interlard, *in-ter-lard'*, V. Mellounc ; bhitor galunc.
Interleave, *in'ter-liv*, V. Panam modem galunc.
Interline, *in'ter-lain*, V. Gitan bhitorborounc.
Interlinear, *in-ter-lin'e-ar*, A. Olim bhitorlo.
Interlocutor, *in-ter-lo'kut-or*, N. Eranchea nanvan uloitolo.
Interloper, *in-ter-lop'ar*, N. Modem aillo (munis).
Intermarry, *in-ter-me'ri*, V. Cazara udexim ecott corunc.
Intermediate, *in-ter-me'di-eitt*, A. Modlo vo modem aslolo.
Interment, *in-ter'ment*, N. Purop; morn.
Interminable, *in-ter-min'ie-bl*, A. Xevott naslolo ; aparampar.
Intermingle, *in-ter-ming'gl*, V. Mellounc; mislonc.
Intermission, *in-ter-mi'shon*, N. Khavallni ; thambni ; khavtem; pidda denvuem.
Intermit, *in-ter-mit'*, V. Thambonc ; soddunc.
Intermittent, *in-ter-mit'ent*, A. Poireacho zor ; vecho euncho.
Internal, *in-tern'al*, A. Bhitorlo ; aplo.
International, *in-ter-ne'shon-al*- A. Paraspara desacho ; paraspradesi.
Internecine, *in-ter-ne'sin*, A. Ecamecac jivesim marcho.

Interpellate, *in-ter'pel-leit*, V. Hoddcunc ; vichar corunc.

Interpolate, *in-ter'po-leit*, V. Fottkiro corunc ; pustocant favo naslelim utram borounc.

Interpose, *in-ter-poz'*, V. Modem galunc ; panchaetdar zaunc.

Interpret, *in-ter'pret*, V. Orth sangunc—, diunc ; vivarunc.

Interpretation, *in-ter-pret-ei'-shon*, N. Orth ; vivaran.

Interpreter, *in-ter'pret-ar*, N. Bhasántar cortolo ; dubashi.

Interregnum, *in-ter-reg'num*, N. Rajantar.

Interrogate, *in-ter'ro-geitt*, V. Vicharunc ; nimgunc.

Interrogation, *in-ter'ro-gei'shon*, N. Vicharnem ; sovall.

Interrogative, *in-ter-rog'at-iv*, A. Vicharcho ; prasna-rup.

Interrupt, *in-ter-rupt'*, V. Bond,—mona corunc, thambounc.

Interruption, *in-ter-rop'shon*, N. Addcoil ; thambounem.

Intersect, *in-ter-sekt'*, V. modem catrunc.

Intersection, *in-ter-sec'shon*, N. modem catornem.

Interstice, *in-ters'tais*, N. Dall. futt ; fursod. [farat.

Interval, *in-ter'val*, N. Avkas, ta-

Intervene, *in-ter-vin'*, V. Bhitor eunc ; addaunc.

Intervention, *in-ter-ven'shon*, N. Modem,—add ennem,—ravnem.

Interview, *in'ter viu*, N. Ulounem, bhett.

Interweave, *in'ter-wiv*, V. Ectta-im vinnunc; mellounc.

Intestate, *in-test'eit*, A. Testament nam kelolo.

Intestine, *in-tes'tain*, A. Bithorlo.

Intestine, N. Ankiddi.

Intimacy, *in'ti-ma-si*, N. Isttogot, amizad ; ennem vochnem.

Intimate, *in'ti-meitt* A. Bhitorlo ; callzacho.

Intimately *in-tim'eitt-li*, AD. Bhitorleau ; callzant ; isttogotin.

Intimation, *in-ti-mei'shon*, N. Janaunni, collounni ; suchana.

Intimidate, *in-tim'id-eitt*, V. Benkddaunc, torjunc ; dogounc.

Intimidation, *in-tim-id-ei'shon'* N Benkddaoni, dogoun.

Into, *in'tu*, PREP. Thuim ; bhitor.

Intolerable, *in-tol'er-ie-bl'*, A. Sosum nozo aslolo.

Intolerant, *in-tol'er-ant*, A. Sosnicai naslolo, sosinaslolo.

Intonation, *in-ton-ei'shon*, N. Tal leachi suru, gaienacho rig.

Intone, *in-ton'*. V. Gaien suru corunc.

Intoxicate, *in-toks'i-keitt*, V. Bebdo zaunc vo corunc.

Intoxication, *in-toks'i-kei-shon*, N. Bebdeponn.

Intractable, *in-tract'ie-bl*, A. Cholounc nozo aslolo ; aplea vadeacho.

Intrench, *int-rench'*, V. Chonn marun tantum ravonc.

Intrenchment, *in-trench'ment*, N. Khondoc.

Intrepid, *in-tre'pid*, A. Calljevont bhienaslolo, doiravont.

Intrepidity, *in-tre-pid'i-ti*, N. Dhoir, nirvonn ; callji.

Intricate, *in'tri-keitt*, A. Cottin, augodd. [augoddai.

Intricacy, *in'tri-ca-si*, N. Tondre ;

Intrigue, *in trig'*, N. Modd, nadd, guddu-lasaum, fott.

Intriguer, *in-trig'er*, N. Kunslavno, lanvddo; naddicho.

Intrinsic, *in-trin'sik*, A. Bhitorlo ; jaticho ; boddicho.

Introduce, *in-tro-dias'*, V. Bhitor galunc—,lottunc,—sirounc; cholounc ; Volloc dacounc.

Introduction, *in-tro-duk'shon*, N; Vorop; sifaras; rig; oromb; toiari.

Introductive, *in-tro-duc'tiv*, A. Orombacho; suruvetcho, vo toiar corcho.

Intrude, *in-triud'* V. Praves zaunc; chora bori rigong, nadduno.

Intruder, *in-triud'er*, N. Naddi, pravesi.

Intrusion, *in-tru'jion*, N. Direit naslelem rigop.

Intrust, *in-trost'*, V. Connainche. adin corunc, suadin corunc.

Intuition, *in-tu-i'shon*, N. Sahaj, ollock, antarjnan.

Inundate, *in-un-deit*, V. Aunr eunc; poriallo eunc. [Aunr.

Inundation *in'un-dei-shon*, N.

Inure, *in-iu'r*, V. Sovoim corunc; gott corunc.

Inutility, *in-iu-til'i-tti*, N. Onupeog; nirfollai.

Invade, *in-veid'*. V. Galo galunc rigunc; angar poddonc.

Invalid, *in-va'lid*, A. Osoct, poklo; chacrec upcaro naslolo munis.

Invalidate, *in-va'li-deit*, V. Nacarunc; mekunc; rodd corunc.

Invaluable, *in-ve'lu-ie-bl*, A. Amolic; bhou moladic.

Invasion, *in-ve'zhon*, N. Dhadd galnem; fg. galo galnem.

Invective, *in-vec'tiv*, N. Gall; ocmon.

Inveigh against, V. Galli sonvonc; angar poddonc.

Inveigle, *in-ve'gl*, V. Fuslaunc; piso corunc.

Invent, *in-vent'*, V. Sodun caddunc; goddunc; rochunc.

Invention, *in-ven'shon*, N. Yojon; goddop; kolponna.

Inventive, *in-ven'tiv*, A. Caramoti; mannecar; yuctivont; tojvitvont.

Inventive, N. Goddpi.

Inventory, *in'ven-to-ri*, N. Potti; sivdi; inventar.

Inverse, *in'vers*, A. Porto, upratto; ulto.

Inversion, *in-vor'shon*, N. Upratni; ulotni.

Invert, *in-vort'*, V. Portunc.

Invest, *in-vest'*, V. Bogavoll diunc; veddo galunc; bondabostin dovorunc.

Investigate, *in-ves'ti-geit*, V. Choucosi corunc; sod—, thav geunc.

Investigation, *in-ves-ti-gei'shon*, N. Choucosi; sod; thav.

Investiture, *in-ves'ti-tiuar*, N. Bogavoll dennem.

Inveteracy, *in-vet'a ra-si*, N. Pornom zannem; porneponn.

Inveterate, *in-vet'e-rat*, A. Pornom; adlo; sobar callacho; pallam getolo.

Invidious, *in vid'i-as*, A. Mosri; temoz.

Invigorate, *in-vi'gor-eit*, V. Bolldiunc.

Invincible, *in-cin'si-bl*, A. Jicnozo aslolo.

Inviolability, *in-vi'o-la-bil'i-tti*, N. Hat launm-, moddum nozo asnem; povitr.

Inviolable, *in vi'o-le-bl*, A. Khotaunc nozo aslolo; povitr.

Inviolate, *in-vi'o-leit*, A. Khot naslolo.

Invisible, *in-vi'zi-bl*, A. Distti poddo naslolo.

Invitation, *in-vi-tei'shon*, N. Apounnem; voullie.

Invite, *in-vait'*. N. Apounc; voullic saugunc.

Inviting, *in-vaitt'ing*, A. Voddnecho.

Invocation, *in-vo-kei'shon*, N. Magnnem; ulo.

Invoice, *in'vois*, N. Samnachem list vo potti.

Invoke, *in-vok'*, V. Ulo marunc; magunc; prathunc.

Involuntary, *in-vo'lun-ta-ri*, A. Khoxi naslolo, nennarponnan kelolo.

Involve, *in-volv'*, V. Sircaunc; corandaen galunc; attapunc.

Invulnerable, *in-vul'ner-ie-bl*, A. Topunc—, gai galunc nozo aslolo.

Inward, *in'vord*, A, Bhitorlo.

Inwardly, *in'vord-li*, AD. Bhitor.

Irascibility, *i-ras'i-bil'i-tti*, N. Zolsarai; tiddai.

Iris, *i'ris*, N. Domdubal.

Irksome, *irk'som*, A. Corcoracho; bejaraecho.

Irksomness, *irk'som-nes*, N. Corcar; tondre.

Iron, *ai'ron*, N. Lokondd.

Iron, V. Gomar corunc; fer marunc.

Iron, V. Lokonddacho.

Ironical, *ai-ron'ik-al*, A. Uprodhacho; uprodhi.

Ironmonger, *ai'ern-mong-er*, N. Lokondacho saucar.

Irony, *ai-ro'ni*, N. Akshep; uprodh; fg. vign.

Irradiate, *ir-ra'di-eit*, V. Uzvadd diunc; pracasunc.

Irrational, *ir-ra'shon-al*, A. Budnaslolo; pixeponnacho; monzaticho.

Irrationality, *ir-ra'shon-al'li-ti*, N. Nam somjicai.

Irreconcilable, *ir-re'con-sail'ie-bl*, A. Somadan corunc nozo aslolo; somadan naslolo.

Irrecoverable, *ir-re-ko'ver-ie-bl*, A. Portun—, novean mello naslolo.

Irrefragable, *ir.ref'ra-ge-bl*, A. Zab dium nozo aslolo; gott; pratipal naslolo.

Irrefutable, *ir-re-fiut'ie-bl*, A. Solvounc nozo aslolo; solvonam sarco.

Irregular, *ir-re'gul-ar*, A. Vancddo; caidea-riti add; kram naslolo; khotto.

Irregu'arity, *ir-re'gul-a-ri-ti*, N. Vankddeponn; akram.

Irrelevant, *ir-re'le-vant*, A. Camanc poddo naslolo; vodd noim; chitor.

Irreligious, *ir-re'li-ji-as*, A. Xastr naslolo vo xastrac add aslolo; bogtivin.

Irremediable, *ir-re-me'di-ie-bl*, A Boro zaunc nozo aslolo; somzaunc nozo aslolo; upavavinn.

Irreparable, *ir-re'pa-ra-bl*, A. Sudarum nozo aslolo; nirupavi; gat zalolo.

Irreprehensible, *ir-rep're-hen'si-bl*, A- Guniaum naslolo; sudd; nirmoll.

Irresistible, *ir-re-zist'ie-bl*, A. Add eum—, boll corum nozo aslolo; vattaum nozo aslolo.

Irresolute, *ir-re-zo'liut*, A. Dubavi; dounddollit; chonchol monacho.

Irresolution, *ir-re-zo-lu'shon*, N. Dubau; goll; embaras.

Irreverence, *ir-re've-rens*, N. Ocman; beman.

Irreverent, *ir-re've-rent*, A. Ocmanacho; man dinaslolo.

Irrevocable, *ir-re'vok-ie-bl*, A. Portum—, firaum nozo aslolo; patti caddi namso.

Irrigate, *ir-ri'geit*, V. Udoc galunc vo simponc.

Irritable, *ir'rit-ie-bl*, A. Ragist vo ragar zai sarco.

Irritate, *ir'rit-eit*, V. Rag addunc.

Irruption, *ir-rop'shon*, N. Dhadd; punddai.

Isinglass, *ai'sing-las*, N. Maslle; [cho sar.

Island, *ai'lund*, N. Zuuvo.
Islander, *ai'lend-ar*, N. Zuuvecar.
Isolate, *ai'zo-leit*, v. Veglo corunc; pois cadduno.
Isolation, *ai'zo-lei'shon*, N. Veglachar; eksurponn.
Issue, *ish'u*, N. Xevott.
Issue, v. Bhair soronc; purgottunc; zaunc. [tto.
Isthmus, *isth'mus*, N. Buim gom-
It, *it*, PRO. Tem; hem etc.
Itch, *ich*, N. Koroz.
Itch, v. Korzunc.
Item, *ai'tem*, N Rokom.
Iterate, *it'er-eit*, v. Portun corunc.
Itinerant, *it-i'ner-ant*, N. Poinnari; ganvangaum bounar.
Itself, *it-self'*, PRO. Tench etc.
Ivory, *ai'vo-ri*, N. Hotiacho doddo vo dant.

J

Jobber, *job'er*, N. J. boddbodd.
Jackal, *jak'ol*, N. Colo.
Jakanapes, *jak'on-ieps*, N. Mankodd.
Jackass, *jak'as*, N. Dadlem gaddum; fg. koddo.
Jacket, *jec'et*, N. Bandian.
Jack-fruit, N. Ponos.
Jag, *jeg*, v. Catre galunc.
Jaggery, *jog'er-i*, N. Godd.
Jail, *jeil*, N. Boncoudd.
Jailer, *jei'lor*, N. Carcereiro, boncond rackno.
Jam, *jam*, N. Dos, jam.
Jangle, *jeng'-gl*, v. Zogddonc.
Jar, *jar*, N. Buiaum.
Jar, v. Zogddonc.
Jasmine, *jas'-min*, N. Collo.
Jaundice, *jon'-dis*, N. Caicoi.
Javelin, *jav'lin*, N. Bhalo.
Jaw, *jo*, N. Gal, daddomona.
Jealous, *je'-los*, A. Mosri; niscuchari; cubdi.
Jealousy, *je'los-i*, N. Niscuchar, mosor.
Jeer, *jer*, v. Yeddaunc.
Jeer, N. Yeddaunem, gall.
Jest, *jest*, N. Chesttai; facahdd.
Jest, v. Chesttai corunc; ansear 'galunc.
Jester, *jest'or*, N. Khelgaddo.
Jew, *ju*, N. Judeu.
Jewel, *ju'el*, N. Mannic; trast.
Jilt, *jilt*, N. Pattolli.
Job, *job*, N. Cani; vaur.
Jobber, *job'er*, N. Dalal.
Jockey, *jok'i*, N. Shertichea goddear bounar. [facanddi.
Jocose, *joc-oz'*, A. Chesttaecho;
Jog, *jog*, v. Dolle moddunc.
Join, *join*, v. Mellounc; goddsunc; zomounc.
Joint, *joint*, N. Gantt; sando.
Joke, *jok*, N. Facandd.
Jollity, *jol-li'ti*, N. Ulas.
Jolly *jol'i*, A. Khoxal; ulasacho.
Jolt *jolt*, v. Cochcochunc.
Jostle, *jo'sl*, v. lottunc, addlounc.
Jot, *jot*, N. Caim.
Journal, *jorn'al*, N. Potr, fol.
Journalism, *jor-na-li'zm*, N. Vortamon—potrachem cam.
Journalist, *jor'na-list*, N. Potr boroinar.
Journey, *jor'ni*, N. Eca ganvant than dusrea ganvant vochop; chol-leli vatt, viaz.
Journey, v. Viaz corunc.
Joy, *joi*, v. Sontos, dadosponn; suc; khoxalai.
Jubilant, *ju-bil'ant*, A. Khoxalborit, dadosi.
Jubilee, *jubi'li*, N. Jubleu.
Judge, *juj*, N. Munsubdar, nitidar.
Judge, v. Nit corunc; chintunc.
Judgment, *joj'ment*, N. Nit, zoddti; bud.
Judgment-day, N. Nimano dis: zoddtecho dis.

Judgment-hall, N. Nitichem sal.
Judicial, *ju-d'isi-al*, N. Niticho.
Judicature, *ju'di-kei-tur*, N. Nit corchi podvi.
Judicious, *ju di'shas*, A. Nitivont.
Jug, *jog*, N. Aidon, mog.
Juggle, *jog'l*, V. Khellonc.
Juggler, *jog'lor*, N. Khellgoddo.
Juice, *jus*, N. Sar; ros.
Jujube, *ju'jub*, N. Bor.
Jumble, *jamb'l*, V. Ras corunc; mellounc.
Jump, *jamp*, V Uddi marunc.
Jump, N. Uddop; uddki.
Junction, *jonc'shon*, N. Mell; sondop.
Jungle, *jong'gl*, N. Ran; Oronnem.
Junnior, *ju'ni-or*, A. Dacto.
Junk, *jongk*, N. Pornea razvache cuddke; kharea masache lombe.
Jurisconsult, *ju'ris-con-sult*, N. Xastr zannar.
Jurisdiction, *ju-ris-dik'shon*, N. Nit corcho adicar.
Jurisprudence, *ju-ris-pru'dens*, N. Caidea videia.
Jurist, *ju'rist*, N. Vokil; zannar.
Juror, *ju'ror*, N. Panchaetdar.
Just, *jast*, AD. Sarkem; khorench.
Justice, *jos'tis*, N. Nit; santipon.
Justification, *jos-ti-fi-kei'shon*, N. Bagevontponn.
Justify, *jost'i-fai*, V. Nitivont corunc; bagevont corunc; udaran sangunc.
Jut, *jut*, V. Bhair eunc; mucar soronc.
Juxtaposition, *juks'ta-po-zi'shon*, N. Lagop.

K

Keel, *kil*, N. Tarvachem pond.
Keen, *kin*, A. Baric; umalleacho.
Keenness, *kin'ness*, N. Barcai; umallo.
Keep, *kiip*, V. Dovorunc; dorunc; asunc; posunc; samballunc; faric corunc.
Keep, (An account), Ixeop borounc.
—(Waiting), Usir corunc.
—(A feast), Fest corunc.
—(A part), Veglo dovorunc.
—(Back), Addaunc; lipounc.
—(Company), Pavounc; sangata vochonc.
—(Down), Bond corunc.
—(Off), Pois caddunc.
—(Together), Sangata dovorunc.
—(Up with), Pattlean vochunc.
—(Up), Samballunc; dovorunc; dhir diunc.
Keeper, *kiip'ar*, N. Racnno.
Keeping, *kiip'ing*, V. Samballop; laecponn.
Kernel, *kar'nel*, N. Bim; coi.
Kettle, *ket'tl*, N. Kitli.
Key, *ki*, N. Chavi; upai.
Kick, *kic*, N. Khott; lat.
Kick, V. Khottaunc; khot marunc.
Kid, *kid*, N. Bocddechem por.
Kidnap, *kid'nep*, V. Munxeac chorun voronc.
Kill, *kill*, V, Jivesim marunc.
Kin, *kin*, N. Soiric.
Kind, *kaind*, N. Jinos; soimb.
Kind, A. Doiall; mogall.
Kindle, *kin'dl*, V. Pettounc; funcunc; zollounc.
Kindliness, *kaind'li-ness*, N. Mogalponn; doia.
Kindly, *kaind'li*, AD. Mogan.
Kindly, A. Mogall; doiall.
Kindness, *kaind'ness*, N. Doia; boreponn; mog; upcar.
Kindred, *kind'red*, N. Soiric.
Kindred, A. Soiro vo soiro-dairo.
King, *king*, Rai; raja.
Kingdom, *king'dom*, N. Raz; razvott; fg. vorg.

Kingly, *king'li*, A. Raiacho.
Kings-evil, *kings-ev'l*, N. Catmau.
Kinsfolk, *kins'fok*, N. Soiro-dairo.
Kiss, *kis*, N. umaum ; bej.
Kiss, V. Umaum geunc.
Kitchen, *ki'chin*, N. Randpachi cudd ; cuzin.
Kite, *kait*, N. Gonn. [por.
Kitten, *kit'ten*, N. Mazrachem
Knave, *neiv*, N. Lucho ; thoc.
Knead, *niid*, V. Pitt mollunc.
Knee, *ni*, N. Dimbi ; dompor.
Kneel, *nil*. V. Dimbi galunc.
Knife, *naif*, N. suri ; pishcati.
Knight, *naitt*, N. Sardar.
Knit, *nitt*, V. Vinnunc ; inni galunc.
Knock, *noc*, V. Boddounc ; darar marunc.
—(Down), Portun galunc.
Knot, *nott*, N. Gantt ; shenddo.
Know, *nou*, V. Zanno zaunc ; somzonc.
Knowingly, *nou'ing-li*, AD. Zanno zaun ; somzon.
Knowledge, *no'lej*, N. Zanvai ; bud ; volloc ; somjicai.
Known, *noun*, P. A. Navaddlolo ; voddlo.

L

Label, *le'bl*, N. Naum ; thican ; direcsaum.
Laborious, *la-bo'ri-as*, A. Cottin ; coisttancho.
Labour, *lei'bor*, N. Vaur ; cam ; coistt ; minot.
Labour, V. Vauronc ; cam corunc; coisttavonc; coistt sosunc.
Labourer, *lei'bor-er*, N. Vauraddi; begari.
Labyrinth, *lab'i-rinth*, N. Nagmodicho zago ; gonthallo ; fa. gospargondhol ; revoddkonkem.
Lac, *lac*, N. Lak.
Lace, *lês*, N. Rend.
Lace, V. Rend launc ; bandunc.
Lacerate, *la'ser-eitt*, V. Ghai galunc ; bokrunc.
Laceration, *la-ser-ei'shon*, N. Bokrop : vidarni.
Lack. *lek*, N. Goroz ; chucop.
Lack, V. Goroz asunc ; asonam zaunc ; chuconc.
Lackey, *lek'i*, N. Chacor.
Laconic, *la-con'ik*, A. Thoddeam utrancho ; sanksepacho.
Lad, *led*, N. Burgo ; chedde.
Ladder, *led'ar*, N. Nisonn.
Laden, *led'n*, A. Borlolo.
Lading, *leid'ing*, N. Vojem ; fret.
Ladle, *le-dl'*, N. Doi.
Lady, *lei'di*, N. Saibinn ; bai.
Lag, *leg*, A. Pattlean eupacho; auxi.
Laggard, *lag'ard*, A. Auxi ; patti aslolo.
Lagoon, *la-gun'*, N. Utoll nod ji lagta doriac vo voddle nodic.
Laic, *la'ik*, A. Sounsari.
Lair, *ler*, N. Dhol.
Laity, *lei'i-tti*, N. Loc padrinc cusin caddun; voizachem vo letradachem profisaum corinaslolo loc.
Lake, *leik*, N. Tollem ; khon.
Lamb, *lem*, N. Bocrechem por ; xelli.
Lame, *lêm*, A. Thontto.
Lameness, *lêm'ness*, N. Thonttepon.
Lament, *la-ment'*, V. Roddunc ; churchurouc ; xinn ulounc.
Lamentable, *la'ment-ie-bl*, A. Roddcho, churchuriancho ; dukhaborit, khontiborit.
Lamentation, *la-ment-ei'shon*, N. Roddnem ; pirgonni ; xinn.
Lamp, *lemp*, N. Lampiaum ; divo.
Lamp-black, *lemp'blek*, N. Cazoll.

Lampoon, *lam-pun'*, N. Nindechem potr.
Lance, *lens*, N. Bhalo.
Land, *lend*, N. Bhuim; zago; gaum.
Land, V. Tarva velo utronc vo devonc.
Landlord, *lend'lord*, N. Zamindar; battcar.
Landmark, *lend'mark*, N. Setacho nis.
Landscape, *lend'skeip*, N. Eke nodren pollounc eta titli bhuim vo zago.
Lane, *lên*, N. Golli; oxir vatt.
Language, *leng'gwej*, N. Bhas; uloumem; bolnem; utram.
Languid, *leng'gwid*, A. Mou; mengo; sust; osoct,
Languish, *leng'gwish*, V. Mou—; mengo zaunc; bavonc; boll unnem zaunc.
Languor, *leng'gor*, N. Bavop; osoctai.
Lank, *lengk*, A. Patoll; soddil.
Lantern, *len'tern*, N. Lampiaum.
Lap, *lep*, N. Miri; usco.
Lapse, *leps*, V. Soronc; nisronc; chuconc; poddonc.
Lapse, N. Chuc; nisrop.
Large, *larj*, A. Rund; vodd.
Lascar, *las'kar*, N. Kholasi.
Lascivious, *las-si'vi-as*, A. Mangro; mosto; pozddo.
Lash, *lesh*, N. Chabuc; mar.
Lass, *las*, N. Cheddum.
Last, *last*, N. Moche corchem form.
Last, A. Nimanno; akricho.
Last, V. Togonc, uronc; pavonc.
Latch, *lech*, N. Khill.
Latchet, *lech'et*, N. Fint; dori.
Late, *leitt*, AD. Usram; magir.
Late, A. Sorlolo; adlo.
Lately, *leitt'li*, AD. Edou, nimannem.
Lathe, *leth*, N. Khoddchil, ec macn zantum lancudd etc catorta anim sullsullit anim vaddcullem corta.
Lather, *lath'ar*, N. Fenno.
Latitude, *la'ti-tiud*, N. Vistarop; rundai.
Latter, *let'er*, A. Dusro; edoucho.
Lattice, *let'is*, N. Voddop, totti.
Laudable, *lad'ie-bl*, A. Onod favo zalolo.
Laugh, *laf*, N. Hans.
Laughable, *laf'i-e-bla*, V. Hanscho.
Laughter, *laf'tor*, N. Hanso.
Launch, *lanch*, V. Tarum doriant devounc.
Laundress, *lon'ddress*, N. Moddvoln.
Laundry, *lon'dri*, N. Umbolchi suat.
Laureate, *la'ri-eitt*, A. Dobajeacho potto aslolo.
Lavatory, *lav'a-to-ri*, N. Tost; nahni; fg. dhunnem.
Lavish, *lav'ish*, A. Vichic, chodd khoroch cornar.
Lavish, V. Cont-ixeop nastanam khorchunc; ibaddunc.
Law, *lo*, N. Caido, npordes.
Law-giver, *lo-giv'ar*. N. Caido galnar.
Lawless, *lo'less*, A. Caideavinn.
Lawn, *lon*, N. Ugtti zomin ranna modecot.
Law-suit, *lo'sutt*, N. Corticho process aplo direit mellounchenc.
Lawyer, *lo'yar*, N. Letrad; vokil.
Lax, *leks*, A. Soddil; beporvo; chodd doiall.
Laxity, *leks'i-lti*. N. Soddilai.
Lay, *ley*, V. Galunc; vo dovorunc.
—(Eggs), tantim galunc.
—(Aside), pelean caddunc; samballun dovorunc.

Lay, (Before), mucar galunc.
—(Down), soddunc.
—(Hold), dorunc.
—(In), eettaim corunc.
—(On), bollan marunc.
—(Open), ugcto corunc.
—(Out), bhair galunc; khorchunc.
—(Together), Sangata galunc.
—(Up), dovorunc.
Lay,—(Wastei), pirder corunc; ibaddunc.
Layman, *lei'men*; N. Sounsari.
Laziness, *le'zi-nes*, N. Ausai; beporvo.
Lazy, *le'zi*, A. Ausi'
Lea, *li*, N. Set.
Lead, *led*, N. Xinsem.
Lead, *liid*, V. Cholounc; vatt dacounc; mucar vochonc.
Leader, *liid'ar*, N. Mukheli, vatt dacoinar.
Leading, *liid'ing*, A. Mukhia.
Leaf, *liif*, N. Kholo; pan.
League, *liig*, N. Mell; carar; kos (3 mail).
Leak, *liik*, V. Ponvonc.
Leak, N. Futt, chil. ver.
Lean, *liin*, A. Baric, sirputto; bagottio.
Leaness, *liin'es*, N. Baricai, sirputtai.
Leap, *liip*, V. Uddonc; uddi marunc.
Leap-year, *liip-yer*, N. Upari voros.
Learn, *lorn*, V. Sik; aic,
Learning, *lorn'ing*, N. Sicop; zanvai.
Lease, *liiz*, N. Baddeac divop.
Least, *liist*, A. Bhou lan.
Leather, *le'dar*, N. Chambddem.
Leather, A. Chambddeacho.
Leave, *li'iv*, V. Soddunc.
Leave, (off), thambounc.
—(Out), V. Soddunc.

Leave, N. Rojea.
Leaven, *liiv'un*, N. fug.
Leaven, V. Fugonc.
Lecture, *lec'char*, N. Sicoun dinnem.
Lecturer, *lec'cher-ar*, N. Sicoun dinar.
Ledger, *lej'ar*, N. Ispachem pustoc.
Leech, *li-ich*, N. Zollu.
Leer, *ler*, V. Vanoddo polleunc.
Lees, *liiz*, V. Soreachi mur.
Left, *left*, A. Davo.
Leg, *leig*, N. Paim; Khur.
Legacy, *leg'a-si*, N. Testament corun dovorleli vost.
Legal, *lig'al*, A. Caidea zocto.
Legality, *li-gal'i-tti*, N. Caidea pormonnem asnem.
Legalize, *li'gal-aiz*, V. Caidea pormonnem corunc.
Legally, *li'gal-li*, AD. Sumurti—, caidea pormonnem.
Legate, *le'gait*, N. Pap Saibacho embaixador.
Legation, *le-gei'shon*, N. Vakil cochorecho loc.
Legend, *lej'end*, N. Contha devon aileli purvilea tempar than.
Legible, *le'ji-bl*, A. Vachi sarkem.
Legion, *le'jon*, N. Sena; pongodd
Legislate, *le'jis-leitt*, V. Caido goddunc.
Legislation, *le-jis-lei'shon*, N. Caide banddi.
Legislative, *le'jis-lei-ttiv*, A. Caide roch-che vo goddche.
Legislator, *le'jis-leit'or*, N. Caide galtolo; sastradar.
Legitimate, *le-jit'i-meitt*, A. Caideachem daiz; niz.
Leisure, *li'jar*, A. Fursott; cam naslolo vell.
Leisurely, *li'jar-li*, AD. Soucosaen.

Lemon, *le'mon*, N. Limbo.
Lemonade, *le-mon-eid'*, N. Lemonad.
Lend, *lend*, V. Usnem diunc-
Length, *length*, N. Lambai.
Lengthen, *length'n*, V. Vaddounc vo lamb corunc.
Lengthily, *length'i-li*, AD. Lambaen.
Lengthy, *length'i*, A. Soi-sumar lamb.
Leniency, *li'ni-en-si*, N. Doia; cacut.
Lenient, *li'ni-ent*, A. Doiall; cacuticho.
Lent, *lent*, N. Corezm.
Leopard, *lep'ard*, N. Biptto vag.
Leper, *lep'ar*, N. Coddkar.
Leprosy, *lep-ro'zi*, N. Codd.
Leprous, *lep'ras*, A. Coddio vo coddacho.
Less, *less*, AD. Unno.
Lessee, *les-si'*, N. Baddeac gotolo:
Lesson, *les'n*, N. Lisaum; sicoun.
Lest, *lest*, Conj. pasun.
Let, *let*, V. Soddunc; baddeac diunc.
Let blood, V, Sir marunc.
—(Down), Devounc.
—(Fall), Socdunc.
—(In), Cobul zaunc; rigounc
—(Off), Far marunc.
Lethal, *leth'al*, A. Mornadik; marecar.
Lethargy, *le'thar-ji*, N. Bormit; kumbacarni nid; ausai.
Letter, *let'er*, N. Chitt; acxer; sicop.
Letting, *let'ing*, N. Baddem.
Levee, *lev'i*, N. Socallincho dorbar.
Level, *le'vul*, N. Ecsarki zomiu; fg. map.
Level, V. Unch-socla asa tem caddunc.
Levelled, *le'vulld*, A. Caplolo.
Lever, *li'vor*, N. Latt.
Levigate, *le'vi-geit*, V, Vanttunc; pudd corunc.
Levity, *le'vi-tti*, N. Khali mot.
Levy, *le'vi*, V. Soldad ecttaim corunc.
Lexicon, *leks'i-con*, N. Utranchem pustoc; dicsionar.
Liable, *lai'ie-bl*, A. Chuco sarco.
Liar, *lai'er*, N. Fottkiro munis.
Libel, *lai'bl*, N. Ninde-potr.
Liberal, *li'ber-al*, A. Udar; generoz; sompurn; ugtto.
Liberality, *li-ber-al'i-tti*, N. Udarponn; vechiponn.
Libertine, *li'ber-tin*, N. Cheddiallo; luchcho; pamprel.
Libertinism, *li'ber-tin-izm*, N. Most; sodeponn; lucheponn.
Liberty, *li'bert-ti*, N. Suttca; sotia; apkhoxi.
Libidinous, *li-bid'i-nas*, A. Mosticho, kamacho.
Library, *lai'bra-ri*, N. Livrari,
Librarian, *lai-bre'ri-an*, N. Livraricho adhikari.
License, *lai'sens*, N. Rojea; hukum.
License, V. Hukum diunc.
Licentious, *lai-sens'shias* A. Vaitt chalicho; mosticho; luchcho.
Lick, *lic*, V. Lenvunc; chacunc.
Lid, *lid*, N. Dampnem; mandd.
Lie, *lai*, N. Fott.
Lie, V. Fotti sangunc vo marunc; add poddunc; attapunc.
—(I lie ill), maca vaitt corta.
—(Over), patti galunc.
Life, *laif*, N. Jinn; auc; pran.
Lifeless, *laif'less*, A. Jiv naslolo.
Lift, *lift*, V. Uclunc, ubarunc.
Light, *laitt*, N Uzvadd; divo.
Light, A. Uzvaddacho; hallu; bolaikecho.
Light, V. (Vat), pettounc, (divo) launc.

Lighten, *lait'n*, V. Uzvadd diunc; hallu corunc.
Light-house, *lait-haus*, N. Forel.
Lightly, *laitt'li*, AD. Hallu zaun; voilea voir; sovai; chintinastanam; aumoriadin.
Lightning, *laitt'ning*, N. zoglaunem.
Like, *laic*, AD. Sarco; bori; baxen.
Like, V. Ruchonc; manvonc; boro disonc; apurbai asunc.
Likely, *laik'li*, AD. Sotmandi sarco.
Liken, *laik'n*, V. Sor corunc.
Likeness, *laik'ness*, N. Sarkem.
Likewise, *laik'vaiz*, AD. Legun vo soit.
Liking, *laik'ing*, N. Ruch; morji; khoxi.
Limb, *limb'*, N. Sando; khando.
Limbo, *lim'bo*, N. Limb; patoll.
Lime, *laim'*, N. Chunom.
Lime-stone, N. Chunneancho fator.
Limit, *lim'it*, N. Aker; mitmer, sim, mer.
Limit, V. Sim,—mer galunc; anvlunc; attapunc.
Limited, *lim'it-ed*, A. Oxir; mer—, sim galolo.
Limp, *limp'*, V. Khunttonc; ravonravon cholunc.
Limpid, *limp'id*, A. Nitoll, nirmoll.
Linch-pin, *linch-pin'*, N. Khil.
Line, *lain'*, N. Voll; kus, mer.
Lineage, *lin'e-eij*, N. Kuttom; rogot.
Lineament, *lin'i-a-ment*, N. Akarrup; thondd rup; anglott.
Linear, *lin'i-ar*, A. Regancho, gitancho.
Linen *li'non*, N. Lugott.
Linen, A. Sonnachem.
Linger, *ling'gar*, V. Vogot corunc; patti fudde corunc.
Linguist, *lin'guist*, N. Zaite° bhaso zanno aslolo.
Linguistic, *ling-guist'ic*, A. Bhasecho sobda-sastracho.
Link, *linc*, N. Sanklichi mudi; ganch; fg. sancoll; band.
Link, V. Bandunc; ecttaim corunc.
Linseed, *lin'sid*, N. Sonbiam.
Lint, *lint*, N. Sut; kisoilolo capus.
Lion, *lai'on*, N. Xinm.
Lioness, *lai'o-ness*, N. Xinm-in xinvanchi bhail.
Lip, *lip*, N. Vontt; fg. deg; kantt.
Liquefy, *lik'wi-fai*, V. Koddounc; pattol corunc.
Liquid, *lik'wid*, A. Alo, udcallo; vanvto.
Liquid, N. Vanvchi vo pattol vost.
Liquidate, *lik'wid-eitt*, V. Faric corunc; choucasunc, topasunc, rujvat corunc.
Liquor, *lik'or*, N. Ros, soro.
Lisp, *lisp*, V. Luddbem ulounc.
List, *list*, N. Potti; ixeop.
Listen, *lis'n*, V. Chit diun aicunc.
Listless, *list'less*, A. Khoxi naslolo; bauncho.
Litany, *li'ta-ni*, N. Ladin.
Literal, *li'teral*, A. Utram pormonem aslolo.
Literature, *li'ter-ie-char*, N. Sicop; videa; panditachi mandalli; pustocam.
Literary, *literari*, A. Sikpacho.
Lithografy, *li-tho'gra-fi*, N. Fatrar shapnem, silalo khanavidea vadi.
Litigant, *li'ti-gant*, N. Daviacho,
Litigate, *li'ti geitt*, V. Davo—, khotto carunc, vivadunc.
Litter, *lit'or*, N. Machil; palki.
Little, *lit'l*, A. Lan; supurlem.
Liturgy, *li'ter-ji*, N. Rit; parvad sevadhorm.

Live, *liv*, V. Jieunc; vanchonc.
Livelihood, *liv'li-hud*, N. Udarposonn; jevonkhan.
Liveliness, *laiv'li-ness*, N. Barikai.
Lively, *laiv'li*, A. Suddsuddit; khoxal; uxar.
Lifelong, *laif'long*, A. Sogli jinn togcho.
Liver, *liv'or*, N. Calliz.
Livid, *liv'id*, A. xinseachea rongacho; callso,
Living, *liv'ing*, A. Jivo.
Lizard, *li'zard*, N. Pal.
Lo, *lo*, INT. Polle.
Load, *lôd*, N. Vojem.
Load, V. Borunc; khandar galunc
Load. (With chains), Sancoll galunc.
—(With injuries), Ocmananim boronc.
Loaded, *lod'ed*, A. Borlolo.
Loadstone, N. Voddcho fator.
Loaf, *lof*, N. Unddo.
Loan, *lon*, N. Usnni vost.
Loath, *loth*, V. Voncaro yeunc; canttallonc.
Loathing, *loth'ing*, N. Voncaro.
Loathsome, *loth'som*, A. Voncareacho.
Local, *lo'kal*, A. Ganvantlo.
Locality, *lo-kal'i-tti*, N. Suat; gaum.
Lock, *lok*, N. Talem, khulop.
Lock, V. Talem marunc.
Locomotive, *lo-co-mo'tiv*, N. Dunvrachi gaddi.
Locust, *lo'kust*, N. Toll.
Lodge, *loj*, V. Ravonc; biddar asunc; biddar diunc.
Lodger, *loj'ar*, N. Baddecar.
Lodging, *loj'ing*, N. Biddar; ghor.
Loft, *loft'*, A. Unch ubar.
Logic, *lo'jic*, N. Tarka sastr; niasastr.
Logical, *lo'jic-al* A. Ruzu corcho.
Logician, *lo'gi-shan*, N. Tarkasastri.
Loin, *loin*, N. Penkott.
Loiter, *loi'tar*, V. Vogot corunc.
Lone, *lo'n*, A. Ecsuro.
Long, *long*, A. Lamb—(before) sobar vell adim.
Long, V. Laleurc; urba asunc.
Longish, *long'ish*, A. Lambso.
Longitude, *lon'gi-tiud*, N. Lambai.
Look, *luk*, V. Polleunc; distt galunc; disonc.
—(About), eusin-tensin polleunc.
—(Back), patti polleunc.
—(Down), socla polleunc.
—(For), sodunc.
—(In the face), thondac dolle launc.
—(Out), patti fudde polleunc.
—(To), chintunc; patieunc.
Look, N. Thondd; distt, rup.
Looking-glass, N. arso.
Loom, *lum*, N. Mag.
Loose, *lus*, A. Soddil; gott noi aslolo fg. aple khoxecho; mosticho.
Loose, *lus*, V. Soddunc; soddil corunc.
Loosely, *lus'li*, AD. Zagrutai nastanam.
Loosenes, *lus'ness*, N. Soddilai; hagon, most.
Lop, *lop*, V. Benddunc.
Loquacious, *lo-kwai'shas*, A. Boddboddo gozali marcho.
Loquacity, *lo-kwa'si-ti*, N. boddboddnem, zauc.
Lord, *lord*, N. Saib; suami, sardhar.
Lose, *luz*, V. Hogddaunc; padd zaunc; noistt zaunc.
Loss, *loss*, N. Hogddaunem; luscon; noistt.
Lot, *lott*, N. Sort; odrustt; vantto.
Lotion, *lo'shon* N. Duunchem vocot.

Lottery, *lot'e-ri*, N. Sort.
Loud, *laud*, A. Voddlea, uncha tal leacho.
Loudly, *laud'li*, AD. Voddlean.
Lounge, *lo-unj*, V. Becar bonvonc.
Louse, *laus*, N. Vu.
Lout, *laut*, N. Holko munis.
Love, *lov*, N. Mog, apurbai.
Love, V. Mog—, priti—, apurbai corunc.
Loveliness, *lov'li-ness*, N. Mogalponn ; apurbai.
Lovely, *lov'li*, A, Mogall vo mogacho ; sobit.
Loving, *lov'ing*, A. Mog-corcho ; apurbaecho.
Low, *lo*, A, Topkotto ; unno ; sovai ; bhou osoct ; motvo.
—(Voice), Socoilo tallo.
Low, AD. Socol.
Lower, *lo'ar*, V. Devounc ; socol caddunc ; dukest zaunc.
Lowliness, *lo'li-ness*, N. Kircollai; unneponn.
Loyal, *loi'al*, A. Niskoptti ; patienicho ; niz ; visvasi,
Loyalty, *loi'al-ti*, N. Niskopott ; Khoreponn ; visvasponn.
Lozenge, *lo'zenj*, N. Mittai ; pipirmitt.
Lucid, *lu'sid*, A. Uzvadacho ; nitoll.
Luck, *lâc*, N. Odrustt ; nosib.
Luckily, *lâk'i-li*, AD. Odrusttan ; nosiban.
Lucky, *lâk'i*, A. Odrusttacho ; feliz.
Lucrative, *lu'krat-iv*, A. Adavacho.
Lucre, *lu'ker*, N. Addau.
Lucubration, *lu-ku-brei'shon*, N. Diveachea uzvaddac kelelem cam—, pustoc.
Luculent, *lu'ku-lent*, A. Porzollit; nitoll.
Ludicrous, *lu'ci-kras*, A. Ansouncho ; chesttaeancho.
Lug, *lug*, V. Voddunc ; lottunc.
Luggage, *lag'eij*, N. Samonn.
Lugubrious, *lu-gu'bri-as*, A. Ducaborit ; chintest.
Lukewarm, *liuk'warm*, A. Unso ; selmoddo ; fg. ausi.
Lukewarmness, *liuk'worm-ness*, N. Ausai.
Lull, *lâl*, V. Ganna gaunc ; nidounc ; fuslannc.
Luminary, *lu'min-a-ri*, N. Divtti; pontti ; divo.
Luminous, *lu'mi-nas*, A. Uzvaddic ; porzollit ; diptivont.
Lunar, *lu'nar*, A. Chondrimacho
Lunatic, *liu'na-tic*, A. Luv aslolo piso ; veddo.
Lunch, *lanch*, N. Follar ; tiffin.
Lung, *lang*, N. Popis.
Lurch, *lorch*, N. Connisttaecho akar.
Lure, *liu-ar*, N. Voddni ; lonch ; ans.
Lurid, *lur'id*, A. Sanvlo ; kallsar
Lurk, *lark*, V. Liponc.
Lurking-place, N. Lipchi suat.
Luscious, *lu'shas*, A. Chodd ruchicho. chi khoxi.
Lust, *last*, N. Most ; cam ; cuddi-
Lustful, *lost'ful*, A. Mosticho ; bhailando.
Lustre, *lost'er*, N. Porzoll ; voddlem castisal. nirvonni.
Lusty, *lost'i*, A. Gott ; mozbut;
Luxurious, *laks-u'ri-as*, A. Kami; chonchol ; sodo.
Luxury, *loks'u-ri*, A. Most; cuddicheo khoxeo ; pozddeponn.
Lye, *lai*, N. Khar ; gudd.

M

Mace, *mes*, N Eoc danddo zaca asta zodd xinseachi etc mutt ; zaifollachea follachi suki cat.
Macerate, *ma'se-reitt*, V. Bizounc ; fg. coisttaunc.

Machinate, *mak'i-neitt,* A. Euzunc, rochunc, sodun caddunc.
Machination, *mak-i-nei'*xion, N. Rochi maudavoll.
Machine, *ma-shin',* N. Makn.
Machinist, *ma-kin'ist,* N. Yantram cortolo, choloitolo.
Mackerel, *mak'er-el,* N. Baugddo.
Mad, *medd,* A. Piso, mot naslolo.
Madam, *ma'dam,* N. Saibinn; bhai.
Madden, *med'n,* V. Piso corunc.
Mad-house, N. Piseanchem ghor.
Madness, *med'ness,* N. Piseponn.
Magazine, *mag'a-zin,* N. Daru khanneu; ugrann.
Magi, *ma'gi,* N. Teg-rai.
Magic, *ma'jic,* N. Devcharpoun; ghadd videa.
Magician, *ma-ji'shan,* N. Ghaddi; fitis cornar.
Magistrate, *ma'jis-treitt,,* N. Munsubdar, nitidar; adikari.
Magnanimity, *mag-na-nim'i-ti,* N. Monachem thorponn, voddlem mou.
Magnanimous, *mag-nan'im-as,* A. vodd monacho, doiravont.
Magnet, *mag'net,* N. Chumbac, fator zo apnna eusilean locondac voddta.
Magnetize, *mag'net-aiz,* V. Voddchi socott launc.
Magnificence, *mag-nif'i-sens,* N. dobazo; voddponu, tharai; tej.
Magnificent, *mag-nif'i-sent,* A. Dobajeacho; voddponnacho.
Magnify, *mag'ni-fai,* V. Vacanddunc, porcondunc; uclun matear dorunc.
Mahomedan, *ma-ho'me-dan,* N. Musolman. [aucuar.
Maid, *meid,* N. Cheddum, choli
Maid-servant, N. Chacorn.
Mail, *meil,* N. Topal; locouddachem anglem.

Maimed, *meim'd,* A. Thontto.
Main, *mein,* A. Mukia.
Mainly, *mein'li,* AD. Mukia zaun.
Maintain, *mein'tein,* V. Dovorunc; samballunc; posunc, khondit sangunc.
Maintenance, *mein'ten-ens,* N. Dispoddto gras; udarposonn.
Majestic, *ma-jes'tik,* A. Manacho; poddvecho; moriadicho.
Majesty, *ma'jes-ti,* N. Voddponn; rai.
Majority, *majo'ri-tti,* N. Voddlo vantto; pirai.
Make, *meik,* V. Corunc; caddunc.
—(Against), luksanac poddonc.
—(Amends), faricponn diunc.
—(Away with), soddunc.
—(For), isilean voch.
—(Free with), aumoriadi cholonc.
—(Over), adin corunc.
—(Out), somzonc.
—(Ready), toiar corunc, faricponn diunc, nicheu corunc.
—(Use of), upeog corunc.
Make way, suat corunc.
Make, N. Corop.
Maker, *meik'ar,* N. cornar; rochnar. [lolo.
Malapert, *mal'a-pert,* A. Loznas-
Malapropos, *mal-ap'ro-pos,* A. Camac poddonaslolo.
Malaria, *ma-la'ria,* N. Vaitt varea udexim ailolo zhor.
Malcontent, *mal'con-tent,* N. Dadoxi naslolo, khottea monacho.
Male, *meil,* A. Dadlo.
Malediction, *mal-e-dik'shon,* N. Xirap; maldisaum.
Malefactor, *mal-e-fec'tor,* N. Guneuncar; morticar.
Malevolence *ma-lev'o-lens,* N. Vaitt khoxi; uiscuchar; khotteponn.
Malice, *ma'lis,* N. Vicottai; khottepon, naddgepoun, mosor.

Malicious, *ma-li'shas*, A. Malizioz, vaitta monacho, vicottaecho.
Malign, *ma-lain'*, V. Bodlam galunc ; chaddieo sangunc.
Malignity, *ma-lig'ni-tti*, N. Khotteponn ; vicottai.
Malleable, *mal-li-ie'bl*, A. Mou.
Mallow, *mel'o*, N. Pettarlechem zadd.
Maltreat, *mal-trit*, V. Dogododgaunc ; nisttnraen-cholounc.
Maltreatment, *mal-trit'ment*, N. Coisttounem ; dogd ; nistturai.
Man, *men*, N. Munis ; dadlo.
Man, V. Munis diunc ; rakon corunc.
Man-of-war, N. Monvar.
Manacle, *man'a-kl*, N. Biddi ; khoddo.
Manage, *man'eij*, V. Cholounc.
Manageable, *man'eij-ie-bl*, A. Choloi sarco.
Management, *man'eij-ment*, N. Kharkanno ; cholounnem.
Manager, *man'eij-ar*, N. Choloinar ; director.
Mane, *mein*, N. Manenche kens.
Mange, *meinj*, N. Khoroz ; rum.
Manger, *meinjar*, N. Khavonn ; khaunni.
Mangle, *meng'gl*, V. Cuddke corunc; gai galunc.
Mango, *mang'go*, N. Ambo ; ambli.
Mango-stone, N. Par.
Manhood, *men'hud*, N. Munxeponn ; voddli pirai.
Mania, *ma'ni-a*, N. Pixeponn.
Manifest, *man'i-fest*, A. Ugtto ; porgott.
Manifest, V. Porgott corunc ; dacounc.
Manifestation, *man-ni-fes-tei'-shon*, N. Ugddapo—, decol cornem.
Manifesto, *man-i-fest'o*, N. Daclo.
Manifold, *man'i-fold*, N. Sobar pautti chodd ; veglo.
Manipulate, *man-nip'u-leitt*, V. Hatanim corunc ; kamavunc.
Mankind, *men-kaind'*, N. Munxecull.
Manliness, *men'li-ness*, N. Nirvonn ; dhoir.
Manly, *men'li*, A. Nirvonni ; dhoiravont.
Manner, *men'ar*, N. Jinos ; fg. marog ; pormonnem ; fg. bhas ; moriad ; sovoim.
Manœuvre, *ma-nu'ver*, N. Kovat; hicmot.
Manse, *mens*, N. Padrichem ghor.
Mantle, *men'tl*, N. Vol.
Manual, *man'u-al*, A. Hatanchem.
Manual, N. Hat pustoc ; rozaracho manual.
Manufactory, *ma-nu-fek'to-ri*, N. Karkanno.
Manufacture, *man-nu-fec'char*, N. Hatan corchem cam.
Manufacture, V. Silpan—, cosben corunc.
Manure, *man-iuar'*, N. Xen ; sarem ; gobor.
Manuscript, *man'u-script*, N. Hatan boroilelem. (pustoc etc).
Many, *me'ni*, A. Sobar; zaite ; chodd.
Map, *mep*, N. Map ; deschitr.
Mar, *mar*, V. Pir der corunc ; ducounc; bigddunc.
Marasmus, *ma-ras'mus*, N. Khevad ; jinjni.
Marauder, *ma-rad'ar*, N. Lutt cornar.
Marble, *mar'bl*, N. Paconnacho fator ; gutti.
March, *march*, V. Pamvlam uddoun cholunc.
March, N. March ; cholni.
Mare, *mer*, N. Goddi.

Margin, *mar'jin*, N. Deg; pamoti.
Marginal, *mar'jin-al*, A, Degecho ; Coddecho.
Marine *ma-rin'*, A. Doriacho.
Marine, N. Tarvacho sipai.
Mariner, *ma'rin-er*, N. Tarvotti.
Maritime, *ma'ri-taim*, A. Doriacho; somudirantlo ; tarvam choloitolo.
Mark, *mark*, N. Kuru ; khunna.
Mark, V. Khunna corunc ; borounc ; chintunc.
Market, *mar'ket*, N. Pentt; bazar.
Marriage, *me'rij*, N. Cazar ; logn; vaddic.
Marriageable, *me'rij-ie-bl*, A. Cazaracho ; savasini.
Married, *me'rid*, A. Cazari.
Marrow, *me'ro*, N. Addantlem tuton.
Marry, *me'ri*, V. Cazar corunc; Cazar zaunc.
Marsh, *marsh*, N. Tollem , chiclacho zago.
Marshal, *mar'shal*, N. Foujicho ; adipati.
Marshy, *marsh'i*, A. Chiclacho.
Martial, *mar'shal*, A. Zuzacho.
Martyr, *mar'tir*, N. Martir sumurti pasun melolo.
Martyrdom, *mar'tor-dom*, N. Martirpon ; fg. coistt ; vollvolle.
Martyrology, *mar-tor-ol'o-ji*, N. Martiranchem pustoc.
Marvellous, *mar'vel-as*, A. Ojapacho.
Masculine, *mas'cu-lin*, A. Purus jaticho ; dadlo.
Mash, *mesh*, N. Borsonnem.
Mask, *mask*, N. Moiem.
Mask, V. Moiem galunc; liponnc
Masquerade, *mas'ker-eid*, N. Moiencarancho chombo ; tomaso.
Mason, *mei'sn*, N. Pidreir.
Mass, *mas*, N. Mis ; ras ; zomo.
Massacre, *mas'sa-kor*, N, Maramari, zomeachi khuni.
Massacre, V. Borochbor sobaranc jivesim marunc.
Mass-book, N. Misal.
Massive, *mas'siv*, A. Chodd ; bhari.
Mast, *mast*, N. Kunvo.
Master, *mas'tor*, N. Dhoni ; ghorcar; voddil.
Master, V. Khalto corunc ; borem somzonc.
Masticate, *mas'ti-keitt*, V. Chabunc ; fg. rovont corunc.
Mastication, *mas-ti-kei'shon*, N. Chabnem ; fg. rovont.
Mat, *met*, N. Mandri ; dalli.
Match, *mech*, N. Ujeachi caddi ; cazaracho carar ; zodden.
Match-box, N. Fosfor.
Mate, *meitt*, N. Sangati.
Material, *ma-ti'ri-al*, N. Jinos.
Material, A. Amgi ; angacho ; cuddicho.
Materialism, *ma-te'ri-al-izm*, N. Dehatmavad , anatmamat.
Materials, *ma-te'ri-als*, N. Samonn.
Maternal, *ma-ter'nal*, A. Maiecho vo avoicho.
Mathematical, *ma-the-ma'ti-cal*, A. Gonnitacho.
Mathematics, *ma-the-ma'tics*, N. Gonnit corchi videa.
Matins, *ma'tins*, N. Ofis.
Matricide, *mat'ri-said*, N. Aple avoic jivesim marnar.
Matriculate, *ma-tric'u-leitt*, V. Matrikl corunc ; listar naum borounc.
Matriculation, *ma-tric-u-lei'-shon*, N. Namvanchi potti.
Matrimony, *mat'ri-mo-ni*, N. Cazaracho sacrament.
Matron, *me'tron*, N. Bai ; danddgi bail.
Matter, *met'er*, N. Prakrit ; anatmo ; vost.

Matter, v. Goroz asunc.
Mattock, *met'ok*, N. Picas.
Mattress, *met'res*, N. Gozddi; culchaum.
Mature, *ma-chuar'*, A. Pico.
Maturely, *ma-chuar'li*, AD. Borem chintun.
Maturity, *ma-chiu'ri-tti*, N. Picop; borgoli.
Maudlin, *mad'lin*, A. Soro pielolo; bebdo.
Maund, *mond*, N. Monn.
Maw, *mo*, N. Ganzo.
Maxim, *mak'sim*, N. Mull; bij; sutr, vachan.
May, *mei*, V. Zaunc puro.
Meadow, *me'dou*, N. Chorvacho zago; tonnachem moidan.
Meagre, *mi'gar*, A. Baric; suko; bhou lan.
Meal, *mil*, N. Jevonn; pitt.
Mean, *min*, N. Modem.
Mean, A. Modlo; unno; imtto.
Mean, v. Xevott asunc; orth asunc. [vott.
Meaning, *min'ing*, N. Orth; xe-
Meanness, *min'ness*, N. Unneponn; kircolai; imtteponn.
Means, *mins*, N. Upai.
Measles, *mi'zlz*, N. Urvurem.
Measurable, *me'jar-ie-bl*, A. Mezi sarco.
Measure, *me'jar*, N. Map; zoc; upai.
Measure, V. Zoc geunc; mezunc.
Measured, *me'jard*, A. Maplolo vo mezlolo.
Measurer, *me'jar-ar*, N. Mapeli; mapnar.
Meat, *mitt*, N. Mas.
Mechanic, *me-kan'ik*, N. Silpi; silpicar.
Mechanics, *me-kan'iks*, N. Chacra samarthi.
Mechanism, *mek-an'izm*, N. Yantrachi rochi; zukti.
Medal, *med'ul*, N. Arluc.
Meddle, *med'l*, V. Rigonc; misoll zaunc.
Mediate, *me'di-eitt*, V. Modest—, raibari zaunc; fuslaunc.
Mediately, *me'di-eitt-li*, AD. Dusrea vorvim.
Mediation, *me'di-ie-xion*, N. Viniot, mozot.
Mediator, *me'di-eit-or*, N. Modem yetolo, modest.
Medical, *me'dical*, A. Boro corcho; voizacho.
Medicate, *med'i-keitt*, V. Vocot dinnc.
Medicinal *med'i-si-nal*, A. Boro corcho.
Medicine, *med'i-sin*, N. Voctanchi videa. voçot.
Mediocre, *me'di-o-kr*, A, Sumaracho.
Mediocrity, *me-di-ok'ri-tti*, N. Soisumar
Meditate, *med'i-tteit*, V. Niall corunc; borem chinturc.
Meditation, *med'i-tei'xion*, N. Niall, dhyan; chinton.
Medium, *me'di-am*, N. Modli vost; dalal.
Medley, *med'li*, N. Gusop; gondoll.
Meek, *mik*, A. Bolo; lin.
Meekness, *mik'ness*, N. Boleponn, movallponn.
Meet, *mit*, V. Mellunc. [bha.
Meeting, *mit'ing*, N. Zomat; sa-
Melancholy, *mel'an-co-li*, N. Khont; dukh; sonkirnai.
Melancholy, A. Chintest; dukhest.
Mellifluous, *mel-if'lu-as*, A. Monv-vanvtalo; fg. godd-godd moum.
Mellow, *mel'o*, A. Pico; mou.
Melodious, *me-lo'di-as*, A. Gayeanacho; suadic.

Melody, *mel'o-di*, N. Gayan; gayanacho jinos.
Melon, *me'lon*, N. Chibud.
—(Water melon,) Calling.
Melt, *melt*, V. Coddounc; movallaunc.
Member, *mem'ber*, N. Membr; sando; fg. vantto.
Membrane, *mem'brein*, N. Cat.
Memorable, *mem'or-ie-bl*, A. Ugddasacho; navaddic.
Memorial, *me-mo'ri-al*. A. Ugddas corchi chit; ugddas; arji.
Memory, *mem'o-ri*, N. Ugddas; yad.
Menace, *men'es*, V. Besttaunc; bhieuno launc.
Menace, N. Besttauni.
Menagery, *me-naj'e-ri*, N. Monzatincho zomo.
Mend, *mend*, V. Durus—, sarkem corunc.
Mendicant, *men'di-cant*, N. Izmol magnar; bhicari. [bolcai.
Mendicity, *men-dis'i-ti*, N. Dur-
Menial, *mi'ni-al*, A. Chacrecho; holco.
Mental, *men'tal*, A. Monacho; moticho.
Mention, *men'shon*, V. Ugddas—, athou corunc.
Mention, N. Ugddas.
Mentor, *men'tor*, N. Racnno; xanno, budvont istt.
Mercantile, *mer'can-tail*, A. Veparacho; saucari.
Mercenary, *mer'se-na-ri*, N. Louch khanar; pag diunchem corun dovorlolo munis.
Merchandise, *mer'chand-aiz*, N. Vepar.
Merchant, *mer'chant*, N. Vepari.
Merciful, *mer'si-ful*, A. Cacuticho; doiall.
Merciless, *mer'si-less*, A. Nisttur; cacut naslolo.
Mercilessness, *mer'si-less-ness* N. Nistturai.
Mercurial, *mer-cu'ri-al*, A. Parozacho.
Mercy, *mer'si*, N. Cacut; doia.
Mere, *mer*, A. Matr; focot; besttem.
Merge, *merj*, V. Buddounc.
Meridian, *me-rid'i-an*, N. Donparanchi mandoll.
Meridian, A. Donparancho.
Merit, *me'rit*, N. Punem; punfoll.
Merit, V. Favo zaun geunc.
Meritorious, *me-rit-o'ri-as*, A. Punevont.
Merry, *me'ri*, A. Khoxal; chesttaecho.
Mess, *mes*, N. Jevonn.
Mess, V. Puzadar vo hotelant jeunc.
Message, *mes'eij*, N. Recad; nirop; sangni.
Messenger, *mes'en-jer*, N. Khobor vortolo; portador; sangnar.
Messmate, N. Sangati.
Metal, *met'al*, N. Dhatu; loha.
Metamorphosis, *me-ta-mor'fo-zis*, N. Rup bodlop.
Metaphor, *me'ta-for*, N. Rupac; upam, rupasobd; samand utor.
Metaphorical, *me-ta-for'ik-cal*, A. Samand orthacho.
Metaphysics, *me'ta-fi-zic*, N. Soimba bhailem xastr.
Meteor, *me'ti-or*, N. Neketr; acasacho porzoll.
Methinks, V. Dista.
Method, *me'thod*, N. Kram, anukram.
Methodic, *me-thod'ic*, A. Kramacho, regular.
Metre, *mi'ter*, V. Metr; vers.
Metropolis, *me-tro-po'lis*, N. Rajdhoni; rajpuri.
Metropolitan, *me-tro-po'li-tan*, N. Arcebisp saib.

Mew, *miu*, V. Voddpa bhitor galunc.
Microscope, *mai'kro-skop*, N. Cuscut pollounchem aidon.
Microscopic *mai-cro-scop'ic*, A. Bhou lan.
Midday, *mid'dei*, N. Donpar.
Middle, *mid'dl*, N. Modem ; maz.
Middle, A. Modlo ; sumaracho.
Middle-ajed, A. Modle piraecho.
Middling, *mid'ling*, A. Sumaracho.
Midnight, *mid'naitt*, N. Modeanrat.
Midst, *midst*, N. Modem.
Midwife, *mid-waif*, N. Voizin.
Mien, *men*, V. Tondd ; rup.
Might, *maitt*, N. Podvi ; boll.
Mighty, *mait'i*, A. Podvecho vo podvedar.
Migrate, *mi'greit*, V. Porganvanc vochunc.
Milch, *milch*, A. Dudacho.
Mild, *maild*, A. Nidan, samandanacho ; doiall, lin.
Mildness *maild'ness*, N. Santeponn ; boleponn ; doia.
Mile, *mail*, N. Mail, kosacho tisro vantto.
Militant, *mil-i-tant*, A. Loddai corcho, zuztolo.
Military, *mil'i-ta-ri*, A. Foujicho.
Militate, *mil'i-teitt*, V. Add vo contr asunc.
Milk, *milk*, N. Dud.
Milk, V. Dud caddunc. [no.
Mill *mil*, N. Vattcho fator ; ghan-
Millsped *mil'li-ped*, N. Kotarli.
Millet, *mil'let*, N. Zonddlo.
Million, *mill'yon* N. Dha lakh.
Mimic, *mim'ic*, A. Dusro corta tosem corcho.
Mince, *mins*, N. Cuddkean cuddco corunc.
Mind, *maind*, N. Mot. mon ; khoxi.
Mind, V. Chintunc ; zoton corunc ; porva corunc.
Mindful, *maind'ful*, A. Ugddas corcho.
Mindless, *maind'less*, A. Ugddas naslolo ; chotrai naslolo.
Mine, *main*, N. Bangarachi khon.
Mine, V. Bangar khoudonc.
Mine, A. Mozo.
Mineral, *min'e-ral*, N. Dhatu vo loha.
Mineralogy, *mi-ne-ral'o-ji*, N. Dhatu-Videa.
mingle, *ming'gl* V. Misollunc ; ecttaim corunc.
Miniature, *min'i-ic-char*, N. Lanchitr, najuc rupcar.
Minion, *min'ion* A. Favonaslele apurbaecho.
Minister, *min'is-tor*, N. Ministr ; padri, muniari ; chacor.
Minister, V. Xeva-chacri corunc.
Ministerial, *min-is-te'ri-al*, A. Ministracho ; padricho ; chaccrecho.
Ministry, *min'is-tri*, N. Xeva ; minister ; padriponn.
Minor, *mai'nor* A. Unno ; unne piraecho. [sall.
Mint, *mint*, V. Ortelaum ; tanc-
Minute, *mi-nut'*, N. Minut ; khin ; goddi.
Minute, *mai'niutt*, A. Bhou baric ; sarco.
Minute-hand, N. Khantto.
Minuteness, *mai'niut-ness*, N. Bhou, lan vost ; barcai.
Miracle *mi'ra-cl*, N. Ochoriam, milagr.
Miraculous, *mira'cu-las*, A. Ojapancho ; ochoriancho.
Mire, *maiar*, N. Volea chiclachi zomin.
Mirror, *mi'ror*, N. Arso.
Mirth, *morth*, N. Koxalponn ; dadosponn.

Misadventure, *mis-ad-ven'char*, N. chintinasiolo vaitt soheog; nirbag.

Misanthrope, *mis'an-throp*, N. jadveshi; ecmullo; nirduki.

Misbehave *mis-be-hev'*, V. Anmoriadin cholouc.

Misbehaviour, *mis-be-hev'yar*. N. Khotti chal.

Miscarriage, *mis-ke'rij*, N. Podchem; abort.

Miscarry, *mis-ke'ri*, V. Podchem vochunc; jiconam zaunc.

Miscellaneous, *miss-e-le'ni-as*, A. Sobar thorancho, nanapracarancho.

Miscellany, *mis'sel-la-ni*, N. Nanapracar charchar, khitkutlo.

Mischief, *mis'chif*, N. Tontto; Noistt; ocman.

Mischievous, *mis'chiv-as*, A. Carandaecheo; lusconacho.

Misconduct, *mis-con'doct*, N. Vaitt chal; beabru; guneaum.

Misconstrue, *mis-con'stru*, V. Orth bodlunc. [tto.

Miser, *mai'zor*, N. Sugrati; im-

Miserable, *miz'er-ie-bl*, A. Kircoll; dublo.

Misery, *miz'er-i*, N. Kircollai; doudirponn; dublocai; coistt.

Misfortune, *mis-for'chun*, N. Odrustt; nirbagponn.

Misinform, *mis-in-form'*, V. Fottkiri khobor diunc.

Mislay, *mis-lei'*, V. Chotrae vinn dourunc; sanddonc.

Mislead, *mis-lid*, V. Fottounc; chucounc.

Misprint, *mis-print'*, V. Chucon xapunc.

Mispronounce, *mis-pro-nauns'*, V. Chucon ucharunc.

Misrepresent, *mis-re-pre-zent'*, V. Fottounc; sarkem sangonam zaunc.

Miss, *miss*, N. Bhai.

Miss, V. Chuconc; soddunc,

Missal, *mis'al*, N. Misal.

Misshappen, *mis-shap'n*, A. Vid rup; besurvanno.

Missile, *mis'il*, N. Ec atiar dusreac ducounc uddoilelem zosi baldi, gullo etc.

Mission, *mi'shon*, N. Misaum; daddnem; dutponn.

Missionary, *mi'shon-a-ri*, N. Misionar; munniari.

Misspell, *mis'spel*, V. Chucon soletrar corunc.

Misstatement, *mis-steit'ment*, N. Fottkiri sangni.

Mist, *mist*, N. Dunvri; fg. calloc.

Mistake, *mis-teik'*, N. Chuc; guneaum.

Mistake, V. Chuconc.

Mister, *mis'ter*, N. Saib.

Mistress, *mis'tress*, N. mestin; battcan. [callocacho'

Misty, *mist'i*, A. Dunvrecho;

Misunderstand, *mis-an'dors—tand*, V. Vanoddem somzonc.

Misuse, *mis-iuz*, V. Favo toso npeog corinam zaunc; ocmanunc.

Mite, *mait*, N. Kidd.

Mitigate, *mi'ti-geit*, V. Ollu—, luu corunc.

Mitre, *mi'tor*, N. Bispacho top.

Mitten, *mit'n*, N. lunv.

Mix, *miks*, V. Mellounc.

Mixture, *miks'char*, N. Mellounem; mistur.

Moan, *môn*, V. Dukhin vo khontin luv roddonc.

Moan, N. Roddnem.

Mob, *mob*, N. Urponz; riti pormonnem naslolo zomo.

Mock, *moc*, V. Khebaddam—, chesttaeo corunc; yenddnunc.

Mocking, *moc'ing*, N. yenddaunem; kenddnem.

Mode, *mod*, N. Rit ; rovis.
Model, *mo'del*, N. Nomunno ; dek ; rit.
Model, V. Rup diunc.
Moderate, *mo'de-reitt*, A. Sumaracho ; modlo.
Moderate, V. Purto—, favo titlo corunc ; attpunc.
Moderation, *mo-de-rei'shon*, N. Damun—, odhun dornem ; attapnni ; unno cornem.
Modern, *mod'ern*, A. Novo ; hea callacho.
Modest, *mod'-est*, A. Nirgorvi ; bhiddecho ; mansugecho ; lojist
Modesty, *mod'es-ti*, N. Vinai ; bhid ; moriad ; mansugi.
Modify, *mod'i-fai*, V. Bodlunc ; firaunc.
Modulate, *mod'u-leit*, V. Tallo bodlunc.
Moist, *moist*, V. Sumaracho volo, bizlolo.
Moisten, *mois'n*, V. Bizounc ; volo corunc.
Moisture, *mois'char*, N. Xell ; volsan.
Molar, *mo'lar*, A. Vattcho; khuttcho ; dadhieo.
Mole, *mol*, N. Chamcull ; khot.
Molecule, *mo'li-kul*, N. Cuscutt.
Molest, *mo-lest'*, V. Ducounc ; dosunc ; bejar corunc.
Molestation, *mo-les-tei'shon*, N. corandai ; pidda ; dukh.
Mollify, *mol'i-fai*, V. Mon corunc.
Molten, *molt'n*, A. Coddoilolo.
Moment, *mo'ment*, N. Khin ; goddi.
Momentum, *mo'men-tum*, N. Boll.
Monarch, *mo'narc*, N. Sotevont rai.
Monastery, *mon'as-te-ri*, N. Convent.
Money, *mon'i*, N. Duddu ; nannem.
Monitor, *mo'ni-tor*, N. Chuki colloitolo vo sangtolo.
Monk, *monc*, N. Frad.
Monkey, *monj'ki*, N. Macodd.
Monogamist, *mon'og-a-mist*, N. Eke hostorecho poti.
Monogamy, *mon-og'a-mi*, N. Ecach dadlea codde cazar zaunchi chal.
Monogram, *mon'o-gram*, N. Ec akxer.
Monopolize, *mo-nop'o-laiz*, V. Sattem marunc ; macto—, guto geunc.
Monopoly, *mo-nop'o-li*, N. Mocto ; guto.
Monosyllabic, *mon'o-sil-lab-ik*, A. Ec akxeracho.
Monosyllable, *mon'o-sil-la-bl*, N. Ec akxer,
Monotonous, *mon-ot'on-as*, A. Ecach talleacho.
Monotony, *mon-ot'o-ni*, N. Ecach talleacho jinos ; fg. bejarai.
Monsoon, *mon-sun'*, N. Pausacho temp.
Monster, *mon'stor*, N. Vidrup vost ; rakos.
Monstrous, *mon'stras*, A. Vidrup ; vo rup naslolo ; raksacho.
Month, *manth*, N. Muinom.
Monthly, *manth'li*, A. Muineachea-muinea.
Monument, *mon'u-ment*, N. Yadgiri ; ugddas corchem bandop.
Mood, *mud*, N. Rup ; jinos.
Moody, *mud'i*, A, Ragist ; sonkirn.
Moon, *mun*, N. Chondrim.
—(New moon), Amas.
—(Full moon), Punou.
Moonlight, *mun'lait*, N. Charnem.
Moor, *mur*, N. Renvoll zago ; padd zago.
Moral, *mo'ral*, A. Moral ; nitivi-dea ; niti sastr.

Morass, *mo-ras'*, N. Chiclachi zomin.

Morbed, *mor'bed*, A. Piddecho.

More, *mor*, A. Chodd; bhou chodd vo vodic.

Moreover, *mor-o'vor*, AD. Tache sivai vo tea sivai.

Moribund, *mo'ri-bund*, A. Mo-runc aslolo.

Morning, *morn'ing*, N. Socallim.

Morning, A. Socallincho.

Morose, *mo-roz'*, A. Mengo; J Izodd.

Morrow, *mo'rou*, N. Falea.

Mortal, *mor'tal*, A. Morn aslolo; mornadic.

Mortality, *mor-tal'i-ti*, N. Sobar mornam; mornacho gunn.

Mortar, *mor'tar*, N. Amaldosto; van; chuno.

Mortgage, *mor'geij*, N. Pinhor.

Mortgage, V. Pinhor dourunc.

Mortgagee, *mor-ge-ji'*, N. Munis zache codde bens pinhor dovorlam.

Mortgager, *mor-ge-jar'*, N. Pinhor dovortolo.

Mortification, *mor'tifi-kei-shion*, N. Coistt, piddapidd; cuddichi donddvon.

Mortify, *mor'ti-fai*, V. Duk—, ija diunc; apnacher zoit vorunc.

Mosque, *mosk*, N. Majid.

Mosquito, *mos-ki'to*, N. Zollar; kimos.

Most, *most*, A. Bhou sobar vo bhou chodd.

Mostly, *most'li*, AD. Voddlo vantto.

Mote, *mot*, N. Kaddi; cuscuit.

Moth, *moth*, N. Kidd; kiddo.

Mother, *mo'der*, N. Maim; avoi; mata.

Mother-in-law, N. Sasu-maim.

Mother-tongue, N. Aplea gaunchi bhas.

Motion, *mo'shon*, N. Halop; boll; utt-cadde.

Motive, *mo'tiv*, N. Sobab; caran.

Motto, *mot'to*, N. Saugnem; munni,

Mould, *mold*, N. Sanso.

Mould, V. Rup diunc.

Moulder, *mold'or*, N. Sansean galnar.

Mouldy, *mold'i*, A. Bato mandlolo.

Mound, *mound*, N. Matiechi ras.

Mount, *maunt*, V. Unch vochonc; goddear bosenc.

Mountain, *maunt'ein*, N. Dongor; porvot.

Mountainous, *maun-tein'as*, A. Dongrancho.

Mountebank, *maun'ti-bangk*, N. Fottkiro voiz.

Mounted, *maunt'ed*, A. Ghoddon boslolo.

Mourn, *morn*, V. Roddonc; dukh corunc.

Mournful, *morn'ful*, A. Dukest.

Mourning, *morn'ing*, N. Khont; dukh.

Mouse, *maus*, N. Undir.

Moustache, *mus'tash*, N. Mixio.

Mouth, *mauth*, N. Tondd.

Move, *muv*, V. Alonc; cholounc; soddunc; uchamboll corunc.

Movable, *muv'ie-kl*, A. Alosarco.

Movement, *muv'ment*, N. Halop.

Mover, *muv'or*, N. Haloitolo; choloinar,

Much, *mach*, A. Chodd.

Mucilage, *mu-si-leij'*, N. Pank; gom.

Muck, *moc*, N. Jivem xenn.

Mucous, *mu'kas*, A Pancacho.

Mud, *mod*, N. Kedd; chikol; mati.

Muddle, *mod'dl*, V. Mello corunc; guspaunc.

muddy, *mod'i*, A. Matiecho; chiclacho.
muff, *mof*, N. Hatanchem potem.
muffle, *mof'l*, V. Guttlaunc.
mug, *mag*, N. Mog.
muggy, *mog'i*, A. Xellicho.
mule, *miul*, N. Kochor.
muleteer, *mul-et-iar'*, N. Kochranç ambuddnar.
mulish, *mul'ish*, A. Kochra baxen; aplea vadeacho.
multiple, *mul'ti-pl*, A. Zaite pautti doddo.
multiply, *mul'ti-plai*, V. Multiplicar corunc; choddounc.
multitude, *mul'ti-tiud*, N. Zomo; urponz.
munificence, *mu-ni'fi-sens*, N. Udarponn.
munificent, *mu-ni'fi-sent*, N. Udar.
munition, *mu-ni'shon*, N. Foujichem somonn.
murder, *mor'dor*, N. Khuni.
murder, V. Jivesim marunc.
murderer, *mor'dor-ar*, N. Mort marnar.
murderous, *mor'dar-as*, A. Khuniyecho.
murky, *mor'ki*, A. Callocacho.
murmur, *mor'mor*, V. Gunngunnaunc; chabddaunc; xinn corunc.
murrain, *mo'rein*, N. Voseachi pidda gorvam modem.
muscle, *mos'l*, N. Mam sapesi; pesi.
mushroom, *mosh'rum*, N. Aimbem.
music, *miu'zic*, N. Gayen; vazop.
musical, *miu'zi-cal*, A. Gaianacho; vazpacho.
musician, *miu-zi-shan'*, N. Cantarist; vazpi; musg.
musket, *mos'ket*, N. Bondunc, arm.
musketry, *mos'ke-try*, V. Armancho dar.
muslin, *mos'lin*, N. Molmol.
must, *most*, N. Ros.
must, V. Goroz asunc.
mustard, *mos'tard*, N. Sansvam.
mustard-plaster, N. Sansvancho lep vo papam.
muster, *mos'tor*, V. Fouz pollevunc; hajir zaunc.
mustiness, *mos'ti-ness*, N. Bato
musty, *most'i*, A. Batelolo.
mustability, *mu-tabil'i-ti*, N. Bodlo sarkem.
mute, *miut*, A. Tondd naslolu; mono.
mutilate, *mu'ti-leit*, V. Mottvo corunc; unno corunc; sande catrunc.
mutineer, *miu'ti-ner*, N. Sercaracher vo tharailele authoridadicher bodolnar.
mutinous *miu'ti-nas*, A. Bandi, Futurio.
mutiny, *miu'ti-ni*, N Bondhay, rajbhong.
mutter *mat'er*, V. Gaungunnanc, aple bhitor ulounc.
mutton, *mot'n*, V. Bocrechem mas.
mutual, *miu'chu-al*, A. Eca mecacho.
muzzle, *moz'l*, N. Sonddi, muscor.
my, *mai*, PRON. Mozo.
myriad, *mi'ri-ad* N. Dha hozar.
myrrh, *mirr*, N. Mir; pormollacho ros.
myself, *mai'self*, pron aumch.
mysterious, *mis-ti'ri-as*, A. Guttacho; guddacho; gupit.
mystery, *mis'ter-i* N. Mister poic; gudd; khon.
mystic, *mis'tic*, A. Guttacho.
mystify, *mis'ti-fai*, V. Fottounc, naddunc; dubavon ulounc.

N

Nabob, *na'bob*, N. Nabab; dud-duancar.
Nag, *nag*, N. Supurlo goddo.
Nail, *neil*, N. Naksi; Khilo.
Nail, V. Khilaunc.
Naive, *hei'ev*, A. Sado.
Naked, *nei'ked*, A. Vinglo; ugtto.
Nakedness, *nei'ked-nes*, N. Nagddeponn, Vinglepon.
Name, *nem*, N. Naum; utor.
Name, V. Munnonc; ulo corunc; naum diunc.
Namely, *nem'li*, AD Munge, mul-lear.
Namesake, *nem'seik*, N. Teach nanvancho munis.
Nap, *nep*, N. Loum; zop; thod-di nid.
Nape. *neip*, N. Man.
Napkin, *nep'kin*, N. tonddacho tuvalo.
Narcotic, *nar-co'tie*, A. Nidoun-cho.
Narrate *na-reit'*, V. Sangonc; munnonc.
Narration *na-rei'shion*, N. Con-tha; Sangnem.
Narrow, *ne'rou*, A. Osir.
Narrow, V. Osir corunc.
Narrowness, *ne'rou-ness*, N. Os-rai.
Nasal, *na'zal*, N. Nacacho, na-kio, simro.
Nastiness, *nas'ti-ness*, N. Melle-ponn.
Nasty, *nas'ti*, A. Olsik; mello.
Natal, *na'tal* N. Zolmancho dis.
Nation, *nei'shon*, N. Porza, des-loc.
National, *ne'shon-al*, A. Loca-cho, desacho.
Native, *nei'tiv*, N. Soimbacho; gauncho.
Nativity, *na-tiv'i-ti*, N. Zolm.
Natural, *ne'cher-al*, A. Soimba-cho; niz.
Naturalize, *ne-cher-a-laiz*, V. Desjat, diunc, desi corunc.
Nature, *nei'char* N. Soimb gunn.
Naughty, *no'th*, A. Gorjec pod-do naslolo; auxi.
Nausea, *nos-he'a*, N. Von caro.
Nauseate, *no-she'eit*, V Vonca-ro eunc.
Nauseous, *no'shas*, A. Vonca-reacho; canttalleacho.
Nautical, *no'tical*, A. Tarvan-cho; dartacho.
Navel, *nei'vel*, N. Bombli.
Navigable. *na'vi-ge-bl*, A. Tarum cholo sarco.
Navigate, *na'vi-geit*, V. Tarvan–, patmaren vochun-eunc.
Navigation, *na-vi-gei'shon*, N. Tarvan yennem-vochnom.
Navigator, *na'vi-geit-or*, N. Tar-van vetolo; tarum choloitolo.
Navy, *neiv'i*, N. Tarvam.
Near, *ner*, A. Lagim aslolo; lag-silo.
Near, AD. Lagim; aro.
Near, PREP. Lagim; sorsim.
Nearly, *ner'li*, AD. Lagim-lagim! sumar.
Neat, *nit*, N. Gorvam.
Neat, A. Nitoll; sundor.
Neatness, *nit'ness*, N. Nitollponn vo sundorai.
Necessarily, *ne'ses-sa-ri-li*, AD Avas zaun; chuco nastanam; gorjevontim.
Necessary, *nes'se-sa-ri*, A. Gor-jecho; zai aslolo; zorur.
Necessity, *nes-ses'i-ti*, N. Goroz; acant.
Neck, *nec*, N. Gollo; gordon.
Neclace, *nec'leis*, N. Sorpolli; golleantlem bangar.
Need, *nid*, N. goroz,

Needful, *nid'ful*, A. Gorjecho; gorjevont.
Needle, *nid'l*, N. Sui,
Needy, *nid'i*, A. Dublo; gorjevont.
Nefarious, *ne-fei'ri as*, A. Khotto.
Negation, *ne-gei'shon*, N. nam—, noi munnem; naca munnem.
Neglect. *nig'lekt*, V. Beporva corunc; visor poddonc; ausai. corunc.
Negligence, *neg'li-jens*, N. Visor, ausai; beporvo; befikir.
Negligent, *neg'li-jent*, A. Porva—fikir naslolo.
Negotiate, *ne-go'shi-eitt*, N. Vepar corunc; chali boli corunc.
Negotiation, *ne-go-shi-ei'shon*, N. Ulonnnem; karar; vepar.
Negotiator, *ne-go'shi-eit-or*, N. Kam cortolo; carbari; dalal.
Neigh, *nei*, V. Goddea baxen roddonc.
Neighbour, *nei'bor*, N. Pelo; sezari.
Neighbourhood, *nei'bor-hud*, N. Sezara; lagsili suat.
Neighbouring, *nei'bor-ing*, A. Sezarcho; lagim aslolo.
Neither-nor, *ni'dor-nor*, CONJ. (toni) nam—, (houi) nam.
Neophyte, *ne'o-fait*, N. Novo christaum, [neo.
Nephew, *ne'fiu*, N. Bacho; put-
Nerve, *norv*, N. Sir; fg. boll.
Nervous, *nerv'as*, A. Sirantarancho; fg. bezudd.
Nest, *nest*, N. Guntter; fg. asro.
Net, *net*, N. Zal!.
Nettle, *net'tl*, N. Katcutli.
Nettle, V, Korzunc.
Net-work, *net'work*, N. Zallie sarkem cam.
Neutral, *niu'tral*, A. Bhair aslolo, raulolo; bhailo.
Neutrality, *niu-tral'i-ti*, N. Sambhandi.
Never, *nev'er*, AD. Kedinch.
Nevertheless, *nev'er-thi-less*. CONJ. Oxem astanam; zalearui,
New, *niu*, A. Novo.
New-comer, *niu'com-or*, N. Atam ailolo; pordesi.
Newish, *niu'ish*, A. Novoso.
Newly, *niu'li*, AD. Yedol.
News, *nius*, N. Khobor; pukaro.
News-paper, *nius-pei'pur*, N. Khobrechem potr,
Next. *nekst*, A. Lagsilo.
Next, AD. Lagim vo sorsim; magir.
Nib, *nib*, N. Apar; domos.
Nibble, *nib'bl*, V. Chanchounc.
Nice, *nais*, N. Sarco; sobit; suadic; naznc.
Nicety, *nai'se-ti*, N. Nazucai; sobsi.
Nickname, *nic'nem*, N. Addnaum.
Niece, *nis*, N. Bachi; duvddi.
Niggard, *nig'ard*, A. Sugrati; imtto.
Niggardliness, *nig'ard-li-ness*, N. Sugrat; imtteponn.
Nigh, *nai*, AD. Lagim; sorsim.
Night, *naitt*, N. Rat; ratchea vellar.
Night-mare, *naitt'mer*, N. Horddea-sull.
Nightly, *naitt'li*, A. Ratcho.
Nimble, *nim'bl*, A. Suddsuddit; uxar.
Nimbleness, *nim'bl-ness*, N. Suddsuddai.
Nine, *nain*, A. Nou.
Nip, *nip*, V. Chimtto caddunc; kimchunc.
Nippers, *nip'pars*, N. Chimto.
Nipple, *nip'pl*, N. Chium; horddem; fg. than.
Nit, *nit*, N. Lik.

No, *no*, AD. Noi ; naca ; nam.
Nobility, *no-bil'i-ti*, N. Vodd kulli ; voddponn ; thorai.
Noble, *no'bl*, A. Manadic ; fg. vorto ; voddlo.
Nod, *nod*, V. Tocli halounc vo bagounc ; dolle moddunc ; jemeunc.
Nod, N. Jem.
Noise, *noiz*, N. Bob ; bobatt.
Noisome. *noi'som*, A. Bolaikec vaitt ; canttalleacho.
Noisy, *noi'zi*, A. Bobattieo ; uchamboll,
Nomadic, *no-mad'ik*, A. Bouncho.
Nomenclature, *no'men-cla-chur*, N. Sobdanchem bhanddar.
Nominal. *no'mi-nal*, A. Nanvacho ; utram pormonnem.
Nominally, *no'mi-nal-li*, AD. Bhaileanunch ; nanvanunch.
Nominate, *no'mi-neitt*, V. Munnonc ; nemunc ; nomear corunc.
Nomination, *no-mi-nei'shon*, N. Nomiasaum ; nemni.
Nominee, *no-mi-ni'*, N. Nomiar kelolo.
None, *non*, PRO. Ecloi noi.
Nonsense, *non'sens*, N. Naca zalolo ; zanc ; pixeaponnachim utram.
Nook, *nuc*, N. Conso.
Noon, *nun*, N. Donpar.
Noose, *nuz*, N. Fas ; gantt.
Noose, V. Naddunc.
Nor, *nor*, CONJ. Anim...... nam.
Normal, *nor'mal*, A. Nemacho ; kramacho ; dekhicho. [dag.
North, *north*, N. Uttar disa, bad-
Northen, *north'on*, A. Baddgacho ; norticho.
Nose, *noz*, N. Nac,
Nosegay, *noz'gei*, N. Fulancho gons ; boquet.
Nosology, *no-zol'o-ji*, N. Piddanchem xastr.
Nostril, *nos'tril*, N. Nacacho pudd.
Nostrum, *nos'trum*, N. Gupit vocot.
Not, *not*, AD. Nam ; noi.
Notable, *not'ie-bl*, A. Chotraecho ; vsiesh ; navaddgo.
Notary. *not'a-ri*, N. Tabeliaum ; dabir.
Notation, *no-tei'shon*, N. Chotrai,
Notch, *noch*, N. Catrop.
Note. *not*, Kuru ; nishani ; chotrai ; chitt ; tallo.
Note, V. Kuru corunc ; chotrai diunc. [toc.
Note-book, N. Chotraechem pus-
Noted, *not'ed*, A. Famad ; voddlo.
Nothing. *noth'ing*, N. Cainch nam.
Notice, *no'tis*, N. Khobor ; chotrai.
Notice, V. Collit zaunc ; chotrai diunc.
Notification, *no-ti-fi-kei'shon*, N. Collouni ; jannanni ; decol cornem.
Notify, *not'i-fai*, V. Collounc ; decol corunc.
Notion, *no'shon*, N. Orth ; sicon ; khobor.
Notorious, *no-to'ri-as*, A. Collit ; ugtto ; porgott.
Notwithstanding, *not-with-stand'ing*, PREP & CONJ. Oxem astanam.
Noun. *naun*, N. Naum.
Nourish, *no'rish*, V. Posunc ; jevon diunc ; vaddounc.
Nourishing, *no'rish-ing*, A. Bolaikecho.
Nourishment, *no'rish-ment*, N. Posop ; jevon.
Novel, *no'vul*, A. novo ; ojap.
Novel. N. Contha ; canni.
Novena, *no-vi'na*, N. Noven ; nov disanchem magnem.

Novice, *no'vis,* N. Umedvar; umedvar xastri.
Novitiate, *no'vi-shi-eitt,* N. Novisianchem ghor.
Now, *nau,* AD. Atam.
Now and then, Thodde pautti.
Now a days, Heam disanim.
Nowhere, *no'rer,* AD. Khuinch nam.
Noxious, *nok'shas,* A. Lusconacho; ocmanacho.
Nugatory. *nu'ga-to-ri,* A. Bestto; chesttaecho.
Nuisance, *nui'sans,* N. Bejarai; bejar vo ocman corchi corni.
Null, *nol,* A. Nirfoll; poklo; nirball; radd.
Numb, *nom,* A. Sintid naslolo.
Number, *nomb'or,* N. Anc; zomo.
Number, V. Nambr galunc; ixeop corunc, mezunc.
Numberless, *nom'bar-less,* A. Mezum nozo titlo.
Numeral, *niu'mer-al,* A. Ancancho, numrancho.
Numerator, *niu'mer-eitor,* N. ams, lav; ancnar, mejpi.
Numerous, *niu'me-ras,* A. Sobar vo zaito; chodd.
Nun, *non,* N. Madr. [cho dut.
Nuncio, *nun-shi'o* N. Pap Saiba-
Nunery, *non'o-ri* N. Couvent; madrincho bonglo.
Nuptials *nop'shal* N. Cazar.
Nurse, *nors,* N. Ayah; dudcarn.
Nurse, V. Vagounc; dud diunc; raconc.
Nursery, *nor'se-ri,* N. Burgeanc vagounchem ghor.
Nut, *not,* N. Foll.
Nutmeg, *not'meg,* N. Zaifol.
Nutriment, *nu'tri-ment,* N. Posnne; udorposonn.
Nutrition, *nu-tri'shon,* N. Posonn, posnem.
Nutritive, *nu-tri'tiv,* A. Posouncho, gottaecho.
Nux vomica, *uux'vo-mica,* N. Cazro.

O

O, int. he; aga.
Oak, *ok,* N. Zaddachem naum zaca thodde munttat vraksaraja.
Oar, *or,* N. Volo.
Oath, *oth,* N. Suput; jurament.
Obduracy, *ob'du-ra-si,* N. Nibor cornem fg. darunnai; nistturai.
Obdurate. *ob'du-reit,* A. Nibor--conttin zalolo; fg. nisttur, darunn.
Obedient. *o-be'di-ent,* A. Khalto; aicotolo, mantolo.
Obediently, *o-bi'di-ent-li,* AD. khalto zaun, khalteponnim.
Obeiance, *o-bei'sans,* N. Nomoscar.
Obey, *o-bei',* V. Manunc, aicunc, pratipallunc.
Obituary, *o-bit'u-a-ri,* N. Meleleanchi potti, sivddi-
Object, *ob'ject,* N. Vishai, orth, vost.
Object, V. Addaunc; posond corinam zaunc.
Objection *ob-jec'shon,* N. Add. coll, add, arkot.
Objective, *ob-jec'tiv,* A. Vostuncho; bhailo; khoroch.
Objurgate, *ob-jer'geit,* V. Gauzunc, insunc. solunc.
Objurgation, *ob-jur-gei'shon,* N. Nisanni solnni; besttauni.
Obligation, *o-bli-gei'shon* N. Caido; upcar.
Obligatory, *ob'li-ga-to-ri,* A. Caideacho; gorjecho; corcho.
Oblige, *o-blaij',* V. Formaunc.

Obliging, *o-blaij'ing,* A. Mogall; upcari; voddnecho.
Obligingness, *o-blaij'ing-ness,* N. Mogalponn.
Oblique, *oblik'* A. Vancddo.
Obliquity, *ob'lik-wi-ti,* N. Vancdeponn.
Obliterate, *ob-lit'e-reit,* V. Pusunc, pusun caddunc, gansunc,
Obliteration, *ob-lit-e-rei'shon,* N. Pusop, gansop.
Oblivion, *ob-li'vi-on,* N. Visor.
Oblivious, *ob-li'vi-as* A. Visrauncho; ngdasnaslolo.
Oblong, *ob'long,* A. Lamboddo, lambelo.
Obloquy, *ob'lo-kwi,* N. Addvo, tiddvo.
Obnoxious, *ob-nok'shas,* A. Dustt, nostto; lusconacho.
Obscene, *ob'sin,* A. Pozddo, burso, canttalleacho.
Obscenity *ob-sen'i-ti,* N. Pozddepon, burseponn.
Obscuration, *ob-skur-ei'shon,* N. Calloc poddnem, andhar.
Obscure, *ob-skiuar',* A. Callso; uzvadd naslolo; conttin; unno vo holco.
Obscure, V. Calloc corunc; fg. man ubounc.
Obscurity, *ob-skiu'-ri-ti,* N. Calloc; unneponn.
Obsequious, *ob-ze'kwi as,* A. Siristo cortolo; mantolo, upcari, porcondtolo.
Observance, *ob-serv'ans,* N. Palleoni, pallo.
Observant, *ob-zerv'ant,* A. Man diuncho, zagrut; chotraecho.
Observation, *ob-zer-vei'shon,* N. Chotrai.
Oservatory, *ob-ser-va'tori,* N. Taramgam, vedha salla.
Observe, *ob-sorv',* V. Polleunc; chotrai diunc; samballunc.
Obsolete, *ob'so-lit,* A. Porno; Aprupacho.
Obstacle, *ob-sta'kl,* A. Harcot, addcoll.
Obstetric, *ob-stet'ric,* A. Voizinnicho.
Obstinacy, *ob'sti-na-si,* N. Darrunnai, murdarponn.
Obstinate, *ob'sti-neit,* A. Darrun, aplea vadeacho.
Obstruct, *ob-stroct',* V. Damunc; addcoll galunc.
Obstruction, *ob-stroc'shon,* N. Addcoll.
Obtain, *ob-tein',* V. Zoddunc, mellounc, jiconc.
Obtrude, *ob-trod',* V. Boll corunc.
Obtuse, *ob-tiuz',* A. Dar naslolo; fg: somzo naslolo.
Obviate, *ob'vi-eitt,* V. Chucounc; nivraunc.
Obvious, *ob'vi-as,* A. Collit, decol, ugddapo.
Occasion, *ok-kei-jion,* N. Soheog, vel, ocaziaum.
Occasional, *ok-kei'jon-al,* V. Samiogacho; auchit; kernaim goddtolo.
Occident, *oc'si-dent,* N. Ostomti.
Occupation, *oc-kiu-pei'shon,* N. Cam, vaur; udiog; dando.
Occupied, *oc-kiu-paid* A. Addlolo, cami.
Occupy, *oc'kiu-pai,* V. Vaurunc, cam corunc; camanc launc; occupad asunc.
Occur, *oc-kor',* V. Zaunc, goddonc; motint ennc.
Occurrence, *oc-ko'rens,* N. Bhett, mell; goddni; goroz.
Ocean, *o'shan,* N Doria, somdir.
Octave, *oc'teiv,* N. Oitav; attvo dis.
Oculist, *oc'u-list,* N. Dolleancho voiz.

Odd (number), N. Geddem.
Odd, *od',* A. Tarifecho.
Odds, *odz',* N. Ecannem chodd ontor ; ogllo.
Ode, *od',* A. Pod.
Odious, *o'di-as,* A. Canttallea-cho ; onkatto.
Odium, *o'di-um,* N. Adavot, cusddai ; dusmancai.
Odontology, *o-don-tol'o-ji,* N. Dantanchi videa.
Odorous, *o'dor-as,* A. Pormolla-cho, domdomit.
Odour, *o'dor,* N. Pormoll ; dom-dom.
Of, *of,* PREP. Cho-chi-chem.
Offence, *of-fens',* N. Ocman, duc ; guneaum ; oprad.
Offend, *of-fend',* V. Ocman co-runc ; ducounc.
Offensive, *of-fens'iv,* A. Ocma-nacho ; ducouncho ; cantallea-cho ; zulmecho.
Offer, *of'or,* V. Bettounc ; somor-piunnc ; diunc.
Offering, *of-for'ing,* N. Bett, den-nem.
Office, *of-is,* N. Caido, cam ; udeog ; upcar, ofis.
Officer, *of'is-ar,* N. Foujicho sar-dar ; udiog-car.
Official, *o-fi'shal,* N. Sercaracho, sercari.
Official, N. Camadar ; adikari ; sardar.
Officiate, *o-fi'shi-eit,* V. Ofisiar corunc, cam cholounc.
Officious, *of-fi'shas,* A. Upcari, biddest ; khasgi.
Offing, *of'ing,* N. Toddi poisilean.
Offscouring, *of-scour'ing,* A. Kunddo.
Offset, *of'set,* N. Ancri.
Offspring, *of'spring,* N. Sonsot, burgim.
Often, *of'n* AD. Sobar pautti.
Ogle, *o'gl,* V. Vancddo vo tirso polleunc.
Ogre, *o'gor,* N. Rakos.
Oil, *oil,* N. Tel.
Oil-cake, N. Pendd.
Oilmen, *oil'men,* N. Telcar ; gan-necar.
Oil-mill, *oil'mill,* N. Ghanno.
Ointment, *oint'ment,* N. Molom, bhailean launchem vocot, por-mollachem tel.
Old, *old,* A. Mataro; porno; adlo.
Olden, *old'on,* A Adle sovon-iecho; porno, adlea callacho.
Oligarchy, *o'li-gar-ki;* N. Thodde-ancho adicar.
Olive, *o'lio,* N. Nannelacho ruk; jitafol.
Omega, *o-me'ga,* N. Ant.
Omen, *o'men,* N. Nimit; khunna; odrustt.
Omission, *o-mi'snon,* N. Soddnem; nam corni.
Omit, *o-mit,* V. Corinam zaunc, soddunc, thambounc.
Omnibus, *om'ni-bus,* N. Topolachi gaddi.
Omnipotence, *om-nip'o-tens,* N. Sorvpodvi.
Omnipotent, *om-nip-o'tent,* A. Sorvpodvedar.
Omnipresence, *om-ni'prez'ens,* N. Sorvoi suatar asnem.
Omnipresent, *om-oi-prez'ent* A. Sorvaviapac, sorvaviapi.
On, *on,* PREP Voir; lagim.
On AD Mucar; ravonastanam.
Once, *ons,* Ad ek pautti; atanch; sangata. sovem.
One, *von,* A. Eoc, eclo; folanno.
Oneself, *von'self,* Pro apunn.
Onion, *o'nion,* N. Piyau, cando.
Only, *on'li,* Ad, matr, focot.
Only, A. Ecach.
Onset, *on'set,* N. zulum; angar poddop; iiprasni.

Onward, *on'ward,* AD. Mucar-
Onward, A. Mucavelo.
Opaque, *o-pak',* A. Aspas, arpar diso naslolo.
Open, *o'pn,* V. Ugtto corunc vo ugddunc, suru corunc.
Open, *o'pn,* A. Ugtto; rigo-sarco; porgott; sado.
Opening, *o'pn-ing,* A. Biddem; moddop; futt; suru.
Openly, *o-pn-li,* AD. Des-porgott, lipoi nastanam; bhailean.
Operate, *o'per-eit,* V. Boll assunc, gunn poddonc; boro rigonc vo lagonc.
Operation, *o-pe-rei'shon,* N. Operasaum; corni; cortub.
Ophthalmy, *of-thal,mi,* N Dolleancho ulop.
Opinion, *o-pi'nion,* N. Opiniaum, somzoni, chintna; bud, sangni.
Opium, *o'pi-am,* N. Afin.
Opponent, *op-po'nent,* A. porto; virodhi, contr.
Opportune, *op-or-tun,* A. Favoto vellac boro, laic, upcarto.
Opportunity, *op-por-tun'i-ti,* N. boro vell, somoio, prasang.
Oppose, *op-poz',* V. Addcoll galunc, addaunc, incar corunc.
Opposed, *op-pozd',* A. Addvo; porto; mucavelo.
Opposite, *op'po-zit,* A. Mucavelo; porto; porte vatten.
Opposition, *op-po-zi'shon,* N. Add asnem, yennem; addchon; virodh.
Oppress, *op-press',* V. Bhar-ojem galunc; fg. dogdaunc; coistaunc.
Oppressed, (with debts) Rinnan buddlolo.
Oppression, *op-pre'shon,* N. dogd. zulum; gulamponn.
Oppressive, *op-pres'iv,* A. Dogdauncho; zulum corcho.
Oppressor, *op-pres'or* N. Rodoitolo, dogdaitolo; zulum cornar.
Opprobrious, *op-pro'bri-as,* A. Lozistt; canttaleacho; beabrucho, abru caddcho.
Opprobrium, *op-pro'bri-um,* N. Ocman; loz; beabru.
Oppugn, *op-pun,* V. Contr vo virodd ulounc.
Optative, *op'ta-tiv,* A. Axecho.
Optic, *op'tic,* A. distticho; drusttícho.
Option, *op'shon,* N. Khoxi; vinchop.
Opulence, *op'u-lens,* N. Girescai; dhon, doulot.
Opulent, *op'u-lent,* A. Vodd girest, dhonvont
Or, *or,* Conj vo.
Oracle, *o'ra-cl,* N. Prasad, devvanni.
Oral, *o'ral,* A. Thondacho, thondapasi.
Orally, *o'ral-li,* AD. Thondda pasim.
Orange, *o'renj,* N. Naring; torenj.
Oration, *o-rei'shon,* N. Sermaum; prasang; ulounem.
Orator, *o'ra-tor,* N. Boli uloinar, bolnar; prasanga pandit.
Oratorical, *o-ra-to'ri-cal,* A. Unchi bhasecho.
Oratory, *o'ra-to-ri,* N. Prasanga videa; magnem corchem ghor; kopel, irmit; orotor.
Orb, *orb,* N. Mandd; gullo.
Orbit, *or'bit,* N. Bovanddo.
Orchard, *or'chard,* N. Mollo.
Orchestra, *or'kestra,* N. Orkestr, thodde musg.
Ordain, *or-dein',* N. Formaunc; povitr corunc.
Ordainer, *or-dein'ar,* N. Nemsitolo; ordenasaum cornar.
Ordeal, *or'di-al,* N. Cottin poricxa.

Order, *ó'der,* N. Mandavoll, hukum, ord.
Order, V. Mandduno ; hukum diunc.
Orderly, *or'dor-li,* VD. Favo te porim, craman.
Ordinance, *or'din-ans,* N. Istiar ; raiacho pergaum.
Ordinarily, *or'di-na-ri-li,* AD. Cholte ponnim ; bhou corun.
Organ, *or'gan,* N. Sando ; potr ; orgaum.
Organic, *or-gan'ic,* A. Sande asIolo, sandeacho, angacho, boddicho ; angac zomlolo.
Organism, *or'gan-izm,* N. Sandeachi goddvon, goddavol.
Organization, *or'gan-i-zei-shon,* N. Goddni, rochni, mandavoll.
Organize, *or'gan-aiz,* V. Mandduno ; rochunc, goddunc ; mandavoll corunc.
Oriel, *o'ri-el,* N. Bolcaum.
Orient, *o'ri-ent,* N. Udenti.
Orifice, *o'ri-fis,* N. tondd vo muc.
Origin, *o'ri-gin,* N. Oromb, mull.
Original, *o-ri'jinal,* A. Poilo,, orombacho, muddlacho; soimbacho,
Original, N. Asoll ; nomuno.
Originate, *o-ri'jin-eit* V. Rochunc ; oromb diunc ; zolmounc.
Ornament, *or'na-ment,* N. Surungar ; netton.
Ornament, V. nettounc, surungarunc.
Ornamental, *or-na-ment-al,* A. Nettouncho, surungaruncho.
Orphan, *or'fan,* N. Por, avoi bapui naslolo burgo.
Orphanage, *or'fan-eij,* N. poranchem biddar.
Orthodox, *or'tho-doks,* A. Aputt; fg, sotevont.
Orthodoxy, *or'tho-doks-si,* N. Aputt, sicop vo bavarth.
Oscillate, *os'sil-eit,* V. Yennem tennem alunc, jelunc, ulandond.
Oscillation, *os-cil-lei'shon,* N. Alop, jelni, jel, jompoi.
Osseous, *os'si-as,* A. Nadancho.
Ostensible, *os-ten'si-bl,* A. Dauncho vo dacoi-sarco.
Ostentation, *os-ten-tei'shon,* N. Dacoun; voddvi, boddai vo boddaic.
Ostentatious, *os'ten-tei'zi-as,* A. Dacouncho, mirvonnecho, dobajeacho.
Ostler, *oist'lor,* N. Gaddecar.
Other, *od'op* A. Dusro ; aninc-ek; eor; bodol.
Otherwise, *od'or-waiz,* AD. Nam zalear ; dusre jinsim.
Ottoman, *ot-to'man,* N. Turki.
Ought, *oth,* V. Caido asunc.
Ounce, *ouns,* N. Ons.
Our, *aor,* PRO. Amcho.
Ourselves, *aor-selvz',* PRO. Aminch.
Out, *out* AD. Bhair.
Outbreak, *aut'brek,* N. Uchambollai ; auchit dacoun zosi ragachi, pestichi etc.
Outcast, *aut'cast,* S. A. Bostailolo, zati bhailo; pordesant uddoilolo.
Outflank, *aut'flenc,* V. Veddo galunc.
Outgrow, *aut-gro',* V. Ispa bhair vaddonc; zainam zaunc.
Out-house, N. Mattou; nanni.
Outlaw, *aut'lo* N. Caideachο mozoti bhailo.
Outlay, *aut'lei,* V. Khorchunc.
Outlet, *aut'let,* N. Bhair sorchem muc vo vatt.
Outline, *aut'lain,* N. Sonkshep.
Outlive, *aut'liv,* V. Vanchono ; uprant jieunc,

Outnumber, *aut-nom'bor*, V. Von chodd asunc.
Outrage, *aut'reij*, N. Ocman.
Outrage, V. Ocman corunc.
Outrageous, *aut-rei'jas*, A. Ocmanacho.
Outright, *aut'rait*, AD. Atanch; purtem.
Outrun, *aut'ran*, V. Mucar danvunc; patti galunc.
Outset, *aut'set*, N. Surn.
Outside, *aut'said*, AD. Bhair.
Outside, N. Bhailem rup.
Outskirt, *aut'skort*, N. Aker; conso.
Outspoken, *aut'spo-kn*, A. Ugtto; gupit noi aslolo.
Outstanding, *aut-stand'ing*, A. Baki urta; bhair sorlelem; mukom.
Outstrip, *aut-strip'*, V. Xime bhair sorunc.
Outward, *out'ward*, A. Bhailo.
Outweigh, *aut-wei'*, V. Teai poros chodd vozon zaunc.
Outwit, *aut-wit'*, V. Fottonnc.
Outwork, *aut'work*, N. Bhailem cott.
Oval, *o'val*, A. Tantia sarco.
Oven, *ov'n*, N. Khorn, batti.
Over, *ov'ar*, PREP. Voir, poros chodd; sivai.
Over, *ad*, N. voir, unch.
Overbalance, *o-vor-bal'ans*, N. Vozon vodic zaunc; vodic bharim zaunc.
Overbearing. *o-vor-ber'ing*, A. podvecho; gorvi.
Overcast, *o-vor-cast'*, V. A. sobar cupancho.
Overcharge, *o-vor-charj'*, V. Chodd mol sangunc.
Overcome, *o-vor-com'*, V. Zoit vorunc; jicon khalto corunc.
Overcoat, *o-vor-cot'*, N. Capot; kutaum.
Overdo, *o-vor-du'*, V. Chodd corunc.
Overdrink, *o-vor'drink*, V. Regre bhair pieunc.
Overflow, *o-vor-flo'*, V. Boron bhair votonc.
Overfond, *o-vor-fond'*, A. Chodd apurbai corcho.
Overgrow *o-vor-gro'*, V. Regre vorto vaddonc.
Overhang, *overheng'*, V. Umcollonc; lambounc.
Overhaul, *o-vor-hol'*, V. Durus corcheac barcaen pollennc.
Overhasty, *o-vor-hast'i*. A. Chodd urmott.
Overhead *o-vor-hed'* AD. Mateavoir.
Overhear, *o-vor-hier'*, V. Auchituch aiconc.
Overlay, *o-vor-lei'*, V. Dampunc; launç.
Overlong, *o-vor-long'* A. Chodd lamb.
Overlook, *o-vor-luk'*. V. Maf corunc, bogsunc; beporvo corunc.
Overpower, *o-vor-pau'er*, V. Chenchunc, domaunc.
Oversee, *o-vor-si'*, V. Raconc.
Overseer, *o-vor-si'ar*, N. Racnno; polletolo.
Oversight, *o-vor'saitt*, N. Nodor chuc; soddni,
Oversleep, *o-vor-slip'*, V. Regre bhair nidonc.
Overspread, *o-vor-spred'*, V. Dampunnc.
Overstep, *o-vor-step'*, V. Mere bhair soronc.
Overtake, *o-vor-teik'*, N. Patt dorunc.
Overtask, *o-vor-task'*, V. Chodd vaur diunc.
Overthrow, *o-vor-throu'*, V. Socol nddounc; ibadd corune.

Overtop, *o-vor-top'*, V. Unch sorone.
Overture, *o'vor-tur*, N. Propost,
Overturn, *o-vor-tarn'*, V. Vompto galunc, portunc; FG. nas corunc.
Overvalue, *o-vor-vel'iu* V. Mol vodic corunc.
Overwhelm, *o-vor-whelm'*, V. zoddai galuno.
Owe, *or*, V. Devo asunc.
Owl, *aul*, N. Natuc.
Own, *oun*, A. Aplo; khaski.
Own, V. Cobul zaunc.
Owner *ou'nor*, N. Dhonim.
Ox, *oks*, N. Boil.
Oyster, *oist'or*, N. Calum.

P.

Pace, *pes* N. Tanch; chal.
Pace, V. Cholonc; Bonvonc.
Pacific, *pa-cif'ic*, A. Nidan; soucassecho; somandanacho.
Pacification, *pa-si-fi-kei'shon*, N. sontsonn; somandan.
Pacify, *pa'si-fai*, V. Sostaunc, tharavunc, thondd corunc.
Pack, *pec*, N. Bocxem, pottli; birem.
Pack, V. Pottli bandunc; dambunc; vochonc.
Package, *pek'eij*, N. Pottli; nog.
Packet, *pek'et*, V. Nog bandunc.
Paddy, *ped'i*, N. Bhat.
Pagan, *pei'gan*, N Onbavrthi; Ooncno. [varthponn.
Paganism, *pe'gan-izm*, N. Onba-
Page, *pej*, N. Pazn; chacor.
Page, V. Paznanc anc galunc,
Pageant. *pe'jent*, N. Dobazo. khall.
Pagoda, *pa-go'da*, N. Diul.
Pail, *peil*, N. Collso; baldi.
Pain, *pein*, N. Dhuk; coistt; acant.
—Take pains-minot geunc.
Pain, V. Dukh disonc, duconc.
Painful, *pein'ful*, A. Dukicho ducouncho; coisttauncho.
Paint, *peint*, V. Pintarunc; rong caddunc.
Paint, N. Rong.
Painter, *peint'or*, N. Pintur.
Painting, *peint'ing*, N. Pintur; chitram caddchi videa.
Pair, *per*, N. Zoddem.
Palace. *pa'les*, N. Polas.
Palankin, *pa'lan-kin*, N. Palki, machil.
Palate, *pa'leit*, N. Ruch; kompo.
Palaver, *pa-la'vor*, N. Naca zallo; chesttai; zanc; gozali.
Pale, *pel*, N. Khuntto; khambo, voi.
Pale, A. Oidduvo; dovo.
Paleness, *peil'ness*, N. Dousan.
Palinode, *pal'i-nod*, n. gorje bhailem sangnem.
Palisade, *pa-li-zeid'*, N. Khuntteachi voi vo addo.
Palish, *peil'ish*, A. Douso.
Pall, *pal*, N. Callem cap; vol.
Pall, V. Ruch naslolo zaunc; puro zaunc.
Pallet, *pa'let*, N. Khattlem; antuln.
Palliate, *pal'li-eit*, V. Nib sarunc, nimit sangunc; lipounc; dampun douruuc.
Palliative. *pal'i-eit-iv*, N. Pidda denvounchem vocot, boll moddcho upai.
Palm, *pam*, N. Tallat; madd; cavoto.
Palpable, *pal'pe-bl*, A. Sanspuncho, posevum-yeso.
Palpitate, *pal'pi-teit*, V. Uddonc; dhoddobunc.
Palpitation *pal-pi,-tei'shon*, N. Doddoddo, dobdob.
Palsy, *pol'si*, N. Ar.

Palter, *palt'or*, V. Fottounc, monant copott dourun ulounc.
Paltry, *pol'tri*, A. Olco; kircoll.
Pamper, *pem'por*, V. Khoxe pormonnem cholonc.
Pamphlet, *pam'let*, N. Dacttem pustoc.
Pan, *pen*, N. Cail.
Panacea *pan-a-se'a*, N. Sorv torechem vocot.
Pander *pen'dor*, V. Fuslaunc.
Pane, *pen*, N. Arso.
Panegyric, *pa-ne-ji'ric*, N. Manadic prasang; sermaum.
Panegyrist, *pa-ne-ji'rist*, N. Prasangcar; sermaum sangnar.
Panel *pa'nel*, N. Follem.
Pang, *peng*, N. Vollvolle; attevitte; acant.
Panic, *pen'ic*, N. Thor camp, doddoddo.
Pannier *pa'ni-er*, N. Vellancho panttulo.
Pant, *pent*, V. Korxeunc; laleunc.
Panther, *pen'thor*, N. Bibtto vag.
Pantomine, *pan'to-mim* N. Noclan corcho; nakali.
Pantry, *pen'tri*, N. Dispens, samonn dovorcho cuart.
Pap, *pap*, N. Chium.
Papal, *pa'pal*, A. Papa saibacho.
Paper, *pei'par*, N. Cagot; vortoman potr.
Parable, *pa'ra-bl*, N. Vopar, gudd.
Paraclete, *pa'ra-clit*, N. Deu Spirit sant.
Parade, *pa-reid*, N. Kovat; dobazo.
Paradigm, *pa'ra-daim*, N. Nomunno; dek.
Paradise, *pa'ra-daiz*, N. Voincut, sorg.
Paradox, *pa'ra-doks*, N. Sotmandum-naie sarki sangni.
Paragraph, *po'ra-graf*, N. Vantto; bhag.
Parallel, *pa'ral-lel*, A. Samamtar; borobor, sarco.
Parallel, V. Somamtar corunc; sor corunc.
Paralysis, *pa-ral'izis*, N. Ar.
Paralyse, *pa'ra-laiz*, V. Ar-zaunc; fg. boll moddunc.
Paramount, *pa'ra-maunt*, A. Mukia; sotantracho.
Parapet, *pa'ra-pet*, N. Otto, doko.
Paraphernalia, *pa'ra-fer-na'lia*, N. Doti bhair vocol addta tem, dennem.
Paraphrase, *pa'ra-freiz*, N. Vivaran.
Parasite, *pa'ra-zait*, N. Dusreavorvim jietolo, lunchoc.
Parasol, *pa'ra-zol*, N. Sotri,
Parcel. *par'cel*, N. Vantto; nôg.
Parch, *parch*, V. Suconc; lasunc.
Parchment, *parch'ment*, N. Borounc, tuiar kelelem chambddem.
Pardon, *pard'on* N. Maf vo map; bogsonnem.
Pardon, N. Maf corunc, bogsunc; sodduuc.
Pare, *per*, V. Catrunc, unnocorunc,
Parent, *pei'rant*, N. Avoi vo bapui avoi-bapui.
Parentage, *pa'rent eij*, N. Kuttom; soin.
Parhelion, *par'he'li-on*, n. Suria sarkem; prati surio.
Pariah, *pa'ri-a*, N. Mar.
Parish. *pe'rish*, N. Firgoz, igroz.
Parishioner, *pe-rish'n-ar*, N. Fregez, firgojecho munis.
Parish-priest. N. Vigar.
Parity. *pa'ri-ti*, N. Sarkem.
Park, *parc*, N. Voddleli suat.
Parliament, *par'la-ment*, N. Raja sabha, parlament.
Parlour, *par'lor*, N. Ulounchem sal.

Parochial, *pa-ro'ki-al*, A. Firgo-jecho.
Parody, *pa'ro-di*, N. Nocol, kel-davni.
Parol, *pa-rol'*, N. Bhas ; utor.
Paroxysm, *pa'roks'izm*, N. Bhar ; vodd.
Parricide, *pa'ri-said*, N. Bapaicho morticar, bapaic jivesim mar-nar.
Parrot, *pe'rol*, N. Kir.
Parry, *pe'ri*, V. Chucounc.
Parse, *pars*, V. Vakiache vantte sangunc.
Parsimony, *par'si-mo-ni*, N. Sug-rat ; imttepon.
Parson, *par'son*, N. Protestant padri. [caido.
Part, *part*, N. Vantto ; cuddco ;
Part, V. Cuddke corunc ; vegla-char corunc ; doxim corunc.
Partake, *par-teik'*, V. Vantto geunc ; zoddunc.
Partial, *par'shal*, A. Tonddac polloun cortolo, nitivont noi aslolo, lonch khauncho ; eoc vantto.
Partiality, *par-shal'i-ti*, N. Taraf-dari, asambudh, favo noi tosi nit.
Particle, *par'ti-kl*, N. Lan cuddco ; particul.
Particular, *par-tik'iu-lar*, A. Pratek. vises ; sarco, aprup.
Particular, N. Eiclo, vingod munis.
Particularly, *par tik'iu-lar-li*, AD. Vodic corun, veses zaun.
Partisan, *par'ti-zan*, N. Eca fanc-savancho membr.
Partition, *par-ti'shon*, N. Vantto ; khonn.
Partitive, *par'ti-tiv*, V. Vantte corcho, vantteacho.
Partly, *part'li*, AD. Ordokuro, thoddo—thoddo.
Partner, *part'nar*, N. Vantteli, bagidar.
Partnership, *part'nar-ship*, N. Sangat.
Parturition, *par-tu-ri'shon*, N. Bauntteor.
Party, *par'ti*, N. Fancsaum.
Pass. *pas*, V. Passar zaunc ; vo-chonc ; utronc ; rigonc ; cho-lounc ; mucar diunc ; posond corunc ; bodlunc ; soddunc.
Passable, *pas'ie-bl*, A. Vochoe sarco.
Passably. *pas'ie-bli*, AD. Sumar.
Passage, *pas'sej*, N. Vatt, marog. vantto.
Passenger, *pas'en-jer*, N. Vatt-sur, viaj cornar.
Passingbell *pas'ing-bell*. N. Mor-nachi ghantt.
Passion, *pe'shon*, N. Vaitt gunn-vaitt voddni, coistt, paixaum, (Suamia J. C.) ; rag, zall.
Passionate, *pe'shon-eit*, A. Apur-bai corcho ; uchambollaecho.
Passport, *pas-port*, N. Rahadari passa-port.
Past, *past*, A. Pattlo, adlo.
Paste, *peist*, N. Moullelem pitt ; grut.
Paste-board, *pest bord*, N. Datt cagot.
Pastime, *pas'taim*, N. Khell, khuxalai.
Pastor, *pas'tor*, N. Gounli.
Pastoral, *pas-to'ral*, A. Gounli acho.
Pastry, *pes'tri*, N. Polli ; mittai
Pasturage, *pas'tur-eij*, N. Chor-vacho zago.
Pasture, *pas'char*, V. Chorounc.
Pat, *pet*, N. Thapuddunc.
Pat, N. Thap, thapott.
Patch, *pech*, N. Cuddco, copo.
Pate, *peit*, N. Matem.
Paten, *pe'ten* N. Paten.

Patent, *pei'tent,* A. Rahadari; porgott.
Patent, N. Potto.
Paternal, *pa-ter'nal,* A. Bapaicho; bapai sarco.
Paternoster, *pa'ter-nos-ter.* N. Amchea bapa.
Path, *path,* N. Osir vatt.
Pathetic, *pa-thet-ic,* A. Movall, vo movallauncho.
Pathos, *pa'thos,* N. Boctiponn; cacut; movallponn.
Patience, *pei'shens,* N. Sosnicai.
Patient, N. Piddest; sonsnic munis.
Patriarch, *pe'tri-arc,* A. patriarc.
Patrimony, *pa'tri-mo-ni,* N. Patrimon; daiz; vit.
Patriot, *pe'tri-ot.* N. Aplea desacho mog cornar.
Patriotism *pei'tri-ot-izm,* N. Aplea gauncho mog.
Patrol, *pa-trol',* N. Gaunche vo cotache racnenc soldadanchi. bonvodd.
Patron, *pei'tron,* N. Patron, racnno; sambauttolo, xerati.
Patronage, *pei'tron-eij,* N. Asro; adar, mozot.
Patroness, *pei'tro-ness,* N. Xaratin, xecai.
Patronize, *pe'tron-aiz,* V. Asro diunc, mozot corunc; raconc.
Patter, *pat'or,* V. Dadda-dadda zaunc.
Patern, *pet'ern,* N. Nomunno.
Pauch, *pau-uch,* N. Ganzo; poscotto.
Pauper, *pau'por,* N. Dublo; gorib; orfaun.
Pause, *poz,* V. Matso ravonc.
Pave, *peiv,* V. Pettunc, fatrachi ladi galunc.
Pavement, *pev'ment,* N. Petleli dhorn vo vatt.
Pavilion, *pa-vil'yon,* N. Tombu.
Paw, *po,* N. Dauli.
Pawn, *pon,* V. Penhor dourunc.
Pawn, N. Pinhor.
Pay, *pei,* N. Pag, muzri; inam.
Pay, V. Faric corunc.
—(Penalty), Sicxea sonsunc.
—(For), Baddeac geunc
Payable, *pei'ci-bl,* A. Faric cocho.
Payment, *pay'ment,* N. Pag, muzri; dennem.
Peace, *pis,* N. Soucasai, somandau; sontos.
Peace, IN; V. Ogoch rau.
Peaciful, *pis'ful,* A. Soucasaecho, somandanacho; nidau.
Peacock, *pi'cok,* N. Mor.
Peak, *pik,* N. Dongrachi aker, pont; domos.
Peal, *piil,* N. Goroz; avaz.
Pearl, *porl,* N. Motim.
Pearl-fisher, *porl-feish-ar,* N. Motiam caddnar.
Peasant, *pe'zant,* N. Setcamti.
Pebble. *peb'bl* N. Gunddo; gutti.
Peccable, *pek'a-bl,* A. Patoc adari sarco.
Peccadillo, *pek-a-dil'lo,* N. Lan patoc.
Peculate, *pe-kiu,leit,* V. Nagounc.
Peculiar, *pe-kiu'li-ar,* A. Aplo khaxa, hud, vises.
Peculiarity, *pe-kiu'li-ari-ti,* N. Visesh-gunn, svadorm.
Peculiarly, *pe-kiu'li-ar-li,* AD. Vishesim; bhou corun.
Pecuniary, *pe-kiu'ni-a-ri,* A. Duddvancho.
Pedagogue. *ped'a-gog,* N. Pantoji.
Pedant, *pe'dant,* N. Zanvaechi boddai dacoinar.
Pedantry, *ped'antri,* N. Zanvaechi boddai.
Peddler, *ped-lar,* N. Bonvon vicnar.

Pedestal, *pe'des-tal*, N. Khambeacho paim ; pedd.
Pedestrian, *pe-des'tri-an*, N. Pai vatten cholnar.
Pedigree, *pe'dig-ri*, N. Soinachi vo cuttumbachi khobor.
Peel, *piil*, V. Solunc. sal caddunc.
Peep, *piip*, V. Tellunc ; nodor marunc.
Peep, N. Telnem.
Peer, *per*, V. Disonc, barcaen polleunc.
Peer, A. Sarco ; ecach jinsacho.
Peevish, *pii'vish*, A. Doscho, bejar corcho.
Peevishness, *pii-vish'ness*, N. bejarai.
Peg, *peg*, N. Khunttì.
Pelf, *peef*, N. Duddu ; girescai.
Pelican, *pel'i-can*, N. Pannolli.
Pell-mell, *pel'mel*, AD. Yennem tennem ; eke ordin noi.
Pellucid, *pel-lu'sid*, A. Aspas discho, asar pasar.
Pelt, *pelt*, V. Fatraunc, gunddeanim maraunc.
Pelt, *pelt*, N. Cat.
Pen, *pen*, N. Pen ; gorvancho veddo.
Penal, *pe'nal*, A. Sikxecho.
Penalty, *pen'al-ti*, N. Sicxa.
Penance, *pen'ens*, N. Pirajit ; faricponn ; cuddichi donddvonn.
Pencil, *pen'sil*, N. Laps, pensil.
Pendant, *pen'dant*, N. Pened, amblo, carab.
Pendant, A. Umcallto, lambto.
Pendulum, *pen'du-lam*, N. Dolcho bhar.
Penetrable, *pen'e-tre-bl* A Rigosarco.
Penetrability, *pen'e-tra-bi-li.ti*, N. Rigo sarkem.
Penetrate, *pen'e-tr-eit*, V. Rigonc ; parcunc.
Penetration, *pen-e-trei'shon*, N. Rigop; fg. barcai, somjicai.
Penetrative, *pe'ne-trei-tiv*. A. Baric ; somzonecho.
Peninsula, *pen-in'su-la*, N. Unvo.
Penitence, *pe'ni-tens*, N. Pirajit ; faricponn.
Penitent, *pe'ni-tent*, A. Pirajit cortolo cumsar zatolo.
Penitential, *pe-ni-ten'shal*, A. pirajitacho; dukicho.
Penknife, *pen'naif*, N. Canvet.
Pennant, *pen'ant*, N. Supnrlem bonder ; naum.
Penny, *pen'i*, N. Penni.
Pensile, *pen'sail*, A. Umcoln, lambonn.
Pension, *pen'shon*, N. Pensaum
Pensive, *pen'siv*, A. Chintest; khontiborit.
Pentup, *pent-op*, A. Damplolo.
Pentagon, *pen'ta-gon*, N. Pauch conxeanchem (rup.)
Penultimate, *pen'ul-ti-meit*, A. Nimannea adlo.
Penumbra, *pen-um'bra* N. Saullisi.
Penurious, *pe-nu'ri-as*, A. Upai naslolo ; sugrati.
Penury, *pen'iuri*, N. Dublocai, ducoll, dolddir.
Peon, *pi'un*, N. Pedo ; sipai.
People, *pi'pl*, N. Loc ; porza.
People, V. Locan borunc.
Peopled, A. Loc asunc.
Pepper, *pep'er*, N. Mirim.
Peppermint, *pep'er-mint*, N. vortelaum.
Peradventure, *per-ad-ven'char*, AD. Goddiec ; Odrusttan.
Perambulate, *per-am'bu-leit*, V. Bonvonc.
Perceive, *per-sev'*, V. Polleunc ; voucone.
Percentage, *per-sent'eij*, N. Xecddeac.

Perception, *per-sep'shon*, N. Volloc ; somjicai.

Perceptive, *per-sep'tiv*, A. Vouconcho.

Perch, *porch*, V. Bosonc.

Perch, N. Col.

Perchance, *per-chans'*, AD. Goddiec.

Percolate, *per'co-leit* V. Gallunc.

Percussion, *per-ku'shon*, N. Pett.

Perdition, *per-di'shon*, V. Perdisaum ; sanddni, nisontonn.

Peregrinate *pe're-grin-eit*, N. Eke suater than dusre suater bonvonc.

Peregrination, *pe-re-gin-ei'shon*, N. Jatra ; pois vochnem ; musafari.

Peremptorily, *pe'remp-to-ri-li*, AD. Khonchit, ecdom.

Peremptory. *pe'remp-to-ry*, A. Khondit.

Perfect, *per'fect*, A. Sompurn ; uttim ; vorto.

Perfect, V. Sompurn corunc

Perfection, *per'fec-shon*, N. Sompurnai ; vorteponn.

Perfectly, *por'fect-li*, AD. Sompurnaen ; purtem.

Perfidious, *per'fi-di-as*, A. Gatki, agbati, visvas gatki.

Perfidy, *per'fi-di*, N. Visvas gat.

Perforate, *per'fo-reit*, V. Burac corunc ; fapsunc.

Perforce, *per-fors'*, AD. Bollan.

Perform, *per-form'*, V. Pallunc ; corunc.

Performance, *per-form'ans* N. Pallo dennem ; cortub.

Perfume, *per'fium*, N. Pormoll, cheir.

Perfume, V. Pormoll galuuc vo launc.

Perfunctorily, *per-fungk'to-ri-li*, AD. Zotnaie-viret, beporvean.

Perfunctory, *per-fungk'to-ri*, A. Zotnai naslolo.

Perhaps, *per-haps'*, AD. Goddiec.

Peril, *pe'ril*, N. Risk ; zokom.

Period, *pe'ri-od*, N. Somoi, call, vell.

Periodic, *pe-ri-od'ic*. N. Somoiacho ; nemlelea callacho.

Periodical, *pe-ri od'ik-al*, N. Nemlelea vellachem vortomon |potr, magazin etc.

Perish, *pe'rish*, V. Nas zaunc ; bhosmunc.

Perishable, *pe'rish-ie-bl*, A. Cuso sarco, ibad zai sarco.

Perjure, *per'jur*, V. Fottkiro jurament, suput diunc.

Perjurer, *per'jur-er*, N. Fottkiro jurament dinnar.

Perjury, *per-ju'ri*, N. Soput moddnem, oproman cornem.

Permanence, *per'ma-mens*, N. Urop, ravop.

Permanent, *per'ma-nent*, A. Raucho, urcho, fg. thir.

Permeable, *per'mi-ie-bl*, A. Rigo sarco.

Permeate, *per'mi-eit*. V. Rigonc.

Permission, *per-mi'shon*, N. Rojea ; hucum. [hucum dinnc.

Permit, *per-mit'*, N. Rojea diunc;

Permutation, *per-mu-tei'shon*, N. Bodlop, sodol-bodol.

Pernicious, *per-ni'shas*, A. Vatt; nosthttadic, lusconacho.

Peroration, *pe-ro-rei'shon*, N. Sompaddni; nimanem sangnem.

Perpendicular, *per-pen-di'kiu-lar*, A. Ubo, nitt.

Perpetrate, *per'pe-trait*, V. Adarunc ; corunc.

Perpetual, *per-pe'chu-al*, A. Sasnancho, nkhondit, sorvcallim.

Perpetuate, *per-pe'chu-eit*, V. Okhondit corunc ; sodancal lagunc.

Perpetuity, *per-pe'chu-i-ti*, N. Sasonn,

Perplex, *per'pleks*, V. Dubavonc; gusponc.

Perplexity, *per-pleks'i-ti*, N. Dubau; tondre.

Perquisite, *per'kwi-sit*, N. Dusre faide vo adau.

Perron, *per'ron*, N. Mettan.

Persecute, *per'se-kiut*, N. Dogdaunc; rodounc.

Persecution, *per-se kiu'shon*, N. Coistt; dogd, dumalo.

Persecutor, *per'se-kiu-tor*, N. Dogdaitolo, piddapidd, dinnar, tras ditolo.

Perseverance, *per-se-ve'rans*, N. Thirasonn, thirponn.

Persevere, *per-se-vier'*, V. Thir ravunc. [Thir.

Persevering, *per-se-vier'ing*, A.

Persist, *per-sist'*, V. Gansunc, zorounc; lagun asunc.

Person, *per'son*, N. Zonn; rup.

Personal, *per'son-al*, A. Aplo; khaski.

Personally, *per'son al-li*, AD. Ostogim.

Personification, *per-son-i-fi-kei' shon*, N. Munxeagunnam rup, jan rup

Perspective, *per-spek'tiv*, A. Distt; as, axea.

Perspicacious, *per-spi-kei'shas*, A. Baric fg. somzonnecho.

Perspicuouo, *per-spi'ku-as*, A. Somzo sarkem.

Perspiration, *per-spi'rei-shon*, N. Gham, um.

Perspire, *per-spaiar'*, V. Gameunc; umeunc.

Persuade, *per-swed'*; V. Somzaunc; bud diunc.

Persuasion, *per-swe'shon*, N. Khatri zavop, sotmandop;. somzonni.

Persuasive, *per-swe'ziv*, A. Somzai sarco.

Pert, *port*, A. Khoxalborit suddsuddit aumoriadicho.

Pertain, *per-tein'*, V. Favo zaunc; lagonc.

Pertinacious, *per-ti-nei'shas*, A. Dharrun; aplea vadeacho.

Pertinent *por'ti-nent*, A. Laik; camanc yeto,--poddto.

Pertness, *port'ness*, N. Amoriad; loz baudponn.

Perturb, *per-torb'*, V. Uchambollaunc; acantaunc.

Perturbation, *per-turb-ei'shon*, N. Uchambollai; hairan.

Peruke, *per-ruik'*, V. Purn, lambkens.

Peruse, *pe-ruz'*, V. Chotraen vachunc.

Pervade, *perfreid'*, V. Rigonc; rigun bonvonc.

Perverse, *per-vors'*, A. Vaitt; khotto, nostto.

Perversion, *per-ver-shon'*, N. Khotteponn; kusddeponn.

Pervert, *per-vor't*, V. Vaitt khotto corunc.

Pest, *pest*, N. Pest, mari, vocot nasleli pidda.

Pester, *pes'tor*, V. Carandai corunc; canant sempddi galunc.

Pestilence, *pes'ti-lens*, N. Pest, voseachi pidda.

Pestilential, *pes-ti-len'shal*, A Mariechi. voseachi—,zodd pidda.

Pestle, *pes'l*, N. Musoll, amaldosteacho guntno.

Pet, *pet*, N. Bhou priticho vo apurbaecho burgo etc; uchambollai.

Petal, *pe'tal*, N. Pakli. [arji

Petition, *pe-ti'shon*, N. Magnem;

Petition, *pe-ti'shon*, V, Arji, praton corunc.

Petitioner, *pe-ti'shon-ar*, N. Arjecer; praton cornar.

Petrification, *pet-rifikei-'shon*, N. Fator cornem.

Petrify, *pet-ri-fai'* V. Fator, dogodd corunc.

Petroleum. *pe-tro'li-um*, N. Petrol, gauslet tel

Pettiness, *pet-i-ness*, N Holkem mon.

Pettish, *pet'tish*. A. Bejaraecho.

Petticoat, *pet'i-kot*, N. Gagro, vaskin.

Pettfogger, *pet-i-fog'ar*, N. Eoc letrad zo corta lan vo holkim camam.

Petty, *pet-ti*, A. Dacto, supurlo; unno, holco.

Petulance, *pe'tu-lans*, N. Most, dangeponn, mostiponn.

Petulant, *pe'tu-lant*, A. Mosto, nilagro, tovnas.

Pew, *piu*, N. Igorjentli bosca.

Pewter, *piu'ter*, N. Dovem xinsem. [nam.

Phantasm, *fan'tuzm*, N. Colpo-

Phantom, *fan'tom*, N. Dristtav; nasaum; soponn.

Pharmacy, *far'ma-si*. N. Butic

Pharos, *fa'ros*, N. Forel.

Phase, *fez*, N. Disnem, porgott; akar, rup.

Phenomenon, *fe-no'me-non*, N. Acasachamatcar; disop.

Phial, *fi'al*, N. Supurli botl; sinsli.

Philologist, *fi-lal'o-jist*, N. Bhasancho pandit.

Philology, *fi-lal'o-ji*, N. Sobda videa vo xastr.

Philosopher, *fi-los'o-far*, N. Ginean sodnar.

Philosophy, *fi-loz-o-fi*, N. Filzofi.

Phlegm, *flem*, N. Thimpi; dorcol,

Phosphorus, *fos'fo-rus*, A. Fosforacho; fg. raguist.

Phosphorescence, *fos-ror-es'ens* N. Porzoll, pracas.

Photograph, *fo'to-graf*, N. Fotto

Photography, *fo'tog-rafi*, N. Fotto caddchi videa.

Phrase, *frez*. Uchar vakia.

Phraseology, *fre-zial'o-ji*, N. Ucharacho jinos vo rit.

Phrenology, *fre-nol'o ji*, N. Cåpalakshana videa.

Phthisis. *thai'sis*, N. Kevad.

Physic, *fizik*, N. Vocot; bairi.

Physical, *fi-zik'ul*, A. Soimbacho; cuddicho.

Physician. *fi-zi'shan*, N. Voiz.

Physics, *fi'ziks* N. Soimbachi videa.

Physionomy, *fi-zi-og'no-mi*; N. Tonddachem rup.

Physiologica,l *fi-zi-ol'o-ji-cal*, A. Prannacho.

Physiology, *fi-zi'o-lo-ji*, N. Pranna videa.

Piacular, *pi-ac'u-lar*, A. Faricponn dinncho.

Pianoforte, *pi-an'o-for-te*, N. Pian.

Pick, *pic*, V. Vinchunc.

Pick-axe, *pik'eks*, N. Cuddoll; pikandor.

Pickle, *pik'l*, N. Lonchem.

Pickle, V. Lonchem corunc.

Picture, *pic'char*, N. Rejist; rupnnem.

Piece, *piis*, N. Cuddco; copo; cuscutt.

Pier, *pi'er*, N. Khambo; dokko.

Pierce, *pi'ers*, V. Topunc; rigonc.

Piercing, *pi'ers-ing*, A. Cottin (duc); baric; kindri (tallo).

Piety, *pai'e-ti*, N. Bogtiponn; devosponn.

Pig, *pig*, N. Ducor; loitaum.

Pigeon, *pi'jon*, N. Parvo,

Pigment, *pig'ment*, N. Rong.
Pigmy, *pig'mi*, N. Mottvo munis.
Pilaster, *pi-las'tor*, N. Chouras khambo.
Pile, *pail*, N. Ras.
Pile, V. Ras corunc.
Pilfer, *pil'for*, V. Caddunc ; chorunc.
Pilgrim, *pil'grim*, N. Povitr suato pollounc bounnar.
Pilgrimage, *pil'grim-eij*, N. Viaj khuincheai povitr zageao.
Pill, *pil*, N. Gulli.
Pillage, *pil'eij*, V. Luttung, nagounc.
Pillager, *pil'eij-ar*, N. Luttnar.
Pillar, *pil'ar*, N. Khambo; fg. adar.
Pillow, *pil'ou*, N. Uxem.
Pilot, *pai'lot*, N. Pilot, tarum, choloinar.
Pimple *pimp'pl*, N. Muromb pulli.
Pin, *pin*, N. Alfinet.
Pin, V. Alfinet topunc.
Pincer, *pin'serz*, N. Chimtto.
Pinch, *pinch*, V. Chimtto caddunc.
Pinch, N. Chimtto.
Pine, *pain*, V. Bogunc, sucone.
Pine-apple, *pain'ep-l*, N. Annenes.
Pink, *pingk*, A. Cor de roz.
Pink, V. Topunc.
Pinnacle, *pin'ei-cl*, N. Okond matem ; gara voir supurli torr.
Pint, *paint*, N. Ordi botl.
Pious, *pai'as*, A. Boctivont; devosponnacho.
Pip, *pip*, V. Concaronc, sad galunc [guddi.
Pipe, *paip*, N. Pemparem, gudd-
Pipkin, *pip'kin*, N. Toplem ; cunddlem.
Piquant, *pi'kant*, A. Tik, tikvoso; khor fg. baric,
Pique, *pik*, V. Abbar corunc; boddai corunc.
Piracy, *pai'ra-si*, N. Doriantli chori.
Pirate, *pai're-it*, N. Doriantlo chor.
Pish, *int.* Shi.
Pismire, *pis'mair* n. Mui.
Pistol. *pis'tol*, N. Pistol, supurlem arm.
Pit, *pit*, N. Khon, fond.
Pitch, *pich*, N. Tar ; damor.
Pitch, *pich*, V. Boronnc ; maruuc; tar launc.
Pitched, *pich'd* A. Regular.
Pitcher, *pich'er*, N. Sidi, couso.
Piteous, *pi'ti-as*, N. Movall ; movallauncho ; dukest.
Pith, *pith*, N. Sar.
Pithy, *pith'i*, A. Saracho; fg. orthan borlolo.
Pitiful, *pi'ti-ful*, A. Cacuticho; doiall ; holco.
Pittance, *pitt'ens*, N. Izmol.
Pity, *pit'i*, N. Birmot; churchure ; doia.
Pity, V. Birmot disonc ; cacutcorunc.
Pivot, *pai'vot*, N. Bonvor khondi.
Placable, *ple'kei-bl*. A. Somandar corueso.
Placard, *pla'card*, N. Stiar.
Place, *ple's*, N. Suat; gaum; udiog.
Place, V. Galunc ; dourunc.
Placid, *pla'-sid*, A. Soucasaecho.
Plagiary, *pla'-jia-ri*, N. Pustocam velem borop chornar.
Plague, *pleg*, N. *pest* ; Voseachi pidda.
Plague, V. Bejar corunc, khorcor corunc.
Plain, N. Moidan ; camp
Plain, A. Saro ; chalto.
Plaintiff, *plein'-tiff*, N. Firiadi.
Plait, *pleit*, N. Miri ; inni.

Plait, V. doddunc.
Plan, *plen*, N. Nomuno, model; tensaum ; nocxi.
Plane, *plein*, N. Sountoll zomin.
Planet, *ple'-net*. N. Graha, bounchem neketr.
Plank, *plenk*, N. Follem.
Plank, V. Follim galunc.
Plant, *plent*, N. Zadd ; rompo.
Plant, V. Launc, ruk launc ; galunc.
Plantain, *plen'-tein*, N. Kellem. —(tree) kheimbo.
Plantation, *plant-ei'-shon*. N. Lavop, porsum; mollo.
Plash, *plesh*. N. Udcar avaz.
Plaster, *plas'-tor*, N. Lep; chunno.
Plastic, *plas'-tic*, A. Rup dinncho, goddcho.
Plat, *plet* N. Zago.
Plate, *pleit*, N. Bosi ; polgon.
Platform, *plet'-form*, N. Sopo, manch, otto.
Platinum, *pla-ti'-num*, N. Rupea baxen dovem metal. [gonn.
Platter, *plet'-ar*, N. Uttou pol-
Plaudit, *plo'-dit*, V. Tallieo pettunc; xebaski diunc.
Plausible, *ploz'-i-bl*, A. Manopacho, puttvonecho, boro disto.
Play, *pley*, N. Khell ; khoxalai, chesttai, tomaso.
Play, V. Khellonc, chesttaeo cocorunc ; sontos bogunc.
Player, *plei'-ar*, N. Kheugaddi; vaztolo.
Playful, *plei'-ful*, A. Khuxal ; khell-goddo, chesttaeo corcho.
Plea, *pli*, N. Niib.
Plead, *pliid*, V. Argument corunc favorar vo contr.
Pleader, *pliid'ar*, N. Letrad, vokil.
Pleasant, *ple'-zant*, A. Khuxal corcho ; mogall : sohit.
Pleasantness, *ple'-zant-ness*, N. Mogallponn ; khuxalai.
Pleasantry, *ple'-zant-ri*, N. Khuxalponn, chesttai.
Please, *pliiz*, V. Manvonc ; khuxal corunc.
Pleasure, *ple'-jar*, N. Khoxi ; sontos; suc; ruch.
Pleasing, *pliiz'-ing*, N. Khoxal—, dadoxi corop.
Plebeian, *ple-he'-an*, N. A. Annvo ; zomeacho.
Pledge, *plej*, N. Utor, bhas ; zamin,
Plenary, *plen'-a-ri*, A. Purem ; soglem.
Plenipotentiary, *ple-ni-po-ten'-shi-a-ri*, A. Sotantri dut; embaixador.
Plentiful, *plen'-ti-ful*, A, Ras ; sobar; fuscoll.
Plenty, *plen'-ti*, N. Sompurnai ; ras, bhou vo sobar.
Pleonasm, *ple'-on-azm*, N. Choddau.
Plethora, *pleth'-o-ra*, N. Rogta borti ; chodd rogot.
Pliable, *plai'-ie-bl*, A. Bagauncho.
Plight, *plait*, N. Acantacho soheog.
Plod, *plod*, V. Coisttounc.
Plot, *plot*, N. Supurlo zago ; guddmell, fituri.
Plot, V. Guddmell corunc.
Plotter, *plot'-ar*. N. Guddmell cornar.
Plough, *plau*, N. Nangor.
Ploughing, *plau'-ing*, N. Kosop.
Ploughman, *plau'-men*, N. Kostolo munis.
Pluck, *plock*, V. Caddunc ; umttunc.
Plug, *plog*, V. Dampunc.
Plume, *plium*, N. Pac.
Plump, *plomp*, A. Pustti ; motto.

Plunder, *plon'-der*, N. Duspott; nagoun.
Plunder, V. Duspott corunc; zulum corunc.
Plunge, *plonj*, V. Buddounc; buzcaunc; buddonc, fg. poddonc.
Plunge, N. Buddop, buzcoll.
Plurality, *pliu-ral'i-tti*, N. Zomo; voddlo vantto.
Plus, *plos*, AD. Vodic tache vonn.
Plush, *plosh*, N. Lonveuchem lugot.
Pluviometer, *plu-vi-om'-et-er*, N. Pausachem map.
Ply, *plai*, V. Borem corun cholounc; lagonc; minot geun vauronc
Pneumatic, *nin'-ma-ic*, A. Vareacho.
Pocket, *pock'-et* N. Bols.
Pocket, V. Chorunc; fottounc.
Pocket-book, N. Ugddasachem pustoc.
Poem, *po'-em*, N. Kovia.
Poet, *po'-et*, N. Kovi.
Poetic, *po'-et-ik*, A. Koviacho.
Poetry, *do'-et-ri*, N. Kovita.
Poignant, *poin'ant*, A. Coddu; FG. cottin; ducouncho; topcho.
Point, *point*, N. Domos; bonch.
Point, V. Domos corunc; tibo galunc; dacounc.
Pointless, *point'less*, A. Domos naslolo; cheptto; daddo.
Poise, *poiz*, V. Sarkem zocunc vo tolunc.
Poison, *poi'zn*, N. Vic.
Poison, V. Vic galunc vo diunc.
Poisonous, *poi'zn-as*, A. Vicallo.
Poke, *pôk*, V. Concunc, topunc.
Poker, *pok'er*, N. Uzo sarchi boddi.
Pole, *pol*, N. Tenkddi; vanso.
Pole-cat, *pol'ket*, N. Ran-mazor.
Polemical, *po-lem'ik-al*, A. Uzoticho, disputancho.
Police, *po-lis'*, N. Pulis, gaunche rnenechi bondabost.
Policeman, *po-lis'man*, N. Pulis; sipai.
Polish, *po'lish*, V. Pausunc; zogzogit corunc. [zogit.
Polished, *po'lish-d*, A. Saf, zog-
Polite, *po-lait'*, A. Mansuguecho; moriadicho.
Politeness, *po-lait'ness*, N. Mansugi, moriad.
Political, *po-liti'ik-al*, A. Stiticho, rajacho; sercaracho.
Politics, *po'li-ticks*. N. Cholouncho jinos; stiticheo vostu.
Poll, *pol*, N. Navanchi patti; matem vo mateachi patt.
Poll, N. pattier borounc.
Pollute, *pol'liut*, V. Khotauuc; bosttaunc.
Poltroon, *pol-trun'*, N. Bezudd; poupotto, holco, ausi.
Polygamy, *po-lig'a-mi*, N. Bhou poti ou hostoreo asnem, eca dadleac choddi bailo asnem.
Poliglot, *po'li-glot*, A. Sobar bhasancho.
Polygon, *po'li-gon*, N. Sobar conseanchem (rup).
Polytheism, *po'li-the-izm*, N. Sobar devanchem xastr.
Polytheist, *po'li the-ist*, N. Sobar devauc sotmandtolo.
Pommel, *pom'el*, N. Thorum, mutt.
Pommel, V. marunc.
Pompous, *pomp'as*, A. Dobajeacho; doulotichо.
Pond, *pond*, N. Tollem.
Ponder, *pond'ar*, V. Motint vozon corunc; chintunc; niallunc.
Ponderous, *pon'der-as*, A. Bharim; zodd.
Poniard, *pon'yeard*, N. Supurli torsad.

Pontiff, *pon'tif*, A. Pap-saib.
Pontifical, *pou'tif-ik-al*, A. Pap-saibacho.
Pontificate, *pon-tif'ik-eit*, N. Pap-saibachem raz,
Pony, *po'ni*, N. Supurlo goddo.
Pool, *pul*, N. Tollem ; zor.
Poor, *puor*, A. Dublo, gorib, bicari ; kircoll.
Pop, *pop*, N. Lan auchit avaz.
Pop, V. Auchit lan avaz corunc'
Pope, *pōp*, N. Pap Saib.
Popinjay, *pop'in-jei*, N. Kir.
Poppy, *pop'i*, N. Coscosancho ruc ; coscos.
Populace, *po'piu-le.*, N. Chalti porza ; chombo, urponz.
Popular, *po'pu-lar*, A. Locacho vo zomeacho ; locacho istt ; chalto.
Popularity, *po-pu-la'rit-i*, N. Locachi isttogot ; porjec mogall.
Populous, *po'pu-las*, A. Locan borlolo.
Porcelain, *por'se-lein*, N. Bosechem vo chini aidon.
Porch, *porch*, N. Bolcaum ; vorand ; angonn,
Porcupine, *por'ku-pain*, A. Sall.
Porcupine-fish, N. Mutrem.
Pore, *por*, N. Supurle burac catir zantlean gam bhair sorta.
Pork, *pork*, N. Ducrachem mas.
Porosity, *por-oz'i-ti*, N. Rigo sarkem.
Porous, *por'as*, A. Chili aslolo.
Porpoise, *por'poiz*, N. Doriantlo ducor.
Poridge, *po'rij*, N. Ambil.
Poringer, *po'rin-jer*, N. Pir.
Port, *port*, N. Bondir ; chal, chomcon.
Portable, *port'ei-bl*, A. Voro sar- [co.
Portal, *port'al*, N. Darvontto.
Portcullis, *port-cul'is* N. Umcoucho sancou.
Portend, *por-tend'*, N. Khunna ; ojeap, ochoriam.
Portend, V. Adim khunna dacounc.
Porter, *port'ar*, N. Porteir.
Portfolio, *port-fo'lio*, N. Cagdancho chimtto ; ministracho zago vo udiog,
Portico, *por'ti-co*, N. Chauddi ; sopo ; bolcaum.
Portion, *por'shon*, Vantto, bhag.
Portliness, *port'li-ness*, N. Bharau vo voddvicaea choluem.
Portly, *port'li*, A. Pustti ; motto.
Portrait, *por'treit*, N. Sarkem ; noksi.
Portress, *port'ress*, N. Portern.
Position, *po-zi'shon*, N. Suat, zago ; bhes.
Positive, *poz'it-iv*, A. Khondit ; khoro ; dubau naslolo.
Possess, *po-zess'*, V. Asunc ; collonc.
Possession, *po-zes'shon*, N. Cosolii vost bognem vo asnem ; dhonipon ; bogunc batt, duddu, gor etc.
Possessor, *po-zes'or*, N. Bognar. dhoni ; battcar.
Possibility, *pas-i-bil'i-ti*, N. Tank ; cuvet.
Possible, *pos'i-bl*, A. Zaum-et aslolo.
Post, *post*, N. Khambo ; udeog ; topal ; mokam.
Post, V. Topalant galunc, ixeopant zoma corunc.
Postage, *post'eij*, N. Postachi tiket.
Posterior, *pos-ti'ri-or*, A. Pattlo, adlo.
Posterity, *pos-te'ri-ti*, N. Sonsot, fuddli pinddca.
Posthumous, *post'i-mus*, A. Bapui melea uprant zalolo.

Postman, *post'men*, A. Chitti vanttnar, topolacho pedo.
Postmaster, *post'mas-tor*, N. Topal offisacho voddil.
Post-office, N. Topal khatem.
Postpone, *post-pon'*, V. Patti galunc vo dourunc.
Postscript, *post'skript*, N. Chittir assinad kelea uprant boroileli khobor etc.
Posture, *pos'char*, N. Akar; ubi rauchi rit.
Pot, *pot*, N. Moddki; aidon.
Potash, *po'tash*, N. Khar.
Potato, *po'tei-to*, N. Bottato.
Potion, *po'shon*, N. Ek pautt pieunchem vocot.
Pottage, *pot'eij*, N. Cald; sop.
Potter, *pot'ar*, N. Cumbar.
Pottery, *pot'e-ri*, N. Cumbarachem cam.
Pouch, *pauch*, N. Poti; bolos.
Poultice, *pol'tis*, N. Poltis, lep.
Poultry, *pol'tri*, N. Cuncddam.
Pounce, *pauns*, V. Zompoi marunc.
Pounce, N. Reti.
Pound, *paund*, N. Rat, paund.
Pound, V. Pudd corunc; duddaunc, mostunc.
Pour, *por*, V. Votunc; simponc.
Pout, *paut*, V. Khontiborit disonc.
Pout, N. Chintest disnem.
Poverty, *po'vor-ti*, N. Durbolcai, durbollpenn.
Powder, *pau'dor*, N. Pudd; daru; pitto.
Powder, V. Pudd vo pitto corunc.
Power, *pau'or*, N. Podvi, boll, tran.
Powerful, *pau'or-ful*, A. Podvedar, bolladic.
Pox, (Small), *poks*, N. Osuc
Practicable, *prac'ti-ke-bl*, A. Corum-eso; sompo.
Practical, *prec'ti-cal*, A. Corpachea visheant aslolo, camanc poddoso.
Practically, *prac'ti-kal-li*, ADV. Corun dacoun; ritipormonnem.
Practice, *prek'tis*, V. Sovoim; dostur; chal..
Practice, *prak'tis*, V. Sovoim asunc vo corunc; sicounc, cholounc.
Prairie, *prei'ri*, N. Lamb moidan.
Praise, *preiz*, N. Vornon; onod.
Praise, V. Vornunc; xifaraz corunc; xebaski diunc.
Praiseworthy, *preiz'-vor-di*, A. Xebaski favo zalolo.
Prance, *prens*, V. Uddonc; patrad daconnc.
Prank, *prengk*, N. Morji.
Prank, V Patraden nettounc.
Prate, *preit*, V. Gozali marunc; boddbo-ddunc.
Prater, *preit'-ar*, N. Boddboddo.
Prating, *preit-'ing*, N. Gozal.
Pray, *prai*, V. Magnem—, rozar corunc.
Prayer, *prei'-ar*, N. Magnem, rozar; praton.
Prayer-book, N. Manual, rozarachem, pustoc.
Preach, *priich*, V. Sermaum sangunc.
Preacher, *priich'-er*, N. Pregador, sermaum cornar.
Preaching, *priich-ing*, N. Sermaum.
Preamble, *pri-am'-bl*, N. Toiari; rig; prastavana, sadar.
Precarious, *pre-kei'-ri-as*, A. Thirnaslolo, sugur noi.
Precaution, *pri-ko'-shon*, N. Chotrai; upai.
Precede, *pre-si-d'*, V. Mucar vochunc, adim corunc.

Precedence, *pre-sid-ens,* N. Man; vinchun caddop. [daklo.

Precedent, *pre'-s-ident*, N. Adlo

Precedent, A. Adlo vo poilo.

Precept, *pri'-sept*, N. Upordes; caido, hucum.

Preceptor, *pri-sept'-or*, N. Guru, upadesi; mistir.

Precinct, *pre'-singt*, N. Mitmer; xime lagcho vantto.

Precious, *pre'-shas*, A. Moladic, amolic; mharog.

Precipice, *pre'-si-pis*, N. Coddso, patoll, raholl.

Precipitance, *pre-si'-pi-tans*, N Utavllai, urmottai; doddpadd.

Precipitate, *pre-si'pi-teit*, V. Socol uddounc, unch than seottunc; uddki marunc.

Precipitous, *pre-si'pi-tus*. A. Coddso coso; fg. uttavlo; urmott, bechotur.

Precise, *pri'saiz'*, A. Sarco, goroztea vellar.

Precocious, *pri-co'-shas*, A. Burgeponnim budi pracas.

Precocity, *pri-kos'-i-ti*, N. Calla adli bud.

Preconception, *pre-eon-sep'-shon*, N. Purva colponna.

Preconcerted, *pre-con-sort'-ed*, A. Adim carar kelolo.

Precursor, *pre-kur'-sor*, N. Mucar vetolo; fudde colloitolo.

Predecessor, *pre-di-ses'-or*, N. Adim ailolo adicari.

Predestinate, *pre-des'-ti-neit*, V. Adim vinchun caddunc; nirmunc, purvim euzunc.

Predestination, *pre-des'-ti-nei'-shon*, N. Adim vinchop; nirmiti. purvyojan.

Predetermine, *pre-de-ter'-min*, V. Nirmunc.

Predicament, *pre-dik'-a-ment*, N. Vorg, kram.

Predicate, *pre'-di-keit*, V. Khondit sangunc.

Predict, *pre dikt'*, V. Adim collounc—, sangunc.

Prediction, *pre-dik'-shon*, N. Adim saugni; professi.

Predilection, *pre-di-lek'-shon*, N. Chodd—, vodic mog. apurbai.

Predispose, *pre-dis-poz'*, V. Adim, mucar toiar eorunc, toiar corun dourunc.

Predisposition, *pre-dis-po-zi'-shon*, N. Toiuri, mandavoll.

Predominant, *pre-dom'-i-nant*, A. Vorto, mukia; sodancho.

Predominate, *pre-dom'-i-neit*, V. Vodic boll—, sotea asunc.

Pre-eminent, *pre-em'-i-nent*. A. Uttim, vorto, voilo, visesh.

Preface, *pre-fes'*, N. Adim sangnnem.

Prefect, *pri'-fekt*, N. Perfeit, podser, voddil.

Prefer, *pri-for'*, V. Vinchun caddunc, vodic manounc, boro disunc.

Preference, *pre'-fer-ens*, N. Vinchun caddnem. vodic mol dinnem.

Prefigure, *pre-fig'-or*, V. Mucar—, adim dacounc; pratirup diunc.

Prefix, *pre'-fiks*, V. Mucar borounc.

Pregnancy, *preg'-nan-si*, N. Gurvacher.

Pregnant, *preg'-nant*, A. Gurvar, gorbest.

Prejudice, *pre'-ju-dis*, N. Khoxe zoctem nasop, vaitt.

Prejudicial, *pre-ju-di'shal*, A. Lusconacho, vaitt.

Prelate, *pre'leit*, N. Igorjecho voddil, bisp.

Prelection, *pre-lek'skon*, N. Sicoun; discurs.

Preliminary, *pre-lim'in-a-ri*, A. Muca velo vo mucar vecho; orombacho.
Prelude, *prel'iud*, V. Toiar corunc.
Premature, *pri'ma-chu-ar*, A. Goddop, zavop tempa adim.
Premeditate, *pre-me'di-teit*, V. Adim chintunc, niallunc.
Premise, *pre-miz'*, V. Adim sangunc.
Premises, *pre'mi-zis*, N. Ghor anim zago. [inam.
Premium, *pre'mi-um*, N. Prem,
Premonish, *pre-mon'ish*, V. Adim collounc.
Preoccupation, *pre-oc'kiu-pei-shon*, N. Khor chintna, nibor niall; usco.
Preoccupied, *pre-ockiu'paid*, A. Chintner aslolo; uskeacho.
Preoccupy, *pre-oc'kin-pai*, V. Usco diunc; chintner dourunc.
Preparation, *pre-pa-rei'shon*, N. Toiari; aitomon.
Prepare, *pri-per'*, V. Toiar corunc.
Preponderance, *pre-pon'der-ans*, N. Vodic vozon, bhar, oglepoun. fg. zoit.
Preponderate, *pre-pon'de-reit*, V. Zoit vorunc.
Prerequisite, *pre-re'kui-zit*, N. gorjecheo vostu, zai asleleo vostu.
Prerogative, *pre-ro'ga-tiv*, A. Visesh podvi, sotea; hakh.
Presage, *pre'seij*, N. Adli vo mucaveli volloc, Khuna.
Presage, V. Adim dacounc.
Prescribe, *pre-scraib'*, V. Formaunc; rocet borounc.
Prescription, *pres-crip'shon*, N. Rocet.
Presence, *pre'zens*, N. Hajir asnem.
Present, *p-e'zent*, A. Hazir, atancho. [inam.
Present, N. Dennem; sagvad;
Present, V. Bettounc; decol coruno; mucar galunc.
Presentation, *pre-zen-tei'shon*, N. Bett; sifaz.
Presentiment, *pre-zen'ti-ment*, N. Adli vo muca veli volloc.
Presently, *pre'zent-li*, AD. Atanch; khinna bhitor.
Preservation, *pre-zer-vei'shon*, N. Raconn; samball; jagoun, tharan.
Preservative, *pri-serv'a-tiv*, A. Raccho; samballcho.
Preserve, *pri'serv*, V. Racunc; samballunc.
Preserve, N. Dos, mittai.
Preside, *pri'zaid*, V. Pirjent, mukeli zaunc.
Presidency, *pre'zi-den-si*, N. Mukeliponn; adikari.
President, *pre'zi-dent*, N. Pirjent; mukeli.
Press, *press*, V. Dambunc, chepunc; ganneant galunc; ecar eoc vichar corunc.
Press, N. Xapkhannem; ganno.
Pressing, *press'ing*, A. Zorur.
Pressure, *pre'shar*, N. Dambop; rattavoll; toddaco.
Prestige, *pres'tij*, N. Maya; bhar, tol asnem.
Presume, *pre-zium'*, V. Somzunc, chintunc; chodd patiennc
Presumption, N. Dhornem, kolpouam; ahancar; gorv.
Presumptious, *pri-zum'-shas*, A. Ahankari; gorvist.
Pretence, *pri-tens'*, N. Nib; kopott.
Pretend, *pri-tend'*, V. Sodunc, magunc; zai zaunc.
Pretender, *pri-tend'or*, N. Sodnar; aplem munnar.

Pretension, *pri-ten'shon*, N. Sod, sodni ; davo.

Preternatural, *pri-ter-nei'che-ral*, A. Soimba vorto.

Pretext, *pri'tekst*, N. Nib, nimit.

Pretty, *prit'i*, A. Sobit, sundor.

Pretty, AD. Sumar.

Prevail, *pri'veil*, V. Zoit vorunc ; fg. jiconc.

Prevent, *pri'vent*, V. Addaunc vo addcoll galunc.

Previous, *pri'vias*, A. Adlo vo muca velo.

Previously, *pri'vias-li*, A. Ad. adim.

Prey, *prei*, N. Lutt ; Khan ; sicarechim sucnim.

Prey, V. Luttunc.

Price, *prais*, N. Mol ; kimot.

Prick, *pric*, V. Topunc.

Prick, *pric*, N. Topnem,

Prickle, *prik'l*, N. Cantto ; gamollem.

Pride, *praid*, N. Gorv.

Pride, V. Boddai dacounc, patrad corunc.

Priest, *prist*, N. Padri.

Priesthood, *prist'-hud*, N. Padriponn.

Priestly, *prist'-li*, A. Sacerdoticho.

Prig, *prig*, N. Kopti ; danddi.

Prim, *praim*, A. Chodd sarco.

Primacy, *prai'-ma-si*, N. Voddleponn, vorteponn.

Primary, *prai'-ma-ri*, A, Poilo ; mukhia.

Prime, *praim*, A. Poilo.

Prime, N. Ful.

Primer, *prai'mor*, N. Poilem pustoc.

Primitive, *prim'i-ti-iv*, A. Poilo; mudolcho.

Prince, *prins*, N. Cunvor.

Princess, *prin'cess*, N. Kuvorn.

Principal, *prin'si-pal* A, Mukhia.

Principally, *prin'si-pal-li* AD Vodic corun vo bhou corun.

Principle, *prin'si-pl*, N. Carann vo oromb; mukhia sot.

Print. *print*, V. Xapunc.

Print, *print*, N. Dambun keleli khunna.

Printer, *print'or*, N. Xapnar, xaptolo.

Printing-press, *print'ing-press*, N. Xapkhanne.

Prior, *pri'or*, N. Conventacho voddil.

Prioress, *pri'o-ress*, N. Conventachi voddli madr.

Prison, *pri'zon*, N. Bondcon

Prisoner, *pri'zon-ar*, N. Prez, coidi.

Prithee, *pri'thi*, Int. doia corun.

Privacy, *prai'va-si*, N. Escurai vo escurponn.

Private, *prai'veit*, A. Khasgi ; guttacho ; ecoddo ; ecsuro.

Privation, *prai-vei'shon* N. Chucop ; dogd.

Privilege, *pri'vi-lej*, N. Hak, adicar, man.

Privy, *priv'i*, A. Gupit vo guttacho.

Privy, *pri'vi*, N. Kakus, cumaum.

Prize. *praiz*, N. Prem, inam.

Probable, *pro'be-bl*, A. Zaitso, goddtaso.

Probation, *pro-bei'shon*, N. Porickxa ; tank.

Probationer, *pro-bei'shon-ar*, N. umedvar.

Probity, *pro'bi-ti*, N. Khoreponn ; pramanicponn.

Problem, *prob'lem*, N. Gudd ; umannem.

Problematical, *prob-le-ma'ti-cal*, A. Dubavi.

Proboscis, *pro-bos'is*, N. Hotiachi sonddi,

Proceed, *pro-siid'*, v. Nitt,—mucai Vochunc. ubzonc.

Proceeding, *pro-siid'ing*, N. Chollouni.

Proceeds, *pro'sidz*, N. Cosoleai dandean eottaulolo duddu.

Process, *pro'ses*, N. Firiad; upai.

Procession, *pro-se'shon*, N. Pursaum.

Proclaim, *pro-claim'*. v. Porgottunc, dangro firaunc.

Proclamation, *pro-cla-mei'shon*, N. Pergaum, dangiro.

Procrastinate, *pro-kras'ti-neit*, v. Vogot launc; patti dourunc.

Procrastination, *pro-kras-ti-nei'shon*, N. Callau.

Procreate, *pro'kri-eit* v. Zolmounc.

Proctor, *proc'tor*, N. Eoc letrad sercari vo dormache cortint.

Procure, *pro-ki-uar'*, v. melloun geunc, addun diunc

Procurer, *pro-kiur'ar* N. Dalal.

Prodigal *prod'i-gal*, A. Ibaddio, ogddaunno; divallkor.

Prodigality, *prod-i-gal'i-tti*, N. Ibadd, nas; tounasponn.

Prodigious, *pro-dij'as* A. Ojapancho, novlancho.

Prodigy, *prod'-i-ji*, N. Ochoriam; ojap.

Produce, *prod-i'us*, v. Corunc; mucar galunc; daconnc.

Product, *pro-dokt'*, N. Foil; utponn.

Production, *pro-dok'shon*, N. Dakon; zolmonnem; follaboritponn.

Productive, *pro'doc-tiv*, A. Folladic, sufoll, picavo.

Profanation, *pro-fan-ei'shon*, N. Bosttauni, anovitrponn; dushan.

Profane, *pro-fein'* v. Bosttaunc, coisttavunc.

Profane, A. Pozddo, povitr noi aslolo, vaitt.

Profess, *pro-fes*, v. Ucharunc. collounc; cholounc, porgott angonn corunc.

Profession, *pro-fes'shon*, N. Bhes, udiog; porgott angoun.

Professor, *pro-fes'sor*, Professor, mistir, pandit.

Professional, *pro-fes'shon-al*, A. Bhesacho; bhes, cholouncho.

Proficiency, *pro-fi'shen-si*, N. Poki volloc.

Proficient, *pro-fi'shent*, A. Poko, cobardar

Profile, *pro'fail*, N. Eke torechem rup vo chitr.

Profit, *pro'fit*, N. Adau, faido, nofa.

Profit, v. Adau saunc; upcarac poddonc; upeog corunc.

Profitable, *pro'fit-ie-bl*, A. Adavacho, faideacho.

Profligacy, *pro'fli-ga-si*, N. Khottem—, pozddem jivit.

Profligate, *pro'fli-geit*, A. Khotto; fotting; mosticar.

Profound, *pro-faund'*, a fg. Xannom, vorto; gund.

Profundity, *pro-fund'i-tti*, N. Kholai; vorteponn.

Profuse, *pro-fiuz'*, A. Khorchadic, vechic; khup, puscoll.

Profusion, *pro-fiu'jon*, N. Udhal, bhou khoroch; puscollai.

Progenitor, *pro-jen'i-tor*, N. Bapbapui; purvoz.

Progeny, *pro'je-ni*, N. Burgim, sonsot.

Prognostic, *prog-nos'tic*, N. Goddteleacho sumar; ajmas; achar.

Prognosticate, *prog-nos'ti-keit*, v. Adim—, purvim sangunc; dacounc, acharunc.

Programme, *pro'gram*, N. Purvalik, sucha potr.

Progress, *pro'gress,* N. Fudde cholnem; choddau, vaddni.
Progressive, *pro-gres'iv,* A. Mucar vecho; adavacho.
Prohibit, *pro-hib'it,* V. Addvarunc, mona corunc.
Prohibition, *pro-hi-bi'shon,* N. Addvarop, mona corop.
Project, *pro-jekt',* V. Yojan—, tozvit corunc; mucar soronc.
Project, N. Yojon, tozvit.
Projectile, *pro-jek'tail,* N. Gullo; gulli. [car sorop.
Projection, *pro-jek'shon,* N. Mu-
Prolix, *pro'liks,* A. Lamb; vistarlolo; sobar utrancho.
Prolixity, *pri-liks'i-ti,* N. Lambai; sobar utram.
Prologue, *pro'log,* N. Toiari.
Prolong, *pro'long,* V. Lamb corunc; fudde voronc.
Prolongation, *pro-lon-gei'shon,* N. Fudde vorop; lambai.
Promenade, *pro-me-neid',* N. Bounddi.
Prominence, *pro'mi-nens,* N. Ubarai, unchai.
Prominent, *pro'mi-nent,* A. Mucar poddcho vo raucho; ubar
Promiscuous, *pro-mis'ku-as,* A. Borsilolo, zaiteam jinsancho.
Promise, *pro'mis,* N. Utor; bhas.
Promise, V. Utor diunc, bhasaunc.
Promissory note, *pro'mis-o-ri-not,* N. Vaideachi chitt.
Promontory, *pro'mon-to-ri,* N. Tonk.
Promote, *pro-mot',* V. Vaddounc, choddounc; upcarac poddonc.
Promotion, *pro-mo'shon,* N. Boddti, chodau.
Prompt, *promt,* A. Uxar; toiar.
Prompt, V. Launc; bad sangunc
Promptitude, *promt'i-tiud,* N. Uxarki; toiari.
Promptly, *promt'li,* AD. Vegim.
Promulgate, *pro-mul'geit,* V. Porgott corunc.
Promulgation, *pro-mul-gei'shon,* N. Porgotton.
Promulgator, *pro-mul-gei'tor,* N. Porgott cornar.
Prone, *pron,* A. Vondouncho; laglolo.
Prong, *prong,* N. Cantto.
Pronoun, *pro'naun,* N. Navambodli.
Pronounce, *pro'nauns,* V. Ucharunc, munnonc.
Pronunciation, *pro-non-si-ie'shon,* N. Ucharop.
Proof, *pruf,* N. Ruzvat; daklo.
Prop, *prop,* V. Dinki diunc; samballunc.
Prop, N. Dinki; khambo.
Propagate, *pro-pa-geit',* V. Vaddounc; porgott corunc.
Propel, *pro'pel,* V. Lottunc.
Propense, *pro'pens,* N. Vondavon.
Proper, *pro'por,* A. Pratek, visesh, aplo; moriadicho.
Properly *pto'por-li,* AD. Sarkem; moriadin.
Property, *pro'por-ti,* N. Gunn, sobau; dhon, asti.
Prophesy, *pro'fe-zi,* N. Profesi, muca veli sangni.
Prophet, *pro'fet,* N. Profet. mucavelem sangnar.
Prophetess, *pro'fe-tes,* N. Profetin.
Propitiate, *pro-pi'shi-eit,* V. Faricpoun diunc; gunnacho corunc.
Propitiation, *pro-pi'si-ei-shon,* N. Faricponn.
Proportion, *pro-por'shon,* N. Poddop, mezop; vantto.
Proportional, *pro-por'shio-nal,* A. Mapa vo vanttea pormonnen,

Proportionate, *pro-por'shon-eit,* A. Vantteac poddo sarco.

Proposal, *pro-poz'al,* N. Munnem; bolnem, vachan ; sort.

Propose, *pro-poz',* V. Mucar galunc ; sor corunc.

Proposition, *pro-po-zi'shon,* N. Vakia, fanki ; bud.

Propound, *pro-paund,* V. Porgottunc.

Proprietor, *pro-prai'e-tor,* N. Dhoni; battcar.

Proprietorship, *pro-prai'e-tor-ship,* N. Dhoniponn ; yezmanponn. [ad.

Propriety, *pro-prai'e-ti,* N. Mori-

Propulsion, *pro-pul'shon,* N. Lott.

Prorogate, *pro'ro-geit,* V. Fudde voronc.

Prorogue, *pro-rog',* V. Patti galunc; fudde voronc.

Proscribe, *pro-scraib',* V. Callea panneac daddunc; gaunvabhairo corunc.

Prose, *proz,* N. Gotha; fg. chaltem cam.

Prosecute, *pro'se-kiut,* V. Cauz cholounc, firiad diunc.

Prosecution, *pro-se-kiu'shon,* N. cholounnem ; firiad.

Prosecutor, *pro'se-kiut-or* N. Cauz choloinar, firiad cornar.

Proselyte, *pro'ze-lait,* N. Sins ; novo christaum; pattlaucar.

Prosody, *pro'zo-di,* N. Slokapoddot.

Prospect, *pros'pekt,* N. Akar, rong; prospect ; sangat.

Prospectus, *pros'pec-tus,* N. Nokxa ; nomuuno.

Prosper, *pros'por,* V. Suc—, bagh melluuc, nondunc vosunc.

Prosperity, *pros-pe'-ri-tti,* N. Borcott, bagh, suc, chodd vodd.

Prosperous, *pros'per-as,* A. Suki, sriman. noudto, vosto.

Prostitute, *prös'ti-tiut,* N. Cheddi.

Prostrate, *pros'tr-eit,* V. Sorpott poddouc ; xeuttunc; fg. boll moddunc.

Prostrate, A. Boll naslolo, sorpott poddlolo.

Prostration, *pros-trei'shon* N. Pam-yam poddnem, gann gennem, sorpottni ; boll nasnem.

Protect, *pro'tekt,* V. Racunc ; samballunc, mozot diunc.

Protection, *pro-tec'shon,* N. Samballop; adar, mozot.

Protector, *pro-tekt'or* N. Racnno, racnar.

Protectress, *pro-tekt'tress,* N. Racnarn, pastivontin.

Protest, *pro-test',* V. Khoudit vochun sangunc; addcoll galunc

Protest, N. Portest ; khondit sangnim.

Protestant, *pro'test-ant,* N. Protestant.

Protract, *pro-trekt',* V. Lambai corunc, fudde urosem corunc.

Protraction, *pro-trek'shon,* N. Lambai cornem.

Protrude, *pro-triud',* V. Mucar lottonc.

Protrusion, *pro-tro'jon,* N. Dung, bucott.

Protuberence, *pro-tu-ber'ans,* N. Gantt, mascutt.

Protuberant, *pro-tu'ber-ant,* A. Suz ; mucar sornem.

Proud, *praud,* A. Gorvi.

Prove, *pruv.* V. Ruzvat corunc ; polleunc.

Proverb, *pro'vorb,* N. Munni, opar.

Proverbial, *pro-verb'i-al,* N. Munniencho, oparicho.

Provide, *pro-vaid',* V. Diunc ; toiar corunc, zoton corunc, formaunc.

Provided. *pro-vaid'ed*, A. Borlclo; aslolo.
Provided, CONJ. Zor tor.
Providence, *pro'vi-dens*, N. Devachi sasai.
Provident, *pro'vi-dent*, A. Zoton vo chotrai; budvont.
Providential, *pro-vi-den'shal*, A. Devache sasaecho.
Province, *pro'vins*, N. Zillo, mahal; gaum ; fg. caido.
Provincial, *pro-vin'shal*, V. Zilleacho.
Provision, *pro-vi'jon*, N. Udarposon ; zoton; bondabost.
Provisionally, *pro-vi'zhon-al-li*, AD. Sodeak.
Proviso, *pro-vi'zo*, N. Condisaum.
Provoke, *pro-vok'*, V. Rag addunc uchamboll corunc.
Provocation, *pro-vo-kei'shon*, N. Challauni ; uchambollai.
Provoking, *pro-vok'ing*, A. Uchamboll corcho; korcoracho.
Provost, *pro'vost*, N. Kharcanneacho voddil.
Prow, *prau*, N. Tarvachem ; muc vo tonk.
Prowl, *praul*, V. Choriam bonvonc.
Proximate, *proks'i-meit*, A. Lagsilo, lagim aslolo.
Proxy, *proks'i-*, N. Dalal, bodli.
Prudence, *pru'dens*, N. Bud ; zanvai; xanneponn.
Prudent, *pru'dent*, A. Budvont ; zantto ; xanno.
Prune, *prun*, V. Benddhunc ; boddcaunc.
Pruriency, *pru'ri-en-si*, N. Khoroz ; fg. axea
Pry, *prav*, V. Tellunc ; barcaen pollounc.
Psalm, *salm*, N. Salm, onondachem gaian. [fott.
Pseudo, *su'do*, N. Fottkiro;
Pshaw. *sha*, Int. Che.
Psychology, *si-col'o-ji*, N. Otmeachem xastr.
Puberty, *piu'ber-ti*, N. Cazar zaunchi pirai, pirae borit.
Puberty, A. piraer paulolo, torno.
Public, *pob'lic*, A. Porgott ; sercaracho ; sorv locacho.
Public, N. Lok.
Public-house—, Ducon.
Publican, *pab'li'can*, N. Jakatdar.
Publication, *pab-li-kei'shon*, N. Porgott cornem ; pustoc.
Publish, *pab'lish*, V. Porgott corunc.
Pucker, *pok'ar*, N. Miri.
Puddle, *pod'l*, N. Mellea udcacho vall ; chicol.
Puddle, V. Chiclan mello corunc.
Puerile, *pu-er'ail*, A Burgeaponnacho.
Puff, *pof*, N. Funk.
Puff, V. Funcunc; fg. fugounc, gorvi zaunc.
Pug, *pog*, N. Macodd ; dactto petto.
Pugnacious, *pug-nei'shas*, A. Zogddecar, tocrari.
Puissant, *pui'is-ant*, A. Podvedar vo bolladic.
Pule, *piul*, V. Burgeam porim roddonc.
Pull, *pull*, V. Voddunc ; caddunc.
—(Up,) Umttunc.
—(Down,) Moddun socla uddounc
Pullet, *pul'et*, N. Tolog.
Pulley, *pul'i*. N. Gaddi.
Pullulate, *pul-u'leit*, A. Uzbonc.
Pulp, *polp*, N. Follanchem mass.
Pulpit, *pul'pit*, N. Pulputr.
Pulpous, *pul'pas*, A. Masall.
Pulsate, *pul'seit*, V. Uddonc, fitfittonc.
Pulsation, *pul-sei'shon*, N. Uddop.

Pulse, *pols*, N. Nadd.
Pulverise, *pul're-raiz*, V. Pudd vo pitto corunc; vattunc.
Pump, *pomp*, N. Udoc chepnem
Pump, V. Chepun udoc caddunc.
Pumpkin, *pomp'kin*, N. Dudi; cuuvallo; boblo.
Punch, *ponch*, N. Eke torechem pieop (soro); girbo.
Punch, V. Topunc.
Puncheon, *pon'shon*, N. Pip.
Punctual, *pong'chu-al*, A. Sarco, vogtar; borobor.
Punctuality, *pangk-chu-al'i-ti*, N. Zagrutai, vellar ajir asnem.
Punctuate, *pongk'chu-eit*, V. Tibe galunc. [nem.
Puncture, *pongk'char*, N. Top-
Pungency, *pun'jen-si*, N. Tiksan, tirbottan, mirmire.
Pungent, *pun'jent*, A. Tic, tirbott, mirmirit.
Punish, *pon'ish*, V. Sicxa vo kheastt launc.
Punishment, *pon'isn-ment*, N. Sicxa, coistt, kheastt.
Puny, *pun'i*, A. Lan.
Pupil, *piu'pil*, N. Sins; bhauli.
Puppet, *pop'et*. N. Bombo; sogleam vostunim dusreache sangnem khal aslolo munis.
Puppy, *pop'i*, N. Supurlem sunne; fg. gorvi burgo.
Purchase, *por'cheis*, V. Victem geunc.
Pure, *piu'ar*, A. Nitoll, nirmoll, saf, uttim.
Purgative, *por'ga-tiv*, N. Purgant, bairi.
Purgatory, *por'ga-to-ri*, N. Purgator.
Purge, *porj*, V. Nitoll corunc; bhair galunc.
Purge, N. Bhairi.
Purity *piu'ri-ti*, N. Nitollponn, nirmollponn; moriad.
Purple, *porp'pl*, N. Jamblo rong; tambdo rong. [zonni.
Purport, *por'port*, N. Orth; som-
Purpose, *por'poz*, N. Xevott; nicheu; chintna; sobab.
Purpose, V. Nicheu corunc; xevott asunc.
Purposely, *por'poz-li*, AD. Mudom corun; khoxen zannozaun. [vo theli.
Purse, *pors*, N. Duddvanchi poti
Purse, V. Duddu potient galunc.
Pursue, *per-su'*, N. Daunddaunc; patta-patt vochonc; xevott asunc. [patt lagop.
Pursuit, *per-sut*, N. Cam; patta-
Purulence, *pu'ru-lens*, N. Pu; rendi. [diunc.
Purvey, *por-vei'*, V. Addunc,
Pus, *pos*, N. Pu.
Push, *push*, N. Lottnem, ducolnem; prayatan. [lounc.
Push, V. Lottunc, locaunc; cho-
Pushing, *push'ing* A. Siddnc.
Pusillaminity, *pu'sil-a-mi-nitti*, N. Bemcreponn, abal, holkeponn.
Pusillaminous, *pu'sil-la-mi-nas*, A. Bhiukuro, bemcro, gabro.
Pustule, *pus'tiul*, N. Fodd, pulli; kensolli. [launc.
Put, *put*, V. Galunc, dourunc;
—(To flight), Daunddaunc.
—(To death), Jivesim marunc.
—(Spirit), Dir diunc.
—(A question), Vicharunc.
—(Apart), Kherit dovorunc.
—(By), Sugur corunc.
—(Out), Gonddlac galunc; palounc.
—(In), Bhitor galunc.
—(Off), Fudde voronc; fottounc.
—(Up), Sosunc; mucar galunc; ravonc.
Putrefaction, *piu-tre-feo'shon*, N. Cusop; cusoddai.

Putrefy, *piu'tri-fai*, v. Cusonc.
Putrid, *piu'trid*, v. Cuslolo.
Puty, *pat'i*, N. Guruth.
Puzzle, *poz'l*, v. Gusponc; gonddlong.
Puzzle, N. Gondoll, gusponnem.
Puzzling, *poz'ling*, A. Cottin; dubavacho.
Pygmy, *pig'mi*, N. Mottvo.
Pyramid, *pi'ra-mid*, N. Domsacho khambo.
Pyre, *paiar*, N. Zollvachi ras (moddem ulpaunc.)
Pyx, *piks*, N. Cals.

Q

Quack, *kwek*, v. Ansa baxen roddonc; boddboddunc.
Quack, N. Boddboddo; fottkiro voiz.
Quadrangle, *kwod'rang-gl*, N. Char conxeanchem; chouki.
Quadruped, *kuod'ru-ped*, N. Char paianchi monzat.
Quaff, *kwof*, v. Jiu soddun pieunc. [thortorunc.
Quail, *kwel*, v. Anvlonc; bhieun
Quail, N. Lovo.
Quaint, *kwent*, A. Nazuc.
Quaintness, *kwent'ness*, N. Nazukai.
Quake, *kwek*, N. Camp, thortor.
Quake, v. Camponc.
Qualification, *kwo-li-fi-kei'shon*, N. Gunn-naum—, dennem—, aropnem.
Qualified, *kwa'li-faid*, A. Gunni, gunnadic, gunnest.
Qualify, *kwa'li-fai*, v. Gunn—, naum diunc,, sangunc; aropunc.
Quality *kwa'li-ti*, N. Gunn.
Qualm, *kuom*, N. Voncaro; fg. churchure.
Quantity, *kwan'ti-ti*, N. Poriman praman, map, punj.
Quarrel, *kur-rul* N. Zogddem; loddai.
Quarrel, v. Zogddonc, zuzonc.
Quarrelsome, *kwo'ral-som*, N. Zogddecar.
Quarry, *kiuo'ri*, N. Fator marchi khon.
Quart, *kwort*, N. Botl.
Quartan, *kwar'tan*, A. Poireacho (zor).
Quarter, *kwar'tor*, N. Chouto vantto; pau.
Quarter, v. Char vantte corunc; biddar corunc.
Quarterly, *kwo'tor-li*, AD. Titisrea muineac.
Quash, *kwosh*, v. Mostunc; nattac corunc.
Quaver, *kwa'ver*, N. Camp; attvo vantto.
Quaver, v. (tallo) camponc.
Quay, *kwe*, N. Doko.
Queasiness, *kwe'si-ness*, N. Voncaro.
Queasy, *kwe'zi*, A. Voncareacho
Queen, *kwin'*, N. Ranni.
Queer, *kwer'*, A. Tarifecho; ansouncho.
Quell, *kwel*, v. Khalto corunc; ravonc somadan corunc; fuslaunc.
Quench, *kwench'*, v. Tan bagounc; fg. nivounc, dadoxi corunc.
Querulous, *kwe'ru-las*, A. Xinn ulouncho.
Querist, *kwer'isl*, N. Vichar, cornar.
Query, *kwe'ri*, N. Vichar, pergunt.
Quest, *kwest'*, N. Sodni; vincharop.
Question, *kwest'yon*, N. Vinchar, pergunt.
Question, v. Vicharunc; pergunt galunc.

Questionable, *kwest'yon-a-bl*, A. tocrar aslolo ; dubavi.
Quick, *kwick'*, A. Vegim, ecach faracho ; uxar ; baric chotur.
Quicken, *kwik'n*, V. Ausar corunc ; uttounc ; vanchounc.
Quickly, *kwick'li*, AD. Vegim-vegim ; sott corun.
Quickness, *kwik'ness*, N. Ausar ; uxarki ; barcai.
Quicksilver, *kwik'sil-vor*, N. Paroz.
Quidity, *kwd'i-ti*, N. Sar.
Quiescence, *kwi'es-ens*, N. Soucasai.
Quiet, *kwa'et*, A. Nidan ; soncasaecho.
Quiet, N. Visou ; soncasai ; sosomandan.
Quill, *kwill*, N. Pac.
Quilt, *kwilt*, N. Gozdi culchaum.
Quintessence, *kwint-es'ens*, N. uttim sar.
Quintuple, *kwen'lu-pl*, A. Panch pautti chodd.
Quip, *kwip*, N. Barcai ; chesttai.
Quire, *kwaiar'*, N. Chovis *foli*.
Quirk, *kwork'*, N. Nib.
Quit, *kwit*, V. Soddunc ; faric corunc.
Quit, A. Suttlolo.
Quite, *kwait'*, AD. Sarkem, tosench ; dubau nastanam.
Quittance, *kwit'ens*, N. Fario corop ; inam.
Quiver, *kwiv'or*, V. Camponc ; thortorunc.
Quivering, *kwi'vor-ing*, N. Camp.
Quoit, *koit*, N. Mandd.
Quorum, *kiuo'rum*, N. Zai title zann.
Quota, *kwo'ta*, N. Vantto.
Quotation, *kwo-tei'shon*, N. Daclo; dor-mol sangnem.
Quote, *kwot*, V. Daclo diunc ; moll sangunc.
Quoth, *kwoth*, V. Sanglem.
Quotidian, *kwo-ti'di-an*, A. Dispotto.

R

Rabbi, *rab'bi*, N. Suami.
Rabbit, *rab'bit*, N. Sonso.
Rabid, *re'bid*, A. Piso ; ragist.
Race, *res*, N. Culli ; cuttom; zat
Race, V. Borobor daavunc.
Race-course, *res'kors*, N. Dauncho zago.
Rack, *rek*, N. Roz; chaer; cottin duc; gotto.
Rack, V. Ija diunc, bhong corunc; dogdaunc; voddunc.
Racy, *rei'si*, A. Ruchicho.
Radiance, *ra'di-ans*, N. Porzoll.
Radiant, *ra'di-ant*, A. Porzollit.
Radiate, *ra'di-eit*, V. Kirnam diunc; porzollunc.
Radical, *ra'di-cal*, A. Poiloch; mullan than.
Radius, *ra'di-us*, N. Kirn.
Raffle, *ref'l*, N. Sort.
Raft. *raft*, N. Patti.
Rafter, *raf'tor*, N. Vanso.
Rag, *reg*, N. Pinzlelem lugott ; chindi.
Rage, *reij*, N. Kirod; uchambollai.
Rage, V. Ragan sizonc.
Ragi, *ra'gi*, N. Nachno.
Rail, *rail*, V. Voi galunc ; angar poddonc; galli souvonc.
Rail, N. Dori; grad.
Raillery, *reil'e-ri*, N. Khebaddam, yenddaunem.
Railway, *reil'way*, N. Locondacho marog.
Raiment, *rei'ment*, N. Nesonn ; vostur.
Rain, *rein*, N. Paus.
Rainy, *rein'i*, A. Pausacho vo pausilo.

Raise, *reiz*, V. Ubaruno; banduno; uttouno; maruno; bodti diuno.
Raisin, *rei'zin*, N. Kismis.
Rake, *reic*, N. Moddcoll.
Rally, *ral'i*, V. Novean eottaim zauno; manddunc.
Ram, *ram*, N. Dadlo bokro.
Ram, V. Boddoune; pettunc.
Ramble, *rem'bl*, V. Parpoll bonvonc.
Ramify, *ra'mi-fai*, V. Tallieo futtunc.
Ramp, *remp*, V. Eke vali porim choddonc.
Rampant, *rem'pant*, A Choddavot; nit mer naslolo; pattleam paianim nbo raulolo.
Rampart, *ram'part*, N. Matiecho uddo cotta bounttonec.
Ramrod, *ram'rod*, N. goz.
Rancid, *ran'sid*, A. Ambett; ghannero.
Rancour, *reng'kor*, N. Rag; mosor.
Random, *ren'dom*, A. Akasmat; chintinastanam.
Range, *reinj*, N. Tar; vistarop.
Rank, *renk*, N. Ek ar; bhes; clas.
Rank, A. ispa bhair fancarcho; ambott, choddavot.
Rank, V. Arin galunc; dourunc; ispan dorunc.
Rankle, *reng'kl*, V. Cusonc; uchamboll zaunc.
Ransack, *ran'sek*, V. Lutt corunc; sarkem sodunc.
Ransom, *ren'som*, V. gulam ponnantlo soddounc.
Ransom N. Soddvonn.
Rant, *rent*, V. Uchamboll zaun ulounc.
Ranter, *rent'or*, N. Uchamboll uloinar.
Rap, *rep*, N. Thapott, thap.
Rap, V. Boddouno vo thapttaunc.
Rapacious, *ra-pei'shas*, A. Lutnecho, horboki.
Rapacity, *ra-pa'si-ti*, N. Vodd horbocponn; zulum,
Rape, *reip*, N. Zulmen gott dorop, eke baile codde aple cuddichi khoxi bogop tichea cobluda sivai.
Rapid, *ra'pid*, A. Chodd vegim.
Rapidity, *ra-pid'i-ti*, N. Suddsuddai ; ausar.
Rapier, *re'pi-er*, N. ek lamb osir torsad.
Rapine, *ra'pain*, N. Chori ; nagonn ; lutt.
Rapt, *rept*, V. Porchong poddonc ; lobdonc.
Rapture, *rep'char*, N. Ulas, drust tavo. [zuc-
Rare, *rer*, A. Aprup ; uttim ; na-.
Rarefy, *re'ri-fai*, V. Pattoll corunc.
Rarity, *ra'ri-ti*, N. Aprupai ; pattollai.
Rascal, *ras'cal*, N. Chor, nagounno ; holko munis.
Rase *reiz*, V. Caddunc ; zorounc.
Rash, *resh*, A. Urmott ; chotrai naslolo, onvatt.
Rash, N. Gomollem.
Rashness, *resh'ness*, N. Utavoll ; urmottai.
Rat, *ret*. N. Undir ; chichondor.
Rat, V. Andaz coruno ; insunc.
Rate, *reit*, N. Dor, mol ; jinos.
Rather, *rath'or*, AD. Poros vo vorn.
Ratification, *ra-ti-fi-kei'shon*, N. Posond ; coblat.
Ratify, *ra'ti-fai*, V. Posand corunc ; cobul corunc.
Ration, *rei-shon*, N. Bhatem,
Rational, *re'shon-al*, A. Somjicai vo bud aslolo ; budvont.
Rationalism, *ra'shon-al-izm*, N. Carandvad, hetuvad.

Rationalist, *ra'shon-al-ist*, N Caranvadi.
Rattle, *ret'tl*, N. Khilkullo.
Rattle, V. Gorgorunc ; fg. gozali marunc.
Ravage, *ra'vej*, N. Lutt ; zulum ; nas.
Ravage, V. Lutt—, nas corunc.
Ravager, *ra've-jar*, N. Lutt cornar.
Rave, *rev*, V. Ragan zollonc.
Raven, *rev'n*, N. Caullo.
Raven, V. Lutt orunc ; go'p-gopiam khaunc.
Ravenous, *rav'en-as*, A. Chodd horboki.
Ravine, *ra-vin'*, N. Lamb kholli ; voll.
Ravine, *rev'ing*, N. Sintid naslelem uloup.
Ravish, *re'vish* V. zulmen voddun vorunc ; Khotounc ; bhou khuxal corunc.
Ravishment, *re'vish-ment*. N. Zulum ; boll ; khotaunem ; bhou sontos. [nar.
Raw, *ro*, A. Jivo ; torno ; nen-
Ray, *rei*, N. Kirn ; vagollem.
Razor, *rei'zor*, N. Vakor.
Reach, *rich'*, V. Vistaronc ; pavonc ; canant poddonc.
Reach, N. Vistarop ; socot.
Re-act, *ri'ect*, V. Add eunc vo patti lottunc.
Re-action, *ri-ec'shon*, N. Patti lottop.
Read, *riid'*, V. Vachunc.
Reader' *rid'er*, N. Vachpi.
Reading, *rid'ing* N. Vachop.
Readiness, *re'di-ness*, N. Toiari ; sompepoun ; uxarki,
Ready. *redi*, A. Toiar ; uxar ; nogot.
Real, *ri'al*, A. Khoroch ; niz.
Reality, *ri-al'i-ti*, N. Khoreponnim ; sot ; khoroch.
Realize, *ri'al-aiz*, V. Khorem co run dacunne ; sovoim corunc.
Realm, *relm*, N. Razvottki. razvott ; raz.
Ream, *rim*. N. Rezm.
Reap, *rip*. V. Luvonc ; pic catrunc ; fg. zoddunc ; mellounc.
Reaper, *rip'or*, N. Lunvtolo vo luuvuar.
Reaping-hook, N. Coiti.
Rear, *rer*, V. Vaddounc ; posunc ; bandunc.
Rear, N. Pattli fouz.
Reason, *ri'zn*, N. Somjicai ; mot ; ginean ; carann.
Reason; V. Argument corunc ; xanepounam ulounc
Reasonable, *ri'zn-ie-bl*, A. gineanam zoctem ; carann aslelem.
Reasonableness, *ri'zn-ie-bl-ness*, N. Bud.
Rebel, *re'bel*, N. Patxaiacher kolpololo, fitur; beleban; augodd.
Rebel, V. Sercaracher kolponc.
Rebellion, *re-bel'yon*, N. Colponi, fituri bonddai.
Rebound, *ri-ba'und*, V. Pattim soronc, portonc.
Rebuff, *re-buf'* V. Pois corunc addaunc.
Rebuff, N. Auchit addauni.
Rebuke, *re-bink*, V. Insunc; guneanncari corunc.
Rebus, *re'bus* N. Gudd
Rebut, *ri'bot*, V. Portun diunc; pois corunc.
Recall, *ri'col*, V. Portun apounc; ugddas corunc.
Recant, *re'kant*, V. Ulolelempatti caddunc vo mul corunc.
Recapitulate, *re'capit-iu-leit*, V. Thoddeam utranim novean sangunc; attapunn diunc.
Recapitulation, *re-ca-pit-u-leishon*, N. Samkshep, attap.

Recast, *re-cast'*, V. Portun galunc; portem rup diunc.
Recede, *re-sed'*, V. Patti soronc.
Receipt, *re'sit*, N. Recib, pauti
Receive *re-siv*, V. Gheunc; melunc; bogunc.
Recent, *re'sent*, A. Novo alincho.
Recently, *re'sent-li*, AD. Alim, nicto; thoddo temp zalolo.
Receptacle' *ri-cep'te-kl* N, Dorop; aidon.
Reception, *ri-sep'shon*, N. Gennem gevop.
Recess, *re-ses*, N. Ecsuri suat, contrel.
Recipe, *re'si-pe*, N. Reset.
Recipient, *re si-pi-ent*, N. Aidon.
Reciprocal, A. *re-sip'ro-cal*, A. Ecamecacho.
Reciprocally *.re-sip'ro-cal-li*, AD Ekamecac.
Recital, *ri-sait'al*, N, Sangunemucharop.
Recitation, *re-si-tei'shon*, N. Kirtan; vachop.
Recite, *ri-sait* V. Ucharunc; munnounc.
Reckless, *rek'less*, A. Chotrui nasjolo;'murk.
Recklessly, *rek-les'li*, AD. Chotraeviun.
Recklessness, *rek'less-ness*, N Chotrai nasnem; utavoll
Reckon, *rek'n*, V. Contanc dorunc; mezunc; chintunc.
·(On,) patieunc.
Reckoning, *rek'on-ing*, N. Ixeop, mezop.
Reclaim, *re-cleim'*, V. Portun magounc. sodunc.
Reclamation, *re-cla-mei'shon* N. ulounem, prativad, magnem.
Recline, *ri-clain'*, V. bagounc; bosonc; add poddonc.
Recluse, *re-klos'* A. Vonvasi.

Recognise, *ri-cognaiz'*, V. Volcoue; zauno zaunc.
Recoil, *ri-coil'*, V. Bhieun patti soronc; canttallonc.
Recollect, *ri'col-lekt*, V. Ugddas corunc; attou corunc.
Recollection, *ri'co-lec-shon*, N. Ugddas, attou.
Recommence, *ri-commens'*, V. Novean suru corunc
Recommend, *ri-com-mend*, V. Sifaras corunc; umedin sangunc; mandun geunc.
Recommendable, *ri-com-mend'-ie-bl*, A. Manadic, navaddic.
Recommendation, *ri-com-mend-ie'shon*, N. Sifaras, tarifs, recommendasaum.
Recommendatory, *re-com'mend-a'to-ri*, A. Tarifecho, siparajicho.
Recompense, *ri'com-pens*, N. Foll; inam.
Recompense, V. Foll inam diunc, kelelem faric corunc.
Recompose, *ri'com-poz*, V. Novean borounc; fuslaunc.
Reconcile, *ri'con-sail*, V. Lagim caddunc; ecttaim corunc, somzavunc.
Reconciliation, *ri-con-si-li-ei'shon* N. somjust, ecvott, mell; soncosai.
Recondite, *ri-con'dait*, A. Gupit, gudh. guttacho.
Reconnoitre, *ri-con-noi'tor*, V. Vicharan corunc. sarkem pollenne.
Record, *record'*, N. Daclo; ugddas
Record, V. Daclo dourunc; ugddas dourunc.
Recount, *re'caunt*, V. Saugonc, munnonc.
Recourse, *ri-kors'*, N. Vochun adar magnem; acantaches vellar asro

Recover, *ri-cov'or,* v. Vosul corunc; portun mellounc; piddentlo boro zaunc.
Recovery, *ri-cov'e-ri,* N. Vosuli; gunn.
Recreant, *re'kri-ant,* A. Bezudd; nirvonn naslolo.
Recreate, *re-kri-eit',* v. Khuxal corunc; sontos bogunc.
Recreation, *re-kri-ei'shon,* N. Soucasai; gommot; khuxalaecho vell.
Recriminate. *re-crim'in-eit,* v. Tonddar marunc; guneauncari corunc.
Recruit, *re-krut',* N. Novo soldad.
Recruit, v. Novo corunc; boll diunc.
Recruiting, *re-crut'ing,* N. Nove soldad corop.
Rectangle, *rec'tan-gl,* N. Samkonn.
Rectification, *rec-ti-fi-kei'shon.* N. Sarkem cornem, nittai.
Rectify, *rec'ti-fai,* v. Sarkem corunc, nittier galunc.
Rectitude, *rec'ti-tiud,* N. Nittai; Sarkeponn.
Rector, *rec'tor,* N. Conventacho vo iscolacho voddil.
Recumbent, *re-cum'bent,* A. Boslolo; add poddlolo; ricambi.
Recuperation, *re-ku'per-ei-shon,* N. Portun mellounem.
Recur, *ri-cor',* v. Portun eunc.
Red, *red,* A Tambddo.
Redden, *red'dn,* v. Tambddo corunc.
Reddish, *red'ish,* A. Tambso.
Redeem, *re-dim',* v. Soddounc, soddvon corunc.
Redeemer, *re-dim'ar,* N. Sorvonddar, tarok.
Redemption, *ri-dem'shon,* N. soddvonn.
Red-hot, *red-hot,* A. Tapoilolo, ujea sarco.
Redness, *red'ness,* N. Tambsan.
Redolent, *ri'do-lent,* A. Pormoll eunc.
Redouble, *ri-do'bl,* v. Doddo corunc; don pautti vodic corunc.
Redound, *ri-daund',* v. Bhair vavunc; upcarac poddonc.
Redress, *ri-dress',* v. Sarkem corunc; apos diunc; bhorun diunc.
Reduce, *re-dius'* v. Unno—,baric —, osoct zaunc; khalto corunc.
Reduction, *ridoc'shon,* N. Unneponn; lacharponn.
Redundancy. *redon'dan-si,* N. choddon.
Redundant, *ri-don'dant,* A. Chodcho; vodic ogllo.
Reduplication, *re-du-pli-kei'shon,* N. Doddop
Reed, *rid,* N. Pokli man; noll.
Reek, *rik,* v. Dunvor eunc; ubeunc.
Reel *ril,* v. Camponc; thortorunc.
Refectory, *re-fec'to-ri,* N. Jennachi cund; refeitor.
Refer, *ri-for',* v. Sangunc, nirupunc; mucar galunc; munnonc.
Reference, *re'fer-ons,* N. Saugni; contha, gosht.
Refine, *ri-fain',* v, Baric corunc; nitol corunc.
Refinement, *ri-fain-ment,* N. Nibor barcai.
Reflect, *ri-flect',* v. Patti portunc; vallunc; uzvadd uddounc.
Reflection, *ri-flec'shon,* N. Patti portonem; vallnem; fankin; niall; chotrai.
Reflective, *ri-flec'tiv,* A. Vinchari; yojanacho, nyallacho.
Reform, *ri-form',* v. Dusrem rup—, veglo akar diunc; aslo toso corunc.

Reformation, *re-for-mei'shon,* N. boro—, sarco cornem ; subdi.
Refract, *rifrekt',* V. Firaunc, vancounc, vaneddo corunc.
Refraction, *rifrekt'shon,* N. Vaneddepoun, vaneudd.
Refractory, *ri-frec'to-ri,* A. Pundd ; fotting ; vadio ; darun.
Refrain, *ri-frein',* V. Damunc, doddpunc, attponc ; samvronci baddgunc.
Refresh, *rifresh',* V. Thondd. sitoll corunc ; jiv boronc.
Refreshment, *ri-fresh'ment,* N. Soucasai ; gottai ; follar.
Refrigeratory, *re-fri-jer-a'to-ri,* A. Thondd corcho.
Refuge, *re'fiuj,* N. Asro ; adar ; sasai.
Refuge, A. Asro sodcho; pordesi.
Refulgence, *re-ful'gens,* N. Poizoll.
Refusal, *re-fiuz'al,* N. Naca munnem, portinem.
Refuse, *re-fuiz',* V. Naca munnonc ; cobul zainam zaunc.
Refutation, *re-fut-ei'shon,* N. Miras; modd; paddni.
Refute, *re-fuit',* V. Paddunc ; tonddar marunc ; fott decol corunc.
Regalia, *re-ga'li-a,* N. Raiachi khunna.
Regard, *re-gard',* N. Pollenuc ; distt marunc ; chintunc.
Regard, N. Zoton, apurbai.
Regardless, *re-gard'less,* A. Urmott, chotrai naslolo.
Regency, *ri'jen-si,* N. Raj chelonnem vo raj cholounchi sabha.
Regenerate, *re-jen-ie'reit,* V. Portun zolmaunc; fg. novo corunc.
Regeneration, *re-jen-ne-rei'shon,* N. Novi jinn ; novo zolm.
Regent, *ri-jent,* N. Patxaiache suater raj choloinar.
Regicide, *re'ji-said* N. Raiacho pran caddnar.
Regimen, *re'ji-men,* N. Cholouni, vosounim; raj viavostha.
Regiment, *re'ji-ment,* N. Polttou.
Region, *re'ji-on,* N. Gaum; suat.
Register, *re'jis-ter,* N. Daclo ; potti.
Register, V. Decol corunc.
Registrar, *re'jis trar,* N. Daclo dovornar, rejistrar.
Registration, *re'jist-rei-shon.* N. Daclo dovornem.
Regret, *re-gret',* N. Khont; duk.
Regret, V. Khontounc, duk disonc.
Regular, *re'gu-lar,* A. Caides purto ; riticho nemacho kramacho.
Regularly. *re'gu-lar-li,* AD. Kraman, fovo-tea pormonnem ; chuconastanam.
Regularity, *re-gu-la'ri-ti.* N. Caidea sirpounn, sarkepounn ; manddavoll.
Regulate, *re'gu-leit,* N. Ritiu caidea pormonnem cholounc; tharavunc ; nemunc.
Regulation, *re-gu-lei'shon.* N. Regr ; caido.
Rehabilitate, *re-ha-bil'i-teit,* V. Adle sarco corunc; sotea portun diunc.
Rehearsal, *re-hers'al,* N. Canni munnon polleop.
Rehearse, *re-hers',* V. Sangunc vo munnonc.
Reign, *rein,* N. Razvott.
Reign, N. Raz.
Rein, *rein,* N. Lagop,
Reinforce, *re-in-fors'* V. Fouz choddounc; boll diunc,
Reinforcement, *re-in-fors'ment,* N. Choddouni; boll; adar.
Reject, *re-jekt',* V. Bhair uddounc, contac dorinam zaunc ; magnem aiconam zaunc.

Rejection, *re-jek'shon*, N. Bhair uddop; magielem ʟam munnop.

Rejoice, *re-jois'*, V. Khoxal zaunc; sontos diunc; ulas bogunc.

Rejoin, *ri-join'*, V. Novean entrad zaunc.

Relapse, *ri-leps'*, V. Portun poddonc. [gonc.

Relate, *re-leit*, V. Munnonc; san-

Related, *ri-leit'ed*, A. Soiro; cosolii soirigot aslolo.

Relation, *re-lei'shon*, N. Khobor; soiro; soiric.

Relationship, *re-lei-shon'ship* N. Soirie, soimgun.

Relative, *re'lat-iv*, N Poisile soiro.

Relax, *ri-leks'*, V. Sodil corunc.

Relaxation, *ri-leks ei'shon*, N. Soddilai; soucasai.

Relaxed, *ri-leks'd*, A. Soddil.

Relay, *ri-lei'*, N. Topalache goddo zancam vatec dortat eranc suttca diunc.

Release, *re-liz'*, V. Soddunc, suttca diunc.

Release, N. Suttca; soddonn; soddilai.

Relent, *ri-lent'*, V. Rag nivonc.

Relic, *re'lic*, N. Relic; ugddasachi vost.

Relief, *re-lif'*, N. Adhar; hallu-vai; soddilai.

Relieve, *re-liev'*. V. Hallu corunc; buzvon diunc; bodol corunc.

Religion, *re-li'jon*, N. Religiaum. dhorm; xastr-

Religious, *re-li'ji-as*. A. Xastracho; devosponnacho.

Religious, *re-li'jias*. N. Frad; xastri.

Relinquish, *re-lin'kwish*, V. Soddunc vo sanddunc.

Reliquary, *re-li-kwa'ri*, N. Relicanchem buxet.

Relish, *re'li-sh*, V. Ruchonc; chaconc.

Relish, N. Ruch; Suad.

Reluctance, *ri-lu'ktans*, N. Namkhoni; mosagot, besarmai.

Reluctant, *ri-luc'tant*, A. Khoxi naslolo, besarmi.

Rely, *ri-lai'*, V. Patieunc; visvas dourunc. [uronc.

Remain, *ri-main'*, V. Ravonc;

Remainder, *re-main'dor*, N. Baki; urta tem; usttem.

Remains, *ri-mains'*, N. Moddem.

Remark, *ri-mark'*, N. Chotrai.

Remark, V. Chotrai diunc; motint galunc.

Remarkable, *ri-mark'ie-bl*, A. Chotraecho; navadic; ojapancho.

Remedy, *re'me-di*, N. Upai; vocot; adar.

Remedy, V. Gunn poddonc; upai corunc,

Remember, *re-mem'ber*, V. Ugddas; vo attou.

Remind, *ri-maind'*, V. Ugddas corunc; bud sangonc.

Reminiscence, *re-mi-nis'ens*, N. Ugddas, attou.

Remiss, *re-mis'*, A. Auxi; chotrai naslolo.

Remission, *re-mis'shon*, N. Soddilai, bogsonem.

Remit, *re-mit'*, V. Bogsunc, maf corunc.

Remittance, *re-mit'ans*, N. Addlolo dnddu; hundi.

Remittent, *re-mit'ent*, A. Caddto, vecho euncho.

Remonstrance, *re-mons'truns*, N. Protest; insinnem.

Remonstrate, *re-mons'treit*, V. ensunc; bud diunc; protest coruc.

Remorse, *ri-mors'*, N. Ontoscornacho, kiddo.

Remote *ri-mot′*, A. Poisilo.
Remotely, *ri-mot′li*. AD. Pois.
Removal, *re-muv′al*, N. Bhair caddop.
Remove, *remuv′*, V. Pelean caddunc chuconc; bhair soronc.
Remunerate, *re-miu′ne-reit*, V. Faricponn dinne; farig corunc.
Remuneration, *re-mune-rei′shon*, N. Faricponn; inam; muzri.
Rend, *rend*, V. Pinzunc; moddunc; foddunc.
Render, *ren′der*, V. Ixeop diunc; vapos diunc.
Rendezvous, *ren′de-vou*, N. Mellchi suat.
Renegade, *re′ne-geid*, A. Aplo dhorm soddlolo; fitur; khotto.
Renew, *re-niu′*, V. Portun corunc; sarkem corunc.
Renewal, *re-niu′al*, N. Portun corop.
Renounce, *rinauns′*, V. Patt corunc; soddunc.
Renovate, *re′no-veit*. V. Novo corunc.
Renowned, *re-naund′*, A. Navadic, famad, kirtivont.
Rent, *rent*, N. Baddem; folli; pinzop.
Rent, V. Baddeac diunc.
Renunciation, *re-nun-si-ei′shon*, N. Naca munnem; Soddni.
Repair, *ri-per′*, V. Sori corunc, faricponn diunc, bhorun diunc;
Reparation, *re-pa-rei′shon*, N. faricponn.
Repast, *ri-past′*, N. Jevonn.
Repeal, *re-pil′*, V. Kelolo caido moddunc.
Repeat, *re-pit′*, V. Portun—, dus. reanim mannonc.
Repeatedly, *re-pit′ed-li*, AD. Portun portun; goddie-goddie.-
Repel, *ri-pel′*, V. Addaunc, patti caddunc-
Repent, *ri-pent′*, V. Duk doruno
Repentance, *ri-pent′ens*, N. Patcachi dukh; pirachit.
Repertory, *re′per-to-ry*, N. Banddar.
Repetition, *repetishon′*, N. Novean munuem.
Repine, *ri-pain′* V. Xinn ulounc
Repining, *re-pain′nig*, N, Xinn.
Replace, *ri-ples′*, V. Adle suater novean dourunc.
Replevy, *re-plev′i*, V. [illegible] voddlem bens fians diun portun geunc anim uprant cortin cauz cholounc.
Reply, *ri-plui′*. V. Zabab diunc.
Reply, N. Zabab.
Report, *riport′*, V. Collounc; khobor addunc.
Report, N. Phucaro; khobor; ixeop-cont.
Repose, *ri-poz′*, N. Soucasai.
Repose, V. Soucasai vo suceg geunc.
Repository, *re-poz′i-to-ri*, N. Dovorchi suat.
Reprehend, *re pri-hend′*, N. Guneucari corunc; besttaunc.
Reprehension, *reprihenshon′*, N. Besttaunem.
Represent, *re.pre-zent′*, V. Hajir corunc, mucar galunc; niallac addunc.
Representation, *re-pre-zent-ei′-shon*, N. Dacoun; arji.
Representative, *re-pre-zent-a-tiv* N. Dacoinar, arpidar; somgam cortolo.
Repress, *ri-press′*, V. Boll moddunc; tambounc; domaunc.
Repression, *ri-pre′shon*, N. Domaunc, monam corunc.
Reprieve, *re-priv′*, V. Thoddo temp suttca diunc.
Reprimand, *rep′ri.mand*, V. Insunc.

Reproach, *ri-proch'* v. Guneauncar corunc, lojec galunc; kenunc.
Reproach, N. Ocman; loz.
Reprobate, *re'pro-beit*, v. Sirap poddonc.
Reprobation, *re-pro-bei'shon*, N. Condemnasaum; soddni.
Reproduce, *re-pro-dius'*, v. Fortun ubjaunc; decol corunc.
Reproof, *re-pruf'* N. insop.
Reprove, *reprov'*, V. Guneauncari corunc.
Reptile, *rep'tail*, N. Jival, jivannem; sorpotti monzat.
Republic, *ri-pob'lic*, N. Dha zanachem raj; porjechem raj.
Repudiate *re-pu'di-eit*, N. Bailec soddunc; bhair galunc.
Repugnance, *ripog'nens*, N. Virod; violab; nakhuxi; voncaro.
Repugnant, *re-pug'nant*. A. Khoxi naslolo.
Repulse, *ri-pols'* v. Pois lottunc
Repulsion, *ri-pol'shon*, N. Lottop.
Repulsive, *ri-pol'siv*, A. Lottacho; advarcho.
Reputation. *re-piu-tei'shon*, N. boren naum.
Request, *rikwest'*, V. Magunc.
Request, N. Magnem.
Require, *ri-kwa'iar*, v. Goroz asunc; magonc.
Requisite, *rek'wisit*, A. Gorjecho.
Requisition, *re-kui-zi'shon*, N. Magunem; apounnem.
Requital, *re-kwit'al*, N. Mam; faricponn.
Requite, *re-kwit'*, v. Mam diunc vo faric corunc.
Rescind, *re-sind'*, catrunc, toddunc, pinzunc.
Rescission, *re-si'shon*, N. Moddni; bhong.
Rescript, *re'skript*, N Hucum.
Rescue, *res'kiu*, V. Acantanlo vattaunc; suttca corunc.
Research, *ri-sorch'*, N. Choucosi, doriaft.
Research, V. Choucosi corunc.
Resemblance, *ri-zem'blens*, N. Soimbi gun, sor.
Resemble, *ri-zem'bl*, V. Sarco zaun asunc.
Resent, *ri-zent'*, V. Vaitt voronc vo dissonc; ragar zaunc.
Resentment, *ri-zent-ment*, N. vodd ocman munn sozmonnem.
Reservation, *re-zer-vei'shon*, N. Dovorni, thevni.
Reserve, *ri-zorv'*, V. Samballunc; apnnac dourunc.
Reserved, *re-zorvd*, A. Gupit; guttacho.
Reservoir, *ri'zor-var*, N. Tellem; baim.
Reside, *ri-zaid'*, V. Ravunc; asunc.
Residence, *re'zi-dens*, N. Thicannem, biddar; ravop.
Resign, *re-zain'*, V. Rajinama diunc, soddunc vopsun diunc; sosnicai geunc, Devacho khoxe zocto cholounc.
Resignation, *re-zig-nei'shon*, N. Sosnicai; ekvott; raji zavop.
Resin, *re'zin*, N. Rezin.
Resist, *re'zist*, V. Addaunc, add ulounc; nam attponc.
Resistance, *re-zis'tence*, Add ennem, addavni.
Resolute, *re'zo-liut*, A. Dhoiravont; thir; toiar.
Resolution, *re-zo-liu'shon*, N. Nicheu, rezolusaum.
Resolve, *re-zolv'*, V. Nicheu corunc; duvallunc; orthsangonc.
Resort, *ri-zort'*, V. Asro, adar magonc.
Resound, *ri-zaund*, V. Sadeunc.
Resource, *ri-sors'*, N. Adar, mozot, upai.

Respect, *ri-spect'*, V. Man diunc.
Respect, N. Man.
Respectability, *ri-spect'bi-li-ti*, N. Moriad; man.
Respectable, *ri-spect'ie-bl*, A. Manacho, abrucho.
Respected, *ri-spect'ed*, A. Manbogcho.
Respectful, *ri spect'ful*, A. Manadic; moriadio.
Respecting, *ri-spect'ing*, PREP. Visiant.
Respective, *ri-spect'iv*, A. Apnplo; ek-eicleacho. [Usvas.
Respiration, *re-spi-rei'shon*, N.
Respire, *ri-spaiar'*, V. Usvas soddunc.
Respite, *ris-pait*, A. Thoddea vogtachem somandan.
Response, *ri-spons'*, N. Zabab portipall.
Responsibility, *re-spons-i-bil-i-ti*, N. Zababdari, jamini.
Responsible, *ri-spons'i-bl*, A. Zabsali, zababdar.
Rest, *rest*, N. Nid; soucosai; visou; baki.
Rest, V. Soucosai bogunc; p tiennc
Resting-place, *rest'ing-ples*, N. Soucasai geunchi suat.
Restitution, *res-ti-tui'shon*, N. Restituisaum, porot dennem; faricponn.
Restless, *rest'less*, A. Uchamboll; soucasai naslolo'
Restoration, *res-to-rei'shon*, N. Porot dennem, faricpoun.
Restorative, *res-to-rei'tiv*, A. Gottai diuncho.
Restore, *ristor'*, V. Vapos diunc; boro corunc; gunn poddoso corunc.
Restrain, *ri-strem'*, V. Addunc; patti caddunc; samballunc.
Restraint, *ri-streint'*, N. Addcoll; addaunni.
Restrict, *re-strikt*, V. Anvlunc; mere bhitor dourunc; unno corunc. [lan.
Restricted, *re-strict'ed*, A. Osir;
Restriction, *re-stric'shon*, N. Anvlop, mit-mer; addcoll.
Result, *ri-zolt'*, N. Upjunc, utpon zaunc.
Result, N. Foll; xevott.
Resume, *re-zium'*, V. Porot suru corunc.
Resurrection, *re-sur-rec'shon*, N. jivontponn.
Resuscitate, *re-sus'i-teit*, V. Meleleantlc jivont corunc.
Retail, *ri-teil'*, V. Chilor vicunc.
Retail, *riteil'*, V. Chilor, thoddem thoddem vicop.
Retailer, *ri-teil'or*, N. Chilor vepari.
Retain, *ri-tein'*, V. Dovorunc; assunc.
Retaliate, *re-ta'li-eit*, V. Porteacportem diunc; faricponn geunc!
Retard, *ritard'*, V. Patti caddunc vo dourunc.
Retention, *ri-ten'shon*, N. Patti dourop; urop; mot.
Retentive, *ri-ten'tiv*, A. Dorcho, addauncho, gott mot.
Retentiveness, *ritentiv'ness*, N. Upddass.
Reticence, *re'tisens*, N. Vogo ravnom; munkeponn.
Reticulated, *re-tik-u-leit-ed*, A. Zallie saico. [zall.
Reticule, *re'ti-kuil*, N. Dacttem
Retinue, *re'ti-niu*, N. Boroborche sangati; durbar.
Retire, *ri'taiar*, V. Patti soronc, vochonc; soddunc.
Retired, *ri-taiurd'*, A. Ecsuro; cam-dando soddun boslolo.
Retirement, *ri-ta'iar-ment*, N. Ecsurponn; patti sorop.

Retort, *ri-tort',* v. Porteac portem diunc tonddar marunc.
Retort, n. Porto zabab; nolli.
Retouch, *ri-toch',* v. Nigut vo sarkem corunc.
Retrace, *ri-tres',* v. Patti portonc
Retract, *ri-trect',* v. Patti caddop.
Retractation, *ri-trec-tei'shon,* n. Patti caddop.
Retreat, *re-trit',* v. Patti caddunc; fariconn diunc.
Retreat, *re-trit',* v. Patti soronc.
Retreat, n. Reculhiment, asro.
Retrench, *ri-trench',* v. Unno khoroch corunc.
Retribution, *re-tri-biu'shon,* n. Pag, faricpon, muzuri.
Retrograde, *ret'ro-greid,* a. Patti choltolo, ultto.
Return, *ri-torn',* v. Porot diunc; ixeop diunc; Pavounc.
Return, n. Portonnem; ixeop.
Reunion, *re-iun'ion,* n. Porto ecvott; somandan.
Reunite, *re-iu'nait,* v. Novean ecttaim zaunc; isttogotin jieunc.
Reveal, *re-vil',* v. porgottunc ugddapem corunc.
Revel, *re'vel,* n. Khangiponn.
Revel, v. Jiv soddun borcunc; fg. vaitt khoxeanc lobdonc.
Revelation, *re-ve-lei'shon,* n. Ugddapi keleli vost; porgottnem.
Reveller, *ri'vel-ar,* n. Khangi.
Revenge *ri-venj',* v. Vingaus geunc.
Revenge, n. Vingans, faricponn.
Revenue, *re've-niu,* n. Utpon, yennem, vosul, *reseit.*
Reverberate, *re-ver'be-reit,* v. sadeunc, fancounc.
Reverberation *re-ver-be-rei'shon,* n. Sad; uzvadd poddnem.

Reverence, *Rev'e-rens,* v. Man diunc; nomoscar corunc.
Reverence, n. Man; nomoscar.
Reverend, *rev'er-end,* a. Man favo zalolo.
Reverie, *re'ver-i,* n. Soporn; utteo chintnam.
Reverse, *ri-vers',* v. Portun dourunc; bodlunc; nul corunc.
Reverse, n. Bodlop; portounem; ogddop.
Review, *re-viu,* v. Choucosen polleunc.
Review, n. Choucosi.
Revile, *ri-vail',* v. Galli sonvonc, vaitt ullounc. [nar.
Reviler, *ri-vail-ar,* n. Galli sou-
Reviling, *ri-vail'ing,* n. Gall; sirap.
Revise, *ri-vaiz',* v. Portun polleunc, sarkem corunc.
Reviser *ri-vaiz'ar,* n. Sarkem cornar.
Revision, *revijon,* n. Portun, barcaen pollovnem.
Revive, *ri-va-iv',* v. Portun jiv boronc; fg. nirvonn diunc.
Revocation *re-vok-ei'shon,* n. Nul corop; goddlolo caido moddnem.
Revoke, *ri-vok',* v. Null corunc; patti caddunc.
Revolt, *ri-volt',* v. Sercaracher portonc, bodlonc.
Revolution, *revoliu'shon,* n. Revolusaum; bodlop.
Revolutionary, *re-vo-lu'shon-a-ri,* n. Sercaracher kolponar.
Revolve, *ri-volv',* v. Bounvonc; boundaunc; chintunc.
Reward, *ri-ward'* n. Inam, prem.
Reward, v. Inam vo prem diunc.
Rhetoric, *re'to-ric,* n. Unch bhas.
Rheumatism, *riu'mat-izm,* n. vat, rematizm, vai.

Rhyme *raim*, N. ec-sarco sad akercheam utranim.
Rib, *rib*, N. Bor.
Ribald, *ri'bald*, A. Lucho.
Ribaldry, *li'bald-ri*, N. Khotte-ponn.
Ribbon, *rib'on*, N. Fint; naddo
Rice, *rais*, N. Tanddul, sit.
Rice-water, N. Nis, ton.
Rice-milk, N. Khir.
Rice-grela, N. Pez.
Rich, *rich*, A. Guirest; astic; dobajeacho.
Riches, *rich'iz*, N. Guirestcai; duddu-addco; fg. sompurnai.
Richness, *rich'ness*, N. Sompur-nai; dobazo.
Rick, *ric*, N. Ras; cuddem.
Rickets, *rik'ets*, N. Morlukechi pidda.
Rid, *rid*, V. suttca diunc; meclo zaunc.
Riddle, *rid'l*, N. Umanem; gutt.
Riddle, V. Umanneanim ulounc
Ride, *raid*, V. Goddear bosunc.
Rider, *raid'or*, N. Goddear bos-nar; choddavot volli.
Ridge, *rij*, N. Patt; pattos.
Ridicule, *ri'di-ki-ul*, V. Ansea-chem cortub; olki vost.
Ridiculous, *ri'dik-iu-las*, A. An-so beporvo favo zalolo.
Rifle, *rai'fl*, N. Arm.
Rifle, V. Nagounc.
Rift, *rift*, V. Futt, ver.
Rig, *rig*, V. Toiar corunc (tarum)
Right, *rait*, A. Sarco; nitivont; uzvo nitt.
Right, N. Sotea, nit.
Right, V. Sarkem corunc; mandunc,
Righteous, *rait'yas*, A. Nitivont; gunest, direntacho.
Righteousness, *rait'yas-ness*, N. Nit callzachem nirmollponn.
Rigid, *ri'jid*, A. Coddu; cottin; nisttur.
Rigidity, *ri-jid'i-ti*, N. Cottinai; nistturai.
Rigmarole, *rig'ma-rol*, N. Ecar-ec guddom.
Rigor, *rig'or*, N. Khorai; nisttu-rai.
Rim, *rim*, N. Deg.
Rime, *raim*, N. Don.
Rind, *ranid*, N. Sal.
Ring, *ring*, N, Mudi.
Ring, V. Vazounc.
Ringlet, *ring'let*, N. Nessonn.
Ringworm, *ring'worm*, N. Dad.
Rinse, *rins*, V. Duunc; gansunc.
Riot, *ra'iot*, N. Boball, ucham-bollai; dumxan.
Riotous, *ra'io-tas*. A. Dumxan-nacho; zogddecar.
Ripe. *raip*, A. Pico.
Ripen, *raip'on*, V. Picounc.
Ripeness, *raip'ness*, N. Picop'
Rise, *raiz*, V. Unch nachanc; uttonc; udeunc; jivont zaunc.
Rise, N. Uttop; choddop;
Rising, *raiz'ing*, N. Revolu-saum.
Risk, *risk*, N. Risc, zokom.
Risk, V. Riscar galunc, perigant galunc.
Rite, *rait*, N. Ceremon, igorje-chi rit,
Ritual, *ri'tu-al*, N. Ritichem pustoc.
Rival, *rai'val*, V. Pelea poros vorto zaunc; mosor corunc.
Rival, N. Pelea sarco dando cor-nar; mosri.
Rive, *raiv*, V. Follounc.
River, *riv'or*, N. Noim.
Rivet, *ri'vet*, N. Khillo.
Rivulet, *riv'u-let*, N. Dactti noim.
Road, *rod*, N. Marog; rosto.
Roam, *rom*, V. Parpoll bounvonc.

Roaming, *rom'ing*, A. Parpoll.
Roan, *ron*, A. Chineheohea rongacho; tambso.
Roar, *ror*, V. Goroz: dencaro galunc.
Roar, N, Goroz.
Roast, *röst*, V. Bazunc; fg. zollounc.
Rob, *rob*, V. Nagounc; chorunc.
Robber, *rob'ber*. N. Nagounno; chor.
Robbery, *rob'e-ri*. N. Nagonn; chori.
Robe, *rob*, N. Cobai; capot.
Robust, *ro-bust'*, A. Gott; fustti; Bolladic.
Robustness, *ro-bust'ness*. N. Gottai; dandgueponn.
Rock, *roc*, N. Khoddop.
Rock, V. Halounc-dolounc; zompounc. [uzo.
Rocket, *rock'et*, N. Icmoticho
Rocky, *ro'ki*, A. Fatracho; khoddopan aslolo.
Rod, *rod*, N. Boddi; bett; dando.
Rodomontade, *rod'o-mon-teid*, N. Khali boddai.
Rodomontade, V. Khali boddai ulounc.
Roe, *ro*, N. Bail-chitoll.
Rogation, *ro-gei'shon*, N. Magnem, praton.
Rogue, *rog*, N. Chor; vait munis; lobaddi.
Roguery, *rog'er-i*, N. Luchepon.
Roll, *rol*, V. Lolonc; covolunc.
Roll, N. Covlo.
Roller. *rol'ar*, N. Paut.
Rolling-pin, *ral'ing-pin*, N. Gunsunno.
Roman, *roman*, A. Romacho.
Romance. *ro'mans*, N. Caunim.
Romantic, *ro-man'tic* A. Ojeapancho; chamatcaracho.
Romp, *romp*, V. Uddonc, aumoriaodin khelulnc.
Romp, N. Uddop; nachop.
Roof, *ruf*, N. Gorachem dancnem, tect.
Roof, V. Gorac dancnem galunc.
Rook, *ruk*, N. Caullo.
Room, *rum*, N. Cudd; zago; suat.
Roomy, *rum'i*, A, Iscoll; vistarlolo.
Roost, *rust*, N. Tenkddi.
Root, *rut*, N. Pall.
Root, V. Pallam futtonc vo eunc.
Rooted, *rut'ed*, A. Laglolo; dornino laglolo.
Rope, *rop*, N. Dori, razu.
Ropy, *rop'i*, A. Lagcho; pancott.
Rosary, *roz'a-ry*, N. Cont; ruzai.
Rose, *roz*, N. Roz; gulabachem ful.
Rostrum, *ros'trum*, N. Bonch; tarvachi jib.
Rosy, *roz'i*, A. Gulabi-rongacho.
Rot, *rot*, Cusonc.
Rot, N. Cusop.
Rotate, *ro'teit*, V. Bountonnim vochonc.
Rotation, *ro-tei'shon*, N. Bounddi.
Rotten, *rot'n*, A. Cuslolo,
Rottenness, N. Cusop.
Rotundity, *ro-tund'i-ti*, N. Vadkulleponn.
Rough, *ruf*, A. Daddo; motto; corddo; uchamboll.
Roughness, *rof'ness*, N. Daddeponn; mottai; corddeponn.
Round, *raund*, A. Vaddcullo.
Round, AD. Bountonim.
Round, N. Bounddi; paunddo.
Round-about, A. Bounttonim.
Roundness, *raund'ness*, N. Vaddkulleponn
Rout, *rout*, V. Duspott corunc ecannem pirder corunc.
Route, N. Gondoll; urponz chombo.

Route, *rot*, N. Vatt; marog.
Routine, *ru-tin*, N. Sodancho, sovoimcho dando.
Rove, *rov*, V. Parpoll bouvonc.
Row, *ro*, N. Ar.
Row, *rau*, N. Zogddem; marfar.
Row, *ro*, V. Vole tanddunc.
Rowdy, *rau'di*, N. Uchamboll, zogddecar.
Royal, *ro'ial*, A. Raiacho; voddponnacho.
Royalty, *roi'al-ti*, N. Razvoddki.
Rub, *rob*, V. Gansunc; rogddunc.
Rubber, *robbar*, N. Robor.
Rubbing, *robbing*, N. Gansop.
Rubbish, *rob'ish*, N. Cochro; camanc poddonasleleo vostu.
Rubric, *ru-bric*, N. Tamddi mati; tambddim acxeram, caide.
Ruby, *ro'bi*, A. Tambsu.
Ruby, N. Mannik.
Ruck, *rok*, N. Urponz.
Rudder, *rod'ar*, N. Sukannem.
Ruddy, *rad i*, A. Tambdoch.
Rude, *rud*, A. Jougli; corddo.
Rudiment, *ru'di-ment*, N. Poili sicoun.
Ruffian, *rof'i-an*, N. Luttcar; lucho.
Rug, *rog*, N. Camboll; bornus.
Rugged, *rog'ed*, A. Corkotto; coranduecho.
Ruin, *ru'in*, V. Vibad vo nas corunc; bosmunc.
Ruinous, *ru'in-as*, A. Lusconacho; bongostoll zalolo.
Rule, *rul*, V. Cholounc; razvoddki corunc.
Rule, N. Regr; caido.
Ruler, *rul'ar*, A. Adikari, rejer cornar.
Rumble, *rom'bl*, V. Gorgorunc.
Ruminate, *ru-min'eit*, V. Rovont corunc, portun portun chintunc.
Rummage, *rum'eij*, V. Sodunc; bus geunc.
Rumour, *riu'mor*, N. Pukaro khobor.
Run, *run*, Danvunc; pollonc.
Run, N. Daum.
Runaway, *run-ei've*, A. Poupoto.
Rundlet, *round'let*, N. Lan pip.
Runlet, *ron'let*, Supurli noim.
Rupee, *ru-pi'*, N. Rupoi.
Rupture, *rop'char*, N. Moddop; vingddop.
Rural, *ru'ral*, A. Gauntti.
Ruse, *ruz*, N. Nadd; naddgeponn.
Rush, *rosh*, V. Daumdavim vochunc; buddonc; rigonc.
Rush, N. Bollist dauni.
Rust, *rost*, N. Kolomb.
Rust, V. Kolomb manddop.
Rustic, *ros'tik*, A. Gauntti; bondro.
Rusticate, *ros'ti-keit*, V. Gauvant ravonc.
Rusticity, *rus'tis-i-ti*, N. Bondreponn.
Rusty, *rost'i*, A. Kolmbelolo.
Rye, *rai*, N. Lan goum.
Ryot, *rai'ot*, N. Roit; porza.

S

Sabbath, *sa'bath*, N. Sunvar, sabat.
Sabre, *sei'ber*, N. Tolvar, torsad.
Sacerdotal, *sa-ser-dot'al*, A. Sacerdoticho; gurucho.
Sack, *sec*, N. Gonn; Potem; lutt.
Sack-cloth, *sec-cloth*, N. Mottem lugot, pirajitachem vostur.
Sacrament, *sa'cra-ment*, N. Sacrament.
Sacred, *se'kred*, A. Povitr, benjar kelolo; consagrad kel-lo.
Sacrifice, *sa'cri-fais*, N. Sacrifis; bhett.
Sacrifice, V. Bhettounc; somorpiunc.

Sacrilege, *sa'cri-lej*, N. Povitr vostunchem bastaunem, sacrilej.
Sacrilegious, *sa'cri-le-jias*, A. Povitr vostu bosttauncho; fottkiro.
Sacristan, *sa'krist-an*, N. Sankristaum.
Sacristy, *sa'krist-i*, N. Sankrist.
Sad, *sed*, A. Chintest; dukest.
Sadden, *sed'n*, V. Chintes corunc; ducounc; coisttaunc.
Saddle, *sed'l* N. Jin.
Saddle, V. Jin galunc.
Sadness, *sed'ness*, N. Khont; dukh.
Safe, *sef*, N. Loconddachi pett; bondabostichi snat.
Safe, A. uskea meclo; thir, patienecho.
Safe-conduct, *sef-con'doct*, N. Zamin.
Safe-guard, *sef'gard*, N. Upai; raconn.
Safety, *sef'ti*, N. Segurans, bachavi.
Saffron, *saf'ron*, N. Holod.
Sagacious, *sa-gei'shas*, A. Chotur, barcaecho, budvont.
Sagacity, *sa-gas'i-ti*, N. Chotrai, uxearki, bud.
Sago, *sei'go*, N. Sago.
Sail, *seil*. N. Sidd.
Sailer, *seil'er*, N. Tarum.
Sailor, *seil'or*, N. Kalasi; tarvacho chacor.
Saint, *saint*, N. Bagevont, sant.
Saintly, *saint'li*, A. Bagivontaporim.
Sake, *seik*, N. Passun vo pasot.
Salad, *sa'lad*, N. Salad; Coromb.
Salary, *sa'la-ri*, N. Pag; muzri.
Sale, *sel*, N. Vicri; loilaum.
Salient, *sa'li-ent*, A. Mukhia.
Saline, *sa-lain'*, A. Khar.
Saliva, *sa'lai-va*, N. Timpi, nitu, [lau.
Sallow, *sel'o*, A. Holdduvo.
Salmon, *sa'mon*, N. Xeutto.
Salt, *solt*, N. Mitt; fg. barcai.
Salt, V. Mittac galunc vo launc.
Saltish, *solt'ish*. A. Kharso.
Salt-mine, *solt'main*, N. Mittachi khonn.
Salt-pit, N. Agor.
Saltpetre, *solt'pi-ter*, N. Soltpiter, khoddeanchem mitt.
Salubrious, *sa-lu'bri-as*, A. Bolaikecho, nerozi; pushtticar.
Salutary, *salutari*, A. Bolaikecho; adavacho.
Salutation, *sa-lu-tei'shon*, N. Noman; nomoscar.
Salute, *saliu't*, V. Salam—, nomoscar corunc; bessaum diunc.
Salvation, *sal-vei'shon*, N. Soddvonn, salvasaum; udargoti.
Salve, *salv*, N. Rogddopachem vocot.
Same, *sem*, A. Toch.
Sample, *sempl*, A. Nomuno.
Sanctification, *sanc-ti-fi-kei'shon*, N. Bagevont ponn.
Sanctify. *sangk-ti-fai*, V. Bagevont vo povitr corunc.
Sanction, *sangk'shon*, N. Sasan, praman, cobuli.
Sanctity, *sangk'ti-ti*, N. Santiponn, bagevontponn.
Sanctuary, *sangk'chu-a-ri*, N. povitr zago; kirtichi igroz.
Sand, *send*, N. Reum.
Sand, reum launc; reven dampunc
Sandal, *san'dal*, N. Vann; kaddavo.
Sandy, *send'i*, A. Renvall.
Sane, *sen*, A. Bolaikent aslolo; piso noi.
Sanguinary, *sang'gion-a-ri*, A Rogtaborit; umalleacho.
Sanity, *san'i-ti*, N. Sarki mot.
Sap, *sep*, N. Ros; dik.

Sap. *sep*, V. Pondchean pokrunc.
Sapid, *se'pid*. A. Ruchicho.
Sapient, *sa'pi-ent*, A. Xanno, bud-vont; videavont.
Sapless, *sep'less*, N. Diknaslolo; fg. cappo.
Sapphire, *saf'fiar*, N. Nil.
Sarcasm, *sar'cazm*, N. Kebaddam, Khelkulam.
Sarcophagus, *sarcof'agus*, N. Mornachi pett (fatrachi).
Sardine. *sar'din*, N. Tarlo.
Sardonic *sar-don-ik*, A. Tondda purto; fottkiro.
Sardonyx, *sar'do-niks*, A. Gome-dacho; bollan caddlolo hanso.
Sash, *sesh*, N. Potto.
Satan, *seit'an*, N. Soitan, deuchar; bhut.
Satanic, *sa-tan'ik*. A. Deuncharacho.
Satellite, *sa'tel-lait*, N. Upagraha; fg. lambto. podo.
Satiate, *sa'shi-eit*, V. Dadosi corunc; borunc.
Satiety, *sa-tai'e-ti*, N. Dadoscai.
Satin, *se'tin*, N. Setim, rosim.
Satire. *sa'taiar*, N. Borop, ogunnachim khebaddam corun.
Satiric, *sa-ti'ric*, A. Moscoreancho.
Satisfaction, *sa-tis-fac'shon*, N. Faricponn; pirajit; sontos.
Satisfactorily, *sa-tis-fec'to-ri-li*, AD. Dadoscaen; sumar.
Satisfactory, *sa-tis-fec'to-ri*, A. Dados corcho; laik; sumar.
Saturate, *sa'tur-eit*, N. Bizounc, umllunc; borunc.
Sauce. *sos*, N. Sas; Chetni.
Saucer, *so'sor*, N. Pir.
Saucy, *sos'i*, A. Urmott; coddvo.
Sausage, *so'seij*, N. Lingis.
Savage, *sav'eij*, A. Zongli, monzati sarco; sico naslolo.
Savageness, *se'vej-ness*, N. Ranvottponn, nistturai.

Save, *sev*, V. Racunc, sambal-lunc; sodvon corunc.
Save, PRP. Sivai.
Saving, *sev'ing*, A. Fiance aslolo.
Saving-bank, *sev'ing-bank*, N. Duddu sugur corcho banc.
Saviour, *sev'yor*, N. sorvonddar; taroc.
Savour, *sa'vor*, N. Suad; ruch.
Savoury, *sa'vo-ri*, A. Suadic, ruchicho.
Saw, *so*, N. Korvont.
Saw, V. Chirunc.
Saw-dust, *so'das*, N. Pudd; dull,
Saw-fish, N. Visvon.
Say. *sei*, V. Sangunc, munnonc.
Saying, *sei'ing*, N. Sangnni. munni
Scab, *skeb*, N. Khoroz.
Scabbard, *skab'ard*, N. Torsadichem potem.
Scabby, *skeb'bi*, A. Khorjicho.
Scaffold, *skaf'old*, N. Goll.
Scald, *skold*, N. Ujeacho fodd.
Scale, *skeil*, N. Tagddi; khovlam.
Scale, V. Khovlam caddunc.
Scalp, *skolp*, N. Matcachi cat.
Scaly, *skel'i*, A. Koulam aslolo.
Scamp, *skemp*, N. Lobaddi, fotkiro, nagonnno.
Scamper, *skemp'ar*. N. Pollun vochunc.
Scan, *sken*, V. Mappa pormonnem vochunc.
Scandal. *sken'dal*. N. Scandl, khotti dek: loz; bodlam.
Scandalize, *sken'dal-aiz*, V. Khoti dek diunc; vait disosem corunc; dukh bogonc.
Scandalus, *sken'do-las*, A. Khoti dek diuncho.
Scanty, *skent'i*, A. Motvo; aprup; osir; imto.
Scantiness, *skent'i-nes*, N. Motvoponn, imttoponn; unneponn.
Scapegrace, *skep'gres*, N. Fikir naslolo munis.

Scapular, *skap'u-lar*, N. Bentin.
Scar, *skar*, N. Mau.
Scarce, *skers*, A. Unno ; aprup.
Scarcely, *skers'li*, AD. Rigvench; teach vellar.
Scarcity *skers'i-ti*, N. Unnau ; ducoll.
Scarf, *skarf*, N. Xelo ; lens.
Scarify, *ska'ri-fai*, V. Bocrun rogot caddunc.
Scarlet, *skar'let*, A. Bhou tambdo.
Scatheless, *sketh,les*, A. Noistta vinn.
Scatter, *sket'ar*, V. Simpddaunc ; simponc.
Scavenger. *ska'vin-jar*, N. Marog zaddnar; bougi.
Scene, *sin*, N. Song ; Nattoc ; distt.
Scenery, *sin'eri*, N. Dacoun ; dristti vishar.
Scent, *sent*, N. Pormoil.
Scent, V. Pormoil—, domdom galunc.
Sceptic, *sep'tic*, N. Dubavi.
Scepticism, *sep'ti-si-zm* N. Dubau.
Sceptre, *sep'tor*, N. Rajkath.
Schedule, *shed'iul* N. Potli, list.
Scheme, *skim*, N. Plan, opiniaum.
Schism *sizm*, N. Dhormbhed, xastrbhed ; futt.
Schismatic, *siz-mat'ic*, A. Dhormantlo cusin sorlolo.
Scholar, *sko'lar*, N. iscolcho burgo ; zannar.
Scholastic, *sko-last'ic*, A. Videa sallicho.
School, *scul*, N. Iscol, sikcho zago ; pattlau.
Sciatic, *si-a'tic*, N. Ponettachi dukh.
Science, *sai'ens*, N. Videa ; xastr; zanvai.
Scientific, *sai-en-ti'fic*, A. Videcho ; videvont.
Scimitar, *si'mi-tar*, A. Mottvi bagouleli torsad ; coiti.
Scintillate, *sin'til-leit*, V. Uzvadd diunc. [siclolo.
Sciolist, *si'ol-ist*, N. Voilea voir
Scion, *si'on*, N. Ankri ; fg. sonsticho.
Scissors, *siz'arz*, N. Cator.
Scoff, *skof*, N. Moscoreo.
Scoff, V. Moscoreo—, khebaddam corunc. [unc.
Scold, *skold*, V. Hinsunc ; besttaunc.
Scolding, *skold'ing*, N. Besttaunem.
Scolopendra, *sko-lo-pen'dra* N. Vagonni
Scoop, *skup*, V. Pocrunc.
Scope, *skop*, N. Xevott ; suat.
Scorch, *scorch*, V. Ulpaunc ; sucounc.
Score, *skor*, N. Gantt ; ixcop ; rinn.
Score, V. Lann dourunc.
Scoria, *sco'ri-a*, N. Coir ; gu,
Scorn, *scorn*, V. Beporva corunc.
Scorn, N. Beporvo ; desprez.
Scorpion, *skor'pi-on*, N. Vinchu.
Scot, *scot*, N. Tex ; fallo.
Scotch, *scoch*, N. Catrop.
Scoundrel, *skaun'dral*, N. Olko munis, lofangi.
Scour, *skour* N. Gansun nittol corunc.
Scourge, *skorj*, N. Jerbond, mar ; fg. sicsha.
Scout, *skaut*, N. Bedi.
Scowl, *scaul*, V. Askiteancher mireo galunc, tonddar calloc galunc.
Scraggy, *skreg'i*, A. Korbotto.
Scramble, *screm'bl*, V. Hatampaiunim choddunc.
Scrap, *screp*, N. Cuddco.
Scrape, *skreip*, N. Acant ; conisttai.
Scrape, V. Cantunc.

Scraper, *sreip'ar*, N. Cantnem.
Scratch, *screch*, V. Bocrunc; corpunc: fapsunc.
Scrawl, *scrol*, V. Vaneddemtineddem borounc.
Scream, *scrim*, V. Killonch marunc; voddlean roddonc.
Scream, N. Killonch; bob:
Screech, *scrich*. V. Killonch marunc.
Screen, *scrin*, N. Dancnem; pordo; asro.
Screen, V. Raconc; samballunc; lipounc. [condi.
Screw, *scru*. N. Mousud bonvor-
Scribble, *scrib'bl*, V. Coseim borounc.
Scribe, *scraib*, N. Boroinar.
Scrip, *scrip*, N. Chitt; borop.
Scripture, *scrip'char*, N. Povitr pustoc.
Scrofula, *scro-fu'la*, N. Catmau.
Scroll, *scrol*, N. Coullo.
Scrub, *scrob*, V. Gansunc.
Scruple, *scro'pl*, N. Dubau; tondre; churchure; iscrupl.
Scruple, V. Dubavonc.
Scrupulous, *scro'pu-las*, A. Dubavi, tondreant aslolo.
Scrutiny, *scro'ti-ni*, N. Barcaen sodnem; poricxa.
Scud, *scud*, V. Varea borobor ubon vochonc.
Scuffle, *scof'l*, N. Zogddem.
Scull, *scoll*, N Cot-tem.
Sculptor, *scolp'tor*, N. Silpi; cantoinar.
Sculpture, *scolp'char*, N. Cantounchi videa.
Sculpture, V. Cantounc.
Scum, *scom*, N. Coir; fenno.
Scurf, *scorf*, N. Khorbem.
Scurrility, *scu'ril-i-ti*, N. Bursepomn.
Scurritous, *scu'rit-as*, A. Loz naslolo, pozddo.
Scurvy, *scor'vi*, N. Urvur.
Scutcheon, *scuch'-on*, N. Dhal.
Scythe, *saith*, N. Coito; coiti.
Sea, *si*, N Doria, somdir.
Sea, V. Doriacho vo doriantlo.
Seal, *sil*, N. Mhor; fg. gutt.
Seal, V. Mhor marunc; dancunc, bond corunc.
Sealing-wax, N. Lac.
Seam, N. Don deganchi sionn.
Sear, *ser*, V. Sucounc; corpaunc.
Search, *sorch*, V. Sodunc; polleunc; vicharunc.
Searching, *serch'-ing*, N. Sodop; vicharop.
Season, *si'-zon*, N. Vorsacho call vo vantto; vell.
Season, V. Fonna diunc; toiar corunc; mellounc; gott corunc.
Seasonable, *si'-zn-ie-bl*, A. Favo tea vellar.
Seasonableness, *si'zn-ie-bl-ness*, N. Favo te vell.
Seasoning, *si'zn-ing*, N. Fonna divop.
Seasoned, *si'zn-d*, A. Fonna galolo; toiar; gott.
Seat, *sit*, N. Bosca; sisonn; suat.
Seat, V. Bossounc; bosorc.
Seated, *sit'ed*. A. Boslolo.
Secede, *se-sid'*, V. Bhair soronc eca associasaunVantlo etc.
Seclude, *se-cliud'*, V. Bhair galun dampunc.
Seclusion, *se-cliu'jon*, N. Bhair galnem; ecsurponn.
Second, *se'kend*, A. Dusro.
Second, N. Khinn.
Second, V. Mozot diunc.
Secondary, *se'kend-ar-ri*, A. Unne gorjecho.
Secondly, *se'kend-li*, AD. Dusre suater.
Secrecy, *si'cre-si*, A. Gutt; ecsurponn.

Secret, *si'cret,* N. Gupit vo gutt-acho.
Secretary, *se'cre-ta-ri,* N. Munsi; pordani, secretar.
Secrete, *se-cret',* V. Lipounc.
Secretly, *se'cret-li,* AD. Guttan, connanc gomoi nastanam.
Section, *sek'shon,* N. Vautto.
Secular, *se'kiu-lar,* A. Sounsa-ri ; sounsaracho.
Secularize, *se'cular-aiz,* V. Chal-tea camano launc.
Secure, *se-kiu'ar,* A. Soucasae-cho, risk naslolo, gott ; khoro.
Secure, V. Gott dorunc ; thara-vunc.
Security, *se-kiu'ri-tti,* N. Zamm ; racon; soucasai.
Sedan, *se-dan',* N. Palki.
Sedate, *sedeit',* V. Thonddaunc, somandan corunc.
Sedateness, *se-deit'ness,* N. Ni-danai.
Sedative, *se-deit'iv,* A. Dukh devouncho, thondd corcho.
Sedentary, *se'den-ta-ry,* A. Bos-cho.
Sediment, *se'di-ment,* N. Mur, khar, maddi.
Sedition, *se-di'shon,* N. Bonddai. rajbhong. [fiturio.
Seditious, *se'di-shas,* A. Bandi,
Seduce, *se-dius',* V. Naddune, fitrunc, bulounc.
Seducer, *se-dius'ar,* N. Fuslainar, naddnar bulounno.
Seduction, *sidok'shon.* N. Fus-launi, nadd.
Seductive, *si-dok'tiv,* A Fot-kiro ; bulouncho.
Sedulity, *se-du'li-ti.* N. Minotin vaur cornem.
Sedulous *se'du-las,* A. Minoti ; uxar; zagrut.
See. *si,* V. Polleunc ; somzonc ; zoton corunc.
Seed, *sid,* N. Bim ; rov ; fg. sonsat.
Seek, *sik,* V. Sodunc ; axea co-runc ; xevott asunc.
Seem, *sim,* V. Disonc.
Seemliness, *sim'liness,* N. Rup; moriad.
Seemly, *sim'li,* A. Zocto ; favo tosolo.
Seer, *ser,* N. Profet.
Seethe, *sith,* V. Khotkotunc ; attonc.
Segment, *seg'ment,* N. Bhag.
Segregate, *se'gre-geit,* V. Vegllo corunc vo dourunc ; vinchun caddunc.
Seine, *sen,* N. Eo voddlem masli; marchem zall.
Seize, *siz,* V. Dorunc ; lagunc; zopti corunc.
Seizing, *siz'ing,* N. Dorop.
Seldom, *sel'dom,* Ad. Kernaim.
Select, *si-lekt',* V. Vinchun cad-dunc.
Selection, *si-lek'shon,* N. Vin-chop vo vinchui.
Self, *self,* PRO. Apunn.
Selfish, *sel'fish,* A. Apnnacho mog cortolo.
Self-control, *self-control'* N. Aple voir addauni, suddalai.
Self-denial, *self-di-nai'al,* N. Apnnac negar zavop.
Sell, *sell,* V. Vicunc.
Seller, *sel'ar,* N. Vicpar.
Selling, *sel'ing,* N. Vicri.
Selvage, *sel'vej,* N. Lugttachi deg.
Semblance, *semb'lens,* N. Sar-kem ; fg. saulli.
Semicircle, *se'mi-ser-kl,* N. Cir-culachem ord.
Seminary, *se'min-a-ri,* N. Simi-nar, padrinchi sall.
Semitone, *se'mi-ton,* N. Ardo tallo vo ordem vazop.

Senate, *se'neit*, N. Rajasabha; parlamentachem gor.

Senator, *se'neit-ar*, N. Senadacho membr.

Send, *send*, V. Daddunc, pattounc. [voddlo.

Senior, *si'ni-or*, N. Malgoddo;

Sensation, *sen-sei'shon*, N. Bagop.

Sense, *sens*, N. Visovo, bud; orth.

Sensible, *sens'i-bl*, A. Diso sarco; visovo aslolo; budvont; baric.

Sensitive, *sens'i-tiv*, A. Visovo aslolo; movall.

Sensibility, *sens'i-bil-i-ti*, N. Visove, bogchi socot.

Sensual, *sens'u-al*, A. Visoveancho; cuddicho, modacho; vaitt khoxeanc lobdololo.

Sensuality, *sens-u-al'i-ti*, N. Cuddichoo khoxeo; burseponn; pozddeponn.

Sentence, *sen'tens*, N. Opar, munni; formonn, sentens.

Sentence, V. Formonn marunc.

Sententious, *sen-ten'shas*, A. Oparincho; utram meznn uloitolo.

Sentiment, *sen'-ti-ment*, N. Movallai; bhog, mon; munxeponn-

Sentimental, *sen-ti-men'-tal*, A. Bhogcho; movallauncho.

Sentinel, sentry, *sen'ti-nel*, *sen'-tri*, N. Raenno, paro cornar.

Separable, *se'-pa-rei-bl*, A. Veglo cori sarco.

Separability, *se'-pa-re-bil-i-ti*, N. Veglem cori sarkem.

Separate, *se'-pa-reit*, A. Vingodd; veglo.

Separate, V. Veglo galunc; vantto corunc, pois dourunc.

Separately, *se'-pa-reit-li*, AD. Cusin, dosim, veglo.

Separation, *se-pa-rei'-shon*, N. Cusin cornem, caddnem; veglachar.

Sepulchre, *se'-pul-kor*, N. Fond; sepulcr.

Sequence, *si'-kwens*, Pattlao; foll.

Sequestration, *si-kwes-trei'shon*, N. Zopti.

Seraph, *se'-raf*, N. Serafim.

Serenade, *se-re-neid*, N. Gora bhair ratchem gaien.

Serene, *si-rin'*, A. Sitoll, nitoll,

Serenity, *se-rin'-i-ti*, Nitollai; nitoll mollob; fg. soucasai.

Serf, *sorf*, N. Chacor; gulam.

Sergeant, *sar'-jent*, N. Havaldar. sarjent.

Series, *si'-ri-iz*, N. Har; fg. sancoll; zomo.

Serious, *si'-rii-as*, A. Baradic; gorjecho; nibor, khor.

Seriously, *si'-ri-as-li*, AD. Khoreponnim; bharim asun.

Seriousness, *si'-ri-as-ness*, N. N. Bhar; zokom.

Serpent, *ser'-pent*, N. Sorop.

Serpentina, *ser'-pen-tina*, N. Sapus, serpemtin.

Serum, *se'-rom*, N. Tak.

Servant, *ser'vant*. Chacor, xovoc.

Serve, *sorv*, N. Chacri corunc; upcaronc.

Serviceable, *sor'-vis-ic-bl*, A. Upcaro sarco; gorjecho; adavacho.

Servile, *sor'-vail*, A. Holko, unno.

Servility, *sor-vil'-i-ti*, N. Gulamponn. [junt.

Session, *se'-shon*, N. Sosaum,

Set, *set*, A. Khondit; caidea pormonnem.

Set, N. Dis poddop; zaiteo vostu mellun ek aki.

Set, V. Galunc; launc; sarkem corunc; nittier galunc.

Setting, *set'ing*, N. Ostomti.

Settle, *set'tl*, V. Ixeop-cont chucounc; faric corunc; cazar corunc; bosonc; pondac bosonc.

Settled, *set'tled,* A. Khondit.
Settlement, *set'l-ment,* N. Thican cornem ; dot; cazar.
Settler, *set'lor,* N. Porkea gauvantlo eun raunar.
Seven, *se'ven,* N. Sat.
Sever, *se'ver.* V. Doxim corunc.
Several, *se'ver-al,* A. Thoddo ; sobar.
Severe, *se-vi'er,* A. Cottin ; khor ; darun.
Severity, *se-ve'ri-ti,* N. Cottinai; nibrai ; bazoddai.
Sew, *su,* V. Siunc.
Sewer, *siu'or,* N. Gottor.
Sex, *seks,* Dadlo vo bail ; zat.
Sacristan, *sa'cris-tan,* N. Sankristaum.
Shabbiness, *sheb'i ness,* N. Nospachi dublocai, imtteponn.
Shabby, *sheb'i,* A. Chindi ; falli.
Shade, shadow, *sheid, sha'dow,* N. Saulli ; fg. calloc ; porddo ; asro.
Shade, V. Racunc ; saulli corunc.
Shaft, *shaft,* N. Bhali ; thorum ! khambo.
Shag, *sheg,* N. Camboll ; lovenchem lugott.
Shake, *sheik,* V. Alounc ; camponnc.
Shallow, *sha'lou,* N. Utoll asloli suat.
Shallow. A. Utoll.
Sham, *shem.* N. Thoc ; fott; dong
Sham, A. Dongi, fotkiro.
Shambless, *shem'bls,* N. Cosaianchi angodd.
Shame, *sheim,* N. Loz ; opman.
Shame, V. Loz disunc.
Shameful, *sheim'ful,* A. Lojist vo ocmanacho ; alxic.
Shameless, *sheim'less,* A. Pozddo ; loz naslolo.
Shamelessness, *sheim'less-ness,* N. Loz nasuem.
Shampoo, *sham'pu,* V. Rogdunc; damunc.
Shank, *shenk,* N. Paim.
Shape, *sheip,* N. Rup , form nomunno.
Shapeless, *sheip'less,* N. Rup naslolo.
Shard, *shard,* N. Coili.
Share, *sher,* N. Vantto ; zogoll.
Shark, *sharc,* N. Mogor (masli) fg. scrupl naslolo munis.
Sharp, *sharp.* A. Dhar aslolo ; domsacho. fg. bank ; ambott ! ducouncho.
Sharpen, *sharp'in,* V. Pazunc ; dhar caddunc.
Sharper, *sharp'ar,* N. Thoc ; dongi.
Sharpness, *sharp'ness,* N. Dhar; fg. barcai.
Shatter, *shat'or,* V. Cuddkean cuddeo corunc ; khalto corunc.
Shave, *shev,* V. Kadd caddunc ; tasnni corunc.
Shaving, *shev'ing,* N. Capnni.
Shawl, *shol,* N. Shal.
She, *shi,* N. Ronti.
Sheaf, *shif* N. Penddi ; maulli.
Shear, *sher,* V. Loum capunc.
Shears, *shers,* N. Cator.
Sheath, *shith,* N. Potem.
Sheathe *shid,* V. Potcaut galunc.
Shed *shed,* N. Mattou.
Shed, V. Vanvounc ; zoddounc.
Sheep, *ship,* N. Bocri, xeli.
Sheep-fold, *ship'fold* N. Bocreancho gotto vo mangor
Sheepish, *shep'ish,* A. Bollo ; piso.
Sheer, *sher,* A. Khali ; Coddso, deunti.
Sheet; *shit,* N. Antunchi vol ; fol, cagot.
Shelf, *shelf,* N. Khon ; chouc.
Shell, *shell,* N. simpi ; congo ; cotti.

Shell. v. Simpi caddunc
Shell-fish, N. Khubo.
Shelter, *shel'tor*, N. Asor ; adar ; mattou.
Shelter, v. Racanc ; samballunc; adar diunc.
Shelve, *shelv*, v. Konnant dourunc ; bhair uddounc.
Shepherd. *shep'ard*, N. Gounlli.
Shield, *shild*, N. Racon ; asro.
Shift, *shift*, v. Bodlunc ; ennem tennem alounc.
Shift, N. Upai, hicmot ; cholli.
Shifty, *shift'i*, A. Hicmoticho.
Shin, *shin*, N. Paiancho nollo ; donko.
Shine, *shain*, v. Zogzogunc ; porzollunc.
Shining *shain'nig*, A. Zogzoguit.
Ship, *shep*, N. Tarum.
Ship, v, Tarvar chacrec ravonc, tarvar boson vochonc.
Shipwreck, *shep'rec*, N. Tarvachem futtop.
Shipwreck, v. Tarum futtonc vo buddonc;
Shirt, *shart*. N. Komis.
Shiver, *shiv'ar*, v. Camponc, thortorunc.
Shivering, *shiv'er-ing*, N. Campero, thortoro.
Shoal, *shol*, N. Zomo ; ras ; reveachi thodd.
Shock, *shock*, N. Ang caddunc ; addlonc.
Shock, N. Ang caddnem.
Shocking, *shoc'ing*, A. Ducouncho ; canttaloacho.
Shoe, *shu*, N. Mocho ; nal.
Shoe, v. Nal marunc.
Shoe-maker, *shu-meik'ar*, N. Mochi ; chamar.
Shoot, *shut*, v. Far marunc, soddunc.
Shoot, N. Ancri.
Shop, *shop*, N. Loz, posro.
Shop-keeper, N. Posorcar ; lozcar.
Shore, *shor*, N. Vell ; todd.
Short, *short*, A. Mottvo ; lan, thoddo.
Short-sighted, *short-sait'ed*, A. Lagsile distticho.
Shortcoming, *short'com-ing* N Unnepone ; chuc ; guneaum.
Shorten, *short'n*, v. Mottvo vo unno corunc.
Shortly, *short'li* Ad. Vegim ; thoddeam utraraim.
Shortness, *short'-ness*, N. Mottvepone.
Shot, *shot*, N. Gulli ; far.
Shoulder, *shold'-ar*, N. Khand.
Shoulder-blade, N. Buz.
Shout, *shaut*, v. Uel marunc, bobatt marunc.
Shove, *shov*, v. Lottunc, mucar daunddaunc.
Shovel, *shov'l*, N. Cailato.
Show, *shou* v. Dacounc ; sicounc.
Show, N. Dacou ; disop; dobazo.
Shower, *shaw'-or*, N. Pausachi doddog.
Shower, v. Udarponnan diunc ; paus poddonc.
Showy, *shou'-i*, A. Ahancari ; dobajeacho.
Shred, *shred*, v. Fallio vo chur corunc.
Shrew, *shru*, N. Zogddecar bail.
Shrewd, *shrud*, A. Baric ; chotraecho.
Shrewdness, *shrud'-ness*, N. Farcai ; chotrai.
Shriek, *shric*. N. Killonch ; kindri
Shrill, *shrill*, A. Nakiam (uloup): baric.
Shrimp, *shrimp*, N. Galmbi ; suncott.
Shrine, *shrain*, N. Povitr relic galchi pett.
Shrink, *shrink*, v. Anvlonc; patti soronc.

Shrivel, *shriv'-el*, v. (Tondd) vaneddem corunc.
Shroud, *shraud*, N. Khoponn.
Shroud, v. Guttiaunc.
Shrub, *shrob*, N. Jilcutt.
Shrug, *shrog*, v. Buz uclunc.
Shudder, *shud'-or*, v. Thortorunc, camponc.
Shudder, N. Camp, thortoro.
Shuffle, *shaf'-fl*, v. Beli corunc, misllunc; vaneddo cholonc.
Shun, *shan*, v. Canttallon pois corunc, chuconc.
Shunning, *shan'ing* N. Chucop.
Shut, *shat*, V. Dancunc, boudcorunc; veddo galunc.
Shutters, *shat'ors*, N. Zonelanchim daram.
Shy *shai*, A. Logistt; Bezudd.
Shyness, *shai'ness*, N. Bidda; bem.
Sibilant, *si'bi-lant*, A. Fusfuscho.
Sick, *sik*, A. Piddest, vaittacar.
Sicken, *si'kn*, V. Carandai corunc, bejar corunc.
Sickle, *si-kl*, N. Coiti.
Sickle. *sik'li*, A. Bolaiki naslolo.
Sickness, *sik'ness*, N. Pidda; vaitt.
Side, *said*, N. Cus; coddvoll.
Side-board, *said'bord*, N. Samounn dovorchem mez.
Sidelong, *said'long*, A. Vaneddo.
Siege, *sij*, N. Veddo.
Siesta, *sies'ta*, N. Donparchem nidop.
Sieve, *siiv*, N. Chaln.
Sieve, v. Challunc.
Sigh, *sai*, v. Suscar soddunc.
Sigh, N. Suscar.
Sight, *saitt*, N. Distt; rup.
Sign, *sain*, N. Curu; Khunna.
Sign, v. Naum borounc vo asinad corunc.
Signal, *sig'nol*, N. Nixanni; khunna.
Signal, v. Sinal corunc.
Signal, A. Vodd; chotrai-favo zalolo.
Signalize, *sig'nal-aiz*, V. Apnnac famad corunc.
Signature. *sig-nei-char*, N. Asinad, dostocot.
Signet, *sig'net*, N. Mhorechi mudi.
Significant, *sig-ni'fi-cant*, A. Arth aslolo; bharim.
Signification, *sig-ni-fi-kei'shon*, A. Bharim.
Signify, *sig'ni-fai*, v. Orth assunc; somzon eunc; bhar asunc.
Silence, *sai'lens*, N. Vogem ravop; moneponn.
Silence, v. Vogo ravounc; gopchip ravounc.
Silent, *sai'lent*, A. Vogo; gop chip.
Silently, *sai'lent-li*, AD. Choriam; guttan.
Silk, *silk*, N. Sed, Rosim.
Silk, A. Sedacho.
Silk-worm, *silk'worm*, N. Resmacho kiddo.
Sill, *sill*, N. Daracho vato.
Sillines, *sil'-li-ness*, N. Piseponn.
Silly, *sil'li*, A. Piso.
Silver, *sil'vor*, N. Rupem.
Silver, A. Rupeacho.
Silver, v. Rupem caddunc.
Similar, *si'mi-lar*, A. Sarco; bori.
Similarity, *si-mi-la'ri-ti*, N. N. Sarkem.
Simile, *si'mi-le*, N. Vopar.
Similitude, *si-mil'i-tuid*, N. Sor, comparasaum.
Simmer, *si'mor*, v. Soucas khokotaunc.
Simony, *si'mo-ni*, N. Povitr vostunchem vicop.

Simper, *sim'por*, V. Bolliam ansunc. [ecoddo.
Simple, *sim'pl*, A. Sado, chalto;
Simpleton, *sim'pl-ton*, A. Pisoso.
Simplicity, *simpli-si-ti*, N. Sadeponn; nibelponn, bolleponn.
Simplify, *sim,pli-fai*, V. Sado—, sompo corunc.
Simulate, *sim'iu-leit*, V. Bolliam—, dongan corunc.
Simulation, *si-mu-lei'shon*, N. Bolliam cornom, fottkirpoun, dong.
Simultaneous, *si-mul-tei'ni-as*, A. Teach vellar, sovem.
Sin, *sin*, N. Patoc; oprad.
Sin, V. Patoc adarunc.
Since, *sins*, PREP, Than, poriant, pasot. [sattavo.
Sincere, *sinsi'er*, A. Khoro, sado,
Sincerity, *sin-se'-ri-ti*, N. Khoreponn; boleponn.
Sinecure, *si'-ne-kiu-ar*, A. Vavravion, folladic zago, namvachi chacri.
Sinew, *si'-niu*, N. Sir; boll, socot.
Sinful, *sin'-ful*, A. Addvarlolo, vaitt, khotto.
Sinfulness, *sin-ful-ness*, N. Khotteponn.
Sing, *sing*, V. Gaen vo cantar corunc.
Singe, *sinj*, V. Ulpannc, lasunc.
Singer, *sing'-or*, N. Cantarist, gaen cornar.
Singing, *sing'-ing*, N. Gaen, cantar.
Single, *sing'gl*, A. Ecoddo.
Single out, V. Vinchun caddunc.
Singly, *sing'-li*, AD. Kherit-kherit, veglo-veglo.
Singular, *sing'-u-lar*, A. Ecuch; aprup; tarifecho.
Singularity, *sing-gu-la'-ri-ti*, N. Ecadeponn; niralepon; uttamponn.

Sinister, *si'-nis-tar*, A. Ogunnacho; odrusttacho.
Sink, *sink*, V. Buddounc; devounc; fg. rigonc.
Sink, N. Cochreacho zago.
Sinless, *sin'-less*, A. Guneaum—, pap naslolo,
Sinner, *sin'-nor*, N. Patki; papi; papin.
Sip, *sip*, V. Gottunc.
Sip, N. Cuscut; soucas pinnem.
Siphon, *sai'-fon*, N. Nolli.
Sir, *sor*, N. Saiba, senhor.
Sire, *sa'-iar*, N. Maharaj.
Siren, *sai'-rin*, N. Fuslaunchi hostori; patolli.
Sirrah, *sir'-ra*, N. Lucho.
Sirocco, *si-rok'-ko*, N. Fugar corchem varem.
Sister, *sis'-tor*, N. Boin.
Sister-in-law, N. Mouni; bavos.
Sit, *sit*, V. Bosono.
—(Up), Zago ravonc,
Sitting, *sit'-ing*, N. Junt, zomat.
Situation, *sit-u-ei'shon*, N. Suat; udeog; cam.
Six, *siks*, A. So.
Size, *saiz*, N. Voddai, vistar; lambai- rundai.
Skate, *skait*, V. Nisronc.
Skate, N. Nisorcho mocho.
Skeleton, *ski'-li-ton*, N. Pandro; bagottio.
Sketch, *s-kech*, N. Nacsha; risco; thoddi somzonui.
Skiff, *s-kiff*, N. Dactti donn.
Skilful, *s-kil'-ful*, A. Uxar; icmoticho; naddgo; sicpi; anbog aslolo.
Skill, *s-kill*, N. Zantticai; socot, tran.
Skim, *skim*, V. Fenno caddunc; voilea voir polleunc.
Skimmer, *skim'-ar*, N. Doi.
Skin, *skin*, N. Cat; chambddem.
Skin, V. Cat caddunc.

Skinflint, *skin'flint*, N. Imtto munis.
Skinny, *skin'i*, A. Baric; bagottio.
Skip, *skip*, V. Uddonc.
Skip, N. Uddop.
Skirmish, *skirm'ish*, N. Lan loddai.
Skirt, *skort*, N. Vostrachem pond; deg.
Skittish, *skit'ish*, N. Bezudd; lozbando.
Skulk, *skolk*, V. Lipounc; aplo caido corchom chucounc.
Skul, *skul*, N. Cot-tem; kodd-do.
Sky, *skai*, N. Mollob, akas; asma.
Slab, *sleb*, N. Marblacho fator; dacttem follem.
Slack, *slek*, A. Soddil; auxi.
Slackness, *slek'ness*, N. Soddilai; ansai.
Slag, *sleg*, N. Coir; ligit.
Slak, *sleik*, V. Palounc; thambounc; mou corunc.
Slander, *slen'dar*, N. Bodlam; vait khobor; ocman; guneaum.
Slander. V. Bodlam galunc; manar add ulounc.
Slanderer, *slen'der-ar*, N. Bodlami.
Slanderous, *slen'der-as*, A. Bodlamacho, ocmanacho.
Slang, *sleng*, N. Holki bhas.
Slant, *slent*, A. Vaneddo
Slap, *slep*, N. Thapott.
Slap, V. Thapott marunc.
Slash, *slesh*, V. Catrunc; chanchounc.
Slate, *sleit*, N. Borouncho fator vo folli.
Slaughter, *slo'tter*, N. Zomoac jivesim marop.
Slave, *slev*, N. Gulam.
Slave, V. Gulamponn corunc.
Slaver, *sle'vor*, N. Lall.
Slavery, *slev'e-ri*, N. Gulamponn.
Slavish, *slev'ish*, A. Gulamponnacho.
Slay, *slei*, V. Jivesim marunc; mort marunc.
Slayer, *slei'ar*, N. Morticar.
Slaying, *slei'ing*, N. Mort, khunni.
Sledge, *slej*, N. Nisorchi vo-chacram nasleli gaddi.
Sleek, *slik*, A. Telto.
Sleep, *slip*, N. Nid; jom.
Sleep, V. Nidonc; jemounc.
Sleepiness, *slip'i-ness*, N. jom.
Sleepless, *slip'less*, A. Nid naslolo.
Sleeplessness, *slip'les-ness*, N. N. Nid nasnem.
Sleepy, *slip'i*, A. nidest.
Sleet, *slit*, Baric corc.
Sleeve, *sliv*, N. Angostracho hat vo mang.
Sleight, *sleith*, N. Nadd; hicmot.
Slender, *slen'dor*, A. Baric; osoct.
Slenderness, *slen'dor-ness*, N. Ossoctai; unneponn.
Slice, *slais*, N. Fati; cap; cuddko
Slide, *slaid*, V. Nisronc.
Slight, *slaitt*, A. Lan; thoddo; hallu.
Slight, N. Beporvo.
Slight, V. Beporvo corunc.
Slime, *slaim*, N. Mou, chicot mati.
Sling, *sling*, V. Uddounc, marunc.
Sling, N. Gofin.
Slink. *slink*, V. Pollonc.
Slip, *slip*, V. Nisronc, soddunc; guttan vorunc.
Slipaway, V. Pollonc.
—(Out of the memory), V. Visronc.
Slip, N. Nisrop; chuc.
Slipper, *slip'ar*, N. Chinel.
Slippery, *slip'e-ri*, A. Dubavi; nisortto.

Slit, *slit*, V. Catrunc.
Slit, N. Catrop.
Sloop, *slup*, N. Patmar.
Slop, *slop*, N. Simpddailelem udoc; ‹oro, urrak; ras.
Slope, *slop*, N. Deunti.
Sloping, *slop'ing*, A. Deunto.
Sloth, *sloth*, N. Ausai; jem.
Slothful, *sloth'-ful*, A. Auxi; bezudd.
Slouch, *slauch*, N. Bagop; pong; vaneddi chal.
Slough, *slau*, N. Condd.
Sloven, *slo'vun*, A. Burso.
Slow, *slo*, Soucas.
Slowly, *slou'li*, AD. Soucasaen.
Slowness, *slou'ness*, N. Soucosai.
Sluggard, *slo'gard*, A. Auxi.
Sluice, *slos*, N. Chonn udoc addaunchi.
Slumber, *slomb'-ar*, N. Jem; zop.
Slumber, V. Jemeunc, zopir asunc.
Slur, *slor*, N. Khot.
Slut, *slot*, N. Bursi hostori.
Sluttish, *slo'tish*, A. Burso.
Sly, *slai*, A. Naddgo.
Smack, *smeck*, V. Umaum diunc, thapott marunc.
Smack, N. Patmar; ruch; thap.
Small, *smol*, A. Dactto, supurlo.
Smallnes, *smol'ness*, N. Lanponn.
Small-pox, *smol'poks*, Asuc.
Smart, *smart*, V. Cottin dukh bogunc.
Smart, N. Cottin dukh; faric-ponnacho duddu.
Smart, A. Ducouncho; bario; nazuc; cottin.
Smartness, *smart'ness*, N. Zall; cottin dukh; boll; barcai.
Smash, *smesh*, V. Chenchunc; pudd corunc.
Smatter, *smet'-or*, V. Voilea-voir sicunc; nacazalelem uiounc.
Smatterer, *smet'-or-rar*, N. Ardukuro sicpi.
Smear, *smer*, V. Chorob vo tel launc.
Smell, *smell*, N. Pormoll, imsan; vas.
Smell, V. Pormoll geunc; ghanounc.
Smelling, *smell'-ing*, A. Pormollacho; ghannecho.
Smile, *smail*, V. Amburco hansunc.
Smile, N. Amburco hanso.
Smirk, *smork*, N. Addecho vo fotkiro hanso.
Smite, *smait*, V. Addlaunc,
Smith, *smith*, N. Vinnani; lovar.
Smock, *smok*, N. Cholli.
Smoke, *smoke*, V. Voddunc (chirut. viddi, etc.)
Smoke, N, Dunvor.
Smooth, *smuth*, A. Sullsullit; nidan; mogall.
Smooth, V. Sullsullit corunc; fuslaunc; hallu corunc; nib sangunc.
Smoothly, *smuth'li*, AD. Soucasaen.
Smoothness, *smuth'ness*, N. Tellsan; nidanai; fuslaunnem.
Smother, *smo'dar*, V. Fugar corunc; palounc; dampun dounc.
Smoulder, *smol'dar*, V. Bitorlea bitor lasonc.
Smuggle, *smog'gl*, V. Choriam vorunc.
Smut, *smot*, N. Goirom; costoll.
Smutty, *smot'ti*, A. Goiramacho; burso.
Snail, *sneil*, N. Vagonni.
Snake, *sneik*, N. Sorop.
Snap, *snep*, V. Foddunc.
Snap up, V. Gillonc.
Snappish, *snep'ish*, A. Chabcor.
Snare, *sner*, N. Nadd; fas.

Snare, V. Nadduno; sampdduno.
Snarl, *snarl,* V. Gorgoruno.
Snatch, *snech,* V. Oann geune; voddun caddunc.
Sneak, *snik,* V. Chorunc; (away) V. Pollunc. [sunc.
Sneer, *sniar,* V. Deporvean han-
Sneeze, *sniz,* V. Sink cadduno.
Sniff, *sniff,* V. Nacan voddunc.
Snip, *snip,* V. Pont catrunc.
Snivel, *sni'vel,* V. Kirmem vanvunc.
Snore, *snor,* V. Goreunc.
Snoring, *snor-ing,* N. Gorenni.
Snout, *snaut,* N. Sonddi.
Snow, *snou,* N. Dou.
Snow, V. Dou poddonc.
Snub, *snob,* V. Pont catrunc; kimchunc; ravounc.
Snub-nose, N. Chepttem nac.
Snuff, *snaf,* N. Pudd, chimtti; cazvo.
Snuff, V. Pudd voddunc; cazvo caddunc.
Snuff-box, N. Bul; chimttechem boxet.
Snuffle, *snaf'fl,* V. Nakiam ulounc.
Snug, *snog,* A. Guttlaulolo; soucasaecho.
So, *so,* AD. Itlo vo titlo; tea pasun; zor tor.
So small, Tedo lan.
So great, Tedo vodd.
So so, Sumar.
So after, Title pautti.
So soon, Titlem veguim.
So then, Tor.
Soak, *sok',* V. Mou corunc; bizounc; bebdo saur asunc.
Soaking, *sok'ing,* N. Bizounnem.
Soap, *sop,* N. Sabu.
Soap, V. Saban gansunc.
Soapnut, N. Ringo.
Soar, *sor,* V. Unch vossonc; zoit vorunc; gunvonc.
Sob, *sob,* V. Uscaronc.
Sob, N. Uscar.
Sober, *sob'ar,* A. Zotnaen pieuncho; bebdo zainaslolo; sarko moticho; nidan.
Sobriety, *so-brai'e-ti,* N. Alpabojan, thoddem khan-pion; moriad.
Sociability, *so-shi-a-bil'i-ti,* N. Shobati, sangatponn; mogallponn.
Sociable, *so'shi-ebl,* A. Sangatponncho; mogall.
Social, *so'shi-al,* A. Ohongantlo, sangata jiololo, mogall.
Socialism, *so'shal-izm,* N. Samanias-vamil-vamat; astecho oc-vott. [méll.
Society, *so-sai'e-ti,* N. Sangat,
Sock, *sok,* N. Lan mei.
Socket, *sok'et,* N. Nem.
Soda, *so'da,* N. Khar; sod.
Sodalist, *so-da'list,* N. Irmaum.
Sodality, *so-dal'i-ti,* N. Irmandad.
Sofa, *so'fa,* N. Sofa.
Soft, *soft,* A. Mou; movall; nazuc; fuslauncho.
Soften, *so'fun,* V. Mou corunc; movallunc; fuslaunc.
Softly, *soft'li,* AD. Soucasaen.
Softness, *soft'ness,* N. Mousan; soucosai; movallponn.
Soho, *so-ho,* Int. Ah.
Soil, *soil,* N. Zago, dhorn; goliz, khot.
Soiled, *soild,* V. Mhello, allsik; burso.
Sojourn, *so-jorn,* V. Ravunc; biddar corunc.
Sojourn, N. Ravop; bidhar.
Sojourner, *so-jorn'ar,* N. Pordesi.
Solace, *so'lès,* V. buzvon diunc.
Solace, N. Buzvon.
Solder, *sold'ar,* V. Pansounc; mellounc.
Soldier, *sol'jer,* N. Sipai, soldad.

Sole, *sôl*, N. Camoilelem chamddem. [vodd.

Solemn, *so-lem*, A. Dobajeacho;

Solemnity, *so'lem-ni-ti*, N. Dobazo; porob.

Solemnize, *so'lem-naiz*, V. Fest corunc, voddponnan vo dobajean corunc.

Solicit, *so-lis'it*, V. Magunc; fuslaunc; laleunc.

Solicitation, *so-lis-it-ei'shon*. N. Magunem; laleunem; fuslaunem.

Solicitude, *so-lis'it-iud*, N. Fiker, porva, minot, jagrutai, husco.

Solicitor, *so-lis'it-or*, Vokil, letrad.

Solid, *so'lid*, A. Gott; okond.

Soliloquy, *so-lil'o-kui*, N. Ecleachom ulounem; gungunnem.

Solitary, *so'li-ta-ri*, A. Ecsuro; khontist.

Solitary, N. Vouvasi.

Solitude, *so'li-tiud*, N. Ecsurai, ecsuri suat.

Solo, *solo*, N. Ecuch tallo.

Solubility, *so-liu-bil-i-ti'*, N Khiro sarkem.

Soluble, *so'liu-bl*, A. Kiro sarco.

Solution, *so-liu'shon*, N. Coddop; khorop; parkinne; zabab.

Solve, *solv*, V. Coddounc vo khirounc; parcunc, ugtto corunc.

Solvent, *sol'vent*, A. Faric cori sarco.

Sombre, *som'ber*, N. Callso; khontist.

Some, *som*, A. Thoddo, ilo; omco.

Something, Kiteim.

Somewhat, Itlo vo thoddo.

Somebody, Conn eiclo.

Somehow, Coseim punn.

Sometimes, Thoddo pautti.

Somnambulism, *som-nam'-bu-lizm*, N. Sopnant cholop.

Somnolence, *som-no'lens*, N. Jem; zop; nidchi khoxi.

Somnolent, *som-no'lent*, A. Nidrest.

Son, *son*, N. Putr; burgo.

Son-in-law, N. Zanvoim.

Song, *song*, N. Pod; cantig; gaien.

Sonless, *son'less*, V. Vanz; burguem naslolo. [cho.

Sonorous, *so-no'ras*, A. Vazpe-

Soon, *sun*, VD. Veguim.

Soot, *sut*, N. Goirum.

Sooth, *suth*, N. Sot.

Soothe, *sud*, V. Hallu corunc; fuslaunc; nivounc.

Soothsayer, *suth'sei ar*, N. Parki; profet.

Sooty, *sut'i*, A. Goiromacho.

Sop, *sop*, V. Bizounc.

Sop, N. Bizoilolo cuddeo.

Sophism, *sof'iz-m*, N. Portibhas; huzot.

Soporific, *so-po-rif'ic*, A. Nidouncho.

Soprano, *so-pra'no*, N. Voilo tallo.

Sorcerer, *sor'ser-ar*, N. Achar cornar; fitis cornar; garri.

Sorceress, *sor'se-ress*, N. Garrin.

Sorcery, *sor'se-ri*, N. Fitisponn; bhul.

Sordid, *sord'id*, A. Imtto; allsik; kircoll.

Sordidness, *sord'id-ness*, N. Imtteponn; ollsikponn; kircollponn.

Sore, *sor*, N. Ghai; zokom.

Sore, A. Coisttauncho; ducouncho.

Soreness, *sor'ness*, N. Coistt.

Sorrel, *sor'rel*, A. Aiduvoso.

Sorrow, *sor'rou*, A. Duc; khont; churchuro.

Sorrowful, *sor'rou-ful*, A. Khontist, dukest.

Sorry, *so'ri*, A. Dukest; khontist.
Sort, *sort*, N. Thar; jinos,
Sort, V. Eike zatiche kherit corunc.
Sortie, *sor'ti*, N. Bhair sorop.
Sot, *sot*, A. Pieono laglolo.
Sottish, *so'tish*, A. Bebdo; bud naslolo.
Soul, *soul*, N. Otmo; boll.
Sound, *saund*, N. Sad; avaz.
Sound, V. Avaz zaunc; poriksha corunc.
Sound, A. Okond, aputt; naznc; bolaikecho.
Soundness, *saund'ness*, N. Mozbutai; aputtai.
Sounding, *saund'ing*, A. Sadouncho.
Soup, *sop*, N. Cald, sôp.
Sour, *sa'or*, A. Ambott; corcoracho.
Source, *sors*, N. Oromb; zor; carann.
Sourness, *sa'or-ness*, N. Amsann.
Souse, *saus*, V. Udcant buddounc.
South, *sauth*, N. Sul.
Sovereign, *sov'o-rin*, N. Sotantri; patxai.
Sovereign, A. Aple sotecho; uttim.
Sow, *so*, N. Ducorn.
Sow, V, Vomponc.
Sowing, *so'ing*, N. Bim.
Sower, *so'ar*. N. Vomptolo.
Space, *spés*, N. Zago; vell.
Spacious, *spei'xi-as*, A. Vistarlolo; isoll.
Spade, *sped*, N. Khorem; panadon.
Span, *spen*, V. Tanddunc.
Span, N. Tanddop; mottveponn.
Spangle, *speng'gl*, N. Bangarachem pan.
Spare, *sper*, A. Baric; urta to.
Spare, V. Samballunc; chucounc; dovorunc.

Spark, *spark*, N. Kit.
Sparkle, *spar'kl*, V. Porzollunc, Uzvadd diunc.
Sparrow, *spe'ro*, N. Girboji.
Sparce, *spers*, A. Aprub; simpddailolo.
Spasm, *spazm*, N. Camp, campero; voddi.
Spasmodic, *spaz'-mod-ik*, A. Voddincho; campouncho; fg. cottin.
Spatter, *spet'er*, V. Dampunc.
Speak, *spik*, V. Ulounc; ucharunc; sangunc.
Speaker, *spik'ar*, N. Uloinar; prasangar.
Spear, *spiar*, N. Bhalo vo bhali.
Special, *spe'-shial*, A. Pratek; vises; mukia.
Speciality, *spe-shi-al'i-ti*, N. Gunn.
Specially, *spe'shal-i*, ADV. Bhou corun; vodic corun; vises.
Specie, *spi'shi*, N. Xannem.
Species, *spe'shiz*, N. Thor; vorg; zat.
Specific, *spe-sif'ik*, A. Vises vo pratek.
Specific, N. Vises vocot.
Specify, *spe'si-fai*, V. [illegible]rkem sangunc.
Specimen, *spe'si-men*, N. Daclo; nomunno.
Specious, *spe'shas*, A. Bc[illegible] diso sarco.
Speck, *spek*, N. Khot.
Spectacle, *spek'te-kl*, N. Dacoun; distt.
Spectacle, N. Vocl.
Spectre, *spek'ter*, N. Nasaunv; distti poddnem; drishtav.
Speculate, *spek'u-leit*, V. Vepar udeom corunc; voivattunc.
Speculation, *spek'u-lei-shon*, N. Tork, dakshan; colpona; naddboli.

Speculative, *spek'u-leit-iv*, A. Oolponnecho; mansik.
Speculator, *spek'u-leit-or*, N. Vepar—, udeom cornar.
Speech, *spiich*, N. Ulonnchi sokot; bhas; utor; ulounem; sermaum.
Speed, *spiid*, N. Zorurai, ausar.
Speed, V. Chodd vodd zaum.
Speedy, *spid'i*, A. Suddsudit.
Spell, *spell*, N. Moutr.
Spell. V. Soletrar corunc.
Spelling, *spell'ing*, N. Acxerancho uchar, soletrasaum.
Spend, *spend*, V. Khorchunc, duddu moddunc.
Spendthrift, *spend'thrift*, N. Duddu khorchinar, vichec; ibaddi.
Sphere, *sfier*, N. Gulló; mitmer.
Spice, *spais*, N. Pormollachi vost; gorom mosalo.
Spice, V. Fonn dinnc.
Spices, *spai'sis*. N. Sambhar.
Spider, *spai'dor*, N. Vanni.
Spike, *spaik*, N. Conos.
Spill, *spill*, V. Simponc; simpddaunc.
Spin, *spin*, V. Vinnunc; lamb corunc.
Spindle, *spin al*, N. Sut volchi [gaddi.
Spine, *spain*, N. Kono.
Spiral, *spi'ral*, N. Revodd.
Spire, *spaiar*, N. Torr.
Spirit, *spi'rit*, N. Otmo; mon; xovott; gun; soro.
Spirited, *spi'rit-ed*, A. Dhoiravont; uxear.
Spiritless, *spi'rit-less*, A. Jiu naslolo, auxi.
Spiritual, *spi'ri-chu-al*, A. Otmeacho; devosponnacho; povitr; cudd naslolo.
Spit, *spit*, N. Thimpi.
Spit, V. Thimpi uddounc.
Spite, *spait*, V. Ducounc; coisttaunc.
Spite, *spait*, N. Mosor; niscuchar.
Spiteful, *spait'full*, A. Mosri; coddu.
Spittle, *spit'tl*, N. Thimpi.
Spittoon, *spit'tun*, N. Thimpiechem aidon.
Splash, *splesh*, V. Chicol launc.
Splash, N. Chicol.
Spleen, *splin*, V. Boc pottantlo visovo; fg. vaitt morji.
Splendid, *splend'id*, A. Voddponnacho; dobajeacho.
Splendour, *splen'dor*, N. Porzoll; dobazo; voddponn.
Splint, *splint*, N. Cuddeo; souli.
Split, *split*, V. Catrunc; chirunc.
Split, N. Futt; meddop
Split. A. Futtul-lo.
Splutter, *splott'ar*, V. Goddboddiam ulounc.
Spoil, *spoil*, V. Nas corunc; cusonnc.
Spoil, N. Lutt.
Spoke, *spok*, N. Khuutto.
Spokesman, *spoks'men*, N. Boli cornar.
Sponge, *sponj*, N. Doriachom aimbem.
Sponge, V. Aimbean pusunc.
Sponsor, *spon'sor*, N. Podon.
Spontaneous, *spon-tei'ni-us*, A. Aplo khoxen; soimba pormonnem aslolo.
Spoon, *spun*, N. Culer.
Spoonful, *spun'ful*, A. Culer bor.
Sporadic, *spo-rad'ik*, A. Aprup; simpoddlolem.
Sport, *sport*, N. Khell.
Sport, V. Khellunc.
Spot, *spot*, N. Suat; zago.
Spotless, *spot'less*, A. Khot naslolo.
Spotty, *spot'ti*, A. Khot aslolo.
Spouse, *spauz*, N. Poti; gorear.
Spout, *spaut*, N. Aidonachem muc vo tondd.

Spout, v. Bhair sorono.
Sprain, *sprein*, v. Tirponc ; voddonc.
Spray, *sprei*, N. Zhodd.
Spread, *spred*, v. Antullunc, patounc ; vistarunc ; porgott corunc.
Sprightly, *sprait'li*, A. Shidduc ; uxear. [uddop.
Spring, *spring*, N. Kaman ; zhor;
Spring, v. Kirlong ; ubzonc ; uddonc.
Sprinkle, *sprin'kl*, v. Shinraunc.
Sprout, *spraut*, v. Futtonc ; kirlonc.
Sprout, N. Ankri.
Spruce, *spros*, A. Nitoll ; danddi.
Spume, *spom*, N. Fenno.
Spurious, *spu'ri-as*, A. Khoro vo niz noi ; borsillo.
Spurn, *sporn*, v. Beporvo corunc; beporvean soddunc.
Spurt, *sport*, v. Bhair soronc.
Sputter, *spott'ar*, v. Lau vanvonc.
Spy, *spai*, N. Bedi.
Spy, v. Bed geunc.
Squadron, *skwod'ron*, Sovarancho zomo ; tarvam.
Squalid, *skwo'lid*, A. Burso ; kircoll.
Squalidity, *skwa-li'di-ti*, N. Burseponn ; kircollai.
Squal, *skwol*, v. Kinncho marunc.
Squander, *skwon'dar*, v. Nas corunc ; ibaddunc.
Squanderer, *skwon'de-rar*, N. Ibaddi.
Square, *skwer*, A. Chouk.
Square, A. Char conseancho.
Square, v. Chuc corunc, cont cobar corunc.
Squash, *skuosh*, v. Chenchunc ; chiddunc.
Squat, *skwot*, v. Guttli corun bosonc vo ukoddiam bosonc.
Squeak, *skwik*, v. Kirkironc.
Squeamish, *skwim'ish*, A. Nazuk.
Squeamishness, *skwim'-ish-ness*, N. Nazukai.
Squeeze, *skwiz*, v. Pillunc ; ros caddunc ; chiddunc.
Squint, *skwint*, v. Tirso polleunc.
Squinting, *skwint'ing*, A. Tirso.
Squirrel, *skwi'rul*, N. Cháni.
Stab, *steb*, N. Suriecho mar.
Stab, v. Suri topunc.
Stability, *sta-bil'i-ti*, N. Gottai ; thirasonn.
Stable, *ste'bl*, N. Gotto ; tobulo.
Stack, *stek*, N. Ras, punzo ; zomo.
Stack, v. Ras corunc, zomaunc.
Staff, *staff*, N. Bett ; khuntti ; foujichea voddilancho mell.
Stag, *steg*, N. Dadlem merum.
Stage, *steij*, N. Sopo ; unch zago.
Stage-coach, N. Topal gaddi.
Stagger, *steg'ar*, v. Camponc, locon cholonc.
Stagnant, *steg'nant*, A. Tharaulelem.
Stain, *stein*, N. Khot ; ocman.
Stain, v. Khotaunc ; mellounc.
Stainless, *stein'less*, A. Khot naslolo ; nitoll.
Stair, *ster*, N. Iscad. [to.
Stake, *steik*, N. Khambo ; khuntStake, v. Dhir diunc ; khuntti launc.
Stale, *stel*, A, Porno.
Stalk, *stok*, N. Dentt.
Stall, *stoll*, N. Bosca, gotto.
Stammer, *stem'ar*, v. Gageunc.
Stammerer, *stem'er-ar*, N. Gagio ; luddbo.
Stamp, *stemp*, N. Mhor.
Stamp, v. Mhor marunc.
Stanch, *stench*, v. Rogot vaunchem thambounc.
Stand, *stend*, v. Ubo raunc ; raunc ; sosunc.

Stand, N. Ravop.
Standard, *stend'ard*, N. Bautto.
Stanza, *stan'za*, N. Slock; pod.
Staple, *ste'pl*, N. Pentt; ganch.
Star, *star*, N. Neketr.
Starch, *starch*, N. Khol, ganji.
Starch, V. Khol vo ganji galunc.
Stare, *ster*, V. Jiu soddun polleunc.
Stark, *stark*, A. Ghott.
Start, *start*, V. Camponc; ang cadduno; bhair sorono.
Start, N. Ang caddnem; bhair sorop.
Starvation, *star-vei'shon*, N. Bukecheo voddi vo sall.
Starve, *starv*, V. Buken moronc.
State, *steit*, N. Stiti; bhes; sangat.
State, V. Sangonc vo munnonc.
Stately, *steit'li*, A. Voddponnacho.
Statement, *steit'ment*, ixeop; sangnni; somzonni.
Statesman, *stets'men*, N. Montri; rajcarbari.
Statics, *stat'ics*, N. Stiti; xastr.
Station, *stei'shon*, Suat; estesaum; mokam.
Statistics, *sta-tis'tics*, N. Locanchom lek.
Statuary, *stei'chu-ari*, N. Silpi; cantoinur.
Statue, *ste'chu*, N. Imaz.
Stature, *stei'char*, N. Voddai vo lambai.
Statute, *stat'ut*, N. Caido.
Stave, *steiv*, N. Pipachem follem.
Stay, *stei*, N. Ravop vo raunnem; biddar.
Steadfast, *sted'fast*, A. Thir, ghott.
Steadfastness, *sted-fast'ness*, N. Ghottai; thirasonn.
Steady, *sted'i*, A. Thir; ghott.
Steak, *stek*, Masachi fati.
Steal, *stil*, V. Chorunc; nagounc.
Stealing, *stil'ing*, N. Chori.
Steam, *stim*, N. Ub.
Steam, V. Ub bhair soronc.
Steamer, *sti-m'ar*, N. Agbot; vapor.
Steel, *stil*, N. Tikem.
Steel, V. Ghott corunc.
Steep, *stip*, N. Nisorti; dounti.
Steep, V. Bizounc.
Steeple, *stip'pl*, N. Torr.
Steepness, *stip'ness*, Dounti.
Steer, *ster*, N. Paddo.
Steer, V. Cholounc.
Steersman, *sters'men*, N. Choloinar, sukanem dornar.
Stem, *stem*, N. Thambounc.
Stem, N. Lund. (Zaddachem).
Stench, *stench*, N. Ghan.
Step, *step*, N. Panvol; paunddo; upai.
Step, V. Cholonc; rigonc.
Step-mother, N. Mausi.
Sterile, *ste-'ril*, A. Vanz; foll dinaslolo.
Sterility, *ste-ri'li-ty*, N. Vanzponn; unneponn.
Stern, *starn*, N. Tarvacho pattlo bhag.
Stern, A. Khor; tik.
Sterness, *storn'ess*. N. Khorai; tiksaun.
Stew, *stu*, V. Lan ujean sizounc.
Stew, N. Sizoilelem mas; cheddianchem ghor.
Steward, *stu'ard*, N. Carbari.
Stewardship, *stu'ard-ship*, N. Carbarponn.
Stick, *stik*, N. Rot; tonnco.
Stick, V. Launc; lagunc.
Sticky, *stik'i*, A. Pancacho, chicott.
Stiff, *stiff*, A. Bazodd, nibor.
Stiffness, *stiff'ness*, Bazoddai; nibrasan.
Stifle, *sti'fl*, N. Dampun dovorunc.

Stigma, *stig'ma*, N. Dag; khot; ocman.
Stigmatize, *stig'ma-taiz*, V. Ocman corunc.
Still, *still*, A. Nidan.
Still, AD. Aninc; sodanch.
Stillness, *still'ness*, N. Nidanai, soucosai.
Stimulate, *sti'mu-leit*, V. Uchamboll corunc; uttounc.
Sting, *sting*, V. Topunc; kuns launc.
Stinginess, *stin'ji-ness*, N. Sugrat; imtteponn.
Stingy, *stin'ji*, A. Sugrati; imtto.
Stink, *stink*, V. Ghaneunc.
Stink, N. Ghan.
Stinking, *stink'ing*, A. Ghannero; ghannicho.
Stint, *stint*, N. Unneponn.
Stipend, *stip'end*, N. Pagar; muzri.
Stipulate, *sti-piu'leit*, V. Carar corunc.
Stipulation, *sti-piu-lei'shon*, N. Carar; sert.
Stir, *stor*, N. Uchambollai.
Stir, V. Uchamboll corunc; uprasaunc.
Stirrup, *sti'rap*, N. Goddiar bostoch paim dorchi khoinddi.
Stitch, *stich*, N. Suecho pont.
Stitch, V. Sinvonc.
Stock, *stok*, N. Purument.
Stock, V. Addun bhorunc.
Stocking, *stock'ing*, N. Mei.
Stoical, *stoi'cal*, A. Baginaso.
Stoker, *stok'ar*, N. Uzo samballnar, agvallo.
Stole, *stöl*, N. Estol.
Stoled, *sto'lid*, A. Dado; somzo naslolo piso.
Stolidity, *sto-li'di-ti*, N. Daddeponn; piseponn.
Stomach, *sto'mak*, N. Poscotto; pot.
Stone, *ston*, N. Fator, chiro.
Stone, V. Fatraunc.
Stone-fish, N. Palu.
Stony, *ston'i*, A. Fatrancho.
Stool, *stul*, Munnoi; bankin.
Stoop, *stup*, V. Vodduno; galunc.
Stop, *stop*, V. Ravounc; dovorunc; monacorunc.
Stopple, *stop'pl*, N. Gurdi.
Store, *stor*, N. Sompurnai.
Store, V. Ras corunc, ecttaim corunc.
Stork, *stork*, N. Bokem.
Storm, *storm*, N. Vadoll; tufan.
Storm, V. Zulmen cann gounc; angar poddonc.
Stormy, *stor'mi*, A. Tufanacho.
Story, *sto'ri*, N. Canim.
Stout, *staut*, A. Motto; pustti.
Stoutness, *staut'ness*, N. Mottai.
Stove, *stor*, N. Diveachi randon vo chul.
Straggle, *streg'gl*, V. Parpoll bouvonc.
Straighten, *strei'tun*, V. Nitt corunc.
Strain, *strein*, V. Gallunc.
Strain, N. Prayatan.
Strainer, *strei'nar*, N. Curpon; gallni.
Strait, *streit*, N. Doriachi asirai.
Strait, A. Osir. (Marog).
Strand, *strend*, N. Todd.
Strand, V. Toddic addolonc.
Strange, *streinj*, A. Atvo; ojcapancho, chamatcarancho.
Stranger, *strein'jar*, N. Pordesi, bhailo, porko.
Strangle, *streng'gl*, V. Fugar corunc, golleac fas galunc.
Strangulation, *stran-gu-lei'shon*, N. Golleac fas galuem.
Strap, *strep*, N. Chambdeacho tir.
Stratagem, *stra'ta-jem* N. Nadd; fottvonn.

Strategic, *stra-te'jic*, A. Hicmoticho ; zuza samarthecho.
Strategy, *stra'te-ji*, N. Zuzachi hicmot.
Straw, *stro*, N. Sukem tonn ; corord.
Stray, *strei*, V. Vatt chuconc.
Stream, *strim*, N. Noim ; vall ; lott.
Streamlet, *strim'let*, N. Dactto vall.
Street, *strit*, N. Marog, bid.
Strength, *strenth*, N. Ghottai, boll ; tran.
Strengthen, *strent'n*, V. Ghott corunc ; choddounc ; boll diunc.
Strenuous, *stre'nu-as*, A. Dhoiravont ; uxoar.
Strenuousness, *stre'nu-as-ness*, N. Dhoir ; uxearkai.
Stress, *stress*, N. Zoddai ; boll.
Stretch, *stretch*, V. Tanddunc ; vistarunc ; voddunc.
Stretching, *strech'ing*, N. Tanddop ; voddop.
Strew, *stru*, V. Simpddaunc ; vomponc.
Stricken, *strik'un*, A. Ghaiello ; utar piraocho.
Strict, *strict*, A. Khor ; sarco ; khoudit.
Strictness, *strict'ness*, N. Khorai.
Stride, *straid*, V. Lamb paim uddounc.
Strike, *straik*, V. Marunc ; boddounc ; vazounc.
Striking, *straik'ing*, A. Ojeapancho ; somzo sarco.
String, *string*, N. Dori ; cordaum ; sori.
Strip, *strip*, V. Meolo vo nagddo corunc ; nisraunc.
Stripe, *straip*, N. Patt.
Stripling, *strip'ling*, N. Burgo.
Strive, *straiv*, V. Praiatan corunc ; minot corunc.
Stroke, *strouk*. N. Mar, far, dumco, buco.
Stroll, *stroll*, V. Bouvonc.
Strong, *strong*, A. Ghott, bolladic ; cottin ; motto vo voddlo.
Structure, *stroc'char*, N. Goddop, baudop ; mandavoll ; rup.
Struggle, *strog'gl*, V. Loddai corunc ; praiatan corunc.
Struggle, N. Loddai ; zogddem.
Strut, *strat*, V. Gorviponnan cholonc.
Stubborn, *stob'born*, A. Aplea vadeacho ; darrun.
Stubborness, *stob'born-ness*, N. darunnai.
Stud, *stod*, N. Khuntto ; butaum.
Student, *stu'dent*, N. Sicnar, iscolacho burgo.
Studied, *stod'id*, A. Toiar keiolo; khoxecho.
Studious, *stu'di-as*, A. Axecho ; sicpac pettlolo.
Study, *stod'i*, V. Siconc ; toiar corunc.
Study, N. Sicop.
Stuff, *stoff*, N. Samonn. lugott ; vostu.
Stuff, V. Borunc.
Stumble, *stom'bl*, V. Addlonc ; mellonc.
Stump, *stomp*. N. Kutti ; zaddachem mull.
Stun, *stan*, V. Can foddunc.
Stunt, *stant*, V. Vaddonam zaunc.
Stupefaction, *stu-pe-fec'shon*, N. Boirevni ; thattacni, chamatcar.
Stupefy, *stu'pi-fai*, N. Murc vo piso corunc ; ojap zaunc.
Stupendous, *stu-pen'das*. A. Ojapancho.
Stupid, *stu'ped*, A. Doddc, murc somzonaslolo ; piso.
Stupidity, *stu-pid'i-ti*, Doddeponn, murkeponn ; madon.

Stupor, *stu'por*; N. Janc, bhul; ar; ojap.
Sturdy, *stor'di*, A. Ghott; dharun.
Stutter, *stat'tor*, V. Gageunc.
Sty, *stai*, N. Ducracho gudd.
Style, *stail*, N. Bhasecho jinos; rit.
Style, V. Munnonc.
Suasion, *su-ei'shon*, N. Bud.
Suavity, *sua-vi-ty*, N. Goddsan, suad; soucosai, mogallponn; otmeachem suc.
Subaltern, *sub'al-tern*, A. Hata khalcho, socoilo.
Subaltern, N. Aprodan, khala aslolo munis.
Subdivide, *sub-di-vaid'*, V. Portun vanttunc; aninc vantte corunc.
Subdivision, *sub-di-vi'jon*, A. Vantteacho vantto.
Subdue, *sob'diu*, V. Khalto corunc; zoit voronc.
Subject, *sub'ject*, A. Khalto vo khala aslolo.
Subject, N. Porza; roit; irado.
Subject, V. Khalto corunc.
Subjection, *sub-jec'shon*, Khalteponn; jicni; domavni.
Snbjective, *sub-jec'tiv*, A. Motint aslolo; kolpounacho.
Subjoin, *sub-join'*, V. Akeric zoma corunc.
Subjugate, *sub-jiu-geit*, V. Domaunc, jicunc, khalto corunc.
Subjunctive, *sob-junct'iv*, A. Somsayarthacho.
Sublime, *sub-laim'*, A. Unch; vorto, voddponnacho; uttim.
Sublimity, *sab-lai'mi-ti*, N. Unchai, vorteponn, voddponn.
Submarine, *sub'ma-rin*, A. Doria pondlo.
Submerge, *sub'morj*, V. Buddonc; buddounc.
Submertion, *sub-mer'shon*, N. Buddop.
Submission, *sub-mis'shon*, N. Khalteponn.
Submissive, *sab-mis'iv*, A. Khalto, utor aicuncho.
Submit, *sob-mit'*, V. Khalto corunc vo zaunc; dacounc.
Subordinate, *so-bor-di'neit*, A. Khalto, socoilo.
Subordinately, *sub-or'din-eit-li*, AD. Khalteponnim, pangim.
Subordination, *sob-or-di-nei'shon*, N. Khalteponn, pang.
Suborn, *sob'orn*, V. Lonch diunc, nadduno.
Subornation, *sub-or-nei'shon*, N. Fituri.
Subscribe, *sobs-craib'*, V. Naum borounc, soin corunc; manovunc
Subscriber, *subs'craib-ar*, N. Naum boroitolo, soi cornar; suscritor.
Subscription, *subs-crip-shon*, N. Soi, dostakat, suscrisaum.
Subsequent, *sab'se-kwent*, A. Pelo vo dusro.
Subserve, *sub-sarv'* V. Adar diunc; upcarac poddonc.
Subside, *sab-said'*, V. Unno zaunc, thambonc; denvonc.
Subsidiary, *sab-si'dia-ri*, A. Upcari, upcaracho, bortecho, purvannacho.
Subsidy, *sab-si'di*, N. Adar, mozot. kumok.
Subsist, *sob'sist*, V. Togonc, [uronc.
Subsistence, *sob-sis'tens*, N. Udarposonn vo jieuncho upai.
Subsistent, *sob- sis'tent*, A. Asto, aslolo; aple sotecho.
Substance, *sobs'tans*, N. Sar; Mukhia gun; ast.; vost; ros.
Substantial, *sobs-tan'shal*, A Saracho; bharim; ghott; bolaikecho.

Substantiate, *sobs-tan'shi-eitt,* V. Khorem mon dacounc; ruzu corunc.
Substantive, *sobs'tan-tiv.* N. Naum. (Gram).
Substitute, *sobs'ti-tiut,* V. Suater; zaguear galunc; bodlunc.
Substitute, N. Bodli; dalal.
Substitution, *sobs'ti-tiu-shon,* N. Bodlop.
Substerfuge, *sob-ter-fiuj,* N. Nib; chor-upai.
Subterranean, *sobs-ter-ra'ne-an,* A. Dorni pondlo, bhitorlo, patollacho
Subtile, *sob'til,* A. Baric, patol; videavont.
Subtilty, *sob'til-ty,* N. Patollai; baricai.
Subtle, *sat'l,* A. Naddgo; baric.
Subtelty, *sut'l-ti,* N. Baricai; nadgeponn.
Subtract, *sab'trect,* V. Caddunc.
Subtraction, *sob'trec-shon.* N. Caddop. [rad.
Suburb, *so-borb',* N. Xarachi sa-
Subversion, *sub-ver'shon,* N. Moddni, moddop; nas.
Subvert, *sub-vort',* V. Nas corunc.
Succeed, *sac-sid',* V. Magir; patti eunc; zaunc.
Success, *soc-ses',* N. Xevott; yes, zoit.
Successful, *soc-ses'ful,* A. Chintleli vost goddonc.
Succession, *suk-se'shon,* N. Magir, patti ennem.
Successive, *sak-se'siv,* A. Ekapatti eo
Successor, *suk-se'sor,* N. Magir, patti etolo; sucesor.
Succint, *suk-sint',* A. Thoddeam utrancho.
Succour, *sok'ar,* N. Mozot, adar.
Succulence, *suk'culens,* N. Sar, ros.
Succulent, *suk'culent,* A. Rosbort, rosvont, gulgullit, chorbecho
Succumb, *sok-komb',* V. Pondac poddunc, moddon poddunc; morunc.
Such, *sach,* A. Tosolo vo toso.
Suck, *sok,* V. Chinvonc; lunchonc.
Suckle, *sok'l,* V. Vagounc; dud diunc.
Suckling, *sok'ling,* N. Chiuntolo dudacho burgo.
Sudden, *sod'dn,* A. Auchit; ecach faracho; gupit.
Suddenly, *sod'dun-li,* Adv. Auchit vo ecach fara.
Sudorific, *su-do-ri'fic,* A. Gam addcho—, caddcho; gam euuchem vocot.
Suds, *sudz,* N. Sabachem udoc.
Sue, *su,* V. Magonc; firiad diunc.
Suffer, *sof'ar,* V. Sosunc, bhogunc; soddunc.
Suffering, *sof'or-ing,* N. Coistt, dogd; duc.
Suffice, *so-fais',* V. Purto assunc,
Sufficiency, *sof-i'si-ensi,* N. Doscai; zai titlem.
Sufficient, *sof-i'si-ent,* A. Purto vo zai titlo.
Suffocate, *so-fo'keith,* V. Fugar corunc, gusmottaunc, middmiddaunc.
Suffocation, *sof-o-kei'shon,* N. Guspatavni, middmiddni, usmot; ubas, dhap.
Suffrage, *sof'reij,* N. Vot dennem; melelea khatir magnnem; bhic.
Suffuse, *sof-fius',* V. Borunc (ducanim).
Sugar, *shu'gar.* N. Sacor.
Sugar-cane, N. Us.
Suggest, *so'jest,* V. Motint galunc; ugddas corunc.

Suggestion, *so-jes'shun,* N. Sicoun, bud.

Suicide, *sui-said',* N. Jiv dinnem, aplo jiv caddnem.

Suit, *sutt,* N. Firiad, kaifet; arji; magnnem.

Suit, V. mandonc ; sarkem corunc.

Suitable, *sut-ie'ble,* A. Laek ; camac upcaroso.

Suitableness, *sutt-ie'bl-ness,* N. Laekponn.

Suite, *sutt,* N. Saugati ; racne, darbar.

Suiter *sutt'ar,* N. Arjecar.

Sulky, *sol'ki,* A. Chirtest, bejaracho.

Sullen, *sol'ln,* A. Khontiborit, bejar corcho.

Sullenness, *sol'lun-ness,* N. Khont, duc.

Sully, *so'ly,* V. Khotaunc, naum pirder corunc.

Sulphur, *sol'for,* N. Gondop.

Sulphureous, *sul-fu'ri-as,* A. Gondopacho.

Sultry *sol'try,* A. Fugar corcho

Sum, *som,* N. Ixeop, cont.

Sun, V. Ixeop corunc ; cont corunc.

Summarily, *sum-m'ar-ili,* ADV. Samkshepim, atapunn.

Summary, *som'a-ry,* A. Attap ; ausaracho.

Summer, *som'ar,* V. Gim.

Summit, *som'it,* N. Matho, toksi.

Summon, *sa'mon,* V. Apounc.

Summons, N. Apounnem, takid.

Sumptuary, *somp'chu-a-ri,* A. Khorchacho.

Sumptuous, *somp'chu-as,* A. Moladic, sopnic ; dobajeacho ; chodd khorchuucho.

Sumptuousness, *somp'chu-asness,* N. Chodd khorch ; dobazo

Sun, *son,* N. Dis, ; vot.

Sunbeam, *son'bim,* N. Kirn.

Sunburnt, *son'bo-rnt,* A. Corpololo.

Sunset, *son'set,* N. Dis dare Vochnem Vostomti.

Sunder, *son'der,* V. Vingodd corunc.

Sunny, *son'i,* A. Vot poddchoo.

Sunshine, *son'shain,* N. Vot.

Sup, *sop,* V. Ratchem jeunc.

Superabound, *su'per-a-bound,* V. Bhon—, phuscoll zaunc ; boron uronc.

Superabundance, *su'per-a-bandans,* N. Phuscollai, sompunai.

Superb, *su'berb,* A. Voddponnacho, dobajeacho.

Supercilious, *su-per-si'li-as,* A. Gorvistt.

Supererogation, *su-pe-re-ro-geishon,* N. Caidea bailem cam.

Supererogatory, *su-pe-re-ro-ga'-to-ri,* A. Caidea bhailo.

Superficial, *su-per-fi'shal.* A. Voilo, bhailo, bhailea angacho.

Superficies, *su-per-fi'shes,* N. Voilem—, bhailem ang.

Superfine, *su-per'fain,* A. Uttim·

Superfluous, *su-per'fluas,* N. Goroz naslolo, gorje virello.

Superfluity, *su-per-flu'i-ti,* A. Gorje bhaili vost.

Superhuman, *su-per-hiu'man,* A. Munxeachea soimba vorto.

Superintend, *su-per-in-tend',* V. Raconc ; polleunc.

Superintendence, *su-per-in-tendens',* N. Polevni, choucosi, karbar.

Superintendent, *su-per-in-tendent,* N. Poleumnar, carbari.

Superior, *su-pe'ri-or,* N. Voddil, mostoc; malgoddo.

Superior, A. Vorto, voilo.

Superioress, *su-pi'ri-o-ress,* N. Voddiln

Superiority, *su-pe-ri-o'ri-ty*, N. Voddilponn ; vorteponn.

Superlative, *su-per'la-tiv*, A. Bhou chodd.

Supernatural, *su'per-ne'che-ral*, A. Soimba vorto vo bhailo.

Superscription, *su-per-scrip'-shon*, N. Voilem vo bhailem borop.

Supersede, *su-per-sid*, V. Goroz naslolo corunc vo suater dokoi zaunc.

Superstition, *su-per-sti'shon*, N. Achar.

Superstitious, *su-per-sti'shas*, A. Acharacho.

Supervision, *su-per-vi'zhion*, N. Polevni, choucosi.

Supine, *su-pain'*, A. Udaro poddnem ; fg. auxi.

Supper, *sap'or*, N. Nimannem jevon.

Supplant, *sup'plent*, V. Nadd viden dusreachi suat geunc.

Supplement, *sup'le-ment*, N. Puraunni, choddauni.

Supplicate, *sup'pli-keit*, V. Magunc, prathunc.

Supplication, *sup'pli-kei'shon*, N. Magnnem, prarthan, vinoti.

Supply, *sop-lai'*, V. Diunc ; borunc.

Supply N. Sompurnai ; bodli.

Support, *sop'port*, V. Bhar geunc, samballunc ; sosunc, niudunc ; nistarunc.

Support, N. Tenco, tenki, dhir, adar.

Supportable, *sop-port'ie-bl*, A. Sosum yeso, tallcho.

Supporter, *sop-port'ar*, N. Dhir vo adar dinar.

Suppose, *su-poz*, V. Ajmas corunc ; chintunc, sotmandunc,

Supposition, *sop-po-zi'shon*, N. Ajmas, kolpona.

Supposititious, *sop-po'zi-ti-shas*, A. Fottkiro ; khoro noi aslolo, dhongi.

Suppress, *sep'press'*, V. Caddun uddounc, rodd corunc ; lipounc.

Suppression, *sop pre'shon*, N. Caddni, moddni, bhong; thambni.

Suppurate, *su-pu-reit'*, V. Picunc, pulennam eunc.

Suppuration, *sup-pu-rei'shon*, N. Picnem, pulavni.

Supremacy, *su-pri'ma-si*, N. Mukhelipoun, poileponn, vorteponn.

Supreme, *su-prim*, A. Vorto ; somestam voilo ; mukheli.

Sure, *shu'ar*, A. Khoro, dubau naslolo.

Surely, *shu'ar-li*, ADV. Dubavavin.

Surety, *shiu'ar-ti*, N. Zamin, zamindar.

Surface, *sor'feis*, N. Voilem vo bhailem ang.

Surfeit, *sor'fit*, V. Jiv soddun khaunc.

Surfeit, N. Khaugiponn ; mirounem ; dadosoai.

Surgeon, *sor'jon*, N. Voiz ; gai curar cornar.

Surgery, *sor'je-ri*, N. Voijiponn

Surliness, *sor-li'ness*, N. Laslelem tondd.

Surly, *sor'li*, A. Laslelea tonddacho.

Surmize, *sor-maiz'*, N. Parkonnem.

Surmount, *sor-maunt'*, V. Polltodd marunc, jiconc, joit vorunc.

Surmountable *sormaunt'ie-bl*, A. Jico sarco.

Surname. *sornem'*, N. Alcunch, cuttumbachem naum.

Surpass, *sor-pass'*, V. Jiconc, zoit vorunc.

Surplice, *sorplis,* N. Suplicis.
Surplus, *sor'plas,* N. Urta tem, baki.
Surprise, *sor-praiz',* V. Ojap corunc; angar poddonc.
Surprise, N. Ojap, novol.
Surrender, *sor-ren'dar* soddun diunc, adin corunc.
Surreptitious, *sur-rep-ti'shas,* A. Patti dovorlolo; guttacho.
Surround, *sor-raund',* V. Veddo galunc; bountonnec vochunc.
Surtax, *ser'teks,* N. Eoc kerit chodoilolo dondd.
Survey, *ser-vei',* V. Topasunc, mapun mol tharannc.
Surveyor *sor-vei'ar,* N. Muzimdar, topasnar.
Survive, *ser-vaiv',* V. Vanchonc; uprant, jiennc.
Susceptibility, *sos-sep-ti-bi'li-ti,* N. Nazucai; socot;
Suceptible, *sus-sept'ti-bl,* A. Nazuc, gunnacho
Suspect, *sos-pect',* V. Dubavonc.
Suspend, *sos-pend',* V. Lambounc, umcallaunc; monam corunc; caddunc.
Suspension, *sos-pen'shon,* N. umcallop, monam corop.
Suspicion, *sos-pi-shon',* N. Dubav
Suspicious, *sospi-shas,* A. Dubavi.
Sustain *sos-tein',* V. Dourunc; sosunc; posunc; cholounc.
Sustenance, *sos'te-nens,* N. Udarposonn; khan; sahai.
Sutler, *sot'lor,* N. Fouji sangata vochun jeunna-khanacheo vostu vicnar.
Suture, *so'tur,* A. Ecttaim sinvop
Swab, *swob,* N. Saronn.
Swab, V. Kittoll corunc; zaddunc.
Swaddling clothes, N. Angatleo; fallieo.
Swain, *swein',* N. Naddear.
Swallow, *swo'lo,* V. Gillonc; sosunc.
Swallow, N. Sherec, svpurlem sucnnnem.
Swamp, *swemp,* N. Chiclacho zago.
Swamp, V. Buddounc.
Swan. *swon',* N. Hans.
Sward, *sword',* N. Tonnacho zago.
Swarm, *sworm,* N. Hind; urponz
Swarm, V. Bhair soronc.
Swarthy, *swarth'i,* A. Callso; ulpollo.
Sway, *swei,* V. Podvi cholounc; dolounc.
Sway, N. Cholounem; adhicar.
Swear *swer,* V. Soput diunc; sirap galunc.
Swearing, *swer'ing,* N. Soput; gali.
Sweat, *swet,* N. Gam, um; coistt; vaur.
Sweat, V. Gameunc; coisttounc.
Sweep, *swip,* V. Zaddunc, coir Caddunc.
Sweepings, *swip'ings,* N. Costoll.
Sweet, *swit,* A. Godd; suadic; dulob.
Sweeten, *swit'n,* V. Godd corunc.
Sweetmeat, *swit'mit,* N. Mittai, dos.
Sweetness, *swit'ness,* N. Goddsan, suad.
Swell, *swell',* V. Suzonc, subam zaunc; gorvan boronc.
Swelling, *swell'ing,* N. Suz.
Swerve, *swerv,* N. Chuc.
Swift, *sweft',* A. Vegim choltolo; suddsuddit.
Swiftness, *swift'ness,* N. Suddsuddai.

Swill, *swill'*, V. Jiv soddun pieunc.
Swim, *swim'*, V. Pieunc, ufeuno.
Swimming, *swim'ing*, N. Pieunem.
Swindle, *swind'l*, V. Fottounc, chorunc.
Swine, *swain'*, N. Ducor.
Swing, *swing'*, V. Dolonc; ennemtenem alonc.
Switch, *swich'*, N. Gollo sarki bonvorkhondi.
Swoon, *swun*, V. Jint marunc; tocli gunvonc.
Sword, *sword*, N. Tulvar, torsad.
Sycophancy, *si'ko-fan-si*, N. Chaddi; gulamponn.
Sycophant, *si'co-fant*, N. Fuslaunar, chaddi cornar. [zomo.
Syllable, *sil'a-bl*, N. Acxerancho
Symbol, *sim'bol*, N. Nomuno.
Symmetry, *sim'me-tri*, N. Poddop: manddavoll.
Sympathize, *sim'pa-thaiz*, V. Cunvallunc, apurbai disunc, vollonc.
Sympathy, *sim'pa-ti*, N. Vondovni, moipas, apurbai.
Symphony, *sim'fo-ni*, N. Vazpacho mell.
Symptom, *simp'tom*, N. Khunna.
Synod, *si'nod*, N. Sabha.
Synonym, *si-no-nim*, A. Ecach orthacho.
Synopsis, *si-nop'sis*, N. Tarjumo, sankshep.
Syntax, *sin'teks*, N. Utranchi manddavoll.
Synthesis, *sin'the-zis*, N. Mellounem. [chal.
System, *sis'tem*, N. Rit, pracar,

T.

Tabby, *teb'bi*, A. Sobar ronganeho.
Tabernacle, *ta'ber-na-cl*, N. Sagrad, sacramentachi pett; tombu.
Table, *tei'bl*, N. Mez; jevonn.
Table-cloth, N. Mezacho tuvalo.
Tableland, *tei bl-lend*, N. Moidan.
Tacit, *ta'sit*, A. Gupit.
Taciturn, *ta'si-torn*, A. Vogo; mono.
Taciturnity, *ta-si-torn-i-ti*, N. Vogem ravop; monspoun.
Tack, *tek*, V. Copo marunc.
Tack, N. Dactto khillo.
Tackling, *tek'ling*, N. Tarvachem samon.
Tact, *tect*, N. Trann; bud
Tactics, *tec'tics*, N. Fouz manddchi videa.
Tag-rag, *teg-reg*, N. Urponz.
Tail, *teil*, N. Xempddi.
Tailor, *tei'lor*, N. Dorji, alfiad.
Taint, *teint*, V. Khotaunc; mellounc; cusounc.
Taint, *teint*, N. Khot; cusop.
Take, *teik*, V. Geunc; vorunc; dorunc; sosunc.
Tale, *teil*, N. Cannim.
Talebearer, *te-il-be'rar*, N. Chaddieo sangnar.
Talent, *ta'lent*. N. Somzoni, mot, guinean.
Talk, *tolk*, N. Ulounem, gozal.
Talk, V. Ulounc, gozali sangunc.
Talkative, *tok'a-tiv*, N. Boddboddo; chodd uloinar.
Talker, *tok'ar*, N. Uloinar
Tall, *toll*, A. Lamb, unch.,
Tallness, *toll'ness*, N. Unchai; lambai.
Tallow, *tel'lo*, N. Chorob.
Talon, *te'lon*, N. Chopco.
Tamarind, *ta'ma-rind*, N. Amsann.
Tamarind-tree, N. Chinch.
Tame, *teim*, A. Sado, gorvasi.
Tame, V. Sado vo gorvasi cornar.

Tameness, *teim'ness,* N. Sadeponn.
Tamer, *teim'ar,* N. Sado vo gorvasi cornar.
Tamper, *temp'ar,* V. Beli corunc; naddunc; fuslaunc.
Tan, *ten,* N. Chambddem camais corunc.
Tangle, *teng'l,* N. Addcoll; comisttai.
Tangle, V. Gusponc.
Tank, *tenk,* N. Tollem.
Tankard, *teng'kard,* N. Ec voddlem pieunchem aidon.
Tanner, *ten'ar,* N. Chamddem camais cornar.
Tap, *tep,* N. Thap.
Tap, V. Thapddunc.
Tape, *teip,* N. Firt.
Taper, *teip'ar,* N. Baric vat.
Taper, A. Domsacho.
Taper, V. Domos zaun ontoronc.
Tapestry, *tei'pest-ri,* N. Porddo.
Tape-worm, *teip-uorm,* N. Patim.
Tar, *tar,* N. Damor.
Tardiness, *tard'i-ness,* N. Soucosai, aucas.
Tare *ter,* N. Gutlailelea vosturachem vozon.
Target, *tar'get,* N. Mocun caddchem tatt.
Tariff, *ta'riff,* N. Zokatichi potti.
Tarnish, *tar'nish,* V. Khotaunc; oxig corunc. [bounc.
Tarry, *ter'i,* V. RaVonc; tham-
Tart. *tart,* N. Ambott. coddu.
Tartness, *tart'ness,* N. Amsann.
Task, *tasc,* N. Cam.
Task, V. Cam diunc.
Taste, *teist,* N. Ruch, suad; somjicai. ;
Taste, V. Chaconn polleunc ruch geunc; poricxa corunc.
Tasteful, *teist'ful,* A. Ruchic suadic.
Tasteless, *teist'less,* A. Ruchnasolo: capo.
Tatter, *tett'ar,* N. Chindi lugot.
Tattle, *tett'tl,* V. gozali marunc.
Taunt, *to'nt,* V. Ocman corunc; lojeo galunc; beneddaunc.
Taunt, N. Ocman, loz.
Tavern, *ta'vern,* N. Soreachem ducarn.
Tavern-keeper, N. Ducarncar.
Tawdry, *to'dri,* A. Dispacho.
Tawny, *to'ni,* A. Callso.
Tax. *teks,* N. Zocat.
Tax, V. Zocat galunc.
Tea. *ti,* N. Chau.
Teach, *tich,* V. Secounc; collit corunc; dacounc.
Teacher, *tich'er,* N. Mestir, sicoinar.
Teaching, *tich'ing,* N. Sincoun.
Teak-tree, *tiik'tri,* N. Saulo.
Team *tiim,* N. Zoddem.
Tear, *ti'er,* N. Duc.
Tear, *ter,* V. Pinzunc; tuttounc.
Tear, *ter,* N. Falli, pinzop.
Tease, *tiiz,* V. Chavounc; bejar corunc.
Teat, *tiit,* N. ChiunV, bomb.
Technical, *tek'ni-cal,* A. Vidiecho.
Tedious, *ti'di-as,* A. Corandaecho, corcorancho.
Teem, *tiim,* V. Boron asunc.
Tegument, *teg'u-ment,* N. Dancnem.
Telegraph, *tel'e-graf,* N. Tar, tantr topal.
Telescope, *te'les-cop,* N. Durbin.
Tell, *tell,* V. Munnonc vo sangonc.
Temerity, *te-me'riti,* N. Utavoll; dandgeponn; zobor dosti.
Temper, *temp'ar,* V. Paunim vo parVoll diunc; unno corunc; misllunc.
Temper, N. Sobau; gunn; morji.

Temperament, *tem'perament*, N. Caletri; suabhav; sobau.

Temperance, *temp-a-rens*, A. Alphabhojan, thoddem jeonem —, pinnem.

Temperate, *temp'e-reit*, A. Somandonacho; nidan; thondd.

Temperature, *temp'er-ei-char*, N. Havo, ghormapraman.

Tempered, *tem'pord*, A. Hadgillem; attaplelem.

Tempest, *tem'pest*, N. Tufan, vaddol, modd.

Temple, *tem'pl*, N. Igroz, Devachem ghor; divul.

Temporal, *tem'po-ral*, A. Sounsari; sorta tosolo; callacho.

Temporary, *tem'po-ra-ri*, A. Thoddea vellacho, doń disancho.

Temporize, *tem'po-raiz*, V. Fudde dovrunc; patti gallunc.

Tempt, *tempt*, V. Naddunc; tallnent galunc. [nadd

Tempter, *tempt'ar*, V. Tallni;

Ten, *ten*, A. Dha.

Tenacious, *te-nei'shas*, A. Ghott, mozbut, bazodd; caicott.

Tenacity *te-nas'i-ti*, N. Ghottai, chicottai.

Tenant, *te'nant*, N. Baddeachea garant raunar

Tend, *tend*, V. Racunc, zoton corunc; xevott asunc.

Tendency, *ten'den-si*, N. Vondavonn.

Tender, *ten'dor*, A. Mou, movall.

Tender, V. Bettounc, mucar galunc.

Tenderness, *ten'der-ness*, movallai, movall mon; apurbai.

Tendon, *ten'don*, N. Xir.

Tenement, *te'ne-ment*, N. Ghor; rauchem biddar.

Tenet, *te'net*, N. Munni, proverb.

Tenfold, *ten'fold*, A. Dha pautti.

Tennis, *ten'nes*, N. Chendduncho khell.

Tenor *te'nor*, V. Dusro tallo; jinos; orth.

Tense, *tens'*, N. Call.

Tension, *ten'shon*, N. Voddop. fg. prayatan.

Tent, *tent*, N. Tombu.

Tentative, *ten'tativ*, A. Bulouno, fuslaunno.

Tenth, *tenth*, A. Dhavo.

Tenuity, *ten-u'-iti*, N. Pattolai barcai.

Tenure, *ten'iuar*, N. Onbogcho jinos.

Tepid, *te'pid*, A. Unso, ubmoddo.

Tepidity, *te-pi'diti*, N. Xellmoddai, ubmoddai; unnim bhokti

Tergiversate, *ter'ji ver-seith*, V. Nib sangunc, ang chucounc; path portunc.

Term, *torm*, N. Aker; utor; vaido.

Term, V. Munnounc.

Termagant, *ter'magant*, N. Zogddecarn bail, rakxin.

Terminal, *tor'mi-nal*, A. Akercho.

Terminate, *ter'mi-neitt*, V. Cobar corunc; mitmer galunc.

Termination, *ter-mi-nhei'shon*, N. Sompaunni, sompni; xevott.

Terminology, *ter-mi-no'lo-ji*, N. Paribhas; sobd.

Terrace, *te'reis*, N. Sountoll zago garachea matear.

Terrestrial, *ter-res'trial*, A. Sounsaracho; buincho.

Terrible, *ter'ri-bl*, A. Birancull; tortoreancho.

Terrify, *ter'ri-fai*, V. Tortorunc, beneddaunc.

Terror, *ter'ror*, N. Bem, bhirant, campero.

Terse, *ters*, A. Nitoll; mottvo.
Tertian, *ter'shan*, A. Poireacho.
Testaceous, *testeishas*, A. (Ghott) simpiecho.
Testament, *tes'ta-ment*, N. Testament; carar.
Tester, *tes'tor*, N. Testament cornar.
Testify, *tes'ti-fai*, V. Sakshi diunc; khondit sangunc.
Testimonial, *tes-ti-mo'ni-al*, N. Siparezichem potr; certificad.
Testimony, *tes'ti-mo-ni*, N. Govai, sakshi.
Tetanus, *te'ta-nus*, N. Dhonki.
Tether, *thet'ar*, N. Danvem.
Text, *tekst*, N. Mull gramth, test; povitr pustocachim utram.
Textile, *teks'tail*, A. Vollallo; vinlolo.
Texture, *teks'chur*, N. Vollullem lugot.
Than, *den*, *conj*, V. Poros, vorn, ki.
Thank, *thenk*, V. Upcar mandunc; argam diunc.
Thankful, *thenk'ful*, A. Upcari, argam attouncho.
Thankfulness, *thenk'ful-ness*, N. Upcarponn.
Thanksgiving, *thenks-giv'ing*, N. Argam divop.
Thatch, *tech*, N. Corord.
Thatch, V. Corrdo, galunc.
Theatre, *thi'ie-tr*, N. Thiatr, khell, dacon.
Theft, *theft*, N. Chori.
Theme, *thim*, N. Irado.
Then, *den*, ADV. Tea vellar, tedoll; mager; tor.
Thence, *dens*, VDV. Thoim than; tantlean'
Theologian, *thi-o-lo'ji-an*, N. Thiolg, devjnani.
Theological, *thi-o-lo'ji-cal*, A. Devasamandi.
Theology, *thi'o-lo-gi*, N. Devjnan.
Theory, *thi-o'ri*, N. Yukti. xastr; kolponna.
There, *der*, ADV. Thoim.
Thereabout, ADV. Thoim lagim, sumar.
Thereafter, *der-aft'or*, ADV. Magir, uprant.
Thereby, *der'bai*, ADV. Tache, vorvim' [pasun.
Therefore, *der'for*, ADV. Tache
Thermometer, *ther-mo'me-tor*, N. Gormenchem map.
Thesis, *the'zis*, N. Paksh, khondit, uchar.
They, *dei*, PRO. Te. tim.
Thick, *theek*, A. Datt, motto.
Thicken, *thick'n*, V. Datt vo motto corunc.
Thickness, *thick'ness*, A. Dattai; gottai.
Thief, *thiif*, N. Chor.
Thieve, *thiiv*, V. Chorunc, collonastanam vorunc.
Thigh, *thai*, N. Zang.
Thimble, *thim'bl*, N. Didal.
Thin, *thin*, A. Patoll; baric.
Thin, V. Patoll vo baric corunc.
Thing, *thing*, N. Samonn vost.
Think, *think*, V. Chintunc, niallunc.
Thinker, *think'ar*, N. Chintnar.
Thinnes, *thin'ness*, V. Pattolai, barcai.
Third, *thord*, A. Tisro.
Thirst, *thorst*, N. Tan.
Thirsty, *thar'sty*, A. Tanelolo.
This, *dis*, PRO. Ho.
Thistle, *this'l*, N. Canti.
Thither, *thi'der*, ADV. Thoim.
Thorn, *thorn*, N. Cantto.
Thorny, *thor'ni*, A. Cantteancho.
Thorough, *tho'ro*, A. Khoroch; sompurn.
Thoroughly, *tho'ro-li*, ADV. Purtem, ecannem.

Thou, *dau*, PRON. Tum.
Though, *dou*, CONJ. Zori tor.
Thought, *thot*, N. Chintna, mot.
Thoughtful, *thot'ful*, A. Chintest; budivont.
Thousand, *thausond'*, A. Hozar.
Thrall, *throll'*, N. Chacor gulam.
Thrash, *thresh'*, V. Boddounc; marunc.
Thread, *thred*, N. Sut, dago.
Thread, V. Sut galunc.
Threadbare, *thhred'ber*, A. Chirdi; porno.
Threat, *thret*, N. Besttauni.
Threaten, *thret'en*, V Bettaund, bhiraut launc.
Three, *tri*, A. Tin ; teg.
Threshold, *thresh'hold*, N. Umbar ; aromb.
Thrift, *thrift*. A. Jagauni, thevni, Sugrat. [vosti.
Thrifty, *thrift'i*, A. Cosricho, gor-
Thrill, *thrill*, V. Campounc ; ang caddunc.
Thrill, N. Camp ; ang-caddop.
Thrive, *thraiv*. V. Nondonc, vosonc, suclac poddonc.
Throat, *thrut*, N. Gongtto ; gollo,
Throb, *throb*, V. Uddunc, dobddotunc, fittfitunc.
Throne, *thron*, N. Siasonn; sodri.
Throng, *throng*. N. Khett ; ur. pouz.
Throng, V. Khett zaun vochunc; borobor cholonc.
Throttle, *throt'-tl*, V. Fugar corunc, usvas suttonam-so corunc.
Throughout, *thru-autt*, AD. Sogleun.
Throw, *throu*, V. Uddounc, soddunc, socol uddounc.
Thrust, *throst*, V. Topunc, bhitor galunc.
Thumb, *thomb*, N. Akonddo.
Thump, *thomp*, V. Tapott marunc.
Thump, N. Tapott,
Thunder, *thon'-dor*, N. Goddgoddo.
Thunder, V. Goddgoddunc; goddgoddo eunc.
Thunderbolt, *thon'-dor-bolt*, N. Viz ; zoglaunnem.
Thunderstruck, *thon'-dor-strok*, V. Thottacun polleunc; ojap zaunc.
Thus, *dos*, AD. Oxem vo toxem ; he jinsim.
Twart, *twort*, V. Addaunc, incar corunc,
Twart, AD. PREP. ADD ; Virodh.
Thy, *dai*, PRO. Tuzo.
Thyme, *daim*, N. Tumbo.
Tiara, *ti-a'-ra*, N. Mocutt.
Tick, *tick*, N. Kidd, ulloe ; udar.
Ticket, *tick'-ct*, N. Chitt, tiket.
Tickle, *tick'-l*, V. Khorzunc; fusiaunc, muyeunc.
Tide, *taid*, N. Bhorti.
Tidiness, *taid'-di-ness*, N. Nittolai ; manddavoll.
Tidings, *tai'-dings*, N. Khebor.
Tie, N. Bandunc; ghot corunc; ecost corunc.
Tie, N. Bandop, bandpas; gant ; fint ; gorvat.
Tier, *ti'-er*, N. Ar ; thor.
Tiger, *tai'-gor*, N. Vag.
Tight, *taitt*, A. Ghott, orn.
Tighten, *taitt'-n*, V. Ghott, corunc; ornun bandunc.
Tightly, *taith'-li*, AD. Ornun.
Tide, *tail*, N. Nollo.
Tile, V. Nolle galunc.
Till, *til*, AD. Munnosor, ittun ; porian.
Till, V. Camais corunc, cusunc, nangrunc.
Till, N. Duddnanchi pet vo govet.
Tillage, *til'eij*, N. Camaisponn, setcamot.
Tilt, *tilt*, N. Pakaddi.

Timber, *timb-ar*, N. Lancudd, moder.
Time, *taim*, N. Vell; fursott; somoio.
Timely, *taim'-li*, AD. Vegim; poiloch.
Timepiece, *taim'-pis*, N. Goddial, reloz.
Timid, *tim'-id*, A. Bezud.
Timidity, *ti-mid'-i-ti*, N. Bezud-dai.
Tin, *tin*, V. Coloi caddunc.
Tin, N. Togodd, potrem.
Tincture, *tingk'-char*, N. Rong; ros; coddo.
Tinge, *tinj*, V. Rong launc.
Tingle, *tin'-gl*, V. Zollonc.
Tinkle, *tink'-kl*, V. Muyeunc.
Tinner, *tin'-or*, N. Ooloicar.
Tinsel, *tni'sel*, N. Begodd.
Tip, *tip*, N. Pont, domos.
Tip, V. Domos corunc; thodde duddu diunc sagund cosl.
Tippet, *tip'pet*, N. Khauda velem vostur.
Tipple, *tip'l*, V. Jiv soddun soro pieunc.
Tipsy, *tip'si*, A. Bebdo.
Tiptoe, *tip'to*, N. Bottanchem pont vo thembi.
Tirade, *ti-reid'*, N. Lamb ulounnem.
Tire, *tai'ar*, N. Mateacho muddaso; potto.
Tire, V. Puro corunc vo zaunc.
Tired, *tai'ard*, A. Puro zalolo.
Tiresome, *tai-ar'som*, A. Coisttancho; bejaracho; augodd.
Tissue, *ti'shu*, N. Vovllelem lugott; vollop.
Titbit, *tit'bit*, N. Amrut.
Tithe *tuid*. N. Dantlem ec foll; cosolei vostucho davo vantto;
Title, *tait'tl*, N. Titl, naum.
Titter, *tit'ar*, V. Bhitorlea bhitor ansonc.
Tittle-tattle, *tit-tl-,tat-tl*, N. Gozali.
Titular, *tit'u-lar*, N. Nanvancho; titl aslolo.
Toad, *tod*, N. Manka, bebo.
Toast, *to'st*, V. Unddeachi fati torrar corunc; saud corunc.
Tobacco, *to-bac'co*, N. Pan, dumtti.
Today, *tu'dei*, Ad. Aiz.
Toddy, *tod'di*, N. Sur; niro
Toe, *to*, N. Botachem pont.
Toga, *to'ga*, N. Dil capot, mucom bhailem angostr purvilea Roman locachem.
Together, *tu-ge'der*, Ad. Sangata; codde; sonvem.
Toil, *toil*, N. Vaur.
Toil, V. Coistti zaunc, vaurounc.
Toilette, *toi'let*. N. Netton vonettounchem.
Toilsome, *toil-som*, A. Coisttancho.
Token, *tok'n*, N. Ugdass; khunna.
Tolerable, *tol'e-rei-bl*, A. Sosue sarco; sumaracho.
Tolerance, *tol'e-rans*, N. Sosnicai; sosop.
Tolerant, *tol'e-rant*, A. Sosnic.
Tolerate, *tol'e-reit*, V. Sossunc; raji zaunc.
Toll, *toll*, N. Zocat.
Toll, V. Soucas gantt marunc.
Tomb. *tumb*, N. Fendd; gori.
To-morrow, *tu'mor-ro*, Ad. Fules.
Tone, *to'n*. N. Gaianacho jinos; Tallo; fg boll.
Tongs, *tongs*, N. Chimito.
Tongue, *tong*. N. Jib; bhas.
Tonsure, *ton.sar*, N. Fiad, curou.
Too, *tun*, Ad. Legun, soith.
Tool, *tuul*, N. Aidon, atiar, samonn.
Tooth, *tuth*, N. Dant.

Toothache, *tuth'eik*, N. Dantachi fodda-fodd.
Toothless, *tuth'less*, A. Dantnaslolo; bonchro.
Top, *top*, N. Matem, tocli.
Top, V. Sogieam voir soronc.
Tope, *top*, V, Chodd soro pieunc,
Topic, *top'ic*, N. Vost; sangat.
Topsyturvy, *top'si-tor-vi*, Ad. Vompto udaro.
Topography, *to'pog-ra-fi*, N. Suatechi navarnnan.
Torch, *torch*, N. Uzvaddi, diutti.
Torment, *tor'ment*, N. Dogd, coistt.
Torment, V. Coisttaunc; dogdaunc.
Tornado, *tor-na'do*, N. Girgirem varem.
Torpid, *tor'pid*, A. Soirann naslolo; nidest; auxi.
Torper, *tor'por*, N. jem; fg. ausai.
Torrent, *tor'rent*, V. Vhall lott.
Torrid, *tor'rid*, A. Bhou un, uso, khor.
Torso, *tor'so*, N. Lundd.
Tortoise, *tor'toiz*, N. Kansou,
Torture, *tor'char*, N. Iza, dogd, coistt.
Torture. V. Iza diunc; dogdogaunc.
Toss, *toss*, V. Alounc (ennem-tennem).
Total, *total*, N. Ottu, zomo.
Total, A. Soglo, sorv; purn.
Totality, *to-tal'i-ti*, N. somest.
Totter, *tot'tor*, V. carcoddunc.
Touch, *toch*, V. Hat launc; apoddonc.
Touch, n. Apoddnem.
Touching, *toch'ing*, PREP. Vishiont.
Touching, A. Lago sarco, movallauncho
Touchy. *toch'i*, A. Àloi sarco.
Tough, *tof* A. Bazodd, nibor couttin.
Toughness, *tof,ness*, N. Bazoddai.
Tour. *tur*, N. Bonvodd, viaz.
Tourist, *tovrist*. N. Viaj ornar.
Tow, *tou*, V. Tarum doriant voddunc. [easilean.
Toward, *tov'ard*, PREP. Thaim,
Toward, A. Sico sarko; sado.
Towel, *tav'ul*, N. Tuvalo; aug puscho cuddco.
Tower, *tau'or*, N. Tor.
Tower, V. Unch vochonc.
Town, *taun*, N. Xar.
Toy, *toi*, N. Kheuchi vost.
Trace, *tres*, N. Khunna, sinal.
Trace, V. sodun caddunc.
Tract, *trect*, N. Gaum; supurlem pustoc.
Trade, *treid*, N. Veper.
Trader, *treid'ar*, N. Vepari.
Tradition, *tra-di'shon*, N. Contha, touddim deuvon aileli saugnni.;
Traduce, *tra'dius*, V. Naum ibaddunc.
Traffic, *traf'fic*, N. Vepar.
Trafic, V. Vepar corunc,
Tragedy, *tra'ji-di*. A. Ducounchem nattoc; hal.
Tragical, *tra'ji-cal*, A. Ducouncho.
Trail, *treil*, N. Khun.
Train. *trein*, V. Siconnc, sovoim corunc; sudarunc.
Train, N. Ag-gaddi; dobazo; dorbar.
Training, *trein'ning*, N. Torbet; sicoun.
Trait, *treit*, N. Soimbgunn.
Traitor, *trei'tor*, N. Gutki; abgatki, gollecapo; fituri.
Traitorous, *trei'tor-as*, A. Gatki, dogolbaji.
Trammel, *trem'el*, N. Addcoll; zall.
Trample, *trem'pl*, V. Mostunc, guddaunc.

Trance, *trans*, N. Drusttavo; zuz, samgram.
Tranquil, *tran'kwil*, A. Thondd, shant, nidan.
Tranquility, *tran'kwil-li-ti*, N. Thonddai, sovostponn.
Tranquilize, *tran'kwil-laiz*, V. Somandan corunc, tharaunc, sostaunc.
Transact, *trans'ekt*, V. Cholounc, corunc.
Transaction, *trans-ekt'shon*, N. Khondd, carar; vepar.
Transcend, *trans'send*, N. Vorto zaunc, vodic-oglo zaunc.
Transcendent, *trans-send'ent*, A. Vorto, uttom; baric, shidduc.
Transcribe, *tran-skraib'*, V. Utrunc, nocol caddunc.
Transcript, *tran-skrit*, n. Nocol.
Transfer, *trans'for*, V. Bodli corunc, dusrea zaguear bodlunc; fudde vorunc.
Transfer, N. Bodlop, utarni, caddun vornem.
Transfiguration, *trans'fig-ur-ei-shon*, N. Rup, akar bodolnem; rupamtar.
Transfigure, *trans-fig-or*, V. Rup, akar bodlunc.
Transfix, *transfiks*, V. Aspas topunc.
Transform, *trans-form'*, V. Rup, akar bodlunc; rupantar corunc.
Transformation, *trans-form-ei'-shon*, N. Rup, bhed; bodlop.
Transfuse, *trans-fiuz'*, V. Vo-, tunc; motint galunc.
Transgress, *trans-gress*, N. Moddunc; beporvo corunc.
Transgression, *trans-gres'shon* N. Moddni, bhong.
Transgressor, *trans.gres'sar*, N. caiddo moddnar, guneamcar.
Transient, *tran'zi-ent*, A. Sortom, danntem, khinnachem.

Transit, *tran'zit*, N. Vochuicholni; marog, vatt, bodlop.
Transition, *tran-zi'shon*, N. Samkram bodlop.
Translate, *trans'leit*, V, Tradúzir corunc, utrunc, bashantor corunc.
Translation, *trans-lei'shon*, N. Bashantor, torjumo; utorlelem pustoc.
Transmarine, *trans-ma-rin*, A. Doria pelo.
Transmigrate, *trans-mi-greit*, V. Dusrea ganvac vochonc,
Transmit, *trans-mit*, V. Vorunc, vahunc, daddunc, pattounc.
Transparent, *trans-pei'rant*, A. Uzvadd, kirnam beddtalo.
Transplant, *trans-plant'*, Eke suate velem caddun dusre suater launo.
Transport, *trans-port'*, V. Eke suater than dusre suater vorunc.
Transport, N. Vornem, vorop.
Transverse, *trans-vers* A. Add colcho vo ardd aslolo.
Transubstantiation, *tran-sub-stan-shi-ei'shon*, N. Draviamtar; unddo anim soro Suam Jesu Christachi cudd zannem.
Trap, *trep*, N. Rateir; fg. nadd.
Trash, *tresh*, N. Chilor vost.
Trashy, *tresh'i*, A. Chillor.
Travel, *trav'l* N. Viaj
Travel. V. viaj corunc.
Traveller, *tra'vel-lor*, N. vatsur.
Traverse, *tra'vers*, V. Bolandunc; negar zaunc.
Tray, *trei*, N. Tatt.
Treacherous, *treach'er-as*, A. Gatki, patieunc nozo aslolo.
Treachery, *trech'e-ri*. N. Gatkeponn.
Tread, *tred* V. Panvlam uddon cholonc; mettan marunc.

Treason, *tre'zon*, N. Traisaum, gat, agbat, viavasgat.

Treasure, *tre'jar*, N. Banddar; thovo.

Treasurer, *tre'je-rar*, N. Tizrer, khajineamcho adikari.

Treat, *triit*, V. Hatan dornno; cholounc, Vagouuc, vosounc.

Treatise, *tri'tiz*, N. Boroilolo discurs.

Treatment, *trit'ment*, N Cholouni, vagauni, chal, kellouni.

Treaty, *tri'ti*, N. Boli, carar, niyam.

Treble, *tri'bl*, A. Tiddo, tin pautti.

Tree, *trii*, N. Ruk, zadd.

Trellis, *trel'is*, N. Sorianchо arro vo voddop.

Tremble, *trem'bl*, V. Camponc; thorthorunc

Tremendous, *tre-mend'as*, A. Birancull; thortoreancho.

Trench, *trench*, N. Khonn, chonn.

Trencher, *trench'ar*, N. Laucddachi bosi; khan: mez.

Trepan, *tre'pan*, N. Surjiaumchi corvont.

Trepidation, *tre-pi-dei'shon*, N. Camp, thortoro.

Trespass, *tres'pas*, V. Caidea bhair dusreachea garant etc. bitor soronc.

Tress, *tres*, N. Inni.

Trial, *trai'al*, N. Zortti corop; choucosi; coistt.

Triangle, *trai-ang'gl*, N. Tin conseanchem rup.

Tribe, *traib*, N. Zat, culli.

Tribulation, *tri-bu-lei'shon*, N. Coistt, sontap, dumalo.

Tribunal, *tri-biu'nal*, N. Sodri, siason.

Tribune, *tri-biun*, N. Porjecho sabhavadi.

Tributary, *tri-biu'ta-ry*, A. Karsumk faric cortolo; khalto.

Tribute, *tri-buit*, N. Kar, sercar potti.

Trick, *trick*, N. Nadd, thocop.

Trickle, *tric'kl*, V. Thembeunc.

Trickster, *trik'star*, N. Thocnar.

Trident, *tri'dent*, N. Cosoleim atiar asun taca canttea porim tindomos.

Trifle, *trai'fl*, N. Chalti vost.

Trifling, *traif'ling*, A. Upcarac poddo naslolo.

Trill, *trill*, N. Talleachi camp.

Trim, *trin*, A. Sarkem; sobit.

Trim, V. Boddcaunc; tocsheo catrunc, sarkem coruuc.

Trinity, *tri'ni-ti*, N. Triudad.

Trio, *tri'o*, N. Tin talleanchem gaen vo vazop.

Trip, *trip*, N. Khep; bounddi.

Tripe, *traip*, N. Ankiddi.

Triple, *tri'ple*, A. Tin puutti chodd.

Tripod, *tri'pod*, N. Tin khuranchi codel vo munnoi.

Trite, *trait*, A. Chalto.

Triturate, *tri-tu-reitt*, V. Vattunc; khuttunc.

Triumph, *trai'ianf*, N. Zoit; yes.

Triumph, V. Zoit voruuc.

Triumphal, A. Zoitvont.

Trivet, *tri'vet*, N. Tin khuranchem aidon.

Trivial, *tri-vi'al*, A. Alko; lan, chalto.

Triviality, *tri-vi-al'i-ti*, N. Alkeponn.

Troop, *trup*, N. Foujicho vantto; urponz; zomo'

Trophy, *tro'fi*, N. Eca zoitacho ugddas vo monument.

Tropical, *tro'pi-cal*, A. Usn; gorom.

Trot, *trot*, N. Uddcon.

Trot, V. Uddcounam marunc.

Troth, *troth*, N. Sot; patieni.

Trouble, *tro'bl*, N. Corondai; tontto; minut.

Trouble, V. Corondai corunc, coisttaunc.
Troublesome, *tro'bl-som*, A. Carandaecho, corcorancho.
Trousers, *trau'sors*, N. Izar, colsaum.
Trow, *trou*, V. Chintunc, somzunc.
Truce, *trus*, N. Thoddo temp zuz bond corop.
Truck, *trak*, N. Dactti goddi.
Trudge, *troj*, V. Coisttavon cholounc.
True, *tru*, A. Khoro, niz, sotevont.
Truly, *truli*, AD. Khorench.
Trumpet, *trom'pet*, N. Trompet, pil-luc.
Trumpet, V. Porgott corunc; dangro firaunc.
Truncheon, *trunch'eon*, N. Danddo; betcatti.
Trunk, *tronk*, N. Lundd (Zaddachem); pett; souddi.
Truss, *tros*, N. Band, penddco.
Trust, *trost*, N. Patieni.
Trust, V. Patieunc.
Trustee, *tros-ti*, N. Dusreanchem batt-vit cholounc nemlolo munis.
Trusty, *tros-ti'*, A. Patie-sarco.
Truth, *truth*, N. Sot.
Truthful, *truth'ful*, A. Sotevont.
Try, *trai*. V. Poricxa corunc; chacon polleunc.
Tub, *tob*, N. Pip.
Tube, *tiub*, N. Nolli.
Tubercle, *ttu-ber'cl*, N. Fodd; suz.
Tuck, *tok*, V. Ucolunc.
Tuck, N. Miri.
Tumble, *tom'bl*, V. Addlon poddonc.
Tumbler, *tom'blar*, N. Vidr, udoo pieunchem aidon.
Tumour, *tiu'mor*, N. Fodd; mascutt.
Tumult, *to'molt*, N. Boball; uchambollai, tirraj.
Tumultuous, *to-mal-tu'as*, A. Boballacho, rajicacho, bomddaecho.
Tun, *ton*, N. Pip.
Tune, *tiun*, N. Vazop; podeonch tallo.
Tunic *tiu'nec*, N. Lob; anglem.
Tunnel, *tan'nel*, N. Dorni pondcho marog.
Turban, *tor'ban*, N. Urmal, pogddi.
Turbid, *tor'bed*, A. Nitoll noi aslolo; ollsic.
Turbulence, *tar'bu-lens*, A. Urmottoi, uchambollai; pamddai.
Turbulent, *tor'bu-lent*, A. Bamddi, pandd, hullvullo.
Turf, *torf*, N. Tonnacho zago.
Turkey, *tor-ki*, N. Perum.
Turmoil, *tor'moil*, N. Tirraj, uchambollai.
Turn, *torn*, N. Bounddop; gunvop; bouvaddo, bodlop.
Turn, V. Bodlonc; gunvlaunc.
Turner, *torn'ar*, N. Cantpi; michinar cosolii vost vost caruor.
Turpitude, *tor'pi-tiud*, N. Olxic vost; olxicponn.
Turtle, *tur'tl*, N. Canson.
Tutelar, *tor-ti-lar*, A. Vazaitolo, ractolo.
Tutor, *tiu'tor*, N. Racnno.
Tweezers, *twiz'ars*, N. Chimtto.
Twig, *twiz*, N. Adar; boddi; bel.
Twilight, *twi'lait*, N. Tinsan.
Twin, *twin*, N. Zounlo.
Twine, *twain*, N. Sutli.
Twinge, *twinj*, N. Zall, contin duk.
Twinkle, *twin'kl*, V. Bitbitaunc, zogzogunc.
Twist, *twist*, V. Revoddunc, vollunc.

Twitch, *twich,* N. Chimtto cadduno.
Two, *tu,* A. Don, dog.
Type, *taip,* N. Nomuno; jinos.
Typography, *ti-po'gra-fi,* N. Xapkhannem.
Tyrannical, *ti-ra'ni-cal,* A. Nisttur.
Tyrannize, *ti-ra-naiz',* V. Dogdogauno; zulum coruno.
Tyranny, *ti'ra-ni,* N. Nistturai; zulum.
Tyrant, *tai'rant,* N. Julumdar, julmi, raza.

U.

Udder, *udd'or,* N. Vuntti.
Ugliness, *ug'li-nes,* N. Vidruppon; olxicponn.
Ugly, *ug'li,* A. Vidrup, besurvanno, rup naslolo.
Ulcer, *ol'sar,* N. Rum, chovond, kinvon.
Ulcerate, *ol'se-reit,* V. Rum galunc; callzac galunc; duk diunc.
Ulterior, *ol'te-ri-or,* A. Fuddlo, magirlo, uprantlo.
Ultimate, *ol'ti-meit,* A. Ximanno, xevottacho.
Umbrage, *om'breij,* N. Saulli.
Umbrella, *am-brella,* N. Sastri.
Umpire, *am'paiar,* N. Juiz khorem vo fott tem sangnar.
Unable, *an-ie'bl,* N. Tanknaslolo.
Unaccomplished, *an-ac-com'plis-hd,* A. Nigut corinaslolo.
Unaccountable, *anac-caunt'ie-ble* A. Sangunc nozo aslolo; zababdar noi aslolo.
Unaccustomed, *an-ac-cos'tomed,* A. Sovoim naslolo
Unacquainted, *an-ac-kwein'ted,* A. Noclo aslolo,
Unanimous, *enna'ni-mas,* A. Ecmonacho; ecchitacho.
Unapproachable, *an-ap-proch'ie-bl,* A. Lagim vocho nozo aslolo.
Unapt, *an-ept',* A. Laic noi aslolo, camanc poddo naslolo.
Unaptness, *an-ept'nes,* N. Nam laicponn.
Unarmed, *anarme'd,* A. Atiaram naslolo.
Unaware, *an-a'ver,* A. Auchit chintinaslolo.
Unbar, *un-bar',* V. Ugtto corunc.
Unbecoming, *anbicom'ing,* A. Noim zalolo; favo noi zalolo.
Unbelief, *an-bi-lif',* N. Onbavarth ponn.
Unbeliever, *an-bi-liv'ar,* N. Onbavarthi.
Unbiassed, *an-bi'asd,* A. Nitivont.
Unbind, *anbaind',* V. Soddunc.
Unblemished, *an-ble'mishd* A. Aile naslolo; nitoll.
Uncertain, *an-ser-tu',* A. Dubavacho.
Uncertainty, *an-ser'tein-ti,* N. Duban.
Unchain, *an-chein',* V. Sancoll Soddunc.
Unchangeable, *ancheinj'ie-bl,* A. boldonanso.
Uncharitable, *an-cha-ritable,* A. Mog naslolo.
Unchaste, *an'cheist,* A. Nitoll, noi aslolo; pozddo.
Uncivilized, *an-si-vi-laizd',* A. Amoriadicho; ranvot.
Uncle, *anc'kl,* N. Tiu; mam.
Unclean, *an-clin',* A. Mello, burso; chiclacho.
Unclouded, *an-claud'ed,* A. Cupant naslolo.
Uncommon, *an-com'mon,* A. Preep; chalto noi.
Unconditional, *an-con-di-shon-al',* A. Asertacho condisaum galinastrmam.

Unction, *anc'shon,* N. Makop. —Extreme Unction—sontesaum.
Uncovered, *an-cov'ard,* A. Vinglo, nagddo.
Uncultivated, *an-coi-tivei'ted,* A. Padd aslolo ; naddcar.
Undecided, *an-di-sai'ded,* A. Dubavacho, dubavi.
Under, *an'dor,* PREP, Socoll, talla, ponda.
Underline, *an-dor-lain',* V. Socla risk marunc.
Undergo, *an-der-go',* V. Sosunc.
Undermine, *an-der-main',* V. Ponda khondonc ; padd oorunc.
Underneath, *an-der-nith',* AD. Ponda.
Understand, *an-ders-tend',* V. Somzonc.
Understanding, *an-ders-tend'-ing,* N. Somzonni, ginean mot.
Undertake, *an-dor-teik'* V. Surn corunc ; apler geunc.
Undertaking, *an-dar-teik'ing,* N. Cam ; cortob.
Undivided, *an-di-vai'ded,* A. Vantti naslolo ; doxim corinaslolo.
Undo, *andu,* V. Soddunc ; bongostoll corunc
Undoubtedly, *on-daut-ed'li,* AD. Dubavavinnem ; dubau nastanam.
Undress, *an-dres',* V. Neson caddunc ; nagddo corunc.
Undulate, *an-diu-leit,* V. Dolunc
Undulation, *an-diu-lei'shon,* N. Dolop.
Uneasiness, *an-iz'i-ness,* N. Husco ; nam boiaiki.
Uneasy, *au-iz'i,* A. Bolaiki naslolo ; huskeacho.
Unedifying, *un-ed-i-fai'ing,* A. Bori dek dinaslolo.
Uneducated, *an-e-diu-kei'ted,* A. Sinconaslolo, nannar.
Unemployed, *an-em-ploid',* A. Becar, cam naslolo.
Unequal, *an'i-kual,* A. Sarco noi aslolo.
Uneven, *an-iv'n,* A. Ec sarco sountoll noi aslolo.
Unexpected, *an-eks-pec'ted,* A. Auchit.
Unfair, *an'fer,* A. Niti zocto noi.
Unfaithful *an-feit'ful,* A. Visvasi noi aslolo.
Unfasten, *an-fas'ein,* A. Soddunc.
Unfavourable, *an-fe'vor-iebl* A. Augunnacho.
Unfit, *an-fit',* A. Upcaro naslolo.
Unfold, *an-fold',* V. Ussounc.
Unfortunate, *an-for'chun-eit,* A. Nirbagi.
Unfrequented, *an-fri-kwen'ted,* A. Ecsuro.
Unfruitful, *an-frut'ful,* A. Nirfoll.
Ungovernable, *an-go-vor'ne-bl,* A. Bargo naslolo.
Ungrateful, *an-greit-ful',* A. Onupcari.
Unhappy, *an-hep'pi,* A. Nirbagi.
Unhealthy, *an-hel'di,* A. Piddest.
Uniform, *iuni'form,* A. Ecach jinsacho.
Uniformity, *iu-ni-for'mi-ti,* N. Ecuch jinos ; ecvott.
Unimpaired, *an-in-perd',* A. Bigddonc naslolo.
Unimpeachable, *an-im-pich'iebl,* A. Guneaum naslolo.
Union, *iu'nion,* N. Ecott, zomo.
Unique, *iu-nik',* A. Sorivinn.
Unit, *iu'nit,* N. Ek.
Unite, *iu-na'it,* V. Ecott corunc.
Unity, *iu'ni-ti,* N. Ecottai.
Universal, *iu-ni-ver'sal,* A. Soglean vistar'olo ; somestancho.
Universe, *iu'ni-vers,* N. Sounsar.
University, *iu-ni-ver'si-ti,* N. Sorv videa sall.

Unjust, *an'jast*, A. Khotto.
Unkind, *an'kind*, A. Nisttur, mog naslolo.
Unknown, *an'noun*, A. Volloc naslolo, atvo.
Unlawful, *an-lo'ful*, A. Caidea zocto noi aslolo.
Unless, *an-les'*, Conj. Sivai.
Unlike, *an-laik'*, A. Sarco noi aslolo.
Unlimited, *an-li'mi-ted*, A. Ispa vorto.
Unload, *an-lod*, V. Usponc; khali corunc.
Unlock, *an-look'*, V. Chavi caddunc.
Unlucky, *an-lok'i*, A. Noxib futtco.
Unmarried, *an-me'rid*, A. Ancuar.
Unmask, *an-mask'*, V. Moiem caddunc.
Unmerciful, *an-mer'si-ful*, A. Nisttur, cacut naslolo.
Unmindful, *an-maind'ful*, A. Ugddas naslolo, chintinaslolo.
Unmixed, *an'miks'd*, A. Aputt, nigoll.
Unnatural, *an-neche-ral*, A. Soimba zocto noi aslolo; racsacho.
Unnecessary, *an-ne'se-sa.ri*, A. Gorje bhailo.
Unoccupied, *an-oku'paid*, A Caim naslolo; ricambo.
Unpleasant, *an-ple'zent*, A. Monanc boro lago naslolo.
Unpopular *an-po'pu-lar*, A. Locac manon naslolo.
Unqualified, *an-kwa-li-faid*, A. Poricxa pasar zai naslolo.
Unravel, *an-re'vl*. V. Meclo zaunc vo doxim corunc.
Unreasonable, *an-ri'zn-ie-bl*, A. Murc, ginena zocto noi aslolo.
Unrestrained, *an-res-traind'*, A. Cholonnc nozo aslolo.
Unrighteous, *an-rai'ti-as*, N. Khotto.
Unripe, *an-raip'*, A. Tornu, horvo.
Unripeness, *an-raip'ness*, N. Torneponn.
Unroll. *an-rol*, V. Usounc.
Unsafe, *an-sef*, A. Sugur noi aslolo.
Unsatisfactory, *an-sa-tis-fec'to-ri*, A. Dadosi noi aslolo.
Unseal, *an-sil'*, V. Ugtto corunc; mor foddunc.
Unserviceable, *an-ser-vis'ie-bl*, A. Camenc poddo naslolo.
Unsettle, *an-set'tl*, V. Dubavac galunc, guspaunc.
Unshaken, *an-sheik'n*, A. Alonaslolo.
Unskilled, *an-skill'd*, A. Anbou naslolo; nennar.
Unsociable, *an-so'sei-bl*, A. Ecmullo, munxean bovom naslolo
Unsound, *an'saund*, A. Bigod dlolo; osoct.
Unstable, *an-stei'bl*, A. Doundolit.
Unstained, *an-stein'd*, A. Khot naslolo.
Unsuitable. *an-sut'ie-bl*, A. Upcarac poddo naslolo.
Untainted *an tein'ted*, A. Cusonaslolo.
Until, PREP. vo conj. Tedon porian.
Untamed, *an-teim'd*. A. Gorvasi noi.
Untie, *an-tai'* V. Soddunc.
Unusual, *an-iu'ju-al*, A. Chalto noi.
Unwell, *an-well*, A. Piddest.
Unwilling, *an-will'ing*, A. Khoxi naslolo.
Unworthy, *an-wor'di*, A. Favo noi aslolo.
Up, *op*, AD, Voir.
Upteraid, *ap-tereid'*, V. Bestaunc.

Uphold, *ap-hold*, v. Dhir vo mozot diunc.
Upon, *a-pon*, AD. Voir.
Upper, *ap'ar*, A. Voilo, vorto, uuch.
Uppermost, *ap'or-most*, A. Bhou ubar.
Upright, *ap'raitt*, A. Nitivont; nitt ubo. [Nit.
Uprightness, *ap'raitt-ness*, N.
Uproar, *op'ror*, N. Uchambollai; vodd bobal.
Uproot, *op'rut*, v. Umpttunc.
Upset, *op'set*, v. Vompto galunc, vo poddonc.
Upshot, *ap'shot*, N. Xevott.
Upside, *op'said*, AD. Vomptem, udarem.
Upstart, *ap'start*, N. Addecho girest; novo bab.
Upwards, *ap'wards*, AD. Voilean.
Urchin, *or'chin*, N. Suparlo burgo,
Urge, *arj*, v. Ball corun; uttounc; mucar galunc.
Urgency, *or'jen-si*, N. Jerurai, goruz.
Urgently, *ar-jent'li*, AD. Vegim.
Urine, *iu'rin*, N. Mut.
Usage, *iu'sej*, N. Chal, sonvoim.
Use, *iuj*, N. Upeog; adau.
Use, v Upeog corunc.
Useful, *ius'ful*, A. Upearnc poddo sarco.
Usefulness, *ius'fulnes*, N. Upeog; prayog.
Useless, *iuz'less*, A. Nirfoll; bestto.
Uselssly, *iuz'less-li*, AD. Besttem.
Usher, *osh'ar*, v. Bhitor voronc.
Usual, *iuj'u-al*, A. Chalto, sodancho.
Usually, *iuj-uali'*, AD. Sodancal.
Usurer, *iuzhar'ar*, N. Vodd lab genar.
Usurp, *userp'*, v. Zalmen vo bollan aplea tabiannt addunc.
Usurpation, *userp-ei'shon*, N. Zalmen posse genem.
Usurper, *user'par*, N. Zulmen genar.
Usury, *u-zhu'ri*, N. Chodd vodd lab.
Utensil, *u-ten'sil*, N. Aidon.
Utility, *iu-ti'li-ti*, N. Adau, upeog.

V.

Vacancy, *vei'can-si*, N. Khali zago; fursot.
Vacant, *vei'cant*, A. Khaii, cam naslolo.
Vacate, *va-keit'*, v. Khali corunc.
Vacation, *va-kei'shon*, N. Rojea.
Vaccinate, *vac-si'neit*, v. Vasin corunc.
Vaccine, *vak-sin*, N. Vasin, dhag.
Vacillate, *va'sil-leit*, v. Yennemtennem alonc; camponc.
Vacillation, *va'sil lei-shon*, N. Dolnem.
Vagabond, *va'ga-bond*, A. Parpoll, ghor-dar naslolo.
Vagary, *ve-ga'ri*, N. Morji: pisai.
Vagrancy, *va'gran-si*, N. Parpoll ponn.
Vague, *va'g*, A Vareacho, dubavi.
Vain, *vein'*, A. Bestto; nirfoll; ahankari.
Vainglorious, *vein-glo'ri-as*, A. Boddaicar, lafango.
Vain-glory, *vein-glo'ri*, N Boddai. mijas.
Vainy, *vem'li*, AD. Besttem.
Valid, *va'lid*, A. Gott, nibar rok. mancullo; molacho.
Validity, *va-li'di-ti*, N. Gottai thirponn, thirsan.
Valley, *vel-li*, N. Gall; dongram modli snat.

Valour, *ve'lor,* N. Doir, nirvonn.
Valuable, *ve'liu-ie-bl,* A. Molacho vo moladic.
Value, *ve'liu,* N. Mol, kimot; preos.
Value, V. Mol vo preos corunc.
Valve, *valv,* N. Covodd (darachem.)
Van, *ven,* A Foujicho muca velo vantto.
Vane, *vein,* N. Vareacho bautto.
Vanish, *ve'nish,* V. Nattac zaunc.
Vanity, *ve'ni-ti,* N. Pokllepoun; dunvor; vostuncho fottkiro mog-
Vanquish, *ven'kuvish,* V. Zioonc zait vorunc.
Vapid, *ve'pid,* A. Pirder zalolo, ruch naslolo.
Vapour, *vei-por,* N. Ub.
Vapour, V Ub bhair soronc.
Variable, *ve-ri-a-bl,* A. Bodol zauncho.
Variableness, *vei'ri-a-bl-ness,* N. Bodlo sarkem.
Variance, *vei'ri-ans,* N. Bodlop; coroodai.
Varicose, *va'ri-kos.* A. Suzullo.
Variegate, *va'ri-e-geit,* V. Veglo veglo rong launc.
Variety, *ve-rai'ie-ti,* N. Jinos.
Various, *vei'ri-as,* A. Veglo veglo, kherit, jinsamvar.
Varlet, *var'let,* N. Chacor, lucho.
Varnish, *var'nish,* N. Varniz.
Vary, *ve'ri.* V. Bodlonc.
Vase, *vez,* N. Aidon, vaz.
Vassal, *va'sal.* N. Roit, kull, porza.
Vast, *vast,* A. Bhou vodd lambdigh
Vastness, *vast'-ness,* N. Bhou vodd lambai-rundai.
Vat, *vet,* N. Voddlem pip.
Vaticinate, *va-ti-si'-neit,* V. Mucar vo adim sangunc.
Vault, *volt,* N. Dornipondcho quart.
Vaunt, *vont,* V. Boddai-dacounc, mijas corunc.
Vegetable, *ve'-je-tei-bl,* N. Verdur, torcari.
Vegetate, *ve-je-teit,* V. Vaddonc.; kirlonc.
Vegetation, *ve-je-tei'-shon,* N. Zaddanchi vaddai.
Vehemence, *ue-he'-mens.* N. Boll; ummallo; uchambollai.
Vehement, *ve-he'-mel,* A. Bolladic; uchamboll.
Vehicle, *ve-hi'-cl,* N. Gaddi.
Veil, *veil,* N. Veu.
Veil, V. Veu gallunc.
Venn, *venn,* U. ser; sokos.
Velocity, *ve-lo'si-ti,* N. damvreponn, turturitai.
Velvet, *vel'-vet,* N. itud.
Venal, *ve'-nal,* A. lonch khannar.
Venality; *ve-nal'-i-li,* N. lonch kaunchem; cusop.
Venerable, *ve'ne-rei-bl,* A. Thor, manacho bagevont.
Venerate, *ve'-nereit,* V. Bhou man dinuc, nomoscar corunc.
Veneration, *ve-ne-rei'-shon,* N. Nomoscar, prannipat, vodd man.
Vengeance, *venj'-ans,* N. Vingans. farioponn.
Venial, *ve'-ni-al,* N. Sompeponnim bogsumcho; upapap.
Venon, *ve'-non,* N. Vic.
Venomous, *ve-no-mas,* A. Vicacho. vicallo.
Vent, *vent,* N. Buras, domplo.
Ventilate, *ven-ti-leit,* V. Varem gaiunc.
Ventricle, *ren'-tri-kl.* N. Poti.
Venture, V. Acantant vochunc.
Venturesome, *ven'-char-som,* A. Dhoiravont.
Veracious, *ve-rei'-shas.* A. Sota-

cho, patiesarco.
Veracity, *ve-ra' ri ti*, N. Sot; patienni.
Veranda, *ve'-ran-da*, N, Varand; balkaum.
Verb, *verb;* N. Criyapad, sobd.
Verbal, *ver' bal* A. Tonddacho, tonddaposi, criyapadacho.
Verbosity, *ver-bo'-zi-ti*, N. Forfornni, boddboddni.
Verdant, *ver'-dant*, A. Pachvea rongacho; fulcho.
Verdict, *ver'-dict*, N. Faisal.
Verdigris, *ver'-di-gris*, N. Colomb.
Verdure, *ver'-dinar*, N. Pachvo rong; torneponn.
Verge, *verj*, N. Cantt; pont.
Verge, V. DenVunc, bagounc.
Verification, *ve-ri-fi-kei'-shon*, N. ruzvat.
Verify, *ve'-ri-fai*. N. Ruzvat vo ruzu corunc.
Verily, *ve'-ri-li*. AD. Nis zaun.
Verisimiler, *ve-ri-si-mi-lar*, A. sotmandiso.
Veritable, *ve'-ri-tei-bl*, A. Khoro; niz.
Vermin, *ver'-min*, N. Kidd.
Vernacular, *ver-na'-kin-lar*, N. gauncho.
Versatile, *vers'-a-tail*, A. Bodlo sarco. tirtiro, variavoilo.
Verse. *vors*, N. Charan slok.
Versed. *vers'-d*, A. siclolo.
Versify, *ver'-si-fai*, V. Slok corunc.
Version, *ver'-shon*, N. Bhasantar. utran.
Vertex, *ver'teks*, N. Aker, tocsi.
Vertical, *ver'-ti-cal*, A, Ubo nitt ubo,
Vertigo, *ver-ti'-go*, N. gunvall.
Very, *ve'-ri*, AD. Bhou: chodd.
Very, A. Toch.
Versicle, *ve'-si-kl*, N. Sus.
Vesper, *ves'-per*, N. Sanz.
Vespers, N. Vesp.
Vessel, *ve'-sl*, N. Aidon; tarum; ser.
Vest, *vest*, N. Nesonn.
Vest, V. Nesounc.
Vestige, *ves'-tij*, N. Khunna, kuru.
Vestment, *vest'-ment*, N. Nisonn, vestiment.
Vestry, *ves'tri*, N. Sancrist.
Veteran, *ve'-te-ran*. A. Mataro anbovacho; lambchacri kelolo.
Veto, *ve'-to*, N. Addvarni.
Vex, *veks*, V. Challonnc dosunc, ducounc.
Vexation, *veks-soi'-shoh*. N. Bong; zall,
Viaticum, *vi-a-ti'-oum*, N. Vattechi bejmi sidori; Saib.
Vibrate, *vai-breit'*, V. alounc, bonvanddunc, campounc.
Vicar, *vi'-car*, N. Vigar.
Vice, *vais*, N. ogunn; guneaum, aibi.
Vicious, *vi'-was*, A, Agunnacho: Khoddio, aibi.
Vicissitude, *vi-si'si-tuid*. N. Hallat, fer, rajgadde.
Victim, *vic'tim*, N. Bhetton, bali.
Victor, *vic'tor*, N. Zoit vornar, jicop.
Victorious, *vic-to'ri-as*, N. Zoitvont, jicnar.
Victory, *vic'to-ri*, N. Zoit, jicop.
Victual, *vic'tu-al*, V. Khan addun diunc,
Victuals, N. Khan, gras.
Vie, *vai*, V. Uddonc.
View, *viu*, N. Distt; xevott.
Vigil, *vi'jil*, N. Besp; adlo dis; zagrutai.
Vigilance, *vi'ji-lane*, Zagrutai; chotrai.
Vigilant, *vi'ji-lant*. A. Zagrut, Chotur.
Vigorous, *vi gor-as*, A. Ghoi: Bolladic.
Vigour, *vig'or*, N. Bolaiki vo

boll ; gottai.

Vile, *vail,* A. Alko, kircoll ; bezudd.

Vileness, *vail'ness,* N. Kircollai ; alkeponn.

Villify, *vil'li-fai,* V. Olko, kircoll corunc.

Villa, *vil'la,* N. Lan sahar, kasbe ; bonglo.

Village, *vil'lej,* N. Vaddo ; gaum.

Villager, *vil'le-jar,* N, Vaddeant raunar.

Villain, *vil'lein,* N. Khotto munis ; lucho.

Vindicate, *vin'di-keitt,* V. Soten sodunc ; hakan porat magunc.

Vine, *vain,* N. Dacanchi val.

Vineyard, *vin'i-yard,* N. Dacancho mollo.

Vinegar, *vin'e-gar,* N. Sirco, vinagr.

Vinous, *vin'us,* A. Dacanchea rosacho.

Vintage, *vin'teij,* N. Dacanchem pic oca vorsachem.

Violate, *vai'o-leitt,* V. Moddunc ; boll cornnc, zulum vo ocmañ corunc.

Violation, *va-io-lei'shon,* N. Ocman ; zulum.

Violator, *va-io-lei'ttor,* N. Ocman cornar, besttainar ; caido moddnar.

Violence, *va-io'lens,* N. Zulum ; zobordosti.

Violent, *va-io'lent,* A. Bolladic ; zulmecho.

Violet, *va'io'let,* Zambli rongacho.

Violin, *va-io'lin,* N Rebec.

Violinist, N. Rebekist.

Viper, *vai'pr,* N. Agio, fg. dustt munis.

Virgin, *var'jin,* N. Ancuar.

Virginity, *vir'gin-i-ti,* N. Ancuaiponn.

Virtual, *vor'chu-al,* A. Gunna vo sokti pormonnem.

Virtue, *var'chiu,* N. Segunn ; gunn.

Virtuous, *vor'chu-as,* A. Segun ; gunnest.

Virulence, *vir'u-lens,* N. Vicacho voso ; coddsan.

Virus, *vi'rus,* N. Vikh.

Visage, *vi'seij,* N. Rup ; tondd.

Viscera, *vis'se-ra,* N. Ankiddi.

Viscid, *vis'sid,* A. Lagcho pancacho.

Visibility, *vi-zi-bil'i-ti,* N. Disteponn, decteponn.

Visible, *viz'i-bl,* A. Discho ; nodrec poddo sarco.

Vision, *vi'zion,* N. Distt ; drusttaVo ; soponn.

Visionary, *vi'zon-a-ri,* A. Urbevont ; uchambollist.

Visit, *vi'zit,* N. Bhett.

Visit, V. Bhettonc ; milakot corunc ; pollounc.

Visitor, *vi'zi-tor,* N. Bhett cornar, milokat cornar.

Vital, *vai'tal,* A. Jiracho. fg. bhon barim. [sande.

Vitals, *vai'talz,* N. Prannache

Vitiate, *vi'shi a-eitt,* V. Khotto corunc, cusounc, ibaddunc.

Vituperate, *vi tu'pe reit,* V. Galli sovonc, hinsunc, kenddunc.

Vituperation, *vi-tu'pe'rei'shon,* N. Beman cornem ; ganjni, keddni.

Vivacity, *vi va'si-ti,* N. Tukaki ; ulasponn ; suddsuddai.

Vivid, *vi'vid,* A. Tuklukit ; loklokit, rosrosit.

Vivify, *vi'vi-fai,* V. JiV dinnc, borunc ; jiv geunc vo borunc.

Vixen, *viks'-n,* N. Coli.

Vocabulary, *vo-ca' bul-a-ri,* N. Sobdakos, vocabular.

Vocal, *vo'cal,* A. Talliacho : vachecho : tonddacho.

Vocation, *vo-kei'-shon*, N. Apounnem, vinchun caddnem ; vondani.
Vocative, *vo'-co-tiv*, A. Apounchem.
Vociferate, *vo'si'fer'eitt*, V. Ardun saugunc, bob marunc.
Vociferation, *vo'si'fer'ei'shon*, N. Bob marnem, bobatt.
Vogue, *vog*, N. Rivaz.
Voice, *vois*, N, Tallo.
Void, *void*, A. Khali, rito ; rod di kelolo.
Void, V. Khali corunc ; red-di corunc.
Volatile, *vo'-la-tail*, A. Uddto ; ubto ; thir naslolo.
Volcano, *vul-ca'-no*, N. Nisvakarma ; ujeachem muc.
Volley, *vol'-i*, N. Thoddeam armancho far borochbor.
Volubility, *vo-lu-bil'-i-ti*, N. Jibechi luslusni : firnem ; girgirnem
Volume, *vo'-lium*, N. Pustoc ; pustocacho bhag voddai.
Voluminous, *vo'lu'mi'nas*, A. Vistarlolo; vodd ; choddam pustocancho.
Voluntary, *vo'lun-ta-ri*, A. Khoxecho.
Volunteer, *vo-lun-ti'er*, N. Khoxecho sipai.
Voluptuary, *vo-lup'tu-a-ri*, N. Camchari, manjecho istt ; cuddir eclo aslolo.
Vomit, *vo'mit*, V. Vonconc.
Vomit, N. Vonc, voncaro.
Vomitive, *vo'mi-tiv*, A. Vonconnchem.
Voracious, *vo-rei'xas*, A. Gilltolo. girastolo ; khangi,
Voracity, *vo-ra'si-ti*, N. Asosponn ; potarponn, khaugeponn.
Vortex, *vor'teks*, N. Bounro ; chakr.
Vote, *vot*, N. Vot ; koblat.
Vote, V. Koblad diunc.
Votive, *vo'tiv*, A. Angounnecho.
Vouch, *vauch*, V. Govai diunc ; zababdar zaunc.
Voucher, *vau'char*, N. Govai zamin.
Vouchsafe, *vauch'seif*, V. Puttvonc.
Vow, *vau*, N. Angoun.
Vow, V. Angoun corunc.
Vowel, *va'ul*, N. Jivakxer.
Voyage, *vo'iej*, N. Viaj, vatt, marog.
Vulgar, *vol'gar*, A. Chalto, sado, sodancho ; olko.
Vulgar, N. Zomo.
Vulture, *vol'char*, N. Gid.

W

Wad, *wed*, N. Chumboll.
Waddle, *wed'dl*, V. Lokonc, dolonc.
Wade, *weid*, V. Udcan peunc.
Wafer, *wei'far*, N. Hostu.
Waft, *woft*, V. Ufeunc.
Wag, *weg*, V. Yennem-tennem alounc.
Wage, *weij*, V. Zuz manddunc.
Wager, *wei'jar*, V. Pont marunc.
Wager, N. Pont.
Waggery, *weg'ge-ri*, N. Ansonchi gozal.
Wages, *wei'jis*, N. Pag, muzri.
Waggon, *weg'gon*, N. Ag-gaddiecho eoc dobo.
Waist, *weist*, N. Combor.
Waistcoat, N. Culet.
Wait, *weit*, V. Ravonc.
Waiter, *wei'tar*, N. Mezar servir zauncho chacor.
Waiting, *wei'ting*, N. Ravop.
Waive, *weiv*, V. Soddunc ; patti galunc.
Wake, *weik*, N. Utlounc ; zago corunc.

Wake, N. Zagrutai.
Wakeful, *weik'ful*, A. Zago.
Wakfulness, *weik'ful-ness*, N. Zagrutai.
Walk, *wolk*, V. Cholonc, bouvonc.
Walk, N. Boundi ; Chal.
Wall, *vol*, N. Vonot.
Wallet, *val'let*, N. Poti.
Wallow, *wol'lou*, V Lollonc.
Walnut, *wal'not*, N. Akrut.
Wan, *won*, A. Calloc vo chintest ; doukuro.
Wander, *won'dor*, V. Parpoll bouvonc.
Wanderer, *won'der-ar*, N. Parpoll mauis.
Wandering, *won'der-ing*, N. Parpollponn.
Wane, *wein*, V. Unno zaunc; denvunc.
Want, *wont*, N. Goroz; fg. acant.
Want, V. zai zaunc ; Khoxi vorunc.
Wanton, *won'ton*, A. Mosticho ; lozbanddo, bailanddo.
Wantonness, *wont-on-ness*, N. Most ; lozbandponn.
War, *wor*, N. Zuz ; loddai.
Warble, *wor'bl*, V. Gayan corunc.
Ward, *word*, V. Chuconne ; pois corunc, raconc.
Ward, N. Chuconnem, raconn ; eoc guard hospitalant.
Warden, *wor'dn*, N. Racnno.
Warder, *word'ar*, N. Parecar.
Wardrobe, *word'rob*. N. Nesonu dovorchi almar.
Ware, *wer*, N. Veparacheo vostu ; samonn.
Warehouse, *wer'haus*, N. Gudaum.
Warfare, *wor'fer*, N. Zuz.
Warlike, *wor'laik*, A. Zuzacho.
Warm, *worm*, A. Un, khor ; tapoillo.
Warm, V. Un corunc; tapounc.
Warmth, *wormth*, N. Gormi, unau,
Warn, *worn*, V. Takit dinnc ; collounc.
Warning, *worn'ing*, N. Bud.
Warrant, *wor'rant*, N. Zamin : hocum.
Warrant, V. Khorem sangunc : thir corunc ; zamin zaunc.
Warrior, *wor'-ri-or*, N. Zuzari.
Wart, *wort*, N. Chamkull.
Wary, *we'-ri*, A. Patti-fudde poi lounncho ; budivont.
Wash. *wosh*, V. duunc ; umbollunc.
Washerman, *wosh'-er-men*, N moddvoll, dobi.
Wasp, *wasp*, N. Gauzil.
Wasp-nest, N. Ganzlauchem malem.
Waste, *weist*, N. Padd suat,
Waste, N. Nasunc, ibaddunc ; khorchunc.
Wasteful, *weist'-ful*, A. Ibadi.
Watch, *woch*, V. Raconc, zago ravonc.
Watch, N. Goddial, zoton.
Watchful, *woch'-ful*, A. Zagrut.
Watchman, *woch'-men*, N. raknno.
Water, *wot'-or*, N. Udoc.
Water, V. Udoc galunc, simponc:
Watered, *wo-'terd*, A. Bizoilolo.
Water-fall, N. Gosgoso.
Water-proof, N. Udoc rigonaso.
Watery, *wot'-o-ri*, A. Udeallo.
Wave, *veiv*, N. Lar.
Wave, V. Alonc dolonc.
Waver, *weiv'-ar*, V. dubavonc : dounddolonc.
Wax, *weks*, N. Menn.
Wax-taper, N. Baric vat.
Way, *wei*, N. Vatt marog ; fg. jinos.
Waylay, *wei-lei'*, V. Vatter lipon bosonc.
Wayward. *wei'-ward*, A. Khotto.

We, *wi* PRO. Amim.
Weak, *wiik*, A. Osoct; bolaiki naslolo.
Weaken, *wiik'-n*, V. Osoct corunc moddunc.
Weakness, *wik'-nes*. N. Osoctai.
Weal, *wil*, N. Dadospoun, bore poun.
Wealth, *welth*, N. Giresai; sompurnai.
Wealthy, *wel'di*, A. Girest, astic.
Weapon, *wep'-on*, N. Atiar.
Wear, *wer*, V. Nesunc, togunc.
Wearied, *wi'-rid*, A. puro zalolo.
Weariness, *wi'-ri-ness*, N. Thocop, jint.
Wearisome, *wi'-ri-som*, A. Coist-tancho.
Weary, *wi'ri*, V. Puro vo cansad corunc.
Weasel, *wi'zl*, N. Mungos.
Weather, *we'dar*, N. Havo; Varem.
Weather, V. Tufanantlean par zaunc.
Weathercock, *we'der-cook*, N Vareacho bautto.
Weave, *wiiv*, V. Vollounc, vinnunc.
Weaver, *wiiv'ar*, N. Vinnpi.
Weaving, *wiiv'ing*. N. Vollop vinnop.
Web, *web*, N. Vanniancheni ghor, lugott.
Wedding-day, *wed'ing-dei*. N. Cazaracho vo resperacho dis.
Wedlock, *wed'lok*, N. Cazar.
Weed, *wid*, N. Cámanc poddonasleleni suparlem zadd.
Week, *wiik*, N. Sumana.
Week-day, N. Sumanacho dis.
Weekly, *wiik'li*, A. Sumanachea sumana.
Ween, *win*, V. Chintunc.
Weep, *wiip*. V Roddunc; doecam gollonnc.
Weeping, *wiip'ing*, N. roddnem, roddop.
Weigh, *wei*, V. Zokunc, vozen corunc.
Weight, *weit*, N. Vozon, bhar.
Weighty, *wei'tti*, A. Voznacho, baradic
Welcome, *wel'com*, A. Boro paulolo.
Welfare, *wel'fer*, N. Sue; bo-repoun.
Welkin, *wel'kin*, Akas, mollob.
Well, *well*, N. Baim.
Well, AD. Borem corun, sobitaen.
Welter, *wel'ter*, V. Lollonc.
Wen, *wen*, N. Guntti; maskatt.
Wench, *wench*, N. Cheddum; cheddi.
Wend, *wend*, V. Vochunc.
West, *west*, N. Ostomti.
Wet, *wet*, A. Volo.
Wet, V. Bisonnc. [volzaun.
Wetness, *wet'ness*, N. Xell,
Whale, *wheil*, N. Maso.
Wharf, *worf*, N. Doko; bondir.
What, *whot*, PRO. Kitem; tem.
Whatever, *whot'ev-ar*, A. Cosoleim; kiteim.
Wheat, *whit*, V. Goum.
Wheedle, *whi'dl*, V. Fuslaunc.
Wheel, *whill*. N. Rod.
Wheel, V. Guunddaunc.
When, *when*, AD. Kernam; zor tor.
Where-there, Khoim-thoim.
Whereas, *wher'es*, C. Kitenc; jernam.
Whereby, *wher'bai*, AD. Zache vorvim
Wherefore, AD. Zache paaun.
Wherein, *wher'in*, AD. Zantum.
Whereof, *wher'of*. AD. Zache visheaut.
Whereupon, AD. Zache uprant.
Wherever, *wher'ev-ar*. AD. Khoinsorni.

Wherry, *wher'ri*, N. Ponev.
Whet, *whet*, V. Gansunc; pazunc; fg. zollounc.
Whether, *whe'der*, CONJ. Zalear.
Whetstone, *whet'stone*, N. Sann-sicho fator.
Which, *which*, A. Khuincho.
Whiff, *whiff*, N. Funk.
While, *whail*, N. Fursot.
Whim, *whim*, N. Morji.
Whimper, *whimp'ar*, V. Pirn-gonc; bob marunc.
Whimsical, *whim'si-cal*, A. Mor-jecho.
Whip, *whip*, N. Chabuc.
Whip, V. Chabucan marunc.
Whirl, *whorl*, N. Gunvop; bonvor.
Whirl, V. Guunc.
Whirlpool, *whorl pul*, N. Bonvor.
Whirlwind, *whorl-wind*, N. Tu-fan.
Whiskers, *whis'kors*, N. Gele-misio.
Whisper, *whis'per*, V. Futfuton ulounc.
Whistle, *whist'sl*, V. Fion vo xellani galunc.
Whistle, N. Fion, xellani.
Whit *whit*, N. Cainch,
White, *whait*, A. Dovo; goro.
White-ant, *whait-ant*, N. Valloi.
Whiten, *wai'tn*, V. Dove corunc.
Whiteness, *whait'ness*, N. Dovo rong.
Whitewash, *whait'wosh*, V. Do-vo corunc; chuno caddunc.
Whither, *whi'dor*, AD. Khoim.
Whitish, *whai'tish*, A. Douso.
Whiz, *whiz*, V. Fusfusunc.
Who, *whu*, PRO. Conn.
Whosoever, PRO. Zo conn.
Whole, *whol*, A. Soglo.
Wholesome, *whol'som*, A. Bo-laikecho.
Wholly, *wind'lass*, AD. Sogloch.
Whoop *wind'mill*, N. Bob

Why, *whai*, AD. Kiteao, vo kitea. pasun.
Wick, *wick*, N. Vat.
Wicked, *wick'ed*, A. Khotto
Wickedness, *wick'ed-ness*, N. Khotteponn.
Wide, *waid*, A. Rund, vistarlolo; poisilo.
Widen, *waid'n*, V. Vistarunc.
Width, *width*, N. Rundai.
Widow, *wi'dou*, N. Randd vo gou meleli hostori.
Widower, *wi'dou-ar*, Randdgo.
Wield, *wild*, V. Cholounc.
Wife, *waif*, N. Potin, bail, gor-carn.
Wild, *waild*, A. Ranvott.
Wilderness, *wild'er-ness*, N. Ran, oronem.
Wildness, *waild'ness*, N, Ran-votpónn.
Wile, *wail*, Fottoun, nadd.
Wilful, *wil'ful*, A. Khoxen ke-lolo; khoxecho.
Wilfully, *wil'ful-li*, AD. Zai monnan; khoxen.
Wilfulness, *wil'ful-ness*, N. Khoxi.
Wiliness, *wai'li-ness*, N. Nadd-geponn.
Will, *will*, N. Khoxi; axea; tes-tament.
Will, V. Khoxi asunc.
Willingly, *wil'ling-li*. A. Khoxen.
Willingness, *wil'ling-ness*, N. Khoxi; sontos.
Wily, *wai'li*, A. Naddgo, thoonar
Wimple, *wim'pl*, N. Madrinchi ven.
Win, *win*, V. Jiconc, zoiz vorunc.
Wince, *wins*, V. Patti sorunc
Wind, *waind*, N. Varem, vau.
Wind, *waind*, V. Vazunc, portunc: bounddaunc.
Windlass, *wind'lass*, N. Chacr,
Windmill, *wind'mill*, N. Varea dantoni.

Window, *win'dou,* N. Zonel, kittki.
Windpipe, *wind'paip,* N. Soknolli.
Windy, *win'di,* A. Vareacho.
Wine, *wain,* N. Dacancho soro; soro.
Wing, *wing,* N. Pacotto; fg vantto.
Wink, *wink,* N. Dolleachem sinal.
Wink, V. Dolle moddunc.
Winnow, *winnow,* V. Vareac diunc; fg. poricxa corunc.
Winter, *winter,* N. Iuvancho cail.
Wipe, *waipe,* V. Pusunc.
Wire, *wa'iar,* N. Aram; sori.
Wisdom, *wiz'dom,* N. Bud; zanvai; ginean.
Wise, *waiz,* A. Budivont; xanno; zantto.
Wish, *wish,* N. Khoxi; axea.
Wish, V. Khoxi vorunc; axennc; khoxi asunc.
Wisp, *wisp,* N. Mutt bhor.
Wistful, *wist'ful,* A. Jiv soddun axetolo.
Wit, *wit,* N. Somjicai; barcai.
Witch, *wich,* N Ghaddin.
Witchcraft, *wich'craft,* N. Bhul; fitisponn.
With, *with,* PREP. Sangata; codde.
Withal, *wi'dal,* AD. Soith.
Withdraw, *with'dro,* V. Patti sorunc. [paunc.
Wither, *wi'dr,* V. Sucounc; ul-
Withhold, *with'held,* V. Patti dovorunc; naca munnono.
Within, *wi'din,* PREP. Bhitor.
Within, AD. Bhitorlean.
Without, *wi'daut,* PREP. Bhair; sivai; kherit.
Withstand, *with'stend,* V. Addaunc; tallunc.
Witness, *wit'ness,* N. Govai.
Witty, *wit'ti,* A. Baric: chest taio corcho.

Wizard, *wi'zard,* N. Ghaddi, fitis cornar.
Woe, *wo,* N. Xirap; maldisaum; duc.
Woful, *wo'ful,* A. Dukest.
Wolf, *wulf,* N. Asvel. [bail.
Woman, *wui'man,* N. Hostori,
Womb, *wumb,* N. Cusvo, pott.
Wonder, *won'dr,* N. Ojap.
Wonder V. Ojap zaunc.
Wonderful, *won'dr-ful,* A. Ojapancho.
Wont, *wont,* N. Sovoim.
Wont, *wont,* A. Sovoiencho.
Wood, *wud,* N. Lancudd; ran.
Wooden, *wu'dn,* A. Lanoddacho
Wool, *wul,* N. Loum.
Word, *word,* N. Utor, sobd.
Work, *werk,* N. Vaur; corni.
Work, V. Vaur corunc, vauronc.
Workman, *wor'kmen,* N. Vauraddi, begari; mannai.
Workshop, *work-shop* N. Mandd Vaurachi cudd.
World, *world,* N. Sounsar.
Wordly, *word'li,* A. Sounsaracho vo sounsarantlo.
Worm, *worm,* N. Kiddo; dont gainddoll.
Worry, *wor''ri,* V. Challounc, bejar corunc.
Worse, *wors,* A. Pastt.
Worship, *wor'-ship,* N. Nomoscar, puja
Worshipper, *wor-ship'ar,* N. Nomoscar cornar.
Worth, *worth,* A. favo to.
Worthily, *wor-di-ly,* AD. Favo to porim.
Worthless, AD. *worth-less,* Mol vo kimot naslolo.
Wound, *wund,* N. Ghai.
Wrangle, *wrang'gl,* V. Zogddonc.
Wrap, *rep,* V. guttlaunc
Wrapper, *rep-pr* N. Guttlaunchem cagot.

Wrath, *rath*, N. Choddnag; kirod.
Wreak, *rik*, V. Vingans genno.
Wreath, *rieth*, V. Revodd galunc vo revoddaunc.
Wreath, N. Copel
Wreck, *rec*, V. Foddunc; perder corunc.
Wrench, *rench*. V. Renddaunc; nibran vollunc.
Wrest, *rest*, V. Forsan vollunc, voddun caddunc.
Wrestle. *res l*, V. Jinzvottonc; zogddonc.
Wretched *rech'ed*, A. Nirbagi, bicari; kiroll.
Wretchedness, *re'tched'ness*. N. Bicarponn, kircollai.
Wriggle, *rig'gl*; V. Renddaunc.
Wring, *ring*, V. Revodd galunc
Wrinkle, *rin'kl*, N. Miri.
Wrist, *rist*, N. Monkutt.
Writ, *rit*, N. Potr; borop.
Write, *r'ait*, V. Borounc.
Writer, *rai'tr*, N. Borpi, boroinar, shennoi.
Writing, *rai'ting*, N. borop, potr.
Wrong, *rong*, A. Fottkiro: chuc aslolo.
Wrong, N. Chuc, ooman.
Wrong, V. Ooman corunc; vaitt corunc.
Wroth *roth*, A. Bhou ragist.
Wry, *rai*, A. Vanceddo.

Y

Yacht *yot*, N. Khuxalaechem tarum.
Yam, *yam*, N. Chinem.
Yard, *yard*, N. Angonn; var.
Yarn, *yarn*, N. Sut; fg. lamb contha.
Yawn, *yon*, N. Zambai.
Ye, *yi*, PRO. Tumim.
Yea, *yea*. Ad. Voi.
Year *ier*, N. Voros.
Yearly *i'er-li*, A. Vorsa-vorsacho.
Yearly, AD. Vorsan-voros.
Yearn, *yern*, V. Laleunc.
Yearning, *yern'-ing*, N. Laleunnem.
Yeast, *yist*. N. Khombir.
Yell, *iell*, V. Boh marunc.
Yell, N. Bob.
Yellow, *iel'-lo*, A. Onduvo.
Yellowish, *iel'lo-ish*, A. Onduvoso.
Yelp, *ielp*, V. Goncunc.
Yeoman, *yo'-men*, N. Battcar
Yes, *ies*, AD. Oi.
Yesterday, *ies'-ter-dei*, A. AD. Cal; Calcho.
Yet, *iet*, CONJ. AD. Anim; torui
Yield, *eild*, V. Soddun diunc patti sorunc.
Yoke, *iok*, N. Zum.
Yoke, V. Bandunc.
Yonder, *ion'-dr*, A. To.
Yonder, Ad. Thoim; laginch
Yore, *ior*, AD. Adim; purvim.
You, *iu*, PRO. Tumim.
Young, *iong*, A. Torno.
Young N. Pil.
Your, **ior**, PRON. Tuzo, tumcho.
Youth, *iuth*, N. Torni pirai; burgo; torno munis.

Z

Zeal, *ziil*, N. Khor mog; otreg suddauddai.
Zealous, *ze'-las*, A. Fikiricho; urbest, axecho.
Zenith, *ze'-nith*, N. Unch suat.
Zero, *ji'ro*, N. Puj, sunya.
Zone, *zon*, N. Band; bhag.